Library Serials Management: Integration and Enhancement through Reorganization

Library Serials Management: Integration and Enhancement through Reorganization

M. Ram

RANDOM

RANDOM PUBLICATIONS
NEW DELHI (INDIA)

Library Serials Management: Integration and Enhancement through Reorganization

---

ISBN 978-93-5111-853-4

Published in 2016 in India by

RANDOM PUBLICATIONS

4376-A/4B, Gali Murari Lal, Ansari Road
New Delhi-110 002
Phone : +9111-43580356, 011-23289044, 011-43142548
e-mail: sales@randompublications.com,
info@randompublications.com, randomexports@gmail.com

Type Setting by : Friends Media, Delhi-110089
Printed at : Mehra Printers, Delhi-110 092

Preface

A "serial" is defined as any publication issued in successive parts which are intended to be continued indefinitely. The nature of serials management is unique within libraries because of its multi-directional workflow. Periodicals are ordered, received, checked in, put onto shelves and maintained for public use. Completed volumes are retrieved at specified intervals, prepared and sent for binding and finally shelved in the stacks or replaced with microfilm or online sources. The combined energy of staff interfacing with the public and performing technical processing is both symbiotic and synergistic. Symbiotic because their work is interdependent, and synergistic because the integration of their work is more productive than their individual parts in the process. Because research is often based on timeliness and urgency, there is also an immediate interconnection between the needs of the public for access to periodicals and the technical process of receiving, shelving and binding periodicals. Bound or current, patrons need to know where an item is at any moment in time and to have timely access to it. Because of this interconnection, librarians have discussed the logical benefit of combining serials processing and public services under a single unit or team. Library literature and conference proceedings make common reference to this trend in looking at serials management.

– Author

Contents

1

Library Cataloguing Theory and Serials Management

INTRODUCTION

This chapter reviews the historical development of basic concepts in descriptive cataloguing and provides an analytical overview of selected cataloguing codes affecting the evolution of cataloguing principles. The main purpose is to explore the basic concepts underlying different codes of cataloguing rules and to provide an understanding of how these codes have developed in accordance with forms of the catalogue.

A clear grasp of the historical development of modern cataloguing codes and an understanding of the evolutionary growth of catalogues are both essential to an understanding of the relevance of cataloguing codes to the new electronic environment. In this context, another aim of this chapter is to acknowledge the role of the catalogue environment on the cataloguing rules and principles, *i.e.*, to see how far the environment in which a catalogue is constructed might influence cataloguing principles.

This chapter is intended to be an introduction to later chapters concerning the conceptual analysis of theories and principles of descriptive cataloguing with regard to the possible influences of the online environment on them. To understand the historical background and to examine the past is very important to any study of cataloguing principles and rules and to the future of code revision.

To quote Svenonius:

- "A well-founded philosophy of catalogue code develop-ment must take cognizance of the past, particularly of those factors which have affected and may continue to affect code design".

Although cataloguing codes have a history as long as the history of libraries, the focus of the present chapter is on the development of codes in the Anglo-American context throughout the nineteenth and twentieth centuries. Two non Anglo-American codes are also introduced to illustrate some other cataloguing traditions which have been different in some basic aspects.

DEVELOPMENTS IN THE NINETEENTH CENTURY

The nineteenth century has been characterised as the formative era of modern catalogues and cataloguing codes. It was a time that revealed a keen interest in catalogues and the involvement of individual libraries and librarians in the compilation of cataloguing codes.

- The transformation of library cataloguing to its present form occurred in the nineteenth century, when it was argued that simple author access was not enough and that a different, more sophisticated, and more elaborate approach was needed.

Although the printed book catalogue was widely in use throughout the nineteenth century, the slip catalogue which was primarily created for the preparation of the printed book catalogue, was gradually found to be more flexible and more suitable. Book catalogues, which were found to be inflexible and in need of constant updating and reprinting, grew less popular in a short space of time.

In addition, the limited number of access points per entry was a major disadvantage of book catalogues. By the end of the nineteenth century the printed card catalogue, although not in a standard form, became the alternative to the printed book catalogue and its use became widespread in the twentieth century throughout the United States as well as in many other countries.

The two most common catalogue forms in the nineteenth century were the classified catalogue and the alphabetical catalogue. The classed or classified catalogue, which was a type of subject catalogue depending on a systematic classification, was used in many British, French and American libraries. In this form of the catalogue, entries were arranged in a systematic order to group together books with subject proximity.

Authors and titles made up accompanying alphabetical indexes. Although the classified catalogue continued its development during the nineteenth century, the difficulties of maintaining it limited its application to a relatively small number of libraries.

On the other hand, a major reason for the development of the alphabetical catalogue lies in the fact that alphabetical order has long been common knowledge and best suited for finding items in the catalogue. Most cataloguing codes developed by individuals or national agencies in modern times have been formulated for alphabetical catalogues rather than classified catalogues.

The nineteenth century was a time when the objectives of the catalogue became more clearly defined. As library catalogues had to be developed in accordance with the users' needs, a first step was to clarify the functions of the catalogue. Thus an essential principle on which rules for entries had to be based was the formulation of objectives for the catalogue.

The concept of one full record per book which was dominant in classified and alphabetical catalogues evolved into multiple entries in the dictionary catalogue. Although the dictionary catalogue had been first introduced by Andrew Maunsell in 1595 in the form of a simple list including authors, added entries and subjects in a single alphabetical sequence, it had its flourishing in the nineteenth century, particularly through the works of Charles Ammi Cutter. In effect, the development of our current cataloguing codes has its roots in the landmark works of a few librarians who formed the theoretical foundations of descriptive cataloguing:

ANTHONY PANIZZI AND THE BRITISH MUSEUM RULES

The beginning of the development of modern cataloguing codes is generally attributed to Sir Anthony Panizzi whose influence in descriptive cataloguing in general, and the theory of cataloguing in particular, is well known to the profession. The British Museum code of 1841 had its roots in preceding rules, and in fact continued practices common in libraries of medieval monasteries. Panizzi took the most useful principles, reshaping and widening them to offer solutions to most of the cataloguing problems of his time.

The *Ninety-One Rules* were drafted by Panizzi for the printed book catalogue of the British Museum and were modified substantially by the Trustees of the British Museum. The rules were a monumental achievement, as they represented the first attempt to codify rules for the compilation of an author catalogue with the inclusion of logical guides for cross references. This system was suited to book catalogues in which only one full entry was provided for each book and other entries were in the form of cross references.

Panizzi's *Letter* to the Earl of Ellesmere which defined the alphabetical catalogue. the concept of 'heading' as the most important bibliographical element in alphabetical catalogues under which other bibliographic data was subsumed in the catalogue. and the objectives and problems of the catalogue of a large library such as that of the British Museum are considered as the first theoretical foundations of descriptive cataloguing.

Throughout his *Letter* Panizzi emphasised the concept of uniformity, whether in the form of author heading, the alphabetical order of headings or in the form of slips or cards, and warned of the difficulties resulting from the lack of uniformity in a catalogue. Panizzi's approach to this concept can be seen in his rules for choice and form of a name.

The focus of Panizzi's code was primarily on the creation of entries based on the information found on the title-page. He selected the title-page as the authoritative source of cataloguing data in the sense that it would offer the same information to all cataloguers.

This was the first approach to standardisation in descriptive cataloguing and has been continued through some of the subsequent codes. Title-page cataloguing was also an indication of the focus of the code on the concept of 'bibliographic unit' and on the finding-list function of the catalogue in that it made for easier retrieval of the item for the user who searched the catalogue with information already obtained from the title page.

The principle of authorship was emphasised as the principal 'organising element' in the catalogue and entries were filed alphabetically by author. When compared to older codes, the treatment of various conditions of authorship that appear on the title-page is, to a considerable extent, complete in Panizzi's code. The principle of *multiple authorship*, although without any differentiation between *joint* and *collective authorship*, is apparent in the code. In fact, the type of publications of that time did not require a clear distinction. however, the 'Anglo-American Code of 1908' and the 'American Library Association Code of 1949' later found this to be necessary. In terms of cataloguing of publications by corporate bodies, the 91 rules do not envision corporate authorship. Instead, corporate entries could be used as a default or as an organising element.

Rule 80:

- All acts, memoirs, translations, journals, minutes, andc., of academies, institutes, associations, universities, or societies learned, scientific, or literary, by whatever name known or designated, as well as works by various hands, forming part of a series of volumes edited by any such society, to be entered, according to the English name of the country and town at which the sittings of the society are held, in the following order....

In contrast to Needham, Carpenter states that this is a misconception to consider the 91 Rules as the first code which explicitly recognised the possibility of corporate authorship. Panizzi suggested the use of *form headings* as the main entry for certain types of publications. Publications such as acts, memoirs, transactions, and minutes published by institutes, universities and learned societies were entered under Academies.

Newspapers, magazines, and annuals under the heading Periodical Publications. and dictionaries under Dictionaries. These form headings, which can be regarded as akin to today's form subject headings, were a means for the bringing together of works of a common nature.

Panizzi used form headings also for anonymous works, which he entered under some catchword from the title. for example, in his rule 33, he prescribed that: "Anonymous publications relating to any act, or to the life of a person whose name occurs on the title of a work, are to be catalogued under the name of such person".

It is generally agreed that Panizzi's *Ninety-One Rules* for the construction of the British Museum catalogue became the source for all subsequent Anglo-American codes. Hyman

"All later catalogers started with Panizzi to compose their codes, and though the debates of his time are still with us, suggested solutions are largely expansions or refinements of the Ninety-One Rules."

CHARLES C. JEWETT AND HIS THIRTY-THREE RULES

It was Panizzi's code that influenced American cataloguers to compile their own codes of cataloguing rules. The rapid growth of libraries in the United States brought the same need for compiling cataloguing codes. Charles Coffin Jewett, then the librarian of the Smithsonian Institution, prepared the first distinct code of cataloguing rules in the United States.

Jewett's code of 1852 entitled *On the Construction of Catalogues of Libraries and of a General Catalogue, and Their Publication By Means of Separate Stereotype Titles. With Rules and Examples* consisted of thirty-three rules, mainly based upon Panizzi's code.

Through minor modifications to Panizzi's rules, Jewett attempted to compose a code of cataloguing rules which would be useful for all American libraries. Another distinct feature of Jewett's code was that it was to be used to prepare both an author listing and an alphabetical listing of subjects.

Jewett continued the work of Panizzi and laid the foundation for the later Anglo-American concept of authorship based upon the principle of intellectual responsibility. Unlike Panizzi, who did not envision corporate authorship, the concept of corporate authorship was reinforced and established more clearly in Jewett's Code. For example, rule 22 prescribed that:

- Academies, institutes, associations, universities, colleges. literary, scientific, economical, eleemosynary and religious societies. national and municipal governments, boards, corporations, and other bodies of men...issuing publications... are to be considered and treated as the author of all works issued by them, and in their name alone.

However, this rule implies that corporate bodies are not authors but should be considered as such. Carpenter has a similar interpretation. To provide effective access to the author/title catalogue, Jewett composed rules for the choice of headings. An interesting and new concept was that, in rule 13, he prescribed that the heading was to be written the transcribed title.

Tait, what makes Jewett modern and in line with catalo-guing codes of recent times, such as CCR and AACR is in the extent to which he separated rules for titles from those for headings.

Another departure from Panizzi is in the entering anonymous works under the first word of the title rather than under catchwords contained in the title. Unlike Panizzi, Jewett did not use form headings for anonymous works. He suggested that anonymous works should be entered under the first word of the title, not an article or preposition.

Jewett emphasised uniformity as an essential issue in cataloguing and suggested all libraries should adhere to same set of rules. Jewett's contribution to author/title cataloguing and the idea of centralised and cooperative cataloguing was in his proposal to prepare stereotype entries for a printed book catalogue. The stereotype blocks that Jewett proposed could be used to print book catalogues for other libraries. In addition to being economically advantageous, this scheme necessitated uniformity in bibliographic description and an agreed code of cataloguing rules.

A technological advance that promises to reduce cataloguing effort tends to be accompanied by a concern for standardization. If the bibliographic records of one institution are to be used by another, they must be constructed according to a uniform style. For Jewett, a code of cataloguing rules exists to promote uniformity, and he formulated what might be called a principle of standardization.

CHARLES AMMI CUTTER AND HIS RULES FOR A DICTIONARY CATALOGUE

The year 1876, besides being the year in which the American Library Association was established, is also a significant date in the Anglo-American history of descriptive cataloguing. in this year Charles Ammi Cutter published his famous *Rules for a Dictionary Catalogue*, a landmark in the continuum of the Anglo-American cataloguing code tradition. Cutter's Rules are undoubtedly the most comprehensive set of rules ever produced by an individual.

Cutter's influence on descriptive cataloguing can be seen in the later design, objectives and principles of cataloguing codes. In his "Preface to the Fourth Edition" of *Rules for a Dictionary Catalogue*, Cutter illuminated cataloguing theory by considering the principle that "The convenience of the public is always to be set before the ease of the cataloger". Svenonius, *"Unlike Jewett, Cutter preferred to view cataloguing as an art needing only a few high-level rules or principles that could be applied by analogy to a variety of situations."* Through his 'Objectives of the catalogue' Cutter reinforced the contention that the catalogue should not only function as a finding list of what exists in a library, but also should assemble 'literary units' by showing what the library has under a given author.

Cutter formulated the objectives of the catalogue as:

- 1. To enable a person to find a book of which either
  - (A) the author
  - (B) the title is known
  - (C) the subject
- 2. To show what the library has
  - (D) by a given author
  - (E) on a given subject
  - (F) in a given kind of literature
- 3. To assist in the choice of a book
  - (G) as to its edition (bibliographically)
  - (H) as to its character (literary or topical)

To achieve these objectives, Cutter offered as practical means:

- Author-entry with necessary references
- Title-entry or title-reference

- Subject-entry, cross-references and classed subject table
- Form-entry and language entry
- Giving edition and imprint, with notes when necessary
- Notes

Cutter anticipated a need to go beyond the limits of the finding-list function and assumed that a library catalogue should assemble all the editions of a work. This can be considered to be an evolutionary step towards the further development of the concept of the functions of the catalogue.

We find in Cutter, fixed for all time, I believe, the two fundamental principles of the modern author catalogue:

- The author catalogue is more than a finding list of separate and particular books. It deals with literary unit and its function is to assemble under a convenient heading all issues or forms of the same literary unit.
- The most satisfactory method of doing this is through the attribution of authorship, using as heading the name, of the person, or corporate body responsible for the work, or using as a substitute for author heading, a conventional name not derived from the title-page but from the literary source of the book or document.

Rules for a Dictionary Catalogue was a relatively comprehensive code that included provision for author, title, subject, form headings, description, and filing. Cutter made one of the most significant contributions to the development of the author catalogue and the establishment of the authorship principle.

He enriched the concept of authorship by using 'main entries' for the fullest bibliographic record and 'added entries' in abbreviated detail. 'Main' and 'added entries' would fulfil both the finding and the assembling functions of the catalogue. To Cutter, the assembling or collocating function of the catalogue, which brought together all works of an author and all editions of a work, was as important as the finding function.

A significant feature of Cutter's *Rules* was that he extended the concept of corporate authorship. This is an indication of the flexibility of the code towards changing conditions in the authorship concept.

Due to an increase in the number of corporate bodies and consequently the number of publications created under their responsibility, it was natural for the code to provide rules for them. Corporate bodies were considered as the authors of works that were published by them: "Bodies of men are to be considered as authors of works published in their name or by their authority".

This concept is a restatement of what Jewett embodied in his Rule 22. Carpenter identifies Cutter as the first theoretician of corporate authorship. Cutter's principle of corporate authorship, as Lubetzky points out, dominated all subsequent Anglo-American codes up to AACR2, which attempted to restrict it to only a few specified categories.

Cutter made no use of form headings for main entry but rather transferred this type of heading to the area of subjects. Like Jewett, he entered anonymous works under the first word of the title, but with an interesting exception in the case of biographies, which he entered not under the first word of the title but under the subject.

Cutter's Rules were designed for the construction of a dictionary book catalogue suited for small and medium-size public libraries with a collection of materials mainly in monographic format. His approach to the dictionary catalogue was to design a code consistent with the dominant printed book catalogues of the time.

Thus, the types of entries he proposed and the kinds of access points he prescribed were relevant to this form of catalogue. The use of a full main entry with abbreviated added entries for the retrieval of bibliographic information was suited to the printed book catalogue. In a book catalogue, the complete bibliographic record would be identified under the main entry and added entries would refer the user to the main entry.

The added entry function before Cutter was performed by cross-references which referred the reader to the main entry record. From the fourth edition of Cutter's rules onward the boundary between the use of added entries and cross references became clearer: added entries to provide added access to a bibliographic record, and cross references for name variations.

Another significant feature of Cutter's Rules was in the provision for short, medium and full entries. This was a requirement that Cutter considered necessary for different library catalogues of that time. It should be noted that a library could choose one option and construct its catalogue according to only one of the prescribed levels of entries.

Cutter took a pragmatic approach towards rules and suggested alternative rules based on the nature and size of the library and the physical form of the catalogue. The three styles of cataloguing that he formulated were a response to such considerations.

Rules for a Dictionary Catalogue became the chief source for later codes in the English language. Lubetzky, like many others, was influenced by Cutter and the principles he proposed in his Code of Cataloguing Rules and to the International Conference on Cataloguing principles are an indication of this influence. Tait, *"The principles laid down by Cutter in 1876 remained almost without challenge until almost the present decade—a testimony to their value."*

THE DEVELOPMENT OF THE CARD CATALOGUE IN THE LATE NINETEEN CENTURY

Parallel to the development of cataloguing codes in the nineteenth century in the Anglo-American countries, an innovation — the introduction of cards for the construction of library catalogues — changed the whole face of American libraries. Although the idea of using slips and cards as a basis for creating the catalogue is not an American invention and goes back to the eighteenth century, when Abbé Rozier employed cards for the compilation of an index of publications of the Paris Académie des sciences in 1775, it was only much later and in the United States that card catalogues became common in libraries for public use. It should be added that slip or hand-written card catalogues were used for the preparation of book catalogues, but not for public use.

After a number of scattered attempts to use printed slips in public catalogues in the second half of the nineteenth century, the card catalogue became commonplace in the United States in the late nineteenth century.

In 1898, the Library of Congress began to provide printed catalogue cards for distribution. Although the service became available to all American libraries by 1898, it was not widely accepted by librarians, due to the various approaches and practices of individual libraries towards author headings, the size of the card, and long delays in shipment. In the last edition of his rules in 1904, Cutter recognised the card catalogue as the way of the future.

By the late nineteenth century, the dictionary card catalogue had been universally accepted as a practical and responsive catalogue. Researchers state:

"By the end of the nineteenth century the pattern of catalogue construction was well defined with subject headings, main entry, literary unit principle, dictionary catalogue, classification, unit cards, added entries, and adequate bibliographical descriptions all well-developed elements".

DEVELOPMENTS IN THE TWENTIETH CENTURY

Cataloguing in the second half of the nineteenth century was characterised by the compilation of a great number of codes which followed more or less the same trend in establishing principles for the construction of library catalogues. There was agreement on a number of general principles, particularly entry under author.

In the twentieth century, a number of significant factors have affected libraries in their operations and practices, including descriptive cataloguing. These factors are: the steady growth in the number of libraries and the size of collections, as an indirect indication of social and technological change.

A rapid increase in the number of publications in book and non-book form which led to the 'information explosion' in the twentieth century and the tendency to, and need for, more and closer international relations. There was a strong trend towards international cooperation and the exchange of ideas in the early twentieth century. The role of national libraries and library associations in formulating bibliographic standards is considered to have been a significant factor in the development of cataloguing codes and the move towards national as well as international standar-disation. In the Anglo-American world, the move towards closer cooperation and formulation of joint codes is a clear expression of such trends in the cataloguing community. Also, availability of printed catalogue cards from the Library of Congress, which was considered by Cutter as "... a great change... the status of cataloguing in the United States" was an important move towards bibliographic uniformity at the national, and later at the international, level.

ANGLO-AMERICAN CODE: CATALOGUE RULES. AUTHOR AND TITLE ENTRIES

As the first attempt at joint compilation of a code of cataloguing rules at an international level, the Anglo-American Code, known as AA or the *Joint Code*, was a response to the common interests and problems in descriptive cataloguing that existed in the United States and the United Kingdom in the late nineteenth and early twentieth centuries.

It was the result of cooperation between the [British] Library Association and the American Library Association in the production of "... a joint code which would bring uniformity into the cataloguing practice of the English-speaking countries". Although the idea came first from Melvil Dewey in 1900, the proposal was made by the [British] Library Association to ALA in 1904.

Unlike most older codes, AA was not formulated for an individual library, rather it was designed for larger libraries of scholarly character. It was, therefore, naturally influenced by other codes, such as Cutter's *Rules,* the *Prussian Instructions*, the *British Museum* code and also the Library of Congress rules, as shown in its preface and throughout the text. Daily, the code:

"... was a largely successful effort to rationalize the rules of several different libraries into one readily followed standard".

It can be said that the Anglo-American Code of 1908 was designed for the construction of author/title card catalogues. The printed card service of the Library of Congress, started in 1898, is considered to have been a significant factor in the rapid proliferation of card catalogues among libraries of different sizes and types. In this situation, the compilation of a joint code which would bring uniformity to the catalogues of different libraries was a welcome event, particularly in the United States.

The code recognised the 'literary unit' as the basis for cataloguing. In this regard, the code preferred as the heading the full, real, baptismal name of the author rather than accepting the name by which the author was identified most commonly on the title pages of works or in reference sources.

A lack of definition of the concept of corporate authorship and also the undefined distinction and inconsistent treatment of institutions and societies were among some of the criticisms made of the code. For example, a difficulty with the rules concerning corporate entry was that buildings and ships were considered as authors?? Most importantly, the principles on which it was formulated were not stated in the code itself. In addition to some inconsistencies and many omissions, its numerous rules made it difficult to understand and use.

ALA CATALOGUE RULES. AUTHOR AND TITLE ENTRIES (ALA DRAFT CODE 1941)

Due to a perceived need for a more detailed and comprehensive code which would cover the various problems encountered by cataloguers, there was increasing demand for the revision of the 1908 code. In 1930 the Library of Congress appointed a subcommittee to study its revision.

Based on cataloguers' experiences in the actual use of the code, work was begun by ALA with the cooperation of the [British] Library Association. Because of the outbreak of World War II, the British could not continue their cooperation. A preliminary edition was published in 1941 and a second American edition was published in the same year as: *ALA Catalogue Rules. Author and Title Entries.* However, because of its adherence to American perspectives and cataloguing tradition, ALA is not considered an international code.

An extremely complex code with an enumeration of cases and what many regard as an over-elaboration of rules, ALA was not welcomed by the cataloguing community. Rather than defining principles, it supplemented and amended the 1908 Code. For example, the definition and the treatment of corporate entry are almost identical to AA 1908. the code was so severely criticised that the situation encouraged Andrew Osborn to write his famous article entitled *"The crisis in cataloguing"*.

This article is considered a classic within the cataloguing community and is very much cited in the literature. Osborn criticised the code's approach towards the provision of various rules for the coverage of different cataloguing cases. Daily restates Osborn's criticism of the code that "What is needed is a set of guiding principles, worked out for the most common cases, which accomplish the basic task of cataloguing without formalistic constraints that perplex the user without adding materially to precise description".

A.L.A. CATALOGUING RULES. AUTHOR AND TITLE ENTRIES (ALA 1949)

Due to the severe criticisms of ALA, a new edition, *i.e.*, the rules for entry was published by the American Library Association in 1949. The Library of Congress had already decided to prepare its own rules for descriptive cataloguing.

Therefore, ALA requested its Catalogue Code Revision Committee to deal only with the revision of part 1 of ALA, taking into account all the criticisms which had been made of it. Thus, the 1949 code covered only rules for entries. In this respect, the code was basically influenced by Cutter's rules for main entry, and his theory that "...the catalogue user was the final arbiter of the form that any specific rule should take".

Although ALA basically followed AA and ALA, it had some new features such as:

- The code chose 'work' as the basis for description. In this regard, it followed AA and took the concept of 'literary unit' from Cutter's rules.
- With regard to the choice of main entry, the code prescribed that the entry was to be made under "...the person or body chiefly responsible for the intellectual content of the book, literary, artistic or musical". Intellectual responsibility was not confined to title page information, rather, the author was usually to be chosen from either the work itself or other sources. In this regard, the concept of principal responsibility was a new idea in ALA.
- It emphasised the concept of corporate versus personal authorship by giving more guidance on the construction of corporate headings. For example, Rule 1 prescribed that: "Enter a work under the name of its author whether personal or corporate".

In the introduction to the code it is stated that, as the dictionary card catalogue was the dominant form of the catalogue in most American libraries, the rules were prepared with that type of catalogue in mind. The main thrust of the Code's rules was the choice of main entry for the author, personal or corporate, who was considered to be chiefly responsible for the intellectual or artistic content of the work.

Added entries were to be made "to enable the user of the catalogue to find a work when incomplete knowledge or imperfect memory of the work, or unfamiliarity with the rules of entry, would prevent ready access to the main entry". References were to be used to provide uniformity and effectiveness in the catalogue.

ALA was criticised for not continuing the trend towards internationalism which AA had tried to achieve at the beginning of the century, especially as the time was more convenient for the code to approach international uniformity and the postwar condition also seemed to be more in need of international cooperation. By abandonment of the agreement reached in 1908 and by adherence to a national tradition, ALA missed a good opportunity for getting closer to uniformity and standardisation.

In his *Headings and Canons. Comparative Study of Five Catalogue Codes*, Ranganathan criticised the ALA Code more than other codes because of redundancies and inconsistencies in its rules. In relation to the lack of sufficient answers to different cataloguing problems, there were many objections to the ALA rules.

The criticism of Osborn did not seem to have a great deal of effect on ALA 1949, for the rules in this code, in the opinion of many, are as pedantic, elaborate, and often arbitrary, as those in the preliminary edition of 1941. The code was constructed on the same formula as AA and ALA but lacked a clear statement of basic principles.

Among major critiques of the code was Lubetzky's report, *Cataloguing Rules and Principles: A Critique of the A.L.A. Rules for Entry and a Proposed Design for their Revision, 1953*. Lubetzky stated that a major shortcoming of the code was that it was "vague in design and weak in structure." Tait Lubetzky criticised the code because of its "proliferation of rules to cover specific cases, and almost complete absence of any principles of entry, in spite of the statement in the introduction. The result is that proliferation also results in inconsistencies".

CODE OF CATALOGUING RULES (CCR 1960)

Lubetzky's *Cataloguing Rules and Principles* which was prepared for the Board of Cataloguing Policy and Research of the American Library Association received general approval. Because of his approach towards the design of an effective code of cataloguing rules, Lubetzky was invited by the ALA Catalogue Code Revision Committee to prepare a new edition of *ALA*. Being influenced by Cutter's 'Objectives', Lubetzky produced his *Code of cataloguing rules, author and title entry: an unfinished draft, 1960,* known as *CCR.*

Lubetzky stated the objectives on which the rules were formulated as follows:

The objectives which the catalogue has to serve are two:

- To facilitate the location of a particular publication, *i.e.*, a particular edition of a work which is in the library.
- To relate and display together the editions which the library has of a given work and the works which it has of a given author.

The two functions are complementary, but both are essential to the effectiveness of the catalogue. Lubetzky adopted Cutter's 'Objectives' with minor changes. Here, the word 'Book' is replaced by the words 'Work' and 'Edition' to give priority to the literary unit concept and to cater for the inclusion of various types of 'non-book' items in the code.

By a clear definition of the main entry concept, Lubetzky tried to remove inconsistencies within Cutter's Code, AA, and ALA in which "the main entry sometimes represents 'work' and sometimes 'edition'". His emphasis was on the 'work' and he considered that a major function for the main entry was the assembling of the editions of a certain work by a certain author.

To Lubetzky, the 'work', rather than the 'edition,' was the primary unit. He assumed that "... the catalogue user is interested in the work represented by the particular publication rather than in its embodiment in any particular edition". In determining the basic principles of his rules, Lubetzky followed Cutter's "convenience of the public" and considered the reader's approach to be an important factor. As CCR was written primarily for the construction of a card catalogue using the concept of a unit cataloguing method, added entries carried far more information than in older Anglo-American codes. Main entry was not considered as the most important entry for a work and lost its importance significantly in the sense that the code avoided the use of the term “main entry”. Instead, it used terms like “entry is made under...” or “... is entered under the person...” However, the significance of the main entry concept in single-entry catalogues, such as union catalogues in hard copies, could not be disregarded. In comparison to the older Anglo-American cataloguing codes, the concept of authorship was broadened and extended to all types of materials in CCR. The utility of such an approach to authorship in the case of non-book materials has been challenged. In this regard, Tait pointed out that:

Certain types of material may not be amenable to or require author entry as such, and one has the impression that CCR occasionally forces author entry, presumably for the sake of consistency.... This would appear to be pushing the authorship concept rather too far, but is almost inevitable within the general framework of the philosophy of CCR.

The code emphasised the concept of corporate authorship. Rule 22 was a general rule for works of corporate bodies. Another concept emphasised in the code was a reliance on title-page information in providing standard cataloguing data. In this respect, Lubetzky followed Panizzi, who was the first to recognise the importance of the title-page. This is in line with the users’ knowledge of or familiarity with books as known or seen by them. In this regard, it is generally said that the cataloguer can avoid the difficulty of determining the intellectual responsibility of the item in hand. However, this approach may be in conflict with the uniformity which is necessary in the assembling of different editions of a work under one form of heading. In relation to the discussion it should be added that, unlike ALA, CCR avoided the subjective judgements required of the cataloguer in distinguishing between different types of multiple authorship. As noted earlier, this was possible by relying on title-page criteria. Because of its logical consistency and its compilation on a solid theoretical basis, CCR received favourable reaction. However, in terms of the alterations that would result in catalogues from the possible implementation of the code, it was criticised by reference librarians who claimed that they would find answering reference questions difficult and by library administrators who preferred the simplification of cataloguing rules and less costly practices.

The CCR was very influential at the time and Lubetzky was hailed as one of the great theoreticians in descriptive cataloguing. Suffice it to say that the principles adopted and internationally agreed upon at the International Conference on Cataloguing Principles, Paris, 1961 were to a large extent influenced by CCR.

THE PARIS PRINCIPLES (ICCP 1961)

As one of the most important events in the history of descriptive cataloguing, the International Conference on Cataloguing Principles (ICCP), Paris, 1961 has had a great impact on the development of current cataloguing codes. ICCP was a response to the need for international agreement on the principles of cataloguing. The conference aimed at providing basic agreement for the compilation of national bibliographies and national codes.

In this regard and in order "to facilitate the international communication of knowledge by achieving the widest possible uniformity in library catalogues and other means of biblio-graphical communication", the Paris Conference has been considered to be one of the most effective attempts in the direction of universal bibliographical control and international standardization in cataloguing.

Due to a number of conflicting issues in different catalo-guing codes and practices, which made the exchange and understanding of bibliographic information difficult at an international level, there was a strong need for some kind of uniformity in national bibliographies and, at a higher level, in the bibliographic universe at large.

The ICCP Report, the Conference intended:

- *... to take the necessary action to ensure:*
  - That cataloguing rules in their countries are established or revised as soon as possible in conformity with the principles laid down by the Conference, and put into practice.
  - That the same principles are taken into account in the compilation of national bibliographies.

Although the physical form of the catalogue was not directly specified in the Principles, it can be concluded that they and their allied recommendations were based on the concept of the card catalogue, the most widely used form of catalogue at the time. It should be added that, by this time, the card catalogue had become an internationally accepted form for the construction of library catalogues. The principles discussed and agreed upon at the ICCP applied mainly to the choice and form of headings and entry words as the most important organising elements in author/title catalogues, which needed uniformity at an international level. The ICCP continued the principles of the older codes in the sense that the emphasis was on alphabetical author/title catalogues and lists of books.

As the first issue in the Statement of Principles the functions of the catalogue were agreed upon as:

- *Functions of the Catalogue:* The catalogue should be an efficient instrument for ascertaining
  - Whether the library contains a particular book specified by
    a. Its author and title, *or*
    b. If the author is not named in the book, its title alone, *or*

c. If the author and title are inappropriate or insufficient for identification, a suitable substitute for the title. and

- Which works by a particular author and
- Which editions of a particular work are in the library.

In relation to the functions of the catalogue and their influence on other cataloguing principles two working papers were presented at ICCP. The two papers, in fact, illustrate the two contradictory approaches which have their root in the long history of cataloguing codes in relation to the functions of the catalogue and the choice and form of main and added entries.

In his working paper, Lubetzky emphasised the second function as the principal element for bringing together different editions of the same work. He considered the 'literary unit' as the basis for description. In this context, different editions and translations of a work should be found together rather than under their own titles. The name of an author must be uniform to bring together all publications by that author. In terms of titles, Lubetzky put emphasis on entering publications under the title as found in the first publication of the work, or where this was not possible, under the accepted 'conventional title.' This would bring together different appearances of exactly the same work.

This approach, of course, has some problems particularly for public library users who usually look for a specific edition or translation of a work and not the original work with a different title they are not familiar with. Verona, who presented the second approach to the function of the catalogue, emphasised the publication in hand as the basis for description.

She stressed that the function of main entries is:

- To represent particular publications, and
- To bring together in the catalogue all publications by one author.

In this context, a certain form of the author's name would group together all publications by the author. To Verona, not the main entries, but added entries would link all editions of a certain literary unit.

In Statements 3 to 12, the ICCP specified the structure of the catalogue and the kinds and forms of entries that were necessary for the effective discharge of the catalogue's functions. Although Principle 2.1 considered the single item important, Principle 2.2 put emphasis on the work. This was a contradictory situation to which the ICCP did not offer an effective solution and to which there were objections.

A significant improvement of the ICCP over AA and ALA was in the definitions that it provided for personal and corporate authorship. In this respect, ICCP put the emphasis on the intellectual responsibility concept of authorship. As opposed to some European traditions, Principles 9.1 to 9.3, that regarded corporate bodies as authors, approached the Anglo-American practice and were accepted by a majority of the national cataloguing committees. Representing the point of view of Hungarian cataloguers, Domanovszky argued against this practice and considered it to be opposed to common practice in everyday speech. The German cataloguing tradition also rejected the concept of corporate authorship in most cases and accepted it only when there was no personal author named in the work and when the title of the work was explicitly related to the corporate body as the originator. On the other hand, Verona was one of the proponents of corporate authorship and later stated that:

A work should be considered to be of corporate authorship if it may be concluded by its character or nature that it is necessarily the result of the creative and/or organizational activity of a corporate body as a whole, and not the result of an independent creative activity of the individual(s) who drafted it.

An interesting issue in the list of topics discussed at ICCP that was not fully acknowledged at the time was the potential impact of electronic information systems upon the process of cataloguing. In his working paper presented at the Conference, Gull discussed the potential impact of electronics, such as machine readable texts and the concept of 'automatic authorship' on cataloguing rules and suggested that the issue be addressed in the design of cataloguing codes.

For example, Gull anticipated that the concept of main entry would be influenced by electronic texts and main entry headings would not be needed for machine readable texts. Gull concluded that: "... cataloguers must fit cataloguing rules to human capabilities and adapt them to changes in technologies.

Indeed, they must enlist the aid of new technologies to assure that cataloguing rules are based on substance rather than form." In the early 1960s, however, the issue was far from clear and did not arouse much comment within the profession. Most subsequent current national cataloguing codes have been compiled on the basis of the ICCP Statements. Although ICCP was regarded as being highly successful in its resolutions and objectives at the time, it was later criticised for some inconsistencies and vagueness. As reported by national cataloguing committees, full conformity to the Statements proved not to be practical, due to variations in cataloguing traditions and practices.

ANGLO-AMERICAN CATALOGUING RULES (AACR 1967)

After ICCP it was time for the English-speaking world to prepare a new set of rules, a second Anglo-American joint code, which could provide for greater uniformity both in library catalogues and in the exchange of bibliographic information between libraries in the English-speaking countries. Based on ICCP and their own cataloguing traditions, the library associations of the United States, Canada and the United Kingdom, with the collaboration of the Library of Congress, provided the groundwork for the compilation of a new joint code which would be applicable at an international level.

Due to some variations in cataloguing practices, the code was published in 1967 in two separate texts: North American and British. One difference between these texts was the departure of the American text from the Paris Principles in its rejection of the entry of a collection under title when such a work had a collective title.

Furthermore, due to the recommendations and require-ments of the Association of Research Libraries (ARL) the impact of the Paris Principles on existing entries for corporate bodies was reduced and there were a few cases in which the code departed from those principles.

The most significant departure was the exemption of certain bodies of an institutional nature from the principle of entry under name and a substitution of a rule of entry under the place in which the institution was situated.

Based on the American cataloguing tradition of entering a work under author rather than title, AACR1 gave entry of collections under compiler when the compiler's name was on the title-page. These exceptions, however, were changed in 1974 and 1975 to bring the code into line with the Paris Principles and to provide uniformity between the two versions.

Unlike AA and ALA, AACR1 was primarily drawn up to respond to the needs of general research libraries and had some features that distinguished it from its predecessors. The needs of smaller public libraries were addressed by the provision of alternative rules as well as more direct headings. Because of a basic difference in approach to the practice of cataloguing, the character of the rules for entry and heading was considerably different.

These differences were summarised as:

- The rules were based on internationally agreed principles,
- Choice of entry and construction of heading were treated as separate problems, except when form subheadings were involved,
- Choice of entry was treated as a problem of determin-ation of authorship responsibility, and
- Construction of heading was treated as a problem of name.

A thorough examination of the code reveals that the rules for entry and heading are substantially based on ALA, Lubetzky's CCR, and ICCP. However, rules for description in AACR1 were formulated on the basis of *Rules for description in the Library of Congress* and its supplementary rules.

The principle of authorship was more clearly enunciated in AACR1, where the primary criterion for determining authorship was 'intellectual responsibility'. As will be discussed later, its handling of this issue was based on conditions of authorship rather than on types of work. Lubetzky, "*... the governing principle in AACR1 is that entry is to be based not on type of publication or work but on the varying conditions of authorship.*" With regard to corporate bodies, as can be seen from the AACR's definition, they were considered as authors in an explicit way.

Although the title-page was chosen as the chief source for determining entries, AACR1 chose the 'work' as the basis for cataloguing. This was apparent throughout the statements of the rules in part I. Lubetzky criticised the definition of authorship in AACR1 in that it based the chief responsibility for a work on its intellectual or artistic content rather than considering the producer as the person chiefly responsible for a work. Through their emphasis on entries under uniform headings and the use of references, the rules were oriented to multiple-entry alphabetical catalogues. However, AACR1 still distin-guished between main and added entries. In explaining the significance of this concept, the framers of the code stated that, both for identification of a single-entry work in multiple entry catalogs as well as for the general needs of libraries and bibliographical and book-trade activities, a standard mode of identifying bibliographical entities was necessary. This standard mode is one of the often stated justifications for the use of main entries in such situations as single-entry bibliographies, book lists, order lists and bibliographic citations. At the time that AACR1 was compiled, the card catalogue was the dominant form of library catalogue and the framers of the code did not take into account the potential impact of automation on library operations, particularly the application of the computer in providing public catalogues.

Daily believed that it was the fate of the code that it was designed for practices of that time and even previous years and not for the coming decades and for the computerised listing of entries. It is worth noting that in the 1960s, the attitude of most librarians towards computerised catalogues was limited to a superficial understanding of the concept of automation, *e.g.*, the ability of computers to perform repetitive tasks with much more precision and speed.

An important factor that disappointed cataloguers in the full adoption of AACR1 was the policy of 'superimposition', declared by the Library of Congress, of continuing the usage of headings which had been constructed according to ALA rules. This policy made trouble for some cataloguing departments in maintaining their catalogues and resulted in numerous inconsistencies in name headings. Soon after the adoption of AACR1 in large libraries, it became apparent that the code was in need of a number of additions and changes. The Library of Congress and the ALA's Division of Cataloguing and Classification approved the need for the addition or change of a number of rules. The British did not welcome the continuous revisions of the rules that were being undertaken in the United States. However, cataloguing trends in the 1970s, such as the introduction of the International Standard Bibliographic Description (ISBD), necessitated that the code should be brought into line with these new trends.

INTERNATIONAL STANDARD BIBLIOGRAPHIC DESCRIPTION (ISBD) (1971)

As one of the major products of the train of activity set in motion by ICCP and elaborated by a Working Group set up by the International Meeting of

Cataloguing Experts, ISBD was developed to specify requirements for the description of publications for the purpose of international communication. The standard assigns an order to the descriptive elements, and specifies a system of punctuation for the description.

It is designed primarily as an instrument for the international communication of bibliographical information not only in library cataloguing but also in book trade activities. ISBD is not a set of cataloguing rules: it does not deal with access points and "does not include any prescription for the heading underwhich a description should appear in a catalogue or other bibliographical list". In addition to the General International Standard Bibliographic Description, IFLA has developed specialised ISBDs for specific types of material.

Many national cataloguing codes have based the rules for description on the general framework of ISBD. Also most national bibliographies are prepared according to this standard. Adherence to these descriptive standards by many cataloguing agencies, whether working in a manual or an automated environment, has provided greater uniformity in the communication and understanding of bibliographical information within countries and between countries. This is essential to Universal Bibliographic Control.

In respond to the requirements of automated systems, which were developing rapidly in the early 1970s, ISBD was designed in a way to facilitate the conversion of bibliographic records into machine-readable form, or as Gorman points out, "to maximize the interchange and processibility of data in the machine environment." This was done through the systematisation of the order of data elements and the punctuation that is used to separate these elements in a record.

Although ISBD is a computer compatible format, many automated systems do not use the ISBD order and/or punctuation, especially when displaying bibliographic records. This is in contrast to the primary aim of the standard. Many online catalogues rearrange the data elements, causing confusion from one system to the next. Much of the criticism of ISBD has been in relation to problems other than automation. Ricard, Lubetzky, Ayres criticised ISBD mostly for the punctuation, the redundancies and repetitive author statement.

ANGLO-AMERICAN CATALOGUING RULES, SECOND EDITION (AACR2 1978)

The second edition of AACR was the result of four years' work by the Joint Steering Committee for Revision of AACR (JSC) which had been set up in 1974 by the American Library Association, the [British] Library Association and the Canadian Committee on Cataloguing, with the support and cooperation of the British Library and the Library of Congress.

Tikku, AACR2 was "the result of the culmination of several factors, which appeared in the 1970's and thus necessitated the production of a revised edition of cataloguing rules". These factors were: piecemeal revision of AACR1. the development of the International Standard Bibliographic Description (ISBD). LC's interest in 'desuperimposition', *i.e.*, allowing for changes to headings established under pre-AACR rules. and the use of computers in libraries.

During the period between the publication of the first and second editions of AACR many changes had taken place, such as the development of MARC formats, the development of computerised catalogues, the growth of centralised and cooperative bibliographic services and the proliferation of new media and nonbook materials, which had significant effects on cataloguing and bibliographic control.

Also, the introduction of ISBD (M), which was incorporated in AACR2, was considered to be a major factor in the move towards Universal Bibliographic Control (UBC). In spite of these factors, AACR2 maintained the same principles and objectives as AACR1 and was based on the work of those who created the first edition.

Gorman, coeditor of the code:

- "AACR2 should be judged not just on its own merits but also as part of a continuum, as part of the 'great tradition' in Anglo-American cataloguing which stretches back to Panizzi, Jewett, and Cutter."

The aims of the second edition of AACR as set out by JSC were:

- To incorporate already agreed revisions to AACR1.
- To harmonize the British and North American texts of AACR1.
- To incorporate international standards and interna-tional agreements.
- To take developments in library automation into account. and
- To incorporate changes arising from proposals for change coming from any source.

In comparison to AACR1, the second edition had the following features:

- AACR2 maintained a more logical and consistent structure than AACR1. In order to provide ease of use for cataloguers, it followed the sequence of the cataloguing process. The rules were divided into two parts: bibliographic description coming as the first part and choice and form of headings as the second. Also the wording, order, and method of construction of the rules were different.
- AACR2 incorporated fully the General International Standard Bibliographic Description in the rules for description, in that it prescribed the same order of elements and punctuation. As "an instrument for the international communication of bibliographical information", this standard is an important factor in achieving bibliographic standardisation and, at a higher level, Universal Bibliographic Control.
- AACR2 was designed for use in the construction of catalogues and

other lists in general libraries of all sizes. With regard to the varying requirements of detail in bibliographic records in different libraries, three levels of description have been provided. These levels, *viz.*, minimum, medium or standard, and detailed or maximum were, in fact, a revival of Cutter's short, medium, and long entries and are applicable to all types of materials. The choice of a level of description was based on "the purpose of the catalogue or catalogues for which the entry is constructed".

- Unlike AACR1, the rules for entry and heading were applicable to all types of library materials. Gorman, the rules and the examples in AACR2 Chapter 21, unlike the book-oriented rules in AACR1, presented an integrated approach to all library materials.
- In AACR2 the concept of authorship was shrinking. This is apparent in the following aspects:
  - In some cases the code replaced the term 'authorship' with the term 'responsibility', which is more comprehensive. A 'statement of responsibility' appeared after the title to indicate the type of responsibility of any one involved in the creation of the item. Also the terms 'Mixed authorship' and 'Shared authorship' that were used in AACR1 were replaced by 'Mixed responsibility' and 'Shared responsibility' respectively.
  - A major difference of AACR2 from the older Anglo-American codes was that editors of collections were no longer regarded as authors. The decision was made in accordance to Statement 10.3 in the Paris Principles. This shrinking of the concept of authorship was a new trend in the family of the Anglo-American codes.
  - In AACR2 the concept of corporate authorship was no longer prevalent, as can be seen in the restriction of cases where main entry was to be under the names of corporate bodies and the increase in the number of cases where serials were given title main entry. In terms of serials, all special rules for entry of serials were removed from the code with AACR2. Thus, rule 6 is not based on authorship. This approach has been criticised by some serials librarians and others on the grounds that it was hard to create relationships among the different publications of a corporate body.
- In accordance with the requirements of the MARC format, AACR2 abolished the dash entry. This was done by prescribing separate entry or multi-level description for items such as supplements, indexes, detached copies and offprints. The dash entry had been used in book and card catalogues and, once the MARC format was introduced, it was abandoned.

AACR2 followed its predecessors, mainly CCR and AACR1, in that the rules for choice and form of access points "apply to works and not generally to physical manifestations of those works, though the characteristics of an individual item are taken into account in some instances".

In spite of the fact that a computer catalogue permits a number of equal access points, the concept of main entry was retained in AACR2. The reasons for this, as presented by the proponents of the main entry concept in JSC's arguments, were on the basis that it is a central principle in conventional cataloguing theory and that it has practical utility in printed book catalogues, in shelf-listing, and in single-entry listings.

However, for those catalogues which are not based on the main entry principle, AACR2 instructed the cataloguer to use the rules in chapter 21 as a guidance for making necessary entries. Although AACR2 deemphasised the traditional concept of main entry and encouraged the use of 'access point' for any entry, it did not ignore its usefulness and states that:

It will be necessary, however, for all libraries to distinguish the main entry from the others when:

- Making a single entry listing
- Making a single citation for a work.

In addition, the concept of main entry is considered to be useful in assigning uniform titles and in promoting the standardization of bibliographic citation. Despite its flaws in a number of aspects, such as not being based on coherent principles, a lack of defined objectives and a lack of integrity, a lack of separate rules for deciding on serials publications access points and inconsistent treatment of the various media, ambiguities which make the rules open to misinterpretations, irrelevance to computerised catalogues, AACR2 obtained overall support among cataloguers and cataloguing educators.

It undoubtedly went further towards achieving standar-disation and internationalisation than AACR1 and even more than any other code. Smiraglia, "AACR2 is an important partner in the international effort to share bibliographic data". The code was considered by *UNISIST Guide to Standards for Information Handling* as one of the standard codes to be used in a multinational context.

The declaration of 'desuperimposition' and the new policy of the Library of Congress towards the closing of its card catalogues beginning from 1980, which later was postponed to 1 January, 1981 was considered an important issue for American libraries. There was a great deal of frustration about the extent to which headings in existing catalogues constructed under older codes would be affected.

At the same time, the advent of online catalogues, as well as the difficulties of maintaining manual systems, encouraged many libraries of different sizes to close or freeze their card catalogues, to adapt themselves to the Library of Congress' policy, and to adopt fully AACR2.

ANGLO-AMERICAN CATALOGUING RULES, SECOND EDITION, 1988 REVISION (AACR2R)

The implementation of AACR2 engendered frustration in many types of library and generated a large amount of literature concerning its problems, shortcomings and flaws. To many cataloguers, the code did not fulfil their cataloguing requirements in a time of rapid movement towards information networks and the international exchange of bibliographic records.

Based on these criticisms and recommendations, the JSC published three separate groups of rule revisions in 1982, 1983, and 1985. These revisions and the complete revision of chapter, published in 1987, made it necessary to provide the profession with a new revision of the code. Thus, the *Anglo-American Cataloguing Rules, Second Edition, 1988 Revision* (AACR2R) was published under the editorship of Michael Gorman and Paul Winkler.

The appearance of the 1988 revision of the *Anglo-American Cataloguing Rules* did not arouse as much enthusiasm as its predecessor (AACR2) had in 1978. Although AACR2R is the result of ongoing revisions, it maintains the same principles and guidelines as AACR2. The major differences relate to the rules for description of some types of materials, notably computer files. Part II has some changes, of which the most important are in the areas of pseudonyms and geographic names as well as the headings for some subordinate corporate bodies and uniform titles for music.

Two major changes in the authorship concept have been addressed in AACR2R. Separate bibliographic identities are to go under their own headings in the catalogue. AACR2R rule 22.2B2 instructs the cataloguer to choose two or more headings for a person who uses a form of his or her name for one type of work and another name for another type of work.

Rule 22.2B3 takes the same approach: the heading for contemporary authors is to be chosen according to the name which appears in the manifestation of the work being catalogued. The aim is to simplify the cataloguer's task and to provide convenient access for the catalogue user.

As the fact that the direct name of a corporate body is more convenient to the catalogue user, AACR2R has taken this approach and suggests that the direct forms of heading be preferred. Rules for geographic names have also been drastically simplified to identify geographic names through addition to the name of the state, province, region, etc. in certain countries

The framers of AACR2R have tried to prepare a set of rules that could be applicable to all types of library materials in all formats and all languages. Thus, in comparison to its predecessors, the code moves further towards internationalism. The code has been adopted by many countries as their national cataloguing standard. It has also been translated into Arabic, Finnish, French, Japanese, Korean, Malaysian, Norwegian, Portuguese, Spanish, Swedish, Urdu and into Afrikaans, Chinese, Italian, Russian and Persian.

NON-ANGLO-AMERICAN CATALOGUING CODES

A number of national cataloguing codes have either been independently written or contain some major departures from the Paris Principles. In this part two non Anglo-American cataloguing codes, *i.e.*, the German cataloguing code will be briefly studied to acknowledge some of the basic concepts underlying cataloguing traditions outside the Anglo-American context.

The German Cataloguing Code

The *Instruktionen fr die alphabetischen Kataloge in der preussischen Bibliotheken* [Instructions for alphabetic catalogues in Prussian libraries, the PI or The Prussian Instructions], which had been in use since 1899, no longer satisfied the requirements of descriptive cataloguing in the second half of the twentieth century.

There was a strong need to adapt, as far as possible, to international cataloguing practice and to take into consideration a more precise treatment of publications, for example, to comply with modern forms and titles of publications and to take into consideration the impact of electronic data processing.

After the Paris Conference and in moving towards an international consistency of cataloguing codes, a new code began to be prepared by the Verein Deutscher Bibliotekare of the Federal Republic of Germany. Among the concepts covered by the new code, two concepts were new to the German cataloguing tradition: entry under corporate name and the filing of entries by computers.

In 1965 cooperation began with the Bibliotheksverband der D D R which was working along the same lines. In 1969 two parts of the code were published as preliminary editions. RAK was produced jointly by commissions of the Verein Deutscher Bibliothekare, of the Deutscher Bibliotheksverb and, and of the Vereinigung Osterreichischer Bibliothekare in 1969. The Rules in RAK apply to libraries of every size and of varying functions. They contain many alternatives for different cases.

RAK is based on the Paris Principles and ISBD. It is said that the code is closer to international recommendations than other cataloguing codes. Johnson reports some of the major differences between RAK and AACR. In terms of authorship, however, RAK continues the German tradition of attributing this concept only to persons.

For corporate bodies, it introduces the concept of 'Urheber' to identify such bodies as either creators or sponsors of anonymous works. The term 'Urheber' came with the introdu-ction of the concept of corporate authorship and was taken over from legal theory and adapted for cataloguing purposes. In this context, the main entry is made under the 'Urheber' only when no personal author is named in the work and only when the title of the work is explicitly related to the corporate body as the originator.

The filing principle in the Prussian Instruction was different from that of other codes in that it was grammatical and not mechanical. In RAK this approach was changed to take advantage of electronic data processing in the filing of large groups of entries in automated catalogues. It is claimed that the RAK filing rules are the first filing rules for catalogues with the application of automation in mind.

To adapt the German code to the online environment and to consider possible changes to RAK, an expert committee was established in 1994 to continue the work of a special Online Expert Group. It is said that the Expert Group is working on possible modification of RAK with radical ideas and concepts which may be challenging the Anglo-American cataloguing tradition.

Among the issues for possible development for online catalogues are:

- The abandonment of the concept of main entry and the relegation of its function to rules for output format. In their present structures the rules for determining main and added entries are said to be too restrictive for online catalogues. For the online catalogue, none of the classic access points such as corporate names, personal names and titles need to be weighted as primary or secondary by means of tags or indicators.
- Indexing for online catalogues, for example, to avoid redundancies in title in the bibliographic description and in the tracing. It should be ensured that rules do not hamper existing data structures, as the many present redundancies do.
- Formatting possibilities and display of bibliographic description. The desired form of lists can be prepared according to the needs of the clientele for whom they are intended and not according to academic citation methods which are not consistent with OPAC displays

It remains to be seen what would be the consequences of such changes for the international exchange of bibliographic data and how far such new rules affect online retrieval of records in a global online environment.

The Japanese Cataloguing Code

The Japanese code, *i.e., Nippon Cataloguing Rules* (NCR), which was compiled in 1977, is not based on the Paris Principles. It is basically for publications in the Japanese and Chinese languages and is based on a *description unit card system* (DUCS) and does not conform to the principle of main entry.

In a catalogue constructed according to this system, multiple entries are created for an item by reproducing the unit card made for it. There are no main entry headings and as many headings as are needed are recorded in the tracing. The descriptive part of the record is created independently of the headings.

Four revisions were carried out in the 1980s and it was revised to be compatible with both the ISBDs and UNIMARC. The last edition, the 1987 edition, is still based on the no main-entry principle. A most notable feature of NCR is in its treatment of bibliographic hierarchy. This novel feature has been incorporated in preparation for online catalogues. Based on the concept of bibliographic hierarchy as derived from the *Reference Manual for Machine-Readable Bibliographic Description* and unlike its 1977 edition, in which the 'physical unit' was taken as the basis for description, this edition has taken the 'work' as the basic unit for description.

In this situation, the physical manifestations of a work are considered subordinate to it. With this approach there is much flexibility for the treatment of bibliographic relationships through a multi-level record.

SUMMARY AND CONCLUSIONS

In studying the historical development of modern catalogues and cataloguing codes, particularly with respect to the physical form of the catalogue, a range of factors and elements have been highlighted as the most important concepts. The development of these concepts, which form the underlying principles of descriptive cataloguing and the design of cataloguing codes, has been substantially based on two funda-mental factors: the form of the catalogue and the nature of bibliographic entities.

These concepts have been subject to constant assessment, reassess-ment and change throughout the history of modern cataloguing:

- *The Alphabetical Catalogue*: The classified catalogue of the early nineteenth century gradually gave way to the alphabetical catalogue, particularly the dictionary catalogue, which has been one of the most popular forms of the catalogue throughout the twentieth century. The development of cataloguing rules in the Anglo-American context for choice and form of entry has been influenced by this type of catalogue.
- *Objectives and Functions of the Catalogue:* The principles on which modern cataloguing codes have been formulated have developed in accordance with the objectives and functions of the catalogue. The older inventory function of the catalogue evolved into a finding function in the early nineteenth century and later also included an assembling function in Cutter's Rules and afterwards. Provisions for the choice of entry in cataloguing codes are based on the objectives and functions of the catalogue and how they should be discharged.
- *The Concept of a Work*: The controversial concept of 'work', as opposed to the concept of 'book' has had significant influence on other concepts and principles in descriptive cataloguing. By giving priority to one concept, other concepts such as the concept of authorship, choice and form of entries and uniform titles are influenced. Inconsistencies are present in some cataloguing codes due to the confusion between 'work' and 'book'.

- *The Concept of Entry:* As the most important means of approaching surrogates of library materials, the concept of entry has become fixed in bibliographic practice. Thus, a significant portion of any cataloguing code is devoted to rules for the construction of entries, which discuss what constitutes the entry and the choice of entry words and access points as well as the form of entry words. Thus, this concept implies the significant notion that there is more than one approach for finding an item in a catalogue.
  - *The Concept of Main Entry*: The question of determining principal responsibility, *i.e.*, the concept of main entry under which the complete catalogue record of an item is entered, has been one of the most important themes in Anglo-American cataloguing codes. With the advent of online catalogues, the value of the main entry has been challenged but with no satisfactory resolution of how to fulfil its functions in its absence.
  - *Number of Access Points Per Work and the Reference Structure of the Catalogue*: As the medium through which the bibliographic record is accessible to the user and the technology of catalogue production has developed from the book catalogue to the card catalogue to the computerised catalogue, there has been more potential for increasing the number of access points by which the complete record is accessible. The author, main entry catalogue, with references, that Panizzi and Jewett found to be the most usable and reasonable eventually evolved into the dictionary catalogue. Development in the application of main and added entries is an indication of better, more flexible and more comprehensive ways of access to bibliographic information.
- *The Concept of Authorship*: This concept is one of the most important organising elements in catalogues and bibliographic lists. A considerable portion of most codes has been devoted to the concept of authorship and to addressing its numerous conditions and problems. Due to the various conditions and complexities of attribution what constitutes authorship in cataloguing is a controversial issue with no satisfactory and comprehensive definition having been established.
  - *Personal Authorship*: Although there has not been consensus as to the definition of what constitutes authorship, this concept has been accepted as one of the most important organising and identifying attributes of a work in the Anglo-American cataloguing tradition, as opposed to oriental traditions. Throughout the evolution of types of authorship, the term has been extended to persons other than writers of works such as editors, compilers of collections, artists, photographers, cartographers and

composers of music. There have, however, been changes in the last two decades so that editors and compilers no longer have the same authorship status as previously.

- *Corporate Authorship*: It was the Anglo-American tradition that extended the concept of authorship to corporate bodies. The concept, though sometimes controversial in definition, was retained for more than a century through the work of Panizzi, Jewett, Cutter, AA, ALA, ALA, ICCP, and AACR1. Although not completely agreed upon, the concept was included in ICCP. The concept has since lost some of its force and, in AACR2, the term 'corporate authorship' has been changed to 'corporate responsibility'.

- *Forms of Heading*: A major portion of each cataloguing code is concerned with the form of the name chosen as heading. This has been a significant contribution, in most codes over the past one hundred and fifty years, towards the achievement of uniformity in bibliographic description and access. In most modern cataloguing codes, it is suggested that a single form of name be used for all the works of an author. Uniform titles are another approach to bringing uniformity in the treatment of the various manifes-tations of a work.
- *The Principle of Standardisation*: A major aim of modern cataloguing codes has been the achievement of standardisation in bibliographic information. This concept has been embodied in different codes in the provision of rules for transcription of cataloguing data from uniform sources, standardisation of bibliographic description, and uniform rules for different types of material. Standardisation has evolved from an internal uniformity within individual catalogues into an international context.
- *Form of the Catalogue*: In relation to the impact of the physical form of the catalogue on the design of cataloguing codes, it can be concluded that, in most cases, the form of the catalogue is either explicitly indicated in the code or can be implied from the predominant form of the catalogue at the time a code was being prepared.

In conclusion, while there have been considerable changes and revisions in rules, cataloguing principles have changed little. Most of the principles formulated in the nineteenth century by Panizzi, Jewett and Cutter have been adopted in our present codes. How does the online environment differ from the manual environment and what are the capabilities of the online catalogue which, as many writers claim in the literature, demand changes in both cataloguing principles and rules?

Such questions and concepts require that, in the first place, a thorough comparison of the two environments be carried out to reveal how far the process of input, storage and output of bibliographic data is different in the new electronic environment. The study of these differences will help to understand better the possible influence of the catalogue environment on cataloguing principles and rules.

ONLINE CATALOGUES AND CARD CATALOGUES: IDENTIFICATION OF AREAS OF SERIALS

This stage is prerequisite to the following chapters, in that it provides the background for the study of the possible influences of online catalogues on both the bibliographic record and on cataloguing principles.

A major aim is to explore the development of online catalogues, their basic features and capabilities and also to reveal the major differences that exist between them and manual catalogues.

This comparison will help identify the differences and similarities in the processes by which a bibliographic record and, on a larger scale, a catalogue, is created, manipulated and made accessible to the catalogue user for searching and retrieval.

In this context, the requirements of online systems which may influence cataloguing rules will also be discussed. A thorough understanding of the conceptual as well as the practical and technical differences and similarities between the online catalogue and the card catalogue will then help in an investigation of the relevance of current cataloguing principles and rules to the online catalogue. It is not the intention of the present chapter to discuss the influence of the features and capabilities of online catalogues on individual cataloguing principles or concepts..

In any comparison between the online catalogue and the manual catalogue, it seems appropriate to choose the card catalogue among the other forms of catalogues as an appropriate approach, because:

- The card catalogue has been and still is one of the most important manual systems in use for more than a century,
- It is the basis from which the present cataloguing standards have been developed, and
- It is the basis on which the structure and contents of online catalogues have been developed, *i.e.*, online catalogues are the logical successors to card catalogues.

It is not the intention of this chapter to reject the merits of the card catalogue. A realistic approach in comparing the online catalogue with the card catalogue should reveal advantages and disadvantages in both catalogues.

Although there is overall support among librarians for online catalogues, most librarians consider having knowledge about the card catalogue to be very useful for an understanding of the origins of the present online system, particularly the structure of the MARC format and how individual records fit into the idea of a catalogue system. This was clearly the case in the general discussions about the card catalogue on the AUTOCAT list, 20 November 1994 to 3 December 1994, commenting on the need to teach the card catalogue in library schools. In fact, an understanding of the origins and underlying concepts from which the present environment has evolved will help us develop catalogue systems based on substantive assumptions. In short, this understanding and comparison of the two environments will help us to reassess, refine and redesign our standards for the construction of catalogues.

John Hickey states:

- "Even if nobody still uses catalogue cards, more of our professional assumptions that we recognize are based upon unit cards and card displays. it helps to have some acquaintance with the previous technology."

It should be noted that online catalogues and card catalogues can be compared from different perspectives and according to different criteria. However, this study will compare them with regard to the processes by which bibliographic records and files are created, manipulated and organised on the one hand and searched, retrieved and displayed on the other. The differences between the online catalogue and the card catalogue will be explored in terms of the input, manipulation and output processes of bibliographic data.

ONLINE CATALOGUES: WHAT THEY ARE

Online catalogues are a norm today. they are not static. they have developed rapidly and will continue to evolve further. By utilising the various capabilities of computers and telecommuni-cations, online catalogues are adding new features that make them totally different from traditional catalogues. Online catalogues are now gateways to larger information systems or, as Hopkins says, they are the 'one-stop information store'.

The online environment is an environment encompassing a wide range of information tools, both bibliographic and non-bibliographic. Library catalogues are now a small but very important component of the evolving online environment and are accessible through different tools in the networked environment, the *public access computer system* (PACS).

The global network is the Internet including various PACS components such as Gopher, WAIS (Wide Area Information Servers), Netscape and Mosaic and other access modes such as Archie and FTP (File Transfer Protocol) tools. The Webpages created by libraries and other information providers are becoming very pervasive and are often used both by librarians and endusers as linking sources for library information.

The same workstation serves as a means of navigating the whole world of the Internet. In the online environment not only are the information tools different from the traditional tools but also the whole concept of access to bibliographic information has changed. Time and location are irrelevant in searching the online environment.

DEVELOPMENTS AND DIRECTIONS OF ONLINE CATALOGUES

As a result of a significant growth in scientific and technological information after the second world war and a resulting expansion in library collections, manual systems could no longer respond effectively to the ever-growing information needs of society.

In terms of fast and effective retrieval of bibliographic information, the card catalogue had many disadvantages. Its large size, complexity and high costs of maintenance made it more and more difficult for libraries to maintain as an up to date searching tool. It became obvious that a more flexible tool was needed to cope with the new conditions of libraries.

It was thus necessary to think of alternative ways of constructing library catalogues that could be cost-effective, manageable and easy to use. Following on the application of computers in other fields, librarians became assured that the computer's theoretical capability to control library operations constituted adequate grounds for embracing a mechanised approach. As Weihs and Howarth point out, "It was necessary to investigate the computer as a relatively cost-effective tool to provide library catalogs."

Computer applications, however, first occurred in library activities other than the provision of public access to the catalogue. Computers were used in libraries mainly for house-keeping types of activities such as circulation control, acquisitions and serial control. This did not directly affect patrons' access to the library catalogue. Library automation began in the early 1960s with the rationale that "If a job could be done by computer, then the number of staff required to work at a defined level of expertise could be reduced".

Although some evidence of automation of library operations other than cataloguing is reported from the 1950s and 1960s, it is the MARC (Machine-Readable Cataloguing) project that has been considered as one of the most important factors in the development of automated catalogues.

With the beginning of the MARC Distribution Service in 1969, large libraries began to utilise MARC magnetic tapes mainly for automated cataloguing in the standard form provided by the Library of Congress. The usefulness of MARC services in cataloguing, along with the increasing availability of computer technology in the late 1960s, led to more developments in automated catalogues.

In response to the needs of small and medium-sized libraries without access to a mainframe computer, centralised cataloguing services gave way to the establishment of bibliographic utilities in the early 1970s.

The Online Computer Library Center, established in 1971, has been considered to be a significant factor in the development of automated catalogues.

With the standard cataloguing services of such bibliographic utilities, libraries were able to utilise the power of computer technology in a cost-effective way.

The proliferation of MARC-based cataloguing led to the realisation of the importance of uniform, standardised bibliographic description as the nucleus of bibliographic services at national and international levels. The growth of bibliographic utilities in the early 1980s as well as developments in telecommunication technology accelerated the move towards centralised MARC-based cataloguing and the need for standardised descriptive cataloguing.

A significant factor further affecting the development of online catalogues was that some libraries began to use MARC bibliographic information for their circulation systems in an online mode. Using short bibliographic records rather than full MARC records for circulation operations, a number of libraries tried to help their patrons in checking whether an item was on loan, on order, or at binding.

This was a form of public enquiry module, which later developed into the online public access catalogue (OPAC). However, as Seal pointed out "The public enquiry module will often replicate the structure of a card or COM [Computer Output Microform] catalogue."

Another major factor leading to the rapid development of online public access catalogues was the contribution, by some library system vendors, of designing and developing public access modules as an important part of their turnkey systems. These vendors tried to incorporate a more sophisticated structure for the public enquiry module with more searching facilities. It should be noted that the early public enquiry systems were not integrated with other library modules, such as acquisitions and serials control.

Due to both the relative success and acceptability of online public enquiry modules, and pressures from patrons and librarians, libraries began to consider developing online public access catalogues (OPACs) with more bibliographic information, *i.e.*, full MARC records and more searching capabilities, such as keyword access and Boolean searching.

The possibility of utilising MARC records as the foundation of bibliographic databases led to the development of the concept of the Integrated Online Library Systems (IOLS) in which "The information that was input at the acquisitions stage would form a basis for the catalogue record which, in turn, would support all library functions. Thus, a number of integrated systems, such as GEAC, ULISYS, ATLAS, DOBIS, NOTIS and VTLS, were established incorporating this modular design.

The overall factors relating to the growing interest in online catalogues have been numerous. It is generally agreed that the most important factors that led to the rapid proliferation and development of online catalogues in the early 1980s were those related to their search, retrieval and display capabilities. Moreover, the opportunity of feedback from librarians and library patrons has provided a continuing momentum for upgrading the structure, contents and capabilities of online catalogues.

Tracing the historical development of online public access catalogues, Hildreth and Matthews identify three generations of OPACs. This categorisation is based on the features and capabilities of online catalogues in the processes of input, storage and output of bibliographic information.

Matthews claims that most of the existing online catalogues are still in the first or second generations and only a few systems have moved beyond first-generation. Added to the three generations identified by Hildreth and Matthews, recent advances in OPACs using graphical user interfaces (GUIs) have introduced a fourth generation to online catalogues.

FIRST-GENERATION ONLINE CATALOGUES

Derived from circulation or cataloguing systems, first-generation online catalogues were in fact computerised card catalogues with almost the same traditional features. In contrast to the patrons' expectations from their use of computerised database systems, these new library catalogues provided limited author, title and controlled vocabulary subject heading access points. For this reason, first-generation online catalogues have been criticised as having no advantages over the card catalogue.

Searching in first-generation online catalogues was essentially based upon pre-coordinated information retrieval principles and was possible only through inputting the exact form of words or phrases. In contrast to searching in card catalogues, the patron had great difficulties as he/she had to input something into the system so that it could respond to his/her query.

As this was possible only through inputting the exact form of words or phrases, which was difficult to remember, searching was not as successful as the searcher expected. Keyword access was not available and refining a search by further limiting it to elements such as date of publication, language or country of publication was not possible. The interfaces, which were usually menu-driven, replicated traditional catalogues in their form of access by providing mainly phrase access to separate subject headings, title, and author indexes. Output and display of search results generally had a single format.

SECOND-GENERATION ONLINE CATALOGUES

With further developments in information technology, it was possible to provide a more sophisticated system for input, storage and output of bibliographic information. Second-generation online catalogues are a departure from traditional card catalogues and incorporate many new features for the provision of effective access.

In contrast to the limited input, storage and output capabilities of first-generation online catalogues, second-generation online catalogues are characterised as being powerful tools for the searching of bibliographic information. Keyword search, Boolean keyword search, cross index search and increasing or reducing of search results are among the features of second-generation online catalogues. Hildreth writes:

Today's second-generation online catalogs represent a marriage of the library catalogue and conventional online information retrieval (IR) systems familiar to librarians who search online abstracting and indexing databases via DIALOG, BRS, ORBIT, MEDLINE, etc.

Improved card catalogue-like searching and browsing capabilities have been joined with the conventional IR keyword and Boolean searching approaches. Many online catalogs support the ability to restrict searches to specified record fields, to perform character masking and/or right-hand truncation, and to limit the results by date, language, place of publication, etc. Also, bibliographic records may be viewed and printed in a number of different display formats.

However, it should be noted that there are a number of major differences between online catalogues and these IR systems that make second-generation online catalogues easier searching tools. With a combination of different search methods, the user is offered possibilities that were not available in first generation online catalogues.

Due to improvements in the design of database management softwares, the structure and content of bibliographic records in second-generation online catalogues may be enhanced by incorporating full records augmented by information such as tables of contents, summaries, content notes, abstracts and links to full electronic texts. Considerable increase in the length of fields was another improvement in second-generation systems.

Interfaces are usually in two modes, menu-driven and command-driven. this makes the interaction between the user and the catalogue more flexible. In terms of user assistance, these catalogues provide more options including, for example, help screens, error messages and suggestive prompts. Ease of use and user-friendliness are two major features of today's second-generation online catalogues.

THIRD-GENERATION ONLINE CATALOGUES

Only a few systems have moved beyond second-generation online catalogues into third-generation online catalogues with enhanced or more sophisticated features. Due to the growing sophistication and availability of technology, new capabilities are being added to online catalogues making them more adaptive to the needs of library patrons. Free text search, enriched database search and simultaneous journal citation searching are among the retrieval capabilities in third generation online catalogues. Furthermore, the mode of interaction has been developed to the point of conversational, adaptive dialogue and the bibliographic format can be tailored according to user preference. Operational assistance such as automatic, context-based correction is also available.

FOURTH-GENERATION ONLINE CATALOGUES

Beginning from the late 1980s, a most recent development in online public access catalogues has been achieved in providing easy access to bibliographic information by using graphical user interfaces (GUIs) such as Windows. These systems, which can be considered as fourth-generation catalogues, have moved away from the traditional menu-type interfaces and are more associated with client server and graphical user interface.

They use WIMP (windows, icons, mouse and pointers) interfaces to speed and simplify searching. With the Windows-style user interface available through PCs (personal computers, *i.e.*, intelligent, and not dumb terminals), there is much more functionality. In these systems the user has the flexibility to click on various buttons, each of which carries a special function.

Nevertheless, these systems do not eliminate but augment the keystroke access. There is also the possibility of using function keys for different purposes when keyboards are involved. In general, access is via mouse or keyboard or a combination of both. Searching capabilities in the Windows version of OPACs are greater than those found in other generations of online catalogues. Pointer capabilities allow the searcher to select exactly the term he/she is looking for, while pull-down menus provide additional options to make searching even more useful. By using scroll bars and pull-down menus, browsing in different indexes is very simple.

With the capability of post-Boolean searching, the search software also attempts to interpret users' search requests in order to present matches of greater or lesser interest to the user. This is called relevance ranking of the search terms. Similar to second and third generation online catalogues, these systems search for terms through using an implicit Boolean 'AND'.

Other Boolean operators such as 'OR' and 'NOT' can also be used to narrow down search results or such search strings can be constructed using the mouse alone. In addition, access has been enhanced by text retrieval qualifiers such as 'language', 'date' and 'form' of the text.

With this feature, it is possible to include new data elements that help in the better identification of the sought item. Integral or add-on text retrieval modules to provide range searching, related term searching, wild card features, adjacency and proximity are supplied by some systems.

One of the recent additional advanced features of fourth-generation OPACs is the 'hypertext' function. Through this function, any word that the user selects or highlights can be used to search all the fields and subfields in all the records in the database for any occurrence of that word. This dynamic feature helps the searcher to navigate the database to find more relevant sources of information.

ONLINE CATALOGUES: HOW THEY DIFFER FROM MANUAL CATALOGUES

There have been some general attempts in the literature of the past decade to briefly compare different types of library catalogues. However, these comparisons have not been concerned with the concepts that underlie the nature and structure of the catalogue. In the following parts, the two types of catalogue will be compared in terms of the creation, manipulation and search/retrieval/ display of bibliographic records.

CREATION AND MANIPULATION OF BIBLIOGRAPHIC RECORDS

Structure and Content of Bibliographic Records

By 'structure of the record' is meant the bibliographic descri-ption consisting of data elements arranged and presented in a given order, such as card catalogue formats and MARC formats. It is generally understood that the medium, via which biblio-graphic records are created, manipulated and made accessible to the searcher, influences their structure and content.

The computer has made possible the enriching of the structure and contents of bibliographic records. While the space limitations of 3" x 5" cards generally restrict the level of data elements to be entered in a record, the content of a bibliographic record in an online catalogue makes it possible and desirable to include more data elements such as those fixed-length data elements indexed in field 008 in the USMARC bibliographic format and even data such as summaries, tables of content, and full texts. This issue has been of major interest to librarians and system designers during the past decade and there have been some proposals in this regard.

User studies of the early 1980s showed that most users of online catalogues would like to have access to tables of contents, back-of-the-book indexes and summaries. Other suggestions have included the titles of essays in collected works or festschriften, book introductions, book jacket material, and the assignment of more subject headings. With the advent and further development of online catalogues it has become possible to assign a larger number of access points to bibliographic records. In comparison to the conventional main and added entries in the card catalogue, any data element in a bibliographic record may be designated as an access point.

MARC Format and Categorisation of Data Elements

As a set of standards for the identifying, storing and communicating of cataloguing information, MARC has significantly contributed to the growth of library automation and to the development of online catalogues. Although the MARC record was conceived as an automated version of the catalogue card, the structure is flexible enough to store bibliographic information in more detailed fields and subfields due to the requirements of automated systems for separate identification of data elements.

While the medium for the card catalogue is the 3" x 5 " card with a fixed, less flexible format, most online catalogues use MARC as a communication format for the exchange of bibliographic information. In this regard, MARC communicates bibliographic information with more flexibility than the card catalogue.

With the machine-readable format, in which the biblio-graphic information on a record has been broken down into fields and subfields, it is possible to separately identify each data element. This approach also allows for inclusion or exclusion of data elements for output as desired.

Based on the MARC format, bibliographic records can be created and tailored according to the specific needs of the library without either discarding standardisation or diminishing the quality of cataloguing.

In the card environment, cataloguing depends on a longer process of manual checking against other catalogues, the ordering of card sets and receiving and interfiling them in the catalogue. This process in online catalogues is done more comprehensively and easily by subscribing to bibliographic utilities or by purchasing MARC products and downloading the needed records into the library's automated system.

MARC records permit a fuller level of description. more data elements to be included in the description and many more data elements to be assigned as access points for retrieval. A MARC record also includes other data, including non-bibliographic data that are used for catalogue maintenance. There is now a trend towards preserving detailed bibliographic records in machine-readable form.

The amount and type of information that constitute a 'full bibliographic record' is certainly open to debate, but since the late 1960s the accepted standard has been the MARC format. The data that can be contained in a MARC record include the entire spectrum of information normally presented on catalogue cards plus a great deal of other potentially valuable categorizing information that can be encoded in fixed elements and elsewhere on record.

However, MARC format has been criticised for being an electronic version of the catalogue card and for its limited accommodation of hierarchically structured information. There are also some problems with the MARC tagging and indexing of data elements that influence retrieval in online databases. Systems may differ from one another in the indexing of fields and it is often difficult to find out what fields are indexed by a given system. This results in retrieval and display problems, leading to user confusion.

Bibliographic Standardization

In comparison to manual systems, the online environment gives much more emphasis to the concept of standardisation. Although the idea of standardised bibliographic description seems to have first appeared with derived cataloguing and the sale of Library of Congress cards in 1898 and later with the introduction of the *National Union Catalogue* (NUC), it was not until the 1970s that the application of computers to library operations and the advent of online catalogues gave to standardisation a much more significant role.

With regard to the description, choice and form of data elements to be included in a bibliographic record, conformity to standards, *e.g.*, cataloguing codes, ISBDs and MARC formats, are vital to online catalogues.

Unlike libraries of two decades ago with their independent card catalogues, libraries of today often create their own catalogue records according to national and/or international standards for the purposes of easy communication of and access to bibliographic information. Now, it is common for libraries of any size to participate in networks. One result of this, as Wajenberg points out, is an ever-increasing pressure to conform to national and international standards.

Uniformity and consistency are basic requirements for effective bibliographical control. The rapid growth of shared cataloguing systems, developments in bibliographic utilities and the need for bibliographic exchange between databases in the last decade has led to a stronger reaffirmation of the value of standardisation in bibliographic records. Standardisation helps bibliographic records to be uniformly created, manipulated, exchanged and retrieved.

As the cataloguing community moves closer to making the ideal of universal bibliographic control a reality through local, regional, provincial, national, continental and international networks, all libraries assume the responsibility of maintaining standards requisite to maintaining the network. Integration and standar-dization are the keywords in the increasing move-ments towards, and promotion of, interconnected telecommunicating automated systems.

Despite this emphasis on the significance of standardisation in the online catalogue, this concept has been considered only in the inputting of data elements in bibliographic description and not in the output and display, whereas in the card catalogue both input and output are standardised.

For example, both the card catalogue and the online catalogue conform to the ISBD standard for the input format, *i.e.*, the order of areas, punctuation and levels of description. However, in online catalogues the output format is not fixed as in card catalogues and may be flexible.

As Gorman and associates state, the standardisation and formalisation of description and access points is crucial to the online environment and to the effective exchange of bibliographic records. As an important concept that has developed over the last hundred years to meet the changing forms of the catalogue and the needs of the profession, standardisation will continue in the future and as Wajenberg points out, at an accelerated pace.

Input Inconsistencies and Level of Tolerance

A major difference between a manual and an automated catalogue lies in the fact that the creation of bibliographic records for online catalogues demands more precision and logic in terms of typography, spelling, punctuation, spacing, coding of fields and subfields.

This is a critical requirement for computerised systems, since such errors can result in a serious separation or an improper sequencing of entries and therefore can lead to the irretrievability of records. In other words, any errors, even if very small, for instance a faulty keystroke, will be magnified in the online catalogue.

However, in a manual system, when filing catalogue cards or when retrieving information, the human brain can often ignore such minor errors and treat them as if they are correct and file them in the right place.

Errors and inconsistencies can be corrected in the process of filing cards, whereas in the automated catalogue there is a lower level of tolerance towards such errors as variations in format, filing and indexing, and literal and logical inconsistencies within the catalogue. In general, the online catalogue is far less forgiving of cataloguing and typographical errors than is the card catalogue.

CONSTRUCTION AND MAINTENANCE OF THE CATALOGUE

Structure and Content of the Catalogue

By 'structure of the catalogue' is meant how the catalogue is built up, the kinds and content of files and indexes constituting it and the relationships of these files and indexes to one another.

For example, a card catalogue, whether in dictionary or divided form, may include different files such as:

- Authors
- References
- Titles
- Subject headings and
- Shelflists

The advent of the online catalogue has given new dimensions to the catalogue's structure. It is generally main-tained that the online catalogue can support a more complex yet more dynamic structure than that of the card catalogue. The online file may be independent and self-contained, it may be related to files of similar scope and structure or it may be integrated with other files such as holdings, circulations, acquisitions and authority files.

The online catalogue provides services that were not part of the traditional library catalogue. Access to circulation information, status information, holding information, indexing of special collections, serials and so on have become possible through the development of the contents and structure of the catalogue.

While the structure of the card catalogue is based on the concept of several discrete entries for a single item, the online catalogue maintains a single-entry structure for a single item but with several indexes as access points to records in the master file.

Emphasising what constitutes the structure of an online catalogue, Svenonius states that:

- In its general sense *structure* refers to an aggregate of elements related, or arranged with respect, to each other... The structure of a catalogue or catalogue database consists of bibliographic, authority, and holdings records arranged in a given order and referencing one another through a variety of syndetic relationships. Thus, filing rules, together with ordering devices, such as the main entry and see and see also references, define a catalogue structure....The structure of biblio-graphic descriptions consists of data elements arranged and presented in a given order. Thus, card catalogue formats and MARC format represent different but related bibliographic structures, the former intended for display and the latter for communication.

In terms of addition to the contents of the catalogue, the online catalogue has a growing ability to enlarge its own scope. Results of a nationwide survey on the use of online catalogues in the United States revealed that respondents were enthusiastic about accessing journal articles, newspaper articles, encyclopaedias, dissertations, films and government documents through online catalogues.

Other studies showed that users wanted the catalogue to be expanded to include journal titles, government publications and dissertations and journal citations, indexes to collections, content services, abstracts and book reviews. Thus, it can be concluded that the contents of the online catalogue will be expanded in parallel with developments in the technology of catalogue construction.

Integration of the Catalogue

Integration has been considered as an important feature of the recent online catalogue in the sense that different parts of the library automated system are integrated through the use and manipulation of the same record as the basis for different library operations. In such an integration, a single master bibliographic record is tagged and can be manipulated for different library operations, such as acquisitions, cataloguing and circulation. A consequence of integration of the online catalogue, as pointed out by Buckland is that bibliographic information in different parts of a library system, as well as other useful information, can be accessible to users and to other libraries. Such a concept indicates the impor-tance of uniformity and standardisation of bibliographic records in the online environment.

Another interpretation of integration in the online environment is related to various methods of access to bibliographic information. In such an integration, different files and databases can be accessible via the same terminal. This concept has opened up a new era in bibliographic services and is considered as a significant factor in the enhancement of the catalogue. There are increasing attempts to build information systems with integrated access to different types of information services. The trend towards the integration of book trade bibliographic databases and A and I services with the online public access catalogue is an approach which makes the library catalogue a window to the whole bibliographic apparatus, a concept not feasible in the manual catalogue. These different kinds of integration have implications for cataloguing principles.

Authority Control

Authority control ensures the consistent use of names, series and subjects. No bibliographic record can be entered into the system until all assigned headings under which it can be searched are verifiable against the approved authority file. In a manual system, it is a time-consuming and costly operation and requires the services of skilled staff.

There are many advantages to authority control in an online catalogue: in terms of maintaining cataloguing operations, it is particularly advantageous when major revisions to name and subject headings have to be done.

In terms of searching, the actual search that the user does is via an authority control file. What the user inputs to the system is automatically switched through the index to the correct form. In the online environment, the authority records are usually linked with bibliographic records.

There are a number of reasons for the resurgent interest in authority control in the online environment. The various difficulties that users have had with searching names and, as Potter points out, the inconsistencies and errors in the records used to build the databases for online catalogues have led to new attention being given to the concept of authority control. For example, the ability to search personal names in either direct order or through initials has led to the enhancement of the scope and structure of authority files.

Another major difference in the process of authority control between a manual system and an automated system is that correction or change of any heading in the card catalogue is a time consuming operation, whereas this task in some automated systems is to a great extent facilitated through a 'global change' which automatically generates a correction or change in all relevant records. Although authority control in the online environment is at an early stage of development and, at present, only a few systems have operational authority control modules, the online catalogue's features and capabilities have given a new dimension to the notion of authority control. Much work needs to be done into the need for authority control in online catalogues. access by name will decrease and the concept of name references will change and the need for authority files in the traditional sense may become less important.

In making the concept of authority control in the online environment clearer, Gorman points out that:

- It is evident that traditional reference structure was designed for premachine catalogues. The ideas that underlie references have been taken over in machine systems and incorporated into the notion of authority files. An authority file consists, very simply, of the approved form of access point for a person, body, or title, together with the references to that approved form and links to other related authority records. We have already seen that, in the computer catalogue environment, the distinction between a main and added entry access point no longer has meaning. The authority record takes this progress a step further. It, in effect, abolishes the distinction between an access point and a reference.... In other words, two of the basic assumptions of traditional catalogue codes—the main entry and the distinction between a heading and a reference—have survived.

Filing Rules and Problems

In any library catalogue, access points are usually filed according to alphanumeric order, which is a conventional arrangement applicable to most information systems accessed by human beings. However, filing is different in the manual catalogue and the automated catalogue. The arrangement of access points has always been of particular interest to librarians and there have been a number of specific filing rules published to date. The *ALA Filing Rules,* The *Library of Congress Filing Rules* developed by John Rather, and the rules developed by the British Library Filing Committee are among the most important. Although developments in filing rules have been strongly in the direction of commonsense and are oriented towards the intelligent user, users actually have major problems in identifying the exact location of a heading in the sequential order of a large card catalogue. In a manual system, filing is flexible and can be executed according to the order which seems desirable to the catalogue user, whereas, in a computer catalogue, it must follow the logic of the computer.

Filing in a manual system follows the principle of *file as if*: that is, the form and order in which access points are arranged is according to the interpretation of the librarian with the supposition that the arrangement would be the most desirable to the user. For instance, the number *3* can be filed as if it were the word *three*. The use of the computer has influenced filing practices and it is generally agreed that the principle of *file as is,* which is necessitated by the introduction of computer filing, has more validity in the computer environment. This principle states that characters or words should be filed as they are and not as if they were something else. for example, the number '3' as *3,* and 'three' as *three.* This realisation of the logical as well as the practical differences between filing in a manual catalogue and a computer catalogue came with the earliest attempts in the application of computers to bibliographical work. Current filing rules, which were developed for manual systems, proved not to be effective in a computer environment.

Users of online catalogues can encounter many problems when searching for bibliographic information. Due to different software specifications, computer-based filing has not been entirely standardised and the burden of thinking, for example, about the exact form of access points and the way punctuation and non alphabetic symbols are treated is left to the user.

In manual filing it is possible, by a simple convention, to ignore stop words such as 'the', 'and', 'of', 'a', 'an', etc. at the beginning of titles whereas, in the computer catalogue, this issue demands special programming and in some cases they are difficult to handle. The treatment of punctuation poses another problem for the computer catalogue. while symbols, such as commas, apostro-phes, periods and hyphens, may cause problems in the manual catalogue, they are considered as characters and are located in their 'logical' places by the computer unless software is created to overcome these difficulties. While the presence or absence of punctuation may be important in access points, they may or may not be important for online display. Diacritics and extended character sets to accommodate non-roman scripts are other important issues in computer filing of entries. In sum, the logical arrangement of data elements in the computer has implications for the form of access points in the online catalogue. As an example, see the treatment of "Sir," which comes before forenames and thus interferes with filing. This can be seen in the change of some rules for the form of headings in the second edition of the Anglo-American Cataloguing Rules.

In fact, the incorporation/modification of some rules in AACR2 concerning the filing of data elements has arisen in response to the requirements of filing in the computer catalogue. For example, the inclusion of given names in parentheses in cases where the initials are not adequate for identification of authors with identical surnames is to respond to computer filing. In terms of conference headings the form and order of the number, the date and the location of a conference in parentheses is an illustration of filing relevant to a computer. The place of numeric identifying elements in music uniform titles, *e.g.*, "Pianos (2)" rather than "2 Pianos", is another example of this issue.

SEARCHING, RETRIEVAL, AND DISPLAY OF BIBLIOGRAPHIC RECORDS

User Interfaces

A significant difference between the online catalogue and the card catalogue comes at the stage in which the user interacts with the catalogue, *i.e.*, bibliographic records can be searched, retrieved and displayed. Online catalogues are here considered to be a great departure from card catalogues and it seems that there will be more developments in this regard in the near future.

While the card catalogue is a self-evident medium with a clear physical existence, the online catalogue is not revealed to the users and is not easy to grasp in their first interactions with it. In an online environment, the user cannot immediately understand the catalogue or its structure, coverage and searching mechanisms unless he/she interacts with the system and tries different options for searching and displaying of bibliographic information.

Despite these limitations of the online catalogue, users show a high degree of satisfaction with the variety of features and capabilities it has at the output stage. *Graphical user interfaces* (GUIs) have made interaction with and use of online systems easier and more desirable. It seems likely that, in the near future, new generations of online catalogues will incorporate intelligent interfaces and sophisticated search/retrieval/display facilities.

Interactivity

Online catalogues have often been defined in the literature as 'interactive' catalogues. In the *Dictionary of Information Technology*, *'interactivity'* is defined as "system or piece of software that allows communication between the user and the computer in a conversational mode." Interactivity is considered as a major advantage of online catalogues over card catalogues. "It is this interaction between the user and the computer system that really sets apart the online catalogue from the other types of library catalogs"

Unlike in the card environment, if the user does not input a query in the system, the system will not respond to him/her. This process, namely the action of inputting a query by the user and responding by the computer, occurs quickly in real time and in a dynamic and progressive way.

In sum, the concept of interactivity in the online catalogue is well defined below:

- "Online catalogues can be reactive and able to respond to the user in an intelligent way. This can be used to indicate what searching options are available, to correct operational errors, to suggest alternative items which might particularly match the search criteria and to guide the user through a long search. The reader can then be given help and feedback from the system itself, without needing to consult library staff. This approach is impossible in a card or a COM catalogue".

With the introduction of the online interactive catalogue, it has also become possible to record how users interact with the system and search the catalogue. In this way, *i.e.*, through 'transaction log' analysis, librarians are able to check how users approach the catalogue and how frequently search terms appear, as well as to examine other aspects of search/retrieval problems, *e.g.*, users' errors and unsuccessful searches. Many catalogue use studies have been and are being done using transaction logs as a means of data collection.

User's Input Errors and the Catalogue's Level of to Lerance

As pointed out earlier, online catalogues are less forgiving than card catalogues in terms of any kind of error, either in the input stage by the cataloguer, or in the searching stage by the user. A general problem with computers is that they are usually unforgiving of errors. if the user makes the smallest of mistakes, they will not necessarily recognise it as a mistake, and even if they do they will often not offer help in correcting the mistake. However, there are systems being developed that recognise errors, display the type of error, and offer help to the searcher.

User Assistance

In comparison to card catalogues, online catalogues have the ability to provide user assistance in a variety of ways and at different levels. Mitev classifies such aids in four categories as 'retrieval aids', 'linguistic aids', 'navigational aids', and 'semantic aids'. This is a major advantage over the card catalogue in that the system can respond to the user's problems and help him/her as to what the next move to achieve the result would be. Online catalogues have developed, over the past decade, different devices for providing help to their users in the different stages of searching the system.

Most online catalogues have the ability to customise help messages, screen displays and system prompts according to the needs of the user. Online assistance enables the user to influence the dialogue at all times in a clear way. This is not possible in manual systems.

User Satisfaction

It is generally stated that there is a higher level of satisfaction with online catalogues than with card catalogues and that users prefer this new form of the catalogue to the traditional card catalogue. Matthews, Lawrence, and Ferguson, over 90% of users like the online catalogue and almost 75% of users rate the online catalogue as being better than the card, book or microform catalogue.

It is also interesting to note that this high level of satisfaction is consistent across all types of libraries. Lewis, in reporting the results of different user studies, states that: "Users have a strong preference for online catalogs over card catalogs, and they very much want the new technology to succeed". Balaam and Burton and Hawkins report user satisfaction with OPACs despite their shortcomings.

A reason for preference of the online catalogue, even in its primitive form, to the card catalogue is related to its search and retrieval capabilities. It is also safe to assume that, as online catalogues continue to mature in terms of user interface, enhanced content and access, the level of satisfaction will be even greater.

Another point worth mentioning is that the result of different online use studies show that use of the catalogue and use of the collection have increased with the introduction of online interactive catalogues. This, in turn, leads to higher user satisfaction as he/she becomes able to fulfil his/her information needs in easier, faster and more effective ways.

A major group of OPAC users are librarians themselves who are among the strong supporters of such systems. In a series of discussions in the electronic mail discussion group PACS-L@UHUPVM1.UH.EDU, 7-20 April 1994 and in response to Nicholson Baker's "Annals of Scholarship: Discards" published in the *New Yorker*, 4 April 1994, concerning the closing or storing of card catalogues, most librarians supported online catalogues as being superior to card catalogues.

Charles Hildreth considers Baker's article to be a nostalgic approach to the historical value of card catalogues. For Hildreth card catalogues represent a dead-end technology and their maintaining would be very expensive. Instead, online catalogues are open-ended, with a pure potentiality that will never reach its 'final' form.

Walt Crawford asserts that online catalogues are ever-evolving systems that, when reasonably well designed, offer substantially better access and, unlike card catalogues, can be maintained as well as improved.

Robin Alston supports online catalogues for their advantages over card catalogues in many ways and states that a major advantage is that most of the key elements on a record in an online catalogue are searchable, while massive amount of information on catalogue cards are not retrievable. Although there are deficiencies in OPACs, as Baker expresses very well from the point of view of a scholar, online catalogues will keep improving, while card catalogues have not any potential for improvement.

Searching and Retrieval Capabilities

With regard to searching capabilities, the online catalogue is a significant departure from traditional library catalogues. One of its most interesting features and a major advantage over the card catalogue, is the ability of the user to search for the needed item in a variety of ways that are not available in the manual catalogue.

Online catalogues are able to generate both a greater number of access points as well as new searching capabilities that enable the user to search the catalogue with little information to hand. In addition to controlled-vocabulary searches by author, title and subject headings, for which relevant indexes have been created and maintained in the online catalogue, it is possible to search bibliographic records through access points such as other title information, series, standard numbers and any other significant data through keyword searching.

In general, although there are still shortcomings in the searching capabilities of online catalogues, particularly in subject searching, the findings of various studies indicate that users show much enthusiasm in online catalogues' searching capabilities. The following types of searches in the online catalogue are not available in the manual catalogue and can help the user to execute a greater variety of searches:

Keyword Searching

Keyword access is a very powerful search tool and can create much greater flexibility for the user to search item(s) of which he/she has not exact information. This is extremely difficult in the card catalogue.

Keywords, *i.e.*, every indexed word in the bibliographic description, mainly headings, titles, other title information, contents notes and subjects, are appropriate alternatives for the catalogue user who cannot match the exact bibliographic information in the catalogue.

When searching the catalogue, it is not necessary for the user to enter the exact form and order of words. while keyword searching is an alternative to controlled-vocabulary searching, it can also act as a complement to it. The potential value of keyword searching has often been highlighted in the literature. For example, reporting the result of a transaction log analysis of the Colorado University Library OPAC, Wallace found that 53% of searches were keyword searches.

In many online catalogues, there are options for limiting keyword searching to fields such as author, title, subject, or cross index. Among these options, title keyword searching provides a useful tool both as a substitute for subject access and for specific items when the exact or full title is not known.

Some online catalogues provide keyword searching of abstracts and a number of systems extend this capability to the entire text of a document, a trend that is becoming common in many online search services. It is extremely difficult to search authors under their forenames in manual catalogues, whereas in online catalogues with keyword access it has become possible to execute such searches. The same capability is available in the online catalogue for searching compound words of which the exact, full form is not known. However, keyword searching has its disadvantages: in some cases too many records may be retrieved and some records may be irrelevant to the searcher's need.

Boolean Searching

Influenced by A&I (*Abstracting and Indexing*) services, many online catalogues have the ability to run Boolean searches. With the use of Boolean operators, such as AND, OR, NOT, it is possible to define subsets of the desired subject or concept when two or more sets are combined.

Specificity is what Boolean searching offers: the user can combine two or more terms in a search statement and narrow or broaden the parameters of the subject of his/her interest. Matthews points out that:

"In most OPACs, a Boolean 'and' is assumed when two or more terms are entered in a search statement, especially if the search is conducted on a single field or type of information, such as author, title, or subject".

Truncation

As in A&I services, some online catalogues permit the user to broaden the set of records to be retrieved by shortening the search word through entering a special truncation symbol immediately after the shortened search word, or before it, or within the word. Most online catalogues perform right-hand truncation implicitly rather than explicitly. This feature of online catalogues provides greater flexibility for the user to broaden access to the necessary information when character-by-character exact match does not help. It should be noted, however, that users have difficulty in understanding and using this type of searching in online catalogues. In some cases, truncation also results in either too many hits or irrelevant records. This has implications for cataloguing principles and rules.

Browse Searching

When the search aim is not specific, the desired results are not precisely known in advance or the correct terms for representing the user's query are not known at the outset, "browse searching is the most useful and preferred approach". Browsing, which is a good feature of the card catalogue, is becoming available in the form of browsable indexes in more and more online catalogues.

The natural searchability that browsing offers satisfies users. In this type of searching, lists of index terms are usually presented in alphabetical order and the searcher can navigate the database by going forward or backward through the desired index until he/she finds the index term which may lead him/her to relevant records.

A novel interface for browsing, which can improve access and the effectiveness of end-user searching, has been developed very recently. Using a GUI, some advanced online systems offer improved searching functionality by providing a multi-windowed view of data stored on a relational database manage-ment system.

This novel interface can help the user to search bibliographic databases in a multi-windowed environment, each of which represents an index of the catalogue with scrollable windows. This approach has the advantage that the user can browse different indexes on the same screen to filter their content and find the most relevant items. Among the indexes are: author, title, publication date, document type, language and subject headings. It would be possible, therefore, to match different indexes and find related documents which have the same values, *i.e.*, identical data elements. This facility helps the user in appreciating the actual contents of the database through its different indexes and removes the problem of search specification using values that are not present.

Hypertext Searching

A most recent addition to searching capabilities in information retrieval systems, including advanced online catalogues, is hypertext searching or 'hypersearch'. Non linear, associative hypertext systems offer a search approach that attempts to more closely mimic human thought processes. It is stated that hypertext, when used with bibliographic records, could overcome the static nature of existing catalogues.

The hypersearch facility, such as that one offered by GoPAC from Data trek, can simply be applied by highlighting a term or clicking on a highlighted term in the record. The system will search for any occurrences of the highlighted term in all fields and subfields or all authority-controlled fields in all records in the database.

The number of postings associated with the term will be indicated or the system will show a brief display of those related records which contain the same term. The term is highlighted in the retrieved records so that the searcher can see in which field it is located and can decide on the relevance of the record to his/her information need.

During the display of related records, the possibility exists for the user to shift his/her focus and to continue a hypertext search on new and more relevant data elements. In this way, the hypertext facility helps users to navigate throughout the catalogue to find possible related works.

Author-title Search

In most online catalogues, there is an option for searching a known item through the author's surname combined with any keyword from the title. This is the clearest way to execute known-item searches. However, in those systems which restrict the search to author surname and the first word of the title, this type of search has the disadvantage of retrieving too many records when the author's surname is a common name, such as 'Smith', 'Johnson', and so on, or the title of the item begins with common words, such as 'Introduction', 'History', and so on. Another disadvantage is that, in most cases, users do not remember the first word of titles and thus fail to use this type of search in online catalogues. Nevertheless, it is very useful, for example, for searching titles on reading lists and it emphasises the importance of surname field.

ID Numbers

Another type of search in some online catalogues is possible through ID numbers. Among possible ID numbers are: call number. *International Standard Book Number* (ISBN). International Standard Serial Number (ISSN). document number. computer system number, *e.g.*, OCLC (Online Computer Library Center), RLIN (Research Libraries Information Network) or WLN (Western Library Network). local system number, *e.g.*, accession number. These types of search are usually performed by library staff.

Other Searching Sapabilities

Other types of searches in online catalogues include full-text searching, proximity searching, adjacency searching which are available only in a few online catalogues. These new searching capabilities in the online catalogue have revolutionised the way in which users search the library catalogue. The results of different use studies indicate that the searching patterns of users in online catalogues have changed. In other words, the online catalogue has affected the ways in which users search for bibliographic information in library catalogues.

Output and Display

Display of bibliographic information is another major aspect in which the online catalogue departs greatly from the card catalogue. Surveying OPACs in a number of Canadian academic libraries, Cherry report that screen display is the best developed area in online catalogues.

The last step at the catalogue, viewing a search result through the display of the bibliographic record(s), is what the user actually gains from the system. The quality of such a display affects the overall usefulness of the catalogue. While the form and content of bibliographic records in the input/output format in the card catalogue are fixed, the online catalogue permits a flexible format, with the possibility of displaying bibliographic information in a variety of ways and at different levels.

The ways in which bibliographic information is presented in the online catalogue in response to searches vary from system to system. Each system has its own techniques for manipulation of a search result. This is impossible in the card technology where space limitations and the fixed form of bibliographic description do not permit any flexibility or manipulation of search results. The level of bibliographic description is usually flexible and can be designed according to the user's needs. On the other hand and from a system perspective, as Boll points out, there is a range of display formats suitable for a computer screen or a page printout rather than a three by five inch card.

Online display formats usually include:

- 'Brief-listing display' which shows, on one or more screens, the overall results of a search through 'author', 'title' and 'date' of publication,

- 'Medium-level display' containing the standard bibliographic description, access points and status and location information, and
- 'Full bibliographic display' which shows full description with all access points, including added entries, and may contain summary and/or table of contents of the item.

Another major difference between the online catalogue and the card catalogue is the way in which data elements in a record make up and represent a bibliographic record. Reynolds points out three functions in this regard: the labelling of data elements, the sequence in which data elements appear and the spacing between them.

The online catalogue can include identifying labels before data elements for distinguishing the bibliographic text in a record. Labels may be highlighted, or displayed in uppercase characters or in a different colour. In relation to the sequence of data elements appearing in a bibliographic record, there is a fairly high degree of uniformity among online catalogues.

As in the card catalogue, the arrangement usually follows the numerical sequence of MARC tags or the ISBD order. Some online catalogues do not incorporate ISBD punctuation on the basis that users do not comprehend such 'secret punctuation'.

However, it should be noted that a number of problems may arise from the differences in the input and output formats in the online catalogue. A problem which would be difficult for the user to understand is that the relationships of headings to bibliographic data may not be clear to him/her.

For example, the role of persons associated with the work or manifestations of a work may not be distinguished in the way these names are displayed on the screen in conjunction with the title of the work. Therefore, the user may miss what he/she is seeking. In short, output in online catalogues is not controlled by cataloguing standards.

Limiting Search Results

Limiting or restricting the search results is a good feature of online catalogues and seems to have been copied from A&I services. Crawford, this capability of online catalogues should be offered or performed only when the search yields a large result. Matthews points out that assisting the searcher in refining or expanding a search shows the powerful capability of the online information retrieval system over the card or COM catalogue.

In terms of refining the search results, the online catalogue has a great advantage over the card catalogue. When many records are retrieved in response to a search, the user may want to restrict them to certain aspects that might seem more relevant to his/her need.

This is not possible in the card catalogue whereas, in most online catalogues, due to the assigning of some subfields in the MARC format as active and searchable, the user has the opportunity of further restricting, reducing or narrowing the search results. For example, the searcher can limit all the search results to works in a particular language, in a particular type of material or all the works published prior to, during or after a given date, or even works of a certain level of difficulty. This is done by specifying certain control fields and other MARC elements that can be used for limiting search results.

With further developments in online catalogues it is expected that the limiting of search results will become more sophisticated and more flexible for the user. In addition to the usual access points available in the card catalogue, more data elements are being indexed and more indexes are likely to be created in the online catalogue.

Sorting Search Results

Another feature of online catalogues is the opportunity offered to the user to sort the search results in the way that will best fulfil his/her need. Most online catalogues can sort the retrieved records according to such data elements as the author, the title and the date. This sorting capability requires that, in addition to usual access points, more data elements be indexed in MARC records in the database.

Some systems, such as OKAPI (Online Keyword Access to Public Information) the experimental OPAC developed at the Polytechnic of Central London, SMART, the US National Library of Medicine catalogue CITE (Current Information Transfer in English), STATUS/IQ, CANSEARCH, PLEXUS provide ranked output and relevance feedback.

They sort and display results of a search in order of highest occurrence of keywords. Given the searcher's judgments of retrieved items as either relevant or irrelevant, some of these systems can be asked to perform another search modified automatically by relevance feedback to provide a new ranked output list.

Status, Holdings and Location Information

A major feature of the online catalogue is its ability to link circulation information to bibliographic and holdings information and to show to the searcher the status and location of the sought item(s). The user of the online catalogue is able to see the status of any volume and/or copy of the item and whether the item he/she is looking for is available on the shelf or it is on loan, on order, at binding, missing or is not for loan. The status information also displays the 'date due' of an item on loan. The online catalogue can also show the location of the item in the library, *e.g.*, on which level and/or in which part it is located. All such information is useful also for stock taking and check-in purposes. These features help the patron, particularly the remote user, saving his/her time in knowing the status and location of the needed item(s).

Access and Availability

Unlike in a manual system, the user of the online catalogue has access to bibliographic, circulation, acquisition, holdings and location information at the same terminal, whether within the library or in other libraries through remote access. Again, this capability may be an indication of the need for uniformity and standardisation of data elements and also the importance of integrity in the structure of different files in the system.

In contrast to the possibilities for online consultation, card technology is a strictly localised medium with many physical restrictions to its use. Almost all libraries have a single set of catalogue cards for a document. To some extent a book catalogue or a COM catalogue might help in making the library catalogue available in different locations but these catalogues are costly to update at regular intervals, particularly when the collection is very large.

Unlike the card catalogue, the online catalogue is accessible through terminals located in different places in the library and outside the library via local area networks (LANs) and wide area networks (WANs). In the online environment it is possible for different users, whether inside the library building or outside it, to use the catalogue online and to even search the same record simultaneously. In terms of access to library catalogues, distance has now become irrelevant. Technology has enabled us to have decentralised access to bibliographic information.

Interconnectivity is one of the most important goals of libraries today and can take different forms. Many library catalogues are now accessible through the different tools in the Internet such as Netscape, Gopher, Mosaic and Telnet. This is a great advantage over the manual system and will continue to expand with further developments in telecommunication allied to a decrease in telecommunication costs.

There is also more flexibility with interconnectivity for the searcher to go from one catalogue to another. This is done through the same catalogue or other catalogues which have a WWW forms-based interface. These developments have brought with them new concepts such as globalisation of catalogues and the 'library without walls'.

With the availability of different types of OPAC systems to remote users over networks, for example, over the Internet, libraries need to conform to a new standard known as Z39.50. This standard is a protocol for information search and retrieval in a client-server environment, and is now moving from a standard to an operational reality. Z39.50 is used by libraries to access and search remote databases.

The WAIS system has implemented the standard to provide a consistent environment with consistent user interface, search and retrieval services. In environments supporting Z39.50 connectivity, the user sees remote catalogues as though they were additional databases available from the local system.

The standard is also being used in different library operations such as technical services, acquisitions and interlibrary loans. In this context, Z39.50 encompasses biblio-graphic databases, full-text documents, even numeric databases. For example, for bibliographic databases, a list of fields needed to exchange information and support those functions has been developed.

With advances in telecommunications and the rapid development of different facilities in the Internet it is now also possible to have access to electronic texts and files stored anywhere in the world. As we move to the end of the twentieth century, more full text services will become accessible through remote databases.

2

Role of Barcode Technology in Library Serials

INTRODUCTION

Barcode technology is reliable and easy to use. It improves accuracy and accelerates the processing time, eliminates the typing errors, decreases the costs and improves the services. During the stock verification period, routine library activities can be carried out without any disturbance. Data-capturing terminal is handy and portable, and there is no problem of scanning the data multiple times. The only disadvantage being like libraries assign simple accession numbers 1 to n for books, R1 to Rn for reports, and S1 to Sn for standards (R and S are the accession series of specific publication type). If libraries carry out stock verification for books alone LibSys has no option to carry out stock verification by an accession series wise. It process as the data and generates a report for all records available in the cataloguing module. Overall, the technology is beneficial for carrying out stock verifications in libraries. Since, there is no human intervention, the verification report generated by the system is perfect and accurate.

BARCODE DATA TRANSFER

The information that can be encoded on the barcodes is rather limited and hence, it is up to the individual libraries to decide what information they need to barcode for efficient handling of collection and for better operation of services. Libraries can use accession numbers of books, the unique information that distinguish their collection, as the vital information entity to barcode their collection. Similarly, the identification number of a user stands distinct for each member, which can be used to barcode the user's cards. Accession number/ borrower number exported from the library database/borrower database is converted to a series of black and white lines by the barcode software.

This can be printed by a dot-matrix/laser printer and pasted on all books and borrower cards. The light beam flashed from the barcode scanner on the barcode label undergoes reflection at the white lines and absorption on the dark bands. This reflected light is collected back and is converted into electric pulses by the photoelectric circuitry of the scanner. Further, these pulses are converted into binary information by the interface circuitry of the scanner before they are fed to the computer, for further processing. So, the information read from barcode acts as a substitute for the same information entered through keyboard, to handle circulation/other routines of the library database.

The barcode technology is essentially a data transfer device and hence, it works in perfect harmony with any of the computerised database systems. Any customisation needed at the user end can be done either by the in-house system personnel or by local solution providers. The barcoding setup includes the barcode scanner to read the barcoded information, its interfacing with the library computer, the software to convert the requisite information to barcodes, and the printer.

The barcode scanners may be classified into different groups like:

- As per design (handheld and fixed-mount).
- As per light source (infrared or visible).

Hand-held scanners contain no moving parts. They are compact, light and cheaper as compared to fixed-mount models. Hence, they are of interest to libraries desiring to optimise their budgetary resources. Infrared scanners can read mutilated labels; however, they need special printers. But recent times saw the dominant categorisation, as per technology, into CCD and laser scanners. In CCD scanners, light from the LEDs is used to read the barcode information, whereas laser light is used in the latter. Accordingly, laser scanners have increased scan width and range (distance from which the labels are scanned), but they are comparatively expensive. The vendors used to offer requisite software to generate barcodes from suggested fields of library database. Since, materials and readers are added only in prescribed number in a library, it will be better to avoid commercial printing of barcode labels.

All required lables can be printed either on normal paper or on purchased blank labels on a dot-matrixllaser printer, as per their availability in the library. While generating lables, provision may also be made to print some other fields like author/title/user riame in normal text to identify the labels easily, as one is more comfortable with text than numbers like accession/identification number. The user cards are normally laminated and to ensure long life of the labels on books (defective labels always lead to wrong/no reading of data), transparent cellotape can be pasted over these.

CODING FORMATS/ SYMBOLOGIES

The different code formats and how the information is encoded in bars is available in the litreature4. The same information can be encoded by different schemes; however, at the user and application level, it doesn't make much distinction and the user may use any of the schemes. The same information can be encoded to and satisfactorily decoded from more than one scheme without hampering efficiency or time. Limitations are imposed by the barcoding software one uses, and it is better to consult the individual operational manual for such information.

Some of the common formats are:

- *Universal Product Code (UPC)*: US standard to encode only digits, UPC-A to encode 12 digits or UPC-E to encode 6 digits.
- *European Article Number (EAN)*: European code to encode digits, available in two variations:. EAN-8 to encode 8 digits and EAN-13 to encode 13 digits.
- *Interleaved 2 of 5. (ITF)*: Supports only numeric characters but can be used for variable length.
- *Code-39*: Encodes capital alphabets, numerical and few special characters like $, +, per cent. Asterisk (*) must be used as the start and stop character. Lowercase alphabets cannot be encoded.
- *Code-1 28*: Encodes both the lower and the upper case letters, numeric and special characters found on the keyboard.
- *Codabar*: Encodes only numeric and few special characters and is the most widely used coding format. Generally, libraries use this symbology to encode books and borrower cards.

BARCODING AT THE IIT KHARAGPUR CENTRAL LIBRARY

The Central Library of the Indian Institute of Technology, Kharagpur, is one of the few libraries in the country to have a huge database of their entire collections. Initially, the computerised issue return of books6 was done by keying in the accession number of books and identification number of borrower, but this mechanism was prone to errors and. also resulted in long queues at the circulation grant desk. Out of the project of ₹ 10 lakh received from AICTE in 1994 for the conversion of the conventional central library into the electronic library, the Library procured 5 CCD barcode scanners and one HP-5Si Mx Laser Printer. It was decided to barcode books and hence, the details of books brought for issue/return were exported from the library database for generating barcode labels with accession number as the key field and the labels were printed on the laser printer using 'Softbar vl' software supplied by the vendor.

The Library also received a consignment of 'Nashua Laser Labels' in 30 labels per page format as gift from one of its alumni settled in US. The system generates three labels for each book to be pasted on the back of title page, secret page and last page. To fasten the process, personnel were given honorarium and encouraged to work overtime/on holidays to barcode the entire book collection. Side by side, new books processed by the technical processing section were also barcoded before release. Out of a special operating fund of ₹ 1 lakh received from the Institute in 1998, all the pending old books were also barcoded.

Now, the entire collection of over 2 lakh books is barcoded. From the academic year 1998-99, all B.Tech and M.Tech students were given a laminated barcoded library identity card and the practice of issuing separate borrower cards as per the entitlement was discontinued.

This facility will be further extended to faculty, researchers, and other staff in near future. This practice not only resulted in saving a large amount of stationery for printing numerous borrower cards but also a total saving of staff time which would have otherwise been spent for filing those cards. The user can have a book in one third of the pre-barcode issue time. The faculty, students and the personnel manning the circulation desk find the barcode technology user-friendly, efficient and fast.

ADOPTION IN OTHER LIBRARIES IN INDIA

Few of the computerised libraries in the country like American Centre, British Council, other ITs, some R&D libraries have already started barcoded circulation. With an investment of less than a lakh, the computerised libraries can procure barcode related hardware and software. A CCD scanner can be purchased for ₹ 15,000 and a laser scanner for ₹ 25,000 with comparable costs for relevant software. It is always better to have a feedback from the nearby libraries who use this technology before procuring one. Also, the potential vendors may be called to give a demonstration of this technology.

The procurement may be carried out in one go or in stages, so that those required for barcoding active collection may be purchased first and on completion of that work, more scanners may be bought. The accrued savings for the first few years will be more than what has been invested. Further, it will also improve the status of the library which will move one step closer to realise the fourth law of library science.

APPLICATIONS OF BARCODING

Barcoding offers a lot of comfort and ease to handle bulk routine tasks efficiently. The application of this technology for issue/return of books is widely identified and practiced in the developed countries of the world. A few of the computerised libraries in our country have also started experiencing the fruits of this technology. It is important to emphasise that this technology is not limited to circulation work. Newnham describes the barcoding of DNA samples in Britain. It is not out of place to ponder over future barcoding applications in a library. With the help of a data gathering device, the barcodes can be used to verify stock, as libraries have to resort to stock verification, at intervals.

If the provision for multiple barcodes or multidimensional barcoding is incorporated to handle call number information also, wrong shelving of books can be autodetected which would help the staff to rectify the same. The individual journal volumes are handled in a library with lots of intricacies. Many a time these issues have to be taken out of the display area for Xerox work. There are also chances of their shelving in wrong cabinets.

These problems are tackled by using a control number for the current journal issues and barcoding them accordingly. A database of journal issues can thus be generated so that their management through cards can be avoided. If the parent institution also has a computerised accounting system, all the bills can be routed after barcoding so that their follow up and processing are done efficiently. Barcoding has come a long way and it is here to stay for faster and efficient library work.

AUTOMATED LIBRARY STOCK VERIFICATION WITH BARCODE AND LIBSYS

The modern technology has enabled automation and integration of the various processes of libraries and information centres to reduce or avoid human intervention and to increase the efficiency and speed. As the libraries provide open access service to make the holdings available to the users, the loss, damage, and misplacement of books are inevitable. To know and replace the lost books, and to maintain balance between various subjects, and to take adequate precautionary measures, it is necessary to do periodical inventory and accounting of the library collection of the library.

The term stock verification thus came into existance with regard to libraries. It is also referred as stock taking, physical verification or checking, stock inspection, and inventory, taking meaning physical checkup of any article on record.

Libraries of Govt. of India and its other organisations has to do a mandatory physical verification of all their holdings as per the following guidelines:

- Complete annual physical verification of books should be done every year in the case of libraries having not more than 20,000 holdings and not fewer than one qualified library staff. In case there is only one qualified staff, the verification may be done as per sub-para.
- Complete physical verification at intervals of not more than three years should be done in the case of libraries having more than 20,000 but not more than 50,000 volumes.
- Sample physical verification at intervals of not more than five years may be done in the case of libraries having more than 50,000 volumes. If such sample verification reveals unusual or unreasonable shortage, complete verification shall be done.

Libraries traditionally perform the periodic stock verification by adopting any one of the following methods: Verification by accession register; using a separate register with accession numbers; slips containing accession numbers; numerical counting; and shelf register cards or shelf list cards. The methods are cumbersome, time-consuming, and error prone as these are done manually.

The automated stock verification procedure adopted at Raja Ramanna Centre for Advanced Technology (RRCAT) library by employing barcode and LibSys facilities library stock verification could be performed easily with less manpower; one person scanned the barcode label (accession number) of documents and other person marked the documents by putting month and year stamp at the inside back cover to ensure that the document was physically verified. Besides, identification of damaged and worn out documents for repair, binding of obsolete volumes, and rearrangement and cleaning can also be done simultaneously. During the stock verification period, the returned (check-in) documents were also verified before shelving. Once the data capturing was over, the verification and generation of report with LibSys could also be done in a short period of time.

IMPLEMENTATION OF BARCODE TECHNOLOGY AND LIBSYS AT RRCAT LIBRARY

To improve the library service and to have an efficient control over the entire operation, the LibSys, which is a commercially available integrated multi-user library automation package, was implemented at RRCAT in 1995. To improve the services further, the barcode technology (print-related automatic identification technology) was implemented in 2000. The hardware installed to implement these technologies at RRCAT are: Laser barcode scanner for reading labels (at circulation counter); portable data capturing terminal with build-in laser scanner for inventory (stock verification); and accessories such as cradle, cable, battery and other items. The softwares for interfacing the data capturing terminal with computer are: PowerGen, SysTools and Label Works for Windows for label designing.

BARCODE AND BARCODE SCANNER

The barcodes are being used effectively to speed up, avoid human error, and automate the processes in industry for production planning control, materials management, purchase/ sale, and inventory control. In libraries, barcode is being used to automate the data-capturing process, for stock verification, and in the circulation counter for issue/return of documents.

A barcode is a sequence of dark bars on a light background or the equivalent of this with respect to the light-reflecting properties of the surface. The coding comprises in the relative widths or spacing of the dark bars and light spaces. A barcode scanner is an optical device that reads the code by scanning a focussed beam of light, generally a laser beam, across the barcode and detecting the variations in reflected light. The scanner converts these light variations into electrical variations, which are subsequently digitised and fed into the decoding unit programmed to convert the relative widths of the digitised dark/light spacings into numbers and/or letters.

BARCODE LABELLING

Each document in a library should be uniquely identified for barcode labelling purpose. Most of the libraries in India use accession number for this purpose. RRCAT has also used the same for printing barcode labels. The labels designed using Label Works for Windows, which supports major barcode symbologies.

Code 128, a high density linear symbology that can encode text, numbers, several functions and the entire 128 ASCII character set was selected for designing the labels. Figure shows the barcode label design specifications.

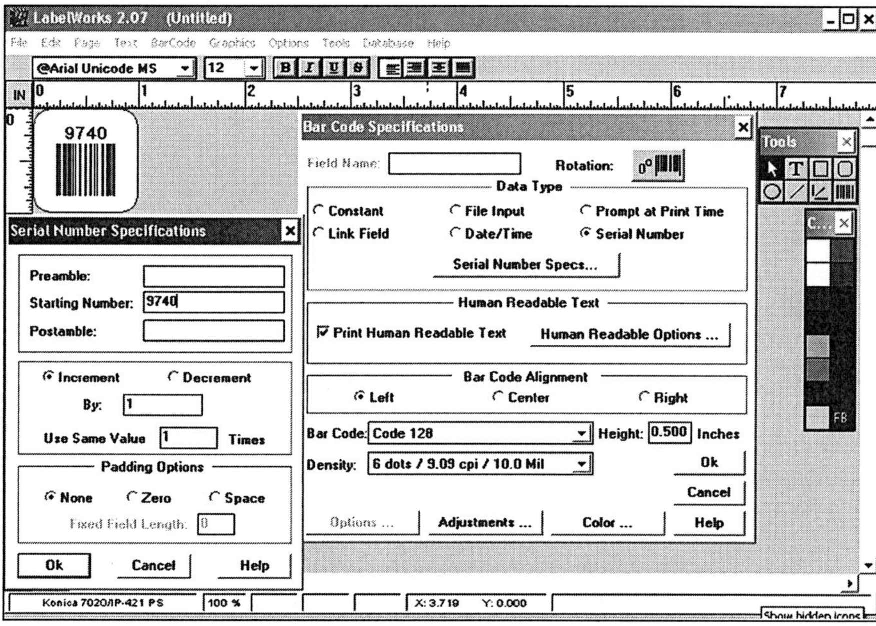

Fig 10.1 Barcode Label Design Specifications

DATA CAPTURING, MODIFICATION AND UPLOADING

The datalogic formula 732 wizard terminal was used to capture the data. The portable data collection laser scanner terminal scans the encoded data and automatically decodes and stores up to 128 KB of data in the memory. As the accession number differs from one to other, the terminal stores approx. 2500 accession numbers. The data was downloaded into the PC using Systool's (software utility for data exchange) and was saved in a data file (*.dat). Later downloads were also appended to the same file. The PowerGen was the other software utility used to build personalised settings as per the requirements.

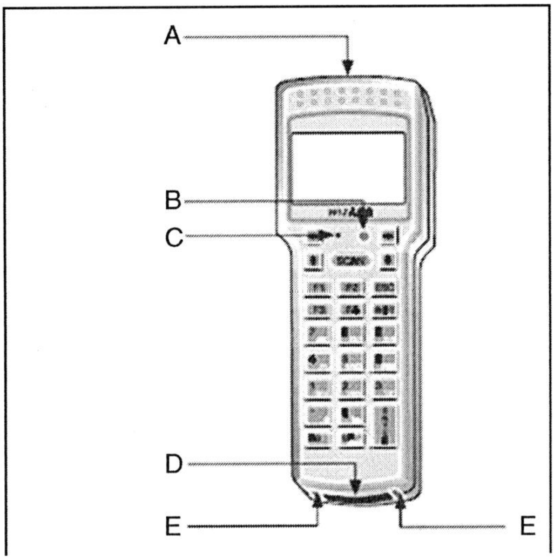

Fig 10.2 Datalogic Formula 732 Wizard Terminal

Notes:

A. Laser beam output window

B. Two colour LED

C. Reset key (shielded)

D. Cradle communications window

E. Contacts for battery recharging

Each document was scanned and stamped (month and year) manually at the inside back cover to avoid duplication. During scanning, the terminal stores the accession number of each document and automatically displays the document number for a moment. If a data scanned is wrong, it can be manually updated or rescanned, and if a document has been inadvertantly scanned multiple times, the terminal simply stores the documents with duplicate accession numbers. The downloaded data in the PC shows a vertical bar '|' (pipe) character after each accession number. The '|' characters were manually removed from the file using the windows text editor. The comprehensive file was then moved to LibSys work file ('wfilexx' directory).

DATA PROCESSING

As the entire collection of RRCAT was catalogued in the LibSys, the data analyses and report generation was carried out through the LibSys cataloguing stock verification module. The initiation of stock verification function is executed at once. This operation sets the system for the big exercise on inventory entails.

Data Analysis

The LibSys provides data verification in two ways; accession numbers one by one, and list of accession numbers in a file. All accession numbers are stored in a file. The system registers accession numbers for verification in the database. After matching the accession number from the file, the LibSys automatically generates an exception case file with extension '*. exp' and saves it in the work file path, i.e., in the wfilexx directory. This file enlists the list of mis-matching accession numbers and wrongly scanned numbers.

Report Generation

As the term stock verification implies only on stock, a list of missing accession numbers is generated against the captured data file. After several cross checkings, the final verification report is prepared in a text (*.txt) file. The flow chart is presented in figure.

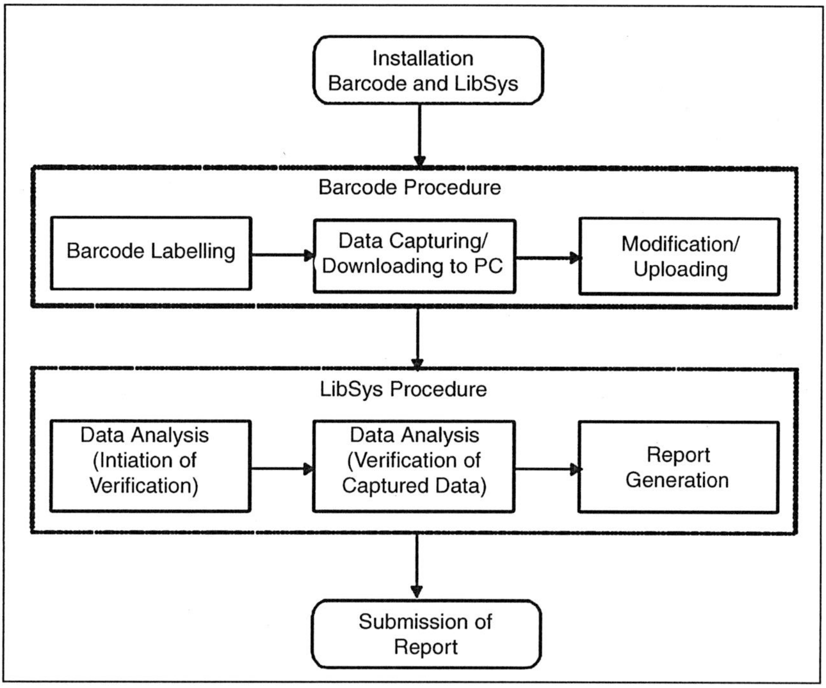

Fig 10.3 Flow Chart of Automated Stock Verification

CONCLUSION

The circulation work in an automated library involves keying in a large amount of data. Sometimes, the library staff at the counter has to retype the same information due to error in data entry. All this results in long queues at the circulation desk in our libraries.

This voluminous work can be handled in a smooth manner in a much less time by the application of barcoding, one of the simplest coding technologies available in the market. The speed of data capture is three times faster than the speed at which a skilled data entry operator can input data' and also the error rate is negligibly small2. The barcode technology originated out of the need of retail stores and big industries to track down their inventory errors in a faster way. Due to the cheap human labour available in our country, the estimated barcoding market was a mere 12 crores in 1995-96', out of which libraries and miscellaneous services accounted for only 1 crore. Libraries need to adopt this technology as it helps retrieve and collect data quickly and efficiently.

3

Impact of Electronic Reserve Collection in Library Serials

ELECTRONIC RESERVE AND ON-DEMAND PUBLISHING

The term 'electronic reserve collection' may be a misnomer as it implies rationed access whereas 'the digital environment removes the need for this form of rationing as a single digitisation can simultaneously be accessed by any number of readers'.

Nevertheless, the term is used to describe collections of resources, including journal papers and extracts from texts and newspapers, that have been digitised and mounted on campus networks to be accessed by students.

The rationale for this is that hard copy can be accessed by only one person at a time but access to digital copy is limited only by the infrastructure required to use it. Electronic reserve collections (ERCs) have been developed with a view to meeting more effectively the needs of large undergraduate classes which rely increasingly on the library for core reading materials. Development of ERCs is more widespread in the US than it is in the UK.

In the early 1990s, many of those developing ERCs in the US considered it 'fair use' to digitize copyright resources and make them available electronically.

The Conference on Fair Use (CONFU) guidelines were intended to formalise this reading of the law but publishers and librarians were unable to agree on guidelines for electronic reserve use of copyright materials (http://www.utsystem.edu/ogc/intellectualproperty/confu.htm).

Nevertheless, many libraries continue to interpret the law in this way (follow links from the following URL for examples http://www.cc.columbia.edu/~rosedale/#Sites). Use of copyright resources in ERCs in the US must now be licensed just as it is in the UK. In the UK, HE ERC developers have assumed that ER use of copyright materials is not 'fair dealing' and guidelines published recently by the Publishers' Association and the JISC confirm that this is so (http://www.ukoln.ac.uk/services/elib/papers/pa/licence/fairnote.html).

Clearly, the cost of obtaining permissions is important to the economic viability of the whole exercise. This cost includes not only the price for using copyright material but also time spent identifying right sholders, seeking permission to use their copyright material and, often, chasing that request. The total figure can be as high as ten times the actual copyright fee. The cost to rightsholders of administering permissions requests is also significant.

At present the Association for Computing Machinery (ACM) grants blanket permission to copy its copyright materials for educational use because the cost of administering applications exceeds the revenue generated. This suggests that if licensing digital use of copyright materials is to become a viable revenue stream for publishers, copyright fees must be relatively high.

Although publishers have been willing to grant permissions free of charge to limited life ER projects, i.e. during development, they charge fees to use their material in ongoing ER services.

This may not be a viable revenue stream but many publishers consider ER use of their material to be a threat to their core business. Charging deters widespread adoption of ER as an alternative to text provision or recommendation. On the other hand, as long as ER systems do not cannibalise publishers' primary income, a streamlined process may actually generate incremental revenue for them.

Another significant cost associated with ERCs is the cost of digitising text. Odlyzko cites an example of a company that will digitise text for $0.60 per page but recent eLib supporting study established £2.50 as a reasonable estimate. Obviously, cost varies with a number of factors such as the cost of identifying and obtaining the original, the condition of the original, the presence or otherwise of special characters, i.e. the degree of manual intervention required to produce a useful file.

If publishers begin to supply their texts in electronic form and offer the facility to buy subsections of texts, then the need for HEIs to digitise a significant amount of text will vanish. However, unless publishers digitise all back runs of journals and text back lists, there will be a need to digitise older material.

At present, developments in delivering texts in electronic form are embryonic, so material selected for reserve collections from texts must almost always be digitised if it is to be delivered in electronic form. However, duplication of effort may be avoided if institutions collaborate.

Very little has been published on the economics of running an ERC. The ACORN Project at Loughborough University compared the costs of traditional and electronic reserve collections of journal papers.

A more comprehensive study of the costs and benefits of ERCs was published as an eLib supporting study in 1998. This study was informed by all eLib studies in the electronic reserves (ER) and ondemand publishing (ODP) programme areas, including ACORN. Another relevant study comparing charging mechanisms was conducted on behalf of a JISC/PA working party following a seminar on pricing in July of that year. This study arose from debate among and between librarians and publishers regarding appropriate pricing mechanisms that would not cannibalise publishers' primary income stream. It considered only licensing of digitised copy from printed books and journals; not licensing of electronic products.

The report from the study called for a pricing mechanism that is 'simple and therefore inexpensive to administer ... susceptible to centralised administration [and produces] predictable costs for users and revenues for rights holders'. Furthermore, the report recommended that two models be adopted to reflect different types of use of digitised material; a 'textbook substitution' model and a 'library substitution' model. The former would be applied to materials that, in print, publishers would expect students to buy.

The pricing mechanism would be based on student numbers and a licence would be granted for a fixed period; probably an academic year. The latter model would be applied to material that, in print, publishers would have expected libraries to buy. In this case, a licence would be granted in perpetuity.

The report referred also to the high cost of digitisation and commended the idea of a central repository of digitised text which would avoid duplication of effort among HEIs and would make it easy for HEIs to identify material for which permission is likely to be granted, as it had been in the past. The report from this study is particularly useful because it resulted from an ongoing collaborative attempt by publishers and HE representative to resolve many issues that hindered progress with ERC developments.

Many of the recommendations in the report appear to have informed the Copyright Licensing Agency (CLA) Higher Education Digitisation White Paper which details the terms on which copyright materials are now licensed by the CLA for digitisation and distribution.

The CLA will continue to require institutions to request rights on a transactional basis and prices will be set individually by publishers. Publishers will differentiate between material that is likely to substitute for sales of texts to libraries and material that is likely to substitute for sales of texts to students. The latter will be more expensive to compensate for many more 'lost sales'.

This differentiation will refer to specific titles; it will not vary between institutions depending on their patterns of use of that title. Thus, although institution A may refer students to title X for further reading while at institution B it is required reading for all students in a class, both institutions A and B will be required to pay at the prescribed rate, be it 'text substitution' or 'library substitution'. This system is not ideal but the alternative, i.e. setting prices with reference to both the title and the institution requesting permission to digitise it would be extremely complex and thus expensive. The CLA White Paper also specifies the format of digitised text; it should be an 'exact page representation' of the print original. As pages designed to be printed tend not to be suitable for on-screen reading students can be expected to print.

At present, students tend to photocopy materials borrowed from a reserve collection so the library could recover print costs from students without increasing student expenditure. However, support for networked printing is likely to be a significant cost associated with the introduction of an ER system.

The CLA does not expect institutions to comply with the 'exact page representation' criterion by creating and delivering bitmapped images from printed originals. The White Paper acknowledges that bitmapped images are large files and thus are bandwidth hungry.

However, licences may specify the degree of qualitative and quantitative accuracy in digitised text. It may be possible to comply with terms by using suitable software and including disclaimers regarding accuracy (and the CLA anticipates that this will be the case) but there is no guarantee that this will be the case. As OCR programs tend to generate errors, it may be necessary to proof-read digitised text. This adds considerably to the digitisation cost. It is not immediately apparent that the eCLA (the name of the new CLA service) will be more efficient than the often criticised CLARCS system for clearing rights in materials to be used in course packs (containing photocopies).

A transactional payment mechanism is expensive. The Copyright Clearance Centre in the US has operated a transactional system for electronic reserve materials since 1997. In addition to any permission fee it charges $5 per request regardless of whether or not permission is obtained and claims that this charge is required to cover costs. The CLA requires from each publisher a mandate to license that publisher's material for use in electronic form in HEIs. The Publishers Licensing Society (PLS) has published a template which publishers can use to mandate the CLA Some of the terminology in this template differs from that used by the CLA, i.e. the PLS refers to a 'Bookshop Materials' model and a 'Library Materials' model instead of, respectively, a 'text substitution' and a 'library substitution' model. One more substantial difference between the CLA White Paper and the PLS mandate is that the latter restricts a licence for 'library materials' to 5 years rather than granting it in perpetuity. The PLS mandate also sets the 'Bookshop Materials' model as default and recommends a default price of 5 pence per page. Thus, libraries will be expected to pay for copyright at a rate of 5 pence per page per student in a class. A single 20-page extract for a class of 200 students would cost £200 (£235 inc. VAT) in copyright fees alone. If widely adopted, the terms of this mandate will probably render ER prohibitively expensive.

HERON

HERON is an eLib-funded project developing a national database and resource bank of electronic texts to be selected and accessed by HEIs throughout the UK. HEIs will supply details of materials that they require in digital form. HERON will obtain permission for their use and will digitise these materials. HERON is collaborating with rights holders and representative bodies to determine appropriate fee levels and conditions of digitised text and to streamline copyright clearance procedures.

The Project will normally clear rights through the CLA and when an institution requires permission to use material that is owned by a publisher or other person who has not mandated the CLA, HERON will seek to secure an agreement directly with the rightsholder.

Thus, when HERON has agreed terms with a publisher and an institution seeks to use material owned by that publisher, HERON can approach the company with confidence not only that permission will be granted but that the terms agreed previously will suffice and no lengthy negotiation will be required. Gradually, HERON will accumulate a collection of such agreements making it more efficient for HERON than for any individual institution to seek to clear rights in material to be included in an ER system. Furthermore, HERON aims to become a repository for digital copy.

HEIs seeking permission to digitise material from the CLA, either through HERON or directly, will be asked by the CLA to place a digital copy in a repository such as HERON so that it may be accessed by other users thereafter, thus avoiding duplication of effort.

Clearly, any future use of the digital copy would also have to be licensed. The model described later in this report is informed by the eLib supporting study of ODP/ER services, by cost and charge developments such as those published by the CLA and the PLS, and by HERON. The economic impact of rationalisation of licence negotiation and of digitisation will be explored using the model as will the ramifications for libraries of the CLA White Paper and the PLS mandate. For example, the textbook substitution model (referred to by the PLS as the Bookshop Materials model) reflects the fact that libraries increasingly provide access to core reading materials that, previously, students would have bought from booksellers. Libraries cannot afford to pay to provide all students with core texts and further reading. The crisis that libraries now face has been precipitated to some degree by student demands that they do so. However, librarians are uncomfortable with the prospect of charging for student reading materials. To do so would be to qualitatively change the role of academic libraries which would then be open to competition from other organisations which charge to supply information. Booksellers also would be affected by a move to supply core texts directly through the library.

INFORMATION GATEWAYS

Very little work has been done on the economics of information (or subject) gateways, also known as portals and hubs. Cataloguing the Internet is an activity undertaken by various types of organisation to attract users to their sites with a view to promoting their primary products/services or enhancing their reputations. Examples of this type of activity include:

- BioMedNet which, offering pointers to useful sites among many other discipline-based services, is effectively a discipline-based Internet community owned by Elsevier Science and funded, in part, by advertising (http://www.biomednet.com/gateways/bac);
- The Wiley student resource centre which includes subject-specific sub-sites each of which revolves around specific high-volume Wiley texts (http://www.wiley.co.uk/products/worldwide/canada/src/index.htm#links);
- Oppedahl & Larson LLP Patent Law Web Server, a site created and maintained by a professional law firm, which includes links to sources about all aspects of intellectual property (http://www.patents.com/index.sht);
- Various HE sites which having created pointers for their own users make them universally available (http://www.stir.ac.uk/infoserv/).

The perceived quality of these types of pointers is related to the site on which they are located. For example, links from an HEI may be considered more credible or impartial than those from a commercial organisation. Information gateways whose primary purpose is to provide pointers to other networked resources without promoting a different primary product would appear to be unique to the UK.

The eLib subject-based gateways (SBGs) have co-ordinated identification and evaluation of Internet resources and provide links to Internet resources within specific subject areas. Every resource which is linked from an SBG has been assessed by an expert in the relevant subject area and deemed to be of high-quality. None of the SBG projects developed an economic model for maintenance and development of a service beyond the grant-funded period. However, an eLib supporting study conducted by Haynes *et al.* evaluated three different models for the transition of the SBGs from project to service status.

These models varied depending on the proposed funding sources. The first was a JISC-funded service, i.e. one which would continue to rely on 100% grant funding. The structure of SBG organisation would remain unchanged.

The second model would increase JISC funding in the first two years with a view to migrating to a service funded 50:50 between JISC and other sponsors. This model includes a considerable degree of rationalisation in the organisation of SBG activities. The third model would end JISC funding and require services to find alternative sources to fund their activities.

The Haynes report recommended that the JISC pursue the second of these models. This required additional JISC funding for two years to employ a managing director who would seek complementary funding for an ongoing service. Many of the functions undertaken individually by eLib SBG projects would be rationalised and centralised to reduce duplication of effort and to allow for greater

PRESERVATION AND ARCHIVING

Acceptable archiving and preservation strategies are essential preconditions to the widespread acceptance of electronic journals by authors and librarians. Many questions relating to archiving and preservation require answers before economic factors can be explored. For example, there is the question of who should archive. Publishers are reluctant to accept what, traditionally, has been a library responsibility.

They are waiting to find out what the role of national libraries will be in a digital environment before they commit themselves in this regard. Furthermore, the long-term commitment of publishers and other stakeholder groups is questionable. It has been suggested that the only way to ensure 'systematic archiving of electronic publishing would be to assign that role to national institutions funded to do so and backed up by legislation'.

The UK research community generally agrees that preservation should be the responsibility of a publicly funded national agency. Preservation issues are of great concern to the UK HE community.

They have been the subject of several eLib supporting studies, of a British Library Research Study and issues continue to be explored by the CEDARS project. Economic modelling however, has not yet been undertaken.

JSTOR

Successful attempt to develop a model for archiving and preservation in electronic form of scholarly journals is JSTOR. One of the aims of JSTOR is to help libraries with space problems. JSTOR is also designed to be a trusted archive. Development of the archive has depended on the cooperation of publishers holding copyright in the journals included therein. It is important to those publishers that JSTOR should not cannibalise subscription income. Thus, current issues of journals are not included in the JSTOR archive. JSTOR operates a 'moving wall' whereby entire backruns of journal issues are included in the archive except those published during the previous X years. Every year the contents from X-1 years ago are added to the archive. The duration of X varies from publisher to publisher but generally is between 3 and 5 years. The JSTOR archive is funded by fees from institutions accessing the contents. The JSTOR team has calculated and compared the costs associated with:

- A centrally managed electronic text archive (including the cost of migrating content to keep pace with technological development);
- Storage, processing, reshelving and maintenance of a hard-copy collection.

A key factor in making JSTOR financially viable is that it is available widely and thus, costs are spread across a large number of institutions both in the US, and now also in the UK. JSTOR aims to be as equitable as possible in pricing access to the archive. Price discrimination is applied with a view to setting prices according to the value derived by each institution.

Thus, institutions are banded according to size and annual access fees are varied on that basis. Pay-per-use was dismissed as a possible pricing mechanism because it 'usually yields prices higher than the marginal cost of providing the product' and JSTOR 'did not want to force students and scholars to have to decide whether it would really be 'worth it' to download and print an article'.

This contrasts with the view that it is prudent to charge a print fee as this discourages indiscriminate use of printing resources, i.e. a fee would encourage users to filter information before rather than after they have printed. JSTOR received start-up funding from the Andrew Mellon Foundation but is expected to be self-sustaining over the longer term.

JSTOR appears to be a pragmatic and useful model for archiving and providing electronic access to backruns of journals. The capacity of JSTOR, however, is limited; currently the project aims to include backruns of a minimum of 100 journals before the year 2000.

To preserve in electronic form and make available worldwide all developments in scholarly communication is a monumental task requiring co-operation on an international scale.

It is notoriously difficult to secure international agreement for any type of activity and it is beyond the scope of this project to explore the ramifications of such an initiative.

PRE-PRINT ARCHIVES

The most famous example of an electronic pre-print archive is the Physics archive developed by Paul Ginsparg at the Los Alamos National Laboratory (LANL) (http://xxx.lanl.gov). The archive is very successful and is used by authors and readers throughout the world.

Development of the archive was funded by a grant from the US National Science Foundation. The full cost of developing and running the archive is not clear. Odlyzko estimated the cost per paper at $5. Then, to pre-empt disagreement on this figure he recalculated using wildly extravagant estimates of the costs of personnel and storage space.

He estimated that the upper limit would be $75, i.e. that it could not possibly cost more than $75 per paper to run such an archive. In the absence of grant funding, a cost-recovery model would be required.

Given Odlyzko's figures, if the international physics community were to subscribe to this service either on an individual or institutional basis, the subscription charge would be small. Nevertheless, the administration of subscriptions would increase the total cost. An alternative model might charge authors to place pre-prints in the archive.

This would be unlikely to succeed however as authors are reluctant to pay page charges even to submit papers tojournals where the benefits of publication are clear. Harnad is trying to establish a similar pre-print archive in the cognitive sciences. This project (CogPrints) is funded by eLib. Other than grant funding, no economic model for a pre-print archive has been published and so no model will be explored here. It should be noted however, that increasing use of preprints effectively transfers the information filtering function either to libraries or to end users.

Publication in a specific journal confers on a paper a mark of quality that is recognised by the readers. When all papers are freely available and unrefereed, the user must seek to identify high quality papers for herself.

The time taken to do so is a cost; thus, in economic terms, preprints are not free. Physicists reading material from the Ginsparg archive tend to read only articles written by colleagues with whose work they are familiar This suggests that they are unwilling to filter the material for themselves. It also makes it difficult for newcomers to establish themselves in the field.

Issues Related to Digital Library Service and Resource delivery

Licensing

The application of national copyright law to the electronic environment is not straightforward; legislation tends to predate the digital era. Furthermore, the business of providing access to copyright materials in electronic form tends to be international. Combined with the Internet 'gift culture' whereby users expect electronic content to be available free of charge, copyright on its own is inadequate for regulating use of copyright materials. Rather than relying on copyright law, content suppliers tend to use licences to detail precisely the terms on which their copyright material is made available to end users.

In the words of Karen Hunter of Elsevier Science, 'publishers view licences 48 and contracts as a more robust, clearer method of resolving what might otherwise be ambiguities as to permitted use and limitations'. Licence terms have important implications for libraries. As the availability of an increasing proportion of library material depends on relationships beyond the organisational boundary, library managers must consider the impact that this has, among other things, on their ability to control budgets and guarantee access beyond the current licence term. Clearly, the pricing model detailed in a licence and the level of prices are important in determining the costs and benefits to licensor and licensee. At present, prices tend to be very high for a variety of reasons including:

- That publishers often tie the price of electronic copy to the print price and offer both formats as a bundle;

- That by becoming the source site, the publisher takes on some of the library roles and costs.

Although pricing is an important element of a licence agreement it is only one of many issues that determine the costs and benefits conferred on the licensor and licensee. At present, pricing models offered by individual publishers vary considerably and are complex. Negotiation on a licence terms requires expertise, and takes a great deal of time. As licensing becomes increasingly important and common so do legal advice and staff with the knowledge and experience required to negotiate favourable and consistent licence terms.

Guidelines published by the US Association of Research Libraries (ARL) in 1997 recommend that institutions 'create a contract team' consisting of 'appropriate staff from the library, legal office, purchasing department and information technology division to provide information and develop contract expertise'. This type of recommendation suggests that licensing electronic resources is very much more expensive in terms of personnel than acquisition of print resources by library staff.

Furthermore, it illustrates the importance to all stakeholders that licences be kept simple and terms be standardised wherever possible. This is the rationale behind CHEST and behind initiatives like the UK National Electronic Site Licence Initiative (NESLI).

NESLI has based its model licence on one developed by a collaborative working party of representatives from the JISC and from the Publishers Association (PA) (http://www.nesli.ac.uk/nesli-licence.html). This model has been revised by NESLI in an iterative process involving all stakeholder groups.

When electronic resources were first offered to libraries by publishers, licences tended to be extremely restrictive with regard, for example, to use and users. This can be understood with reference to the size and importance of the market to academic publishers and the apparent naivety about copyright among users accustomed to the internet 'gift culture'. A great deal of progress has been made towards increased trust, goodwill and understanding between different stakeholder groups.

Librarians have identified licensing issues of importance to them and initiated dialogue with publishers. In the US an informal organisation calling itself the International Coalition of Library Consortia (ICOLC) and representing initially US library consortia, but later also consortia from Australia, the UK and the Netherlands, published a Statement on Current Perspectives and Preferred Practices for the Selection and Purchase of Electronic Infrastructure (http://www.library.yale.edu/consortia/statement.html).

This is essentially a wish list which elicited responses from several publishers thus initiating dialogue which continues at annual meetings of the ICOLC. The most recent (7th) draft of the NESLI model contract, published in September 1998 (http://www.nelsi.ac.uk/nesli7.html) addresses many of the issues raised by the ICOLC 50 and by writers on licensing such as Okerson. For example, terms dictate that access to licensed material will not be withdrawn when subscriptions are cancelled and that licensees will be given the opportunity to subscribe to electronic copy only. NESLI is also considering the type of usage data that it can feasibly provide and is working towards seamless access from OPAC entry to abstracts, Tables of Contents, and full text.

By offering standardised terms, NESLI aims to minimise negotiation costs for both parties but acknowledges that the terms in this contract will not be acceptable to all publishers.

There are often stark differences between the commercial interests of publishers and the library mission and negotiation is not often straightforward. The US experience to date is that negotiation of terms of use of electronic journals is often adversarial and protracted, and the resulting licences are lengthy and complex but clearly there is a willingness to simplify the licensing process and thus reduce costs for all parties.

User Behaviour in the Online Environment

User acceptance is key to the success of digital library resources and services. A resource can be technically impressive but unless it is acceptable to the target audience it will not be used. Research on user needs should be practical rather than hypothetical as potential users' reported needs differ from those of experienced users. Thus, studies which provide access over a sufficient period to allow users to learn and repeatedly use a system are likely to be most useful. Research on user behaviour tends to focus on electronic journals but user needs and behaviour with reference to electronic texts and monographs have also been explored. There is a remarkable degree of consensus among researchers of user behaviour in the online 51 environment. It would appear that researchers consistently identify the same essential pre-requisites for a successful online resource and the same deterrents to use.

Core Functionality

Identification of core functionality is important as journal readers use only those functions that meet their needs. As additional functionality increases production costs and may impact on price, superfluous functions should be avoided.

Users consider the core functions to be the facility to browse, search and print from an electronic journals service. Research repeatedly emphasises the fact that users do not read on screen but prefer to use print copy.

There are various reasons for this, including portability, the facility to annotate and guaranteed future access. Some users claim that a virtual filebox may reduce the need to print.

This would reduce anxiety about accessing materials in the future but does nothing to address the requirement for annotation and portability. Although Butterworth reports that scientists' interest in electronic journals relates primarily to improved functionality and lists linking to references as one of the required functions, the SuperJournal project found that users consider linking to be 'nice to have' rather than essential.

Creating links to references can be expensive especially for journals that are published in PDF format so it is essential that the importance of this feature to users be established.

Critical Mass and Currency

Users consider it essential that any service should offer a critical mass of resources both in terms of breadth and depth. Access to a limited selection of journal titles, whether they be published by a single publisher or by a range of publishers, is not considered sufficient incentive to learn to use a new system. Users also expect an electronic journal service to offer a backfile of a minimum duration. The SuperJournal Project found that users consider the minimum requirement for a journal service to be a backfile of 5–10 years. Others consider the minimum useful backfile to be 25 years. Furthermore, many users expect an electronic journals service to offer a wider range of titles than is currently available in print from the library.

System Performance

System performance is a necessary prerequisite if users are expected to use digital resources and services. Both academics and students are subject to time constraints and users are reluctant to learn to use new systems unless there are clear benefits.

Lowlevel problems demoralise users and it is difficult to entice them back if they have been disappointed. Time taken to download and print materials from a system is also important.

At present many users consider the delay to be excessive and consequently, would not print. Staff from the library at the University of Columbia have found that the online books system is used as a sophisticated catalogue. Users search for items of interest in the digital environment but when they have identified an item and wish to read more than a few lines, they seek a print copy from the library shelf. This finding echoes that, noted earlier, of the ELINOR project at De Montfort University. It is no surprise that users consider the online books system to be an adjunct rather than a replacement for print.

Convenient, Fast Desktop Access to a one-stop Shop

Desktop access is considered to be important as is speed and ease of use. Users prefer not to have to login at all and complicated login procedures invariably deter use. The SuperJournal project found that when users experienced difficulty with the login procedures they did not attempt to use the system again. Furthermore, 90% of requests for user support from the SuperJournal helpdesk were from users who had forgotten their personal ID for logging in.

Having accessed the system, the time taken to identify and retrieve material is important; users are not prepared to follow long chains of links to access relevant content. A single common interface is also an important feature and the interface should be familiar so frequent upgrading and redesign is unacceptable. Furthermore, users expect an electronic journals service to offer seamless discovery and access. The user should have the facility first to identify material that she wishes to read by searching or browsing tables of contents, second to link to the abstract of any items that interests her, and third to link to the full-text of any article that she wishes to read in full.

Format

A significant proportion of electronic journals are delivered as portable document format (PDF) documents especially when the electronic format is produced as a parallel of the print format. It is claimed that PDF is cheap to produce in these circumstances but is inappropriate for electronic delivery especially when pages have two or more columns.

Nevertheless, PDF currently has advantages over HTML. Users of Super Journal service claimed to prefer reading HTML on screen but when offered a document in either HTML or PDF format, the majority selected the latter.

This may be related to the fact that users prefer not to read on screen and print material if they intend to read more than a few lines. Super Journal users claim to prefer prints from PDF because they look like printed journal pages and, unlike HTML documents, they have page numbers.

Benefits of an Electronic Service

Access to digital library resources tends not to be restricted to library opening hours and generally, two or more users may access an item simultaneously. Improved access is considered to be a benefit of digital library services. However, although Super Journal users claimed that access outside library opening hours is important, most use occurred during office hours.

Users also believe that the digital medium should facilitate faster publication; where items are published in both print and digital formats, users expect the latter to be published before or at the same time as the former.

Benefits of Print and Photocopies

Generally, studies of user needs and behaviour in the digital library have revealed a range of different functions associated with print and photocopies that users consider to be 55 important. Until equivalent or improved features are available in an electronic environment many users will remain attached to print. These features include ease of browsing and reading; most current users have been familiar with print since childhood and are skilled in its use. A ubiquitous equivalent level of familiarity and skill is likely to be available to future users who are currently in the primary education system. Studies also report an emotional attachment to print.

Whether or not this attachment will remain among future lifelong users of electronic media remains to be seen. Another feature of print that currently give it an edge is its portability. Users tend not to read at their computers and often read journal papers at home or when travelling.

The facility to annotate a print copy is also important as is the fact that they can legally cache materials for future use. Finally, some users consider presentation in print resources to be superior to that in digital resources. For example, high-quality graphics cannot be satisfactorily reproduced on prints from electronic resources. This is particularly important with regard to colour images.

Disciplines

Although many research findings apply to all users, differences between disciplines should be recognised. The Los-Alamos pre-print archive is commonly cited as an example of discipline-specific behaviour which has contributed to the success of a digital library resource.

There has long been a culture among physicists of distributing preprints. Physicists differ from other sciences in this respect and it is argued that the success of the Los Alamos archive derives in part from 56 this culture.

It is reported also that electronic journals are embraced more readily by those in disciplines that have not been adequately catered for in a print environment, for example musicology and other disciples to which non-printable elements are important. Future research on user behaviour in the online environment should differentiate between users from different disciplines. Unfortunately, initiatives such as ATHENS which are designed to streamline delivery of digital resources can subvert attempts to gather data on different types of user.

MEASUREMENT OF USE AND PERFORMANCE INDICATORS IN THE DIGITAL LIBRARY

International Standards for Performance Measurement

The ability to monitor use and interpret the results is essential if any information resource or service is to be deemed a success or otherwise. Internationally standardised performance indicators have been developed for traditional library services. However, recent studies of usage measurement and performance indicators for digital libraries have found no evidence of standardisation and continue to recommend that international standards be developed and applied.

An initiative in this direction has been taken by the ICOLC who have published guidelines for statistical measures of usage of electronic resources. An eLib supporting study published in 1997 investigated Management Information Systems and Performance Measurement for the Electronic Library. The authors described a three-fold approach to library management with regard to performance measurement:

- The day-to-day needs of library managers;
- The need for information that can be used by planners for forecasting;
- The need for indicators of value for strategic review.

Although they found that some indicators used in traditional libraries can be adapted, it was necessary to devise other 57 new indicators. For example, the number of documents accessed was considered not to be important in an electronic environment; the range and depth of resources available was deemed far more important.

Furthermore, Brophy and Wynne identified a number of issues which must be addressed if progress is to be made in this area. While acknowledging the significant contribution of the eLib programme in this regard, they called for a clearer definition and understanding of what is meant by the term 'electronic library'.

Non-standard Usage Measurement

A requirement for international standards is clear but development of such standards is a lengthy process. While this process is ongoing, each individual digital library initiative requires feedback to inform development and, thus, must unilaterally adopt an approach to performance measurement.

Electronic library projects in the UK, Europe and the USA have used a variety of different definitions and methods of usage measurement and analysis. Thus, neither analyses nor data from different projects can be compared.

Most Internet usage analysis tools are applicable to digital library activities and WWW server log file analysis programs still predominate. In 1997 the eLib supporting study referred to above found that most work in the electronic library field relied on transaction logging for management information.

If users are authenticated (i.e. have usernames and passwords), it is possible using these tools, to monitor individual use by logging the username alongside the URL. Hits can also be time stamped. In this way, an individual's progress can be tracked from page to page. It is possible also, using cookies, for a service supplier to track an individual's movements on the Internet beyond that supplier's site. However, this is likely to be considered a breach of privacy and librarians 58 make it an issue in negotiation with content suppliers. To comply with the library ethos, performance indicators should not rely on information about individuals' reading habits. Many academic subscription services authenticate whole sites by registering and restricting access a list of IP addresses.

Not only does this overcome privacy issues related to individual users as names and time stamps cannot be recorded on accesses, but it also removes the need for costly password management. An alternative means of reducing the cost of authentication in the UK is use of the ATHENS service which provides an individual with a username and password which may be used to access a variety of services.

Unfortunately, use of ATHENS greatly reduces the management information that can be gathered by individual service suppliers. This is deliberate to protect the privacy of individual users. For example, it is not possible for a supplier to monitor use of her service within a specific discipline if neither individuals nor even whole classes are identifiable by user ID.

Limitations of Current usage Measurement Tools

It is important when designing performance measurement activities that they be justified in terms of the benefits derived. Because it is automatic, transaction logging is a cheap way of gathering data in an electronic environment.

Unfortunately, the type of data that can be collected is often restricted by the delivery format. In 1996, when Michigan University intended to test economic models during the TULIP Project, it was unable to do so because 'the Web does not support the kind of data collection required to test economic models'.

Project MUSE is still unable to distinguish between downloading/printing and browsing as the Web is a stateless environment. SuperJournal know that although users claim to prefer HTML documents for onscreen viewing, given a choice of formats, a large majority 59 chooses PDF over HTML. As most users print documents if they intend to read more than a few lines, it can be assumed that they select PDF as a superior format for printing.

Unfortunately, SuperJournal cannot verify this assumption by monitoring use as it is not possible to differentiate downloading from printing. Thus, although data gathering is cheap, as yet, it is also limited. Furthermore, analysis of such data tends to be time consuming and thus expensive and interpretation is not always straightforward.

For example, it may be assumed that more hits indicate a better service, as a high number suggests that users return and that they recommend a site to others but, of course, this may not always be the case. A subject-based gateway which generates search results that closely match a users needs will record very few hits before that user leaves the site satisfied with the result. If the search results supplied are poor and include a number of extraneous links or if the user is required to conduct several searches before she retrieves useful links, the gateway will record many more hits before the user leaves.

However, if a subject-based gateway offers not only access to a database of catalogue records but also holds a local archive, it should record a larger number of hits as users are likely both to search the database and to retrieve local resources. Furthermore, attempts to make more efficient use of internet bandwidth by caching and mirroring can subvert attempts to monitor use. Access to resources from site A from a cache or mirror held at site B will not be included in usage measurement unless site B informs site A about the cache and agrees to supply site A with use data. This type of shortfall makes WWW statistics unreliable or, worse, misleading.

Inferring user Behaviour from Transaction Logs

Use of transaction logs for performance measurement requires digital library practitioners to infer meaning from specific types of user act in a digital environment. For example, A. Dawson of the BUBL service (http://www.bubl.ac.uk) suggests that to view a list of journal issues with dates and contents is the equivalent of browsing a library shelf. He also asserts that searching is a deliberate activity which is not easily mistaken and that to access full-text is a likely indication that the user is reading the article.

The latter assertion is qualified by the acknowledgement that the reader may access text to scan for relevance rather than, necessarily, to read the article. However, Dawson argues that this ambiguity need not influence the accuracy of any performance measure as it applies to all journals. This type of inference helps digital library practitioners to make sense of quantitative data. However, knowledge of user behaviour in the digital environment is limited and it can be dangerous to base inference entirely on assumptions and prior experience. For example, Dawson's assumption that the frequency with which a reader accessing full text is in fact scanning for relevance will apply equally to all journals is contradicted by the findings of the SuperJournal project.

SuperJournal found evidence that the way in which scientists and social scientists use journal elements differs. For example, scientists are more likely than social scientists to identify a relevant article from its title and to print it on that basis. Social scientists more often read the abstract to establish relevance because article titles in the social sciences can be more ambiguous. There may be similar differences in the way that scientists and social scientists approach full text. It is clearly difficult to derive qualitative research findings from quantitative information. Qualitative methods such as interviews and 61 observation should be used to inform assumptions about the meaning of quantitative information and for triangulation.

Training and Awareness

Some of the eLib projects in the Training and Awareness programme area have now migrated to a service model and offer training courses in the use of new technologies for teaching and learning. HEIs are likely to continue to pay for this type of training from staff development budgets.

Training of users in the use of IT is unlikely to fall within the remit of libraries although libraries will probably continue to offer training in information skills and the use of specific resources.

It is beyond the scope of this project to explore the economics of this activity and compare the costs and benefits of training academics and students in the use of electronic and print resources. Clearly, the transition from a traditional to a digital or hybrid library involves dramatic changes in the infrastructure that supports the production and use of information resources. At present people prefer not to read on screen so they print articles from electronic journals.

As resources for teaching, learning and research are increasingly delivered in electronic form there is likely to be a mass shift from photocopying to printing; the latter is more expensive than the former but the total opportunity cost of an individual operating a photocopier is not incurred so costs are probably very similar. As people become more familiar with technology, users may no longer need print copies.

This could lead to a net reduction in the cost of using information. The report of a recent study on the impact of electronic journals on networked printing suggested that one of the reasons for printing material from the Internet is to ensure future access; networked access is not always reliable.

In effect users create a personal print cache of networked resources. The report predicted that improved access to networked resources would 62 reduce the need to print but suggested that it may also increase use of the network, which in turn would increase the print load. The net effect of a combination of such changes is virtually impossible to predict.

Another factor impacting on the economics of digital information is the pace of technological change; new technologies become obsolete at an alarming rate, making it expensive for organisations to meet the changing needs of users. However, technological advances are reducing some costs, for example the cost of storing digital resources.

It is not possible within the scope of this project to estimate the infrastructure costs associated with delivering electronic resources in such an unstable and unpredictable climate. Investment in infrastructure that effectively enables all stakeholders to conduct much of their business electronically will be required. The models described here will be based on the assumption that the HE sector will invest in sufficient infrastructure to support digital/hybrid library activities.

At present there is no coherent model of the digital library, nor is there yet any developed model of the hybrid library. Furthermore, economic issues tend to be tested after solutions have been found to the more pressing technical, cultural and legal issues. Many specific digital library activities are insufficiently mature to have generated economic models. Where a model exists it has been evaluated and where alternatives exist these have been compared.

It is clear that a great deal of progress has been made over the last decade towards a greater understanding of how digital library activities may be integrated in HE. Nevertheless, a considerable amount of work remains, specifically in the areas of preservation and archiving and in standardisation of usage measurement and performance indicators. Conclusions regarding specific issues relating to digital library activities are outlined in the remainder of this report.

4

Evaluation of Online Databases and their Uses in Library Serials

INTRODUCTION

Now a days, libraries are using web technology extensively for user services to provide dynamic services to the remote users. Web technology currently available is helping the libraries to achieve their purposes. Although, web technology available, especially from Microsoft, is easier to setup the applications. It requires less programming skill and, is suitable for librarians. However, there is a need for librarians to get extensive exposure with the computer and communications technology in general and web technology specifically. The advancement in database technology especially RDBMS has made them ideal for library applications. These RDBMS provide simple architecture, easy to design and are equipped with flexible data exchange interface and, thus, present ideal solutions for web-enabled databases in libraries.

BENEFITS OF WEB-ENABLED DATABASES

Web-enabled databases have certain advantages over other means of sharing/publishing information over internet. These advantages are common to bibliographic databases also where libraries can put their OPACs and other databases on web.

L.J.Haravu; Kristin Aantelman and; Chong Ho Yu, the benefits of web-enabled databases are as follows:

- Global/wide access to data with a single user inter face.
- Format in dependent access of data.
- Up-to-minute up dated access of data in real time.
- Dynamic updating of data from many locations.
- Cost-effective way of data sharing.
- Instant feedback from users.
- Seamless links from resource to resource.

- Unlimited download/printing.
- Environmental friendly.

Besides, Ortiz-Repiso and Norm Medeiros have written excellent papers on differences between traditional v/s innovative means of library catalogs, while B. Ramesh Babu, *et al* have presented an overview of web OPACS with their advantages in libraries.

DATABASE TOOLS

In the early days of database development, it was the flat-file system to store data in a single file by using field separators and record separators. Later, such flat-file systems were facilitated by an index in which a single index file stored keywords and pointers to the records that were stored in main file. This made retrieval more efficient, still flat-file systems were seriously inefficient. It showed data-redundancy, poor data control, and did not supported complex data types. After 1960s, two database models were developed in quick succession to solve the limitations of flat-file systems. These database models were Hierarchical Database Model and Network Database Model. The Hierarchical Database composes of a root segment, parent segments and child segments. This model depicts a set of one-to-many relationships between a parent and its children. However, this model has number of limitations. It does not include *ad hoc* querying capability and, a multi-parent relationship is difficult to implement, as in a many-to-many relationship. The Network Database Model attempted to deal with many of the hierarchical model's limitations. The network database structure easily accommodates the multiple child, although, its structural complexities often limit its effectiveness and efficiency. Both of these database models are obsolete now mainly because of their incompatibility with web environment and have been replaced by RDBMS. RDBMS is the current database implementation standard being used for publishing information on the web.

It includes the following features which make it suitable for web environment:

- Provide extremely useful tools for database administration;
- Adhere to powerful query language SQL developed by Microsoft Corporation;
- Compliant with ODBC/JDBC and other database interface tools;
- Work in client/server mode;
- Offer distributed database and distributed processing options; and
- Have referential integrity controls to ensure data consistency and, thus, suitable for web environment.

It is easier to design applications in RDBMS due to the following features:

- Requires less programming skill
- Availability of third party tools, and
- Inbuilt web interface.

These all features of RDBMS have made them ideal for library applications to setup bibliographic database solutions and publishing them over the web. In the early days of library systems development, vendors have designed library applications software by using pre-relational database technology. Still some library systems suppliers are continuing to maintain and develop such products. These proprietary library applications software have their own advantages and disadvantages. However, in the library management systems marketplace, there is a growing trend towards the use of RDBMS as shown in the figures.

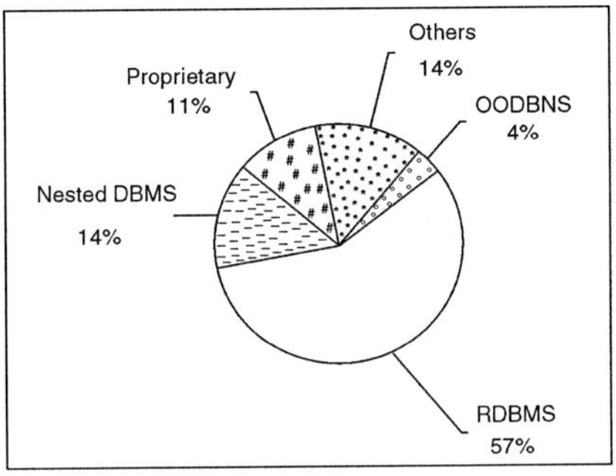

Fig. Type of Databases Used in Library.

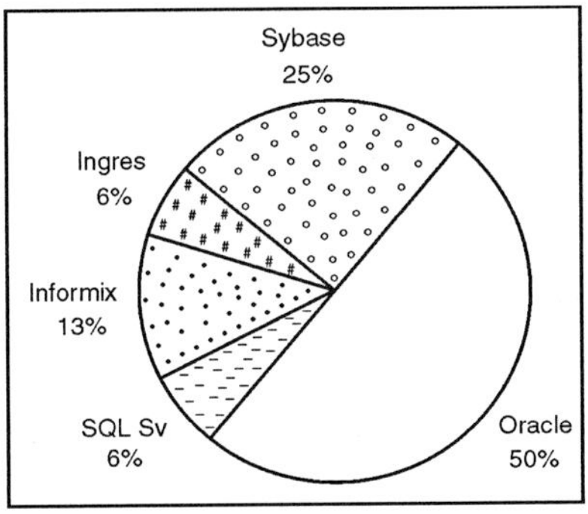

Fig. Use of Various RDBMS in Library Systems.

As per the Gartner list of database management systems, there are 140 products from 67 vendors ranging from pre-relational, relational and, object-oriented databases. The RDBMS accounted three-quarters of the total database market.

Table. Market Percentage of Vendors in DBMS Sector

Company	2000 Market (%)	1999 Market (%)
Oracle	33.8	31.4
IBM	30.1	29.9
Microsoft	14.9	13.1
Sybase	3.2	3.3
Informix	3.0	5.0
Others	15.0	17.3

Table shows that in the relational segment, there are 'Big Five' DBMS vendors which include Oracle, IBM, Microsoft, Informix, and Sybase

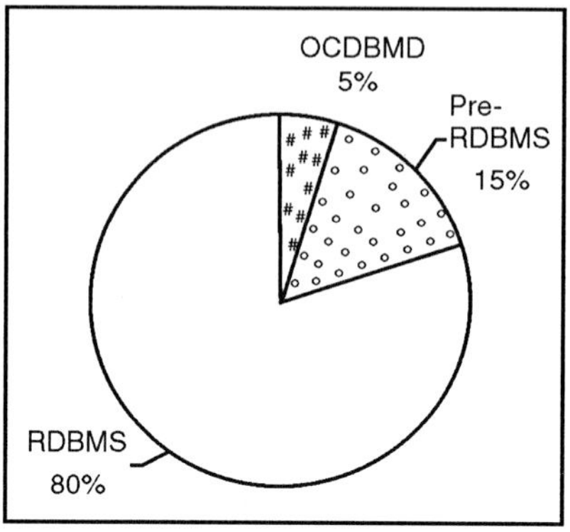

Fig. Worldwide DBMS New License Revenue

Some of the common RDBMS which can be used to design in-house databases in libraries are *MS Access, SQL Server, Oracle, Informix, Sybase, File Maker Pro, SAS,* etc.

However, the selection of suitable RDBMS for library applications depends on:

- The particular library requirements,
- Kind of applications,
- The application level,
- Magnitude of data,
- Nature of data analysis and
- Comprehensiveness and inter-operability.

Other points to be considered while selecting database tools for library applications are easiness, user-friendliness, flexibility and low cost. In most of the cases in libraries where bibliographic databases are dealt with, commonly available consumer database products such as *MS Access*, and *File Maker Pro* are sufficient.

These products can support up to 1GB of data and provide cheaper solutions. However, these database tools are suitable for small databases and not useful for large databases, hence provide limitations in web environment. There are specific database solutions for large databases available from *MS SQL Server, DB2, Oracle, Informix, Sybase,* etc. These database tools support up to several terra byte of data; permit thousands of simultaneous users; work in client/server mode; show natural affinity towards web environment and, thus, suitable for large bibliographic, web-enabled databases in libraries.

However, to design full-text databases in libraries where large files are to be stored and retrieved, these tools do not offer good solutions as most of these tools support 200-255-400 characters field length. Although, many of these tools allow unlimited entries in memo field, the data inside a memo field are not searchable and thus, offer limited utility. In this respect, *MS SQL Server* has extended the searchable field length up to 8063 characters and thus, provide solutions for moderate full-text databases. As a common trend, a number of libraries have been using open source software available either free or on nominal prices.

These database management systems include the most common *mySQL, mSQL* and, recently updated *PostgreSQL*. These database tools are easy to work and run on various platforms such as UNIX, Lynux, NT, etc. Besides, there are some library specific text retrieval database tools for management of full-text large files, generally known as 'Free Form Databases', provide powerful search engine.

Although, in some ways they are at the opposite end of the RDBMS, little database structure imposed on the designer and, thus, provide an easy and readymade database structure. However, they provide some limitations in achieving integration in the modules other than searching such as cataloguing, classification, management module, etc. These software are *BRS/Search, Basis Plus, Status,* etc.

WEB TECHNOLOGY

World Wide Web or WWW or web, sometimes wrongly mentioned as synonymous to internet, is a sub-set of it and is a most promising mode of publishing/sharing of data/information. Now, the web has emerged as the dominant protocol over internet due to its special features like easy interfacing of diverse platforms/technologies; provision to incorporate text, graphics, audio and video, etc.; permitting to access data/information in a non-linear way and; jumping from one document/resource to another through hyperlinks. The superiority of www over other modes of online sharing, *viz.*, e-mail, FTP, Telnet, Gopher, etc., has been well explained by Paul Scully. In fact, web has provided a single user interface to facilitate the user interaction with the databases or systems resources.

The web uses unique URL (universal resource locator) address which facilitates the access of information seamlessly across the diverse platforms in a client-server mode.

The actual data represented in a structured way reside in a powerful computers called server, while the latter is equipped with server tools/software to populate the information over web. The client/user equipped with web browser such as Microsoft Internet Explorer (MSIE) and Netscape Navigator, etc., which interact with the server through common communications protocol TCP/IP over high speed network/internet.

In fact, the client/user sends its query to the server while the latter processes the request and gets the response/results from the database and sends it back to the client/user over the web.

COMPONENTS OF WEB-BASED SYSTEMS

Following components are required for web-based systems:

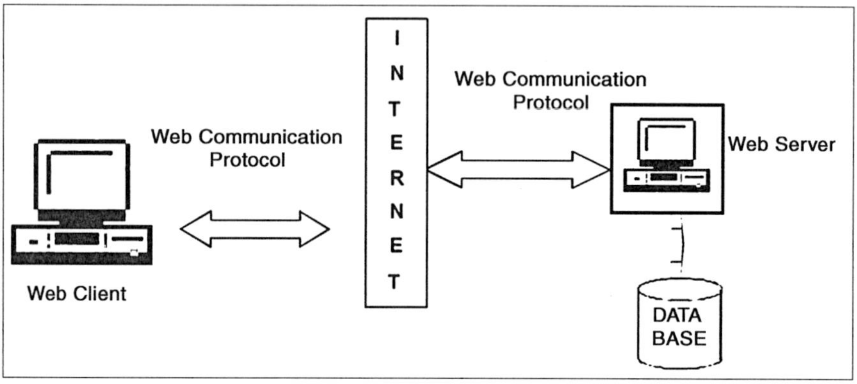

Fig. World Wide Web Architecture.

Web Browser

It is a software that helps users to interact with the server for sending queries and getting results over the web. MSIE and Netscape are the most popular web browsers, both of these are available free.

Web Server

Web server is the software that helps in sharing the system resources/ files over the internet through web browsers. The latter communicate with a web server via the standard Hyper-Text Transfer Protocol (HTTP). In fact, web servers receive queries from the client, process it, get data from databases and send it back to the client over web. The popular web servers are Apache, Microsoft IIS, iPlanet from Sun-Netscape alliance, and newly developed *Zeus* from Zeus Technology Ltd. Although web servers are increasingly found as components within full-featured server operating systems, there are some basic selection points that should be highlighted.

These points are scalability and performance; high availability and reliability; interoperability and open standards; system administration and; security. In fact, there are not much choice in the web server segments as many of them come along with database tools, show natural affinity with the database tools from same vendor, and some other work better with certain platform/operating systems. The widely followed Netcraft web survey, approximately 60 percent of web servers run Apache, with Microsoft's IIS and the Netscape/iPlanet web server as its major competitors. However, Gartner studies have given Netscape/iPlanet a larger share of public web sites, followed by Apache and Microsoft/IIS.

Apache is being used for the public sites of companies such as Merck, American Express, Texaco, Chrysler, and others. However, it is easier to find both Microsoft/IIS and Netscape/iPlanet as the servers for large corporate public web sites when using the lookup facility offered by Netcraft. Also, for intranets, most counts credit Microsoft/IIS and Netscape/iPlanet as the leaders, followed by Apache, IBM's Lotus Domino Go server, and others. Among hot e-commerce sites, E*Trade runs the Netscape/iPlanet server, eBay runs Windows/IIS, and Amazon runs Apache.

WEB AUTHORING TOOLS

Basic web server software does nothing except it sends HTML data in response to a browser request. However, certain other web-authoring and scripting tools are required to extend the functionality of web server to extract the data from databases. These web-authoring tools and scripting tools are required to write web pages and scripts to interact with back-end databases. In early days of web-based applications, *CGI* (common gateway interface) programmes were used extensively to extend the server functionality by allowing web users to interact with the web server to request specific data from the databases.

Although, writing *CGI* programme is difficult and requires programming skill, however, it works with high reliability. Now-a-day, number visual editors are available to generate the web pages and write scripts automatically. The common editors are *Microsoft Front Page, Visual Interdev, Netscape Composer, Web Builder,* etc. Besides, other technologies have been introduced to communicate with the back-end databases. These technologies are Microsoft *Active Server Pages (ASP*) and *Java Server Pages (JSP)* from Sun Micro Systems. Both the technologies have combined the HTML codes with the scripts in a single page and thus, making it easier to interact with back-end databases. During last few years, object-oriented and component based solutions were added to further make it easier to interact with the back-end databases.

These solutions include:

- Microsoft COM/DCOM,
- ActiveX Data Objects (ADO);
- OMA and CORBA (Common Objects Request Broker Architecture) from Object Management Group;
- Sun's EJB (Enterprise Java Beans),
- Java Applets (for client) and
- Java Servlets (for server), etc.

Besides, some database connectivity tools such as ODBC and JDBC have also emerged as in-built features of operating systems, etc.

FREE WIZARDS AND THIRD PARTY TOOLS

Writing HTML codes and scripts for database interaction is the most difficult part, requires programming skill, systems logic and manipulation planning, especially for non-computer professionals. However, a number of free wizards and third party tools are available on internet which can generate hundred of lines of codes automatically with a single click, thus, making it easier for non-skilled users to set up web-enabled database solutions in libraries. Some of the free wizards are Rule Zero, Power ASP, Active Server Pages Tools and Components, etc. Besides, *Microsoft FrontPage* also provides database wizard to generate *ASP* pages/*VBScripts* automatically to interact with back-end databases, while *Visual InterDev* provides a visual interface to develop a web-enabled web site with minimum efforts.

DATABASE SEARCHING IN CENTRAL UNIVERSITY LIBRARIES IN INDIA

In consequence of the recommendation of the National Knowledge Commission, each of the Indian states has at least one fully-funded central university. Now there are 39 central universities. Privately funded and owned statelegislated universities are also being established to cater to the increased demand for higher education. In between there are many universities that are not legislation-based but are authorised by the University Grant Commission to award degrees. Central universities are better-equipped in terms of financial resources, faculty, and infrastructure, and thus have an edge over the usually fund-starved state universities.

The libraries across the globe are challenged to integrate e-resources into their collection, services, and patrons' lives and academic libraries face obstacles when virtual learning environment (VLEs) become "the primary means of interaction between students and universities. Providing access to electronic journals and other e-resources is an important area of librarianship. The design of usable online interfaces is a crucial issue. Traditional library services and printed material are still more effective to researchers in Indian universities than web-based information and resources. Barriers to progress in this area in university libraries in India cannot be overlooked.

NETWORK INFRASTRUCTURE AND STRENGTH

Fast and effective information retrieval to support information sharing requires sound and wide network with adequate bandwidth. The UGC-sponsored Infonet is the mainstay of the academic info-network infrastructure. The UGC has constituted a national committee called the Central Monitoring Committee (CMC) for smooth implementation and execution of information infrastructure.

The CMC has chosen ERNET India to establish information network in universities. The committee has recommended high bandwidth campus wide networks for Internet and external connectivity. So far 149 universities have been provided connectivity with raw bandwidth ranging from 512 KBPS to 20 MBPS. The Inflibnet is administering and funds its cost for all these universities.

ONLINE DATABASES

Out of the eight universities surveyed, seven are members of the UGC-Infonet consortia. The IGNOU, due to its unique character, subscribes to 17 databases of its own. A tabulated picture is given below:

Table. Numbers of Databases in Different University Libraries

Name of the Universities	UGC-Infonet Databases	Self Subscribe Databases	Public Domain Databases
AU	16	0	0
BHU	23	24	–
DU	23	25	41
IGNOU	–	17	52
JMI	21	15	–
JNU	21	15	–
PU	22	–	–
VBU	18	–	–

There are 77 databases in all in these eight universities. But strangely enough only one online database, namely Project Muse, is common to all the universities, and 69 databases are subscribed by single universities. The following Databases are available in seven of the eight university libraries: ACS, AIP, APS, Annual Review, BWP, CUP, IOP, ISID, JCCC, JSTOR, OUP, RSC, SIAM, Springerlink and Taylor and Francis. A tabulated picture is given below:

Table. Percentage of Availability of Online Database

No. of Database	No. of Universities	% of Occurrence
1	8	100 %
16	7	87 %
1	6	75 %
3	5	62.5 %
4	4	50 %
5	3	32.5 %
16	2	25 %
69	1	12.5 %

These are further categorised as:

- Full Text e-Journals - 72.
- Bibliographic Databases 15.
- E-Books 29.
- Total Databases 116.

Of these there are 15 bibliographic/indexing databases, while 29 are e-book databases. There is no single common e-book database available in all eight libraries. Among the bibliographic databases, DELNET and ISID are most popular, which are available in seven libraries, while MathSciNet is subscribed by six university libraries. Exemptions are Assam and Viswabharati Universities. It is natural and normal as each central university located in different region has its own requirements based upon its courses of study and areas of research. The subject needs of the JNU differ from that of Delhi University, while Jamia has its own needs. Need and Specialisation of IGNOU are of quite different nature. Still some of the databases are very common to all universities especially the Project Muse, JSTOR, American Chemical Society, American Institute of Physics, American Physical Society, Annual Review, Blackwell Publishing, Cambridge University Press, Institute of Physics, Oxford University of Press, Royal Society of Chemistry, SIAM, Springerlink and Taylor and Francis.

Retrieval Techniques

Net Server and CD-ROM mirror servers are very popular among the universities. The university libraries under study no longer provide CD-ROM services. Multimedia databases are available only in DU and JNU, while all the eight libraries own and provide access to full text and bibliographic databases.

For academic libraries the two most important consortia are the UGC-Infonet and Indest. All the libraries have self-subscribed as well as consortia based databases, whereas the DU and JNU have also developed in-house databases. Being traditional and general universities under the preview of the UGC, all are members of the UGC-Infonet, while DU is also member of AICTE Indest consortia. All the universities use commercial as well as open source databases while DU and JNU have also their home grown databases. Open source databases are also available there, but the study found that only DU, BHU, IGNOU and JNU host important open source online databases on their web sites.

Other universities are not able to create this kind of facility for their users merely because the staff of these libraries are not conversant with open access sources on the Internet. Databases can be accessed through login and password, but the misuse of these is a common complaint. Therefore, IP access is more suitable.

Now most of the universities allow online access to databases either through their intranet or directly from the Web. Experienced librarians prefer a campus-wide facility for providing access to databases. AU, IGNOU, Jamia, JNU and Viswabharati allow access from limited and specified terminals within campuses. Assam, IGNOU, Jamia, JNU and Viswabharati allow access through campus wide Intranet or Internet with identification and password. Many busy scholars and faculty have less time to visit the library. Therefore, access to online information must be provided on their desktops. This requires campus wide Internet accessibility. Further it was found that AU, BHU, DU, Jamia, JNU, PU and Viswabharati allow IP enabled access while IGNOU databases are password based.

Download Facility

Downloading of the required files is a critical issue. In case of commercial databases it is costly as the host library has to pay per download. But indeed it is an essential facility. It has been found that all the libraries provide downloading of PDF and HTML files, while image downloading facilities are available in all except at BHU and DU. RTF downloading is not permitted by BHU, DU and Jamia Millia Islamia, Whereas word file are not downloadable at BHU, DU and Jamia. DU and JNU provide DBMS software to download the data oriented information.

Data Retrieval Techniques

Some of the universities provide common databases linked through federated search. Only DU has the federated search engine GIST find. In this survey, only DU and PU revealed their online search techniques while the other libraries kept these confidential. DU uses Boolean, Interactive, and Proximity searches, while PU uses quick search. Simple search Advanced/Boolean search in addition to menudriven searches are provided by their vendors. Both these libraries provide facilities for further refinement of large chunks of search output to make the search more precise and relevant. Nevertheless, none of the universities use data mining.

Complexity of Information Retrieval

Indeed information retrieval techniques vary from university to university system. It depends upon both internal and external factor of database.

In the questionnaire about 48 aspects or facilities for information retrieval were identified and the users of these eight libraries were asked to mark their ease of use on the Likert scale as:

- Easy 3.
- Challenging 2.
- Difficult 1.

The mean value of university wise pattern is given below:

Table. Complexity Level of IR in Different University Libraries

Universities	AU	BHU	DU	IGNOU	JMI	JNU	PU	VBU
Mean	2.58	1.95	2.54	2.52	2.22	2.61	2.37	2.34
Std. Deviation	(0.54)	(0.92)	(2.54)	(0.64)	(0.85)	(0.57)	(0.6)	(0.89)

User Orientation

For optimum use of all resources and services of a library, user orientation programmes, especially of new users, are a proven effective measure. User orientation is the most important component in the online databases for the users to gain knowledge and enhance usability of databases. All the university libraries in this study have positively voted for provision of such programmes to help users in the effective use of the retrieval system for information access.

This survey found that orientation programme are conducted by all except AU, BHU, IGNOU, and Viswa Bharati. It is important to note that regular orientation programmes are required to make the users familiar with new feature of new databases. DU conducted programmes as "How to search the online databases," while the Pondicherry library provides instructions in the use of library resources including eresources and effective online searching. BHU conducts programmes on Science Direct and Proquest. DU provides need-based instruction and PU provides general instruction in effective search and the publishers also conducted such programmes to faciliatets searching of their supplied databases.

DU conducts such programmes throughout the years, while PU organises orientation of the users at the beginning of the academic years. PU also offers need based person to person training. It is clear that there is no uniform pattern of conducting user's orientation programmes. Indeed we need a dedicated library staff for online training of library users, especially in the electronic environment.

There are posts of information scientist in universities funded initially by the by UGC. Those hired are mostly from computer science and not conversant with library philosophy and routine. There is an urgent need of a designated post for an online librarian who can provide assistance in using e-resources and may also take care of any aspect of user orientation for sharing and dissemination of library e-resources. The survey showed that none of the library staff has any formal education and training in online searching. Most have learned it on the job, and most have learned by trial and error.

XML AND RELATIONAL DATABASES: USES AND OPPORTUNITIES FOR LIBRARIES

Extensible Markup Language (XML) is becoming an indispensable tool for virtually every type of content that is digitally produced. The advantages of XML for libraries have been well described by others.

On a general level, XML has at least three key advantages:

- *XML is standard.* XML is a subset of Standard Generalised Markup Language (SGML), a well established and highly regarded ISO standard. XML also offers mechanisms to encourage and enforce common definitions of the logical structure of a document so that standards for the documents themselves are easier to apply.
- *XML is extensible.* XML has no limits on the number of markup languages that can be defined using it, and each of these languages can consist of an unlimited number of tags. This flexibility is essential for fostering the widespread adoption of XML and helps explain why XML has been utilised for markup languages in every conceivable subject area, ranging from chess playing to mind reading.

- *XML is well supported.* It seems that almost every serious Web technology is now expected to define its relationship to XML, and XML has fostered an explosion of related technologies. The W3C has made many tools and toolkits freely available to Web developers, and utilities and applications for XML are being developed by a worldwide community of vendors, open source contributors, and other groups that seek to move information across the Web.

XML has been used extensively for authoring standalone documents, but database solutions for storing and managing large collections of materials in XML format are becoming more common. As Bourett, a researcher who tracks developments in XML databases, points out, choosing between an RDBMS and other database options for storing XML often comes down to whether you are working with data or documents.

If the XML content is usually manipulated at the individual field level, needs to be accessed with standard query and reporting tools, and pulls together information from sources that are updated and maintained separately, then a Relational Database Management System (RDBMS) approach may make the most sense.

Examples of this kind of "data-centric" content include purchase orders, flight schedules, and scientific data. If the XML content is largely contained in individual documents, and the content will be edited and updated at the document level, then Object Orientated Databases (OODBMS), Object/ Relational Databases, and other solutions that can maintain XML documents as a more complete unit on the backend will be preferred. Data housed in an RDBMS are typically based on individual rows in tables, using "keys" or "ids" to pull together content dynamically.

Most RDBMS solutions for storing XML assemble XML representations of the data on the fly. Object relational databases and some RDBMS addons, such as Oracle's Internet File System (IFS), step slightly outside of the standard RDBMS tables to work with Binary Large Object (BLOB) or other mechanisms built into the database to store whole XML documents without parceling pieces of it to separate tables.

This allows the document to be stored with all tags and ordering preserved. Of course, the data and document distinction is not absolute, and there are other factors that can influence the choice of a database. An organisation may have built up a high level of Oracle experience, for example, and that would have a huge impact on any data management decisions. Libraries are also in a somewhat unique situation in that they house collections of both data-centric and document-centric materials that may require database solutions.

For example, libraries with finding aids in Encoded Archival Description (EAD) format or full text materials marked up with Text Encoding Initiative (TEI) are more likely to favour "document-centric" solutions and require extensive full text searching capabilities that are more prevalent in OODBMS and Object/ Relational Databases. Libraries are even more likely to deal with content that is "data-centric", such as purchase orders and circulation records; they may already have RDBMSs in place to support the processing activities associated with this data.

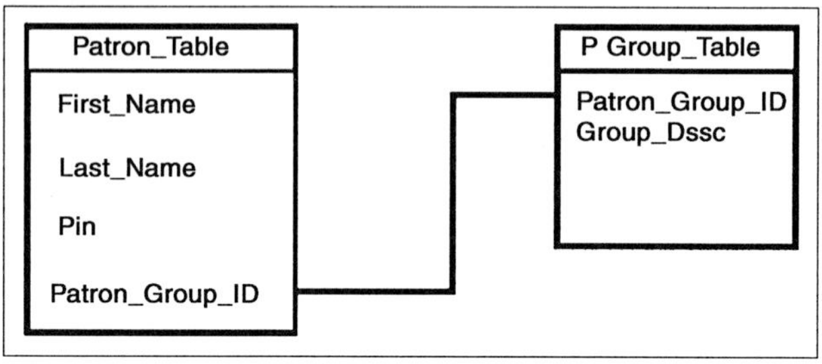

Fig. The Table with Patron Information (Patron Table) is Linked to another Table (Pgroup Table) Describing the Patron Group.

MARC AND XML

The difficulty in separating data from document-based content can be seen in the Machine Readable Cataloguing (MARC) format, one of the library community's most successful and durable standards. Like many document-centric formats, MARC records can carry a lot of text-intensive information. Libraries may even choose to convert MARC records to standalone XML documents in order to take advantage of mainstream XML tools for indexing or for presentation purposes.

On the other hand, MARC records are "data-centric" in the sense that they can often bring together data sources that are maintained outside of the bibliographic description of an item. Authority, holdings and item records, for example, play a key role in helping to define the bibliographic view of the physical and virtual objects in the library's collection, yet these records are often processed and updated separately.

Libraries have begun to explore the use of XML for MARC. Lane Medical Library at Stanford University has created a DTD and released conversion software for converting MARC records to XML documents in an initiative called XMLMARC. K.T. Lam has also proposed a DTD for MARC and suggests that the use of a decentralised authority repository may one day be possible with XML linking technologies.

This would allow libraries to "point" to established names and subjects that could be maintained remotely rather than replicated by each individual library. Clearly, there is interest on the part of libraries in bringing MARC fully into an XML environment. The challenge is to define an XML infrastructure that can handle the amount of materials that libraries catalogue without isolating the content from the transactional processes that libraries use for acquiring and circulating the collection.

Cataloguing records are typically maintained by dozens of library staff and are linked to ordering and circulation processing procedures that involve many updates. Any application of XML that is tied directly to where cataloguing records are maintained and use XML as a means of updating content may need to be "transaction aware" and support a high level of multi-user access.

MIDDLEWARE ALTERNATIVES

A number of middleware mapping tools exist for layering XML representations of information that is housed in an RDBMS on top of individual tables, such as IBM's DatabaseDOM. The middleware typically uses Structured Query Language (SQL) to pull together the fields needed for the XML input/ output. The advantages of this approach are that this greatly increases the number of database systems that a library can select from because all major RDBMSs support SQL, and that this allows great flexibility for moving from one database to another. For formats like MARC, these tools also offer the possibility of using XML technologies without losing the robustness of relational databases for maintaining content and linkages that are updated by multiple users.

The disadvantages of this approach include the overhead required to assemble and disassemble XML documents as they move in and out of the database, and the extra groundwork to define an XML representation that takes full advantage of both the RDBMS and XML technologies. A good example of an XML mapping tool for relational databases is Castor, an open source project from Exolabs.

The mapping file in Castor determines how the XML will be produced from the contents of the RDBMS. In addition to defining whether a field in the RDBMS is to be rendered as a node or an attribute, an ID reference is provided that identifies the records in the appropriate table. Castor is very "Java-centric," which can be an advantage or disadvantage depending on how comfortable an organisation is with the Java platform. By working with Java, a developer can use Castor to render the records in an RDBMS accessible and updatable as XML documents. Databases that can be used with Castor include Oracle, MySQL, and PostgreSQL.

THE WEB AS THE WORLD'S BIGGEST RELATIONAL DATABASE

The way that an RDBMS references rows from multiple tables can be compared to Web links. A Web page is, in some ways, much like an RDBMS "view" of disparate data. From a user perspective, the content is brought together based on a predefined logic and a series of "keys" or "pointers" that identify relevant material.

A dynamically generated Web page comes even closer to the conceptual model of an RDBMS, particularly if much of the content of the page is based on remote network resources retrieved through URLs. For example, a search of a library catalogue on the Web typically involves a cgi-bin programme that dynamically displays results using HTML. Each result record is usually linked to a fuller display via a URL that specifies from where the information is to be retrieved. The linking mechanisms of the Web have recently been leveraged to support the OpenURL framework.

The OpenURL framework has been proposed as an architecture for retrieving references to scholarly works by enabling third parties to provide links for a referenced item. Although OpenURLs have typically been deployed to provide links to the full text of scholarly works, the framework can also be utilised to identify a catalogued item in an ILS. Ex Libris' ALEPH500 System, for example, directly supports OpenURL, and exploratory work has been carried out to generalise the OpenURL framework beyond reference linking scholarly environments.

If the Web can be thought of as an ever-growing RDBMS, and OpenURLs can be utilised to provide "RDBMS-like" standard and precise links between specific items in information systems, then there are possibilities for providing extensive distributed search and retrieval functions in Web-based library services.

For example, a remote database consisting of Library of Congress names and subject headings could be searched within a browser environment, and the results could provide links to items in the local catalogue.

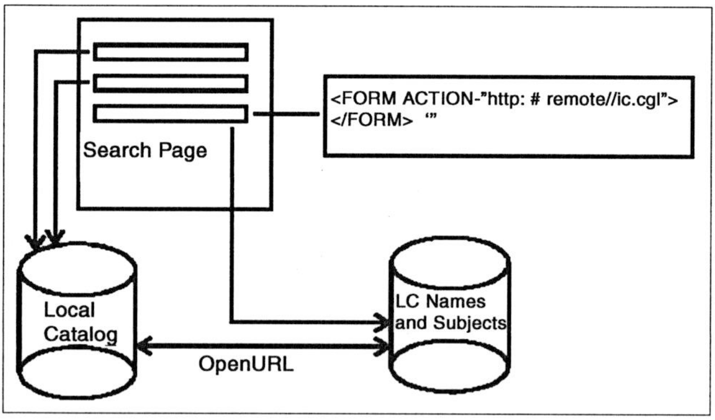

Fig. The Web form is Constructed to Pass some Searches to the Local Catalogue and one against a Remote Database. OpenURLs "Point" back to Local Holdings.

Web-based union catalogues support standardised indexing and searching at a central location. With OpenURLs, links can be made to point to holdings and other localised information within the member library's Integrated Library System.

All of this fits within the RDBMS notion of creating and maintaining data with as little duplication as possible, and linking it together to provide a logical view of the content itself. XML plays a role by greatly enhancing the linking mechanisms of the Web. XML technologies such as Xinclude, Xpath, and Xlink, provide sophisticated methods for drawing on network resources. Xinclude allows the contents of a separate XML resource to be inserted into an XML document based on a link.

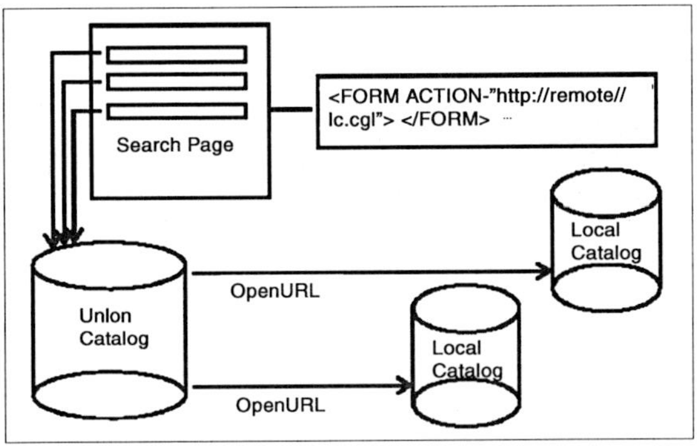

Fig. A Centralized Union Catalogue Provides Searching Services, OpenURL Links to Location-specific Information.

Xpath will be familiar to anyone who has worked with XSTL and other XML stylesheet tools. It allows the creation of expressions for specifying every visual and interface portion of a document. Xlink is the XML linking language and offers much more sophisticated types of linking than currently offered by the familiar HREF and NAME elements found in HTML. Xlink's extended element can name one or more linked resources. The arc element in this example tells an application about the behaviour expected when moving through the linked resources. The role and title attributes are used to describe the function of the linked resource in the context of the local resource. Role is meant to be descriptive to the application and title is meant to be descriptive to the user. In this case, the roles are meant to identify an author's works and biographies. The *acutate* element describes how the resources should appear. The value "onRequest" specifies that the resource should appear when the link is selected, and the value "embed" for the *show* attribute tells the application to insert the specified resource inline within the current document. Finally, an *item* element is used to represent where this particular resource can be found in physical form in the library. If an XML representation of an RDBMS-based library catalogue or other library database is made available, the library can make use of XML linking technologies and other XML tools for manipulating database contents. OpenURL lays the groundwork for using links as virtual keys to content that goes far beyond individual tables, and the content can be as broad as the diversity of the Web itself.

STANDARDS FOR CREATING BIBLIOGRAPHIC DATABASES INDIAN ACADEMIC LIBRARIES UNDER INFLIBNET UMBRELLA

The concept of "standard" in the field of library and information science is interpreted as codes of cataloguing rules, classification schemes, subject headings and various other documents contained recommendations for good library practice, all of which are subject to varying interpretation. But, for another professionals, standards are extremely precise technical specifications for communication between software and machines in an automated information-processing environment.

For example, Operating Systems, TCP/IP, etc. Standards are documented agreements containing technical specifications or other precise criteria to be used consistently as rules, guidelines, or definitions of characteristics, to ensure that materials, products, processes and services are fit for their purpose Field of bibliographic standards are not limited to the rules only but spread up to the authority files such as person names, corporate names, subject headings, classification schemes, series names, institution names, software and standardisation form and format, etc.

In beginning, during the initiation of automation to library professionals, there was not much focus on bibliographic standards and were creating databases in any formats. That affected to the automation of their libraries, which forced them to think over the issue. Now, gradually, the libraries and information centres are realising the importance of bibliographic standards. Centres like Information and Library Network (INFLIBNET), Ahmedabad is playing important role in bringing all libraries together to work on a single platform of standards with linking under one huge national network, *i.e.* UGC-Infonet. INFLIBNET Centre is an Inter-University Centre of University Grants Commission (UGC), working on Academic library system in India. In 1990, UGC launched it as a programme for five years on pilot basis. On June 1996, the programme was recognised as a full-fledged Centre. UGC-Infonet is a project of UGC being implemented by INFLIBNET Centre in collaboration with ERNET (Education and Research Network), New Delhi. It is an Intra-Network of Indian universities and colleges across the country based on the Open IP platform, employing state-of-the-art technologies like IP or TV, enabling online response to queries. The network facilitates Intranet and Internet access to its users on high data rates.

STANDARDS FOR BIBLIOGRAPHIC DATABASE

Well-known simple definition of database is a set of records and record is a set of fields, where, field is a combination of different pieces of information. Bibliographic database is a database of resources available at libraries in print format. With the revolution of information technology in the field of libraries, bibliographic catalogue has come up into the form of bibliographic database. For making compatible with these changes, there, many library institutions have come up with different standards and formats such as CCF, AUSMARC, CANMARC, UKMARC, USMARC, UNIMARC, MARC21, AACR2, ISBD, LCSH, MeSH, etc. Some of the Internationally recognised standards and formats being used by many libraries of different countries for creating databases. As per the INFLIBNET's guidelines following standards are recommended for use:

Standardised Bibliographic Formats

During the inception of the Programme, The Task Group on "Union Catalogue, Data Capturing and Standardisation" was constituted by UGC. The Task Group was assisted by a Sub-Committee on implementation of Common Communication Format (CCF) for data capturing and data exchange. Later on, the Sub-Committee formalised some fields based on CCF and named it as "Guidelines for Data Capturing: a user manual". During the initial stage of automation, Micro CDS/ISIS software (developed by Unesco) were suggested to use for creating bibliographic databases based on the format recommended by the Centre. Simultaneously, other DBMS such as DBase, FoxPro, FoxBase, etc., were also being used by different libraries for creating the databases. In addition, the Centre had also the library house keeping software called "ILMS – Integrated Library Management System" developed on COBOL language on Unix platform, and was distributed freely to the member libraries of the Centre. Later in February 2000, Centre developed another library house keeping software called "SOUL – Software for University Libraries" on Power Builder language on Windows platform by using the client-server architecture to keep in mind the shortcomings being faced in ILMS software. The software is developed based on the format formalised by Sub-Committee of the Task Force. Later, early 2001, The Ministry of Human Resource Development (MHRD), Govt. of India visualises building up a national database of library holdings in the country based on the MARC21 format. Further, after approval the committee directed INFLIBNET Centre to implement the MARC21 format in all libraries of the country. In this regards, the Centre formed the MARC21 Core Group during December 2001, which formalised the fields for implementing it with the SOUL library house keeping software. The main reason for preferring MARC21 over CCF and other formats was that most of the countries in the world use MARC and it is comprehensive having number of fields.

STANDARD FOR RENDERING INFORMATION/ BIBLIOGRAPHIC DESCRIPTIONS

AACR2R, ISBD and CCC are standards for bibliographic descriptions. But, INFLIBNET Centre suggests their participating libraries to follow the Anglo American Cataloging Rules-II (AACRII) Revised version for rendering bibliographic information.

STANDARDISED SUBJECT HEADINGS

Different subject headings list are available, developed by different institutions such as LCSH, Sear's List of Subject Headings, MeSH, Thesaurus, etc. But INFLIBNET suggests to its member library to use LCSH (for generalised subject headings) and Engineering Index, MeSH and thesaurus (for specialised Subject Headings).

STANDARD FOR CLASSIFICATION SCHEMES

There are various classification schemes have been developed by different organisations for classifying the books on different subjects. Functionally, most of the libraries are using the Dewey Decimal Classification (DDC) for assigning the Classification Number to the documents. But, under INFLIBNET umbrella, all the libraries are free to use any classification scheme for classifying the document, as it is very difficult for any library to reclassify the entire collection based on any new scheme. As per the library practice any classification scheme can be used as MARC21 has capability to adopt any kind of classification schemes.

ISO–2709 INFORMATION EXCHANGE FORMAT

This standard specifies the requirements for generalised interchange format that will accommodate data describing all forms of material. It describes a generalised structure designed specifically for exchange of data between processing systems and not necessarily for use as a processing format within systems.

The format may be used for the interchange of records using various communication media. INFLIBNET Centre recommends to follow this Exchange Format for contributing records to the Centre. The exchange format has implemented too with the in-house developed software SOUL for exchanging records. Physical structure of the implemented information exchange format is given below:

Physical Structure

General Structure of the Record:

Leader	Directory	Data Fields	R/S

R/S = Record Separator

Leader

Each record begins with a leader of fixed length of 24 character positions and is the first instance of the ISO 2709 format of a record. It contains:

- *Record length (5 characters):* The length of the record includes the leader, directory, data fields and record separator.
- *Record Status Code:* Always '0' for output files, ignored on input files.
- *Implementation Codes:* These codes are defined for each specific implementation of the ISO 2709 format. Second character position

represents Bibliographic level codes and rest of the character positioned not used. Here, Bibliographic level is defined here as per the INFLIBNET's use. For the MARC21 based records, it follows the description defined for bibliographic level in MARC21 bibliographic format.

- *Indicator length:* This is always '0', because here at INFLIBNET database indicator is not being used. But the value is '2', when we export records from SOUL to MARC21 in ISO 2709 format.
- *Subfield identifier length:* '2' The subfield identifier length. This shows the number of characters being used for the subfield identifier.
- *Base address of data:* A decimal number indicating the number of control characters which precede the variable data fields. This number, when added to the starting address of the record, gives the address of the first character of the variable fields.
- *For user systems:* These character positions are not used. Always '000' in output files.
- *Length of "Length of Datafield" field:* '4' the length of "Length of Datafield" in the directory.
- *Length of "Starting character" position:* '5' the length is "Starting character position" in the directory.
- *Rest:* These character positions are not used. Always sets on '00'.

Directory

A directory entry in this bibliographic record is made up of a tag, length-of-field, and field starting position.

It is of variable length and consists of a series of fixed fields, referred to as "entries". One directory entry is associated with each datafield present in the record. Each directory entry is 12 characters in length and is divided into three parts:

- *Tag:* A three numeric ASCII character code identifying the datafield, which corresponds to the directory entry. In software, names of the fields are being used in alphabetical name, but during the export in ISO 2709 format and display on screen, it converts in three-numeric digit ASCII character code.
- *Length of datafield:* A four digit number showing how many characters are occupied by the datafield, including datafield separator but excluding the record separator code if the datafield is the last field in the record.
- *Starting character position:* A five-digit number giving the position of the first character of the datafield relative to the base address of data, *i.e.*, the first character of the first of the datafields.

Table. Structure of a Directory Entry.

Tag	Field Length	Starting Character Position

Datafields

A datafield consists of subfield and datafield separator:

- Subflield: A subfield consists of a subfield identifier followed by a data string, which is terminated by either another subfield identifier or a field separator. A subfield identifier consists of a subfield identifier flag, *i.e.*, cap (^) sign followed by one another character, that can be alphabet a to z (small or capital) and numeric 1 to 9, INFLIBNET Centre uses here small alphabets. For MARC21 based records "$" graphical sign is used as a subfield identifier.
- Datafield Separator: The datafield separator, *i.e.*, hash (#) sign constitutes the final character of every datafield. ASCII value 30 (character 1/14 of ISO 646) is being used as a field separator in MARC21 based data.

A datafield, which has a single subfield, will be organised as follows:

Subfield Identifier 2 Character	Subfield Variable	Fieldseparator 1 Characters

A Datafield, which has two subfield, will be orgainsed as follows:

First Subfield Identifier 2 Characters	First Subfield Varibale	Second Subfield Identifier 2 Characters	Second Subfield Variable	Field Seperator 1 Character

Record Terminator/ Separator

The record terminator is the final character of the record, *i.e.*, hash (#) sign. It follows the field separator of the final datafield of the record. ASCII 29 (character 1/13 of ISO 646) is being used as record separator in MARC21 based data.

OTHER STANDARDS RELATED TO BIBLIOGRAPHIC DATABASE

There are some other standards related to the bibliographic databases, are given below:

Z39.50 Retrieval protocol

Z39.50 refers to the International Standard, ISO 23950: "Information Retrieval (Z39.50): Application Service Definition and Protocol Specification", and to ANSI/NISO Z39.50. The standard specifies a client/serverbased protocol for searching and retrieving information from remote databases.

OAI (Open Archive Initiative)

The Open Archive Initiative (OAI) for metadata harvesting is a new protocol dedicated to solving problems of digital library interoperability by defining simple protocols, most recently for the exchange of metadata. Although, Z39.50 Information Retrieval Protocol is also one of the harvesting protocols. Some digital library systems are using for retrieving and searching the records for example Maxwell System. It is crucial to explain, discuss, and disambiguate the concepts and terminology used among OAI implementers to harvesting approach to interoperability. The harvesting protocol defined by the OAI is a request/ response protocol with 6 request types, *viz. Identity, ListMetadataFormats, ListSets, GetRecords ListRecord, and ListIdentifiers.* It has defined in such a way to support a common set of principles and a technical framework to achieve interoperability. Although, both the standards are not being used with the INFLIBNET database right now, but being explored to implement it in near future.

PURPOSE OF THE BIBLIOGRAPHIC STANDARDS

Mostly, purpose of using these standards for creating bibliographic databases or suggesting using it at libraries of India, has following reasons behind it:

- Pursuing Universal Bibliographic Control
- Exchange of information among union databases for the purpose of global resource sharing
- Cooperation at the local level, transferring data from one system to another

IMPORTANCE OF THE BIBLIOGRAPHIC STANDARDS

Following bibliographic standards for creating the databases produces following importance:

- It makes uniformity in records;
- It provides better resource sharing between different resource centres.
- It helps in exchanging of records and facilitates it without data loss.
- It helps in creating national/ International bibliographic union database.
- It helps to adopt any system and provides platform interoperability.

DESIGN AND DEVELOPMENT OF WEB-ENABLED DATABASES

Application of computers certainly has improved the ways in which we acquire, process, store and disseminate information in libraries. As a result, we have automated house-keeping operations, catalogue and, user services in libraries.

Moreover, with the advancement in the network technology during last decade, we have started providing user services through various online modes, *viz.*, e-mail, FTP, Telnet, etc. These static/interactive modes of data/information sharing over network have improved the library services and, their popularity among the users. During 1994, libraries began to show their presence on the internet by setting up their web sites. In the beginning, libraries built their web pages by providing mainly static information. However, in the late 1997, libraries began re-engineering their web pages with the intention of providing information from databases in a dynamic manner. Today the advancements in web and database technology have enabled the libraries to share/publish the data/information directly from the databases over the internet.

Now web has become a dynamic platform for information delivery over the internet and very useful for libraries to provide various user services. This paper intends to provide an overview of the database tools available for designing in-house databases in the libraries as well as the web technology for publishing such databases over the web. Besides, the thesis discusses the need of developing in-house databases in libraries, advantages of web-enabled databases, and selection of database tools from RDBMS commonly available.

IN-HOUSE DATABASES IN LIBRARIES

There are a number of ready-made library automation software packages in the market which can be used to automate the library functions and user services. However, many of these packages lack web interface and, thus, do not provide library database access through web. Moreover, these commercial packages provide less flexibility to librarians for making desired changes to the existing databases and to publish the same on the web. An in-house designed database system provides full flexibility to the developer/administrator/librarian and is simpler to install, maintain and, use without having to rely on external support, and also is highly customisable and can be designed to meet local needs. Librarians can also participate in design/development process as now a days easy and user-friendly database tools are available with in-built web interface. As per the survey conducted in order to get a clear understanding of the current role of library web master, 100 percent of the respondents felt that librarians should have some role in web site design and maintenance.

5

Serials Librarian: Libraries and Cloud Computing

AN OVERVIEW

The case studies focused on five networks:

1. The Ohio Public Library Information Network (OPLIN)
2. The West Virginia Statewide Library Network (SLN)
3. Wisconsin's BadgerNet
4. The Maine School and Library Network (MSLN)
5. California's Peninsula Libraries Automated Network (PLAN)

The first four of these are state networks, while the last is regional (in California's San Mateo County).

OHIO PUBLIC LIBRARY INFORMATION NETWORK

OPLIN is a centralised system whose primary function is to provide broadband connections to the main public libraries in the state. In addition, OPLIN is the Internet service provider (ISP) for all the libraries in Ohio and provides access to a set of information databases that libraries might not be able to afford on their own. All of these services are provided at no direct cost to the libraries.

Unlike many other statewide library networks, OPLIN coordinates the acquisition and installation of the physical network connecting libraries to the Internet. It is transitioning those connections to fibre-based Ethernet circuits. As a result, Ohio libraries generally have faster Internet connections than those in many other states: about 60 percent of Ohio libraries report having broadband connections that are faster than 1.5 megabits per second (Mbps), compared with the national average of 45 percent.

WEST VIRGINIA'S STATEWIDE LIBRARY NETWORK

The West Virginia Library Commission (WVLC) established the centralised SLN to provide all of the state's public library systems with broadband Internet connections and a wide variety of technical assistance, including support for the online catalogue. SLN provides Internet access, e-mail communication, and web support to all public libraries in the state. Without SLN, many West Virginia libraries could not operate modern library systems, maintain computer equipment, or offer Internet-based services to users.

The key to SLN's success is a uniform approach to network design and service that lends itself to economies of scale. The WVLC has encouraged all libraries to join the network, enhancing its ability to aggregate demand and further upgrade connections. The WVLC took a similar approach to technology and E-rate support, centralising these services at the state level.

WISCONSIN'S BADGERNET

Wisconsin's public libraries are highly connected to the Internet; all public libraries have at least a 1.5 Mbps connection, and most are planning to increase to at least 3 Mbps before the end of 2009. As of the end of 2008, 97 percent of the state's population could access wireless Internet at their local public library. Perhaps the biggest reason for Wisconsin's success in connecting users to the Internet is the creation of BadgerNet, one of the largest state networks in the country. BadgerNet extends to all of the state's 72 counties, providing next-generation voice, data, and video services to state agencies, local governments, schools, and libraries. It provides a statewide backbone network, as well as middle-mile and last-mile connectivity. This comprehensive end-to-end service is one of the reasons a very high percentage of schools and libraries in the state are connected to BadgerNet.

MAINE SCHOOL AND LIBRARY NETWORK

In 1996, Maine implemented MSLN, one of the first statewide networks to provide connections to the Internet for all schools and libraries. MSLN was later codified by the state legislature and is now funded by a combination of federal (E-rate) and state surcharges on telephone bills. As a result, Maine's libraries have much greater connectivity than is the case in most states; about 75 percent of those that participate in MSLN have one T1 line (1.5 Mbps), and the remainder have two T1 lines (the maximum available through MSLN).

MSLN funds direct local connections from each school and library to two aggregation points operated by the ISP for the State of Maine. The network uses standard T1 connections, which are easy to provision and troubleshoot. By aggregating its purchasing power, MSLN can obtain prices for these circuits far lower than those an individual library could negotiate. The network design and technologies used by MSLN are now under stress because of the growth in Internet demand. Maine is therefore considering shifting to a new network design that would rely on local fibre optic and wireless connections to the Maine research and education backbone network.

CALIFORNIA'S PENINSULA LIBRARIES AUTOMATED NETWORK

The Peninsula Library System (PLS), located in California's San Mateo County, serves the county's eight public library jurisdictions and the San Mateo Community College District. The PLS Administrative Council, composed of library directors from PLS member libraries, is responsible for overseeing PLAN, which currently serves only PLS. All branches of the eight public library jurisdictions in PLS have participated in PLAN since its inception.

Member libraries share the up-front and ongoing maintenance costs of the central system, the connectivity costs of the transmission system, and the support staff that manage and operate the system. PLS created and maintains the network with funds from membership fees, which are derived from city and county property taxes. The PLAN department is responsible for the day-to-day operation of the network, and provides PLS libraries with a variety of telecommunications and broadband services through a centralised information technology (IT) department.

PLS applies for federal E-rate discounts for eligible costs of operating PLAN, excluding Internet access and internal connection costs. PLS initially relied on a traditional hub-and-spoke frame relay design in which the individual libraries (spokes) were served with DS1 (T1) connections. This design has been replaced by a new fibre-based Layer 2 Ethernet service. Each library now has fibre inside the building connecting it to the network. The majority of the libraries connect at 5 Mbps, which is more than triple the 1.5 Mbps (Frame Relay DS1) they had previously. However, a number of larger libraries have implemented 10 Mbps and have already seen usage peak at or near circuit capacity.

LESSONS LEARNED FROM THE CASE STUDIES

Developers of the five networks that served as case studies confronted similar challenges in different settings as they worked to implement their respective solutions. The approaches they used to address these challenges offer valuable lessons for other library systems seeking to initiate, develop, maintain, or improve a network.

In this part, these lessons learned are organised according to seven key characteristics of a successful library network project as revealed by the case studies:

1. Leadership, cooperation, and the ability to learn from past successes
2. Aggregation of demand and services
3. Use of demonstrations
4. Provision of technical support and training for library staff
5. Multiple funding sources
6. Role for library representatives in network governance
7. Involvement of the State Library

While these characteristics emerged as common themes from the case studies, they take varying forms across the five networks, and not every network displays all seven characteristics. These variations among the case studies are as informative as their commonalities. There is no single recipe for the development of a library network; rather, the case studies provide a set of options that libraries interested in forming a network may consider as they go forward.

Options derived from experience with several different networks can be combined to form a solution tailored to the unique circumstances of a particular community, region, or state, meeting the needs of users and increasing the chances for success.

LEADERSHIP, COOPERATION, AND THE ABILITY TO LEARN FROM PAST SUCCESSES

Strong leadership was an essential element in the development of each of the five networks. At the same time, leadership was distributed among different players at the state, regional, and local levels and was not the exclusive domain of one person or organisation. Moreover, cooperation among these players was a hallmark of the effort. The case studies also illustrate how the various organisations involved often drew on the experiences of other successful cooperative projects to help in the development of their network. In the formative stage of the Ohio Public Library and Information Network (OPLIN), public libraries that wanted to emulate successful school and academic networks broached the idea of a public library network with the state library association.

This association, later called the Ohio Library Council (OLC), assumed a leadership role, and two OLC staff members organised planning and advocacy efforts that led to OPLIN's development. The West Virginia Network was the first network to centralise the state's computing and data needs. Statewide Library Network (SLN) leadership acknowledged learning from this first statewide network during the project development. Taking a cooperative approach similar to that applied in the development of OPLIN, Wisconsin's local and regional libraries and State Library officials worked together to define the libraries' role in BadgerNet.

A past collaborative project to establish a distance learning video network was a key factor in the creation of a 1993 Governor's Blue Ribbon Telecommunications Infrastructure Task Force, which in turn recommended the creation of BadgerNet. The Maine School and Library Network (MSLN) was also the result of cooperation between statewide library associations and the State Library agency. Finally, the member libraries of California's Peninsula Library System (PLS) developed the Peninsula Libraries Automated Network (PLAN) based on their past success with a common circulation and catalogue system.

Perhaps the most important factor contributing to the success of PLAN is the spirit and habit of cooperation among PLS members. Since 1982, member libraries have been cooperating to operate a joint circulation system. Such collaborations require that libraries engage in significant give-and-take to modify longstanding local policies and procedures so as to accommodate a centralised system. This habit of collaboration led to the success of other collective endeavors, including PLAN.

AGGREGATION OF DEMAND AND SERVICES

Aggregation of demand is an acknowledged successful approach to network management.

Among its benefits are:

- Improved planning.
- Support for a business case for providers to deploy broadband.
- More affordable pricing.
- Sharing of costs.

Aggregation of demand allowed the establishment of each of the five successful networks profiled here, and its benefits have contributed to the networks' continued success. For example, MSLN aggregates library traffic to two nodes, which results in lower recurring expenses for Internet access. Aggregation offers other, less obvious benefits. An example is streamlining and standardisation of members' E-rate participation. All of the statewide networks profiled here regularly file for E-rate discounts on behalf of their members or offer assistance to members in doing so. A centralised application relieves the burden on individual libraries. MSLN files an aggregated application for federal E-rate discounts and an application for Maine's state universal service fund. Wisconsin files one aggregated E-rate application that includes every K-12 school district and public library on BadgerNet (about 910 sites), and also completes all the required follow-up. Considering that the most frequently cited reason for libraries' non-participation in the E-rate programme is the complexity of the process, this is a very real benefit with tangible results. Standardisation is a key requirement for aggregation. OPLIN, MSLN, PLS, and BadgerNet require the same router configuration for every library site; SLN requires that all members have the same network equipment; and every school and library on BadgerNet has the same standard Ethernet interface. Standardisation avoids the logistical challenges associated with customisation. It also allows for aggregation of technical support services.

The benefits of aggregating technical support are readily apparent in West Virginia, where these services are typically beyond the means of individual public libraries with limited budgets and staff expertise. MSLN employs a shared project manager to provide planning guidance to individual libraries, a service that would otherwise be too costly for individual libraries.

USE OF DEMONSTRATIONS

OITP's past research suggests that technology demonstrations are necessary to convince a library's community to support a major new effort such as a regional or statewide network. Such demonstrations, while providing essential training to library staff, also serve a critical outreach and public relations function. For example, during the initial phase of network development, OPLIN staff members visited libraries around the state to demonstrate how access to the Internet would help their users. While demonstrations can be very helpful in growing network membership, their usefulness does not end with the network's establishment. OPLIN and SLN representatives continue to provide information on network services and their use at annual conferences and meetings. Other library systems offer ongoing training on new resources provided via the network and on how library staff can use these resources to improve library services and ultimately benefit the library's patrons. Demonstrations can also help achieve the network's sustainability when used as an advocacy tool for continued funding and support of network projects.

PROVISION OF TECHNICAL SUPPORT AND TRAINING FOR LIBRARY STAFF

Library networks are complex technical entities that support many users and applications; it is unreasonable to expect local library staff, especially those in smaller or rural libraries, to provide comprehensive technical support for the network. All the networks profiled here provide members with some level of technical support and training in how to solve technical problems. The level of support ranges from handling all network problems to training local librarians in problem solving. Two of the networks—PLAN and Badger Net—continuously monitor network traffic and respond with solutions when they are needed.

The case studies demonstrate several innovative approaches to supporting large networks:

- In a centralised model, OPLIN manages a support center that offers members a first line of defence for network troubleshooting.
- MSLN employs one circuit rider whose responsibilities include focusing on resource poor libraries with the most serious problems and developing technical skills among local library staff.
- SLN has network support staff in offices throughout the state and, like MSLN, works to develop the technical skills of library staff.
- In Wisconsin, regional library systems serve as the first point of contact to assist with troubleshooting and the installation of new equipment and software.
- In California, PLS meets the need for network-level support only; its member libraries all have technical support staff on site.

MULTIPLE FUNDING SOURCES

The networks profiled here rely on various revenue streams, such as grant funds, telecommunications settlement funds, universal service funds, state general funds, and local library funding. The five networks were established in economically favourable times, when state and other funds were more readily available for large capital projects than is the case today.

Nevertheless, all the networks face the challenge of securing ongoing funding. Even Maine, which has the most stable source of funding (state and federal universal service funds), struggles with balancing the need for increased network services with limited funding resources. The major sources of funding for the statewide networks have historically been state tax funds and universal service funds (both the federal E-rate programme and state-based programmes).

During the last year, however, tax revenues have decreased sharply in almost every state, and both OPLIN and SLN were in danger of losing significant state funding. California's PLS, funded primarily by member fees derived from local property taxes, has yet to see any significant reductions as assessments of property lag at least one year behind tax collections. Federal universal service funds are relatively stable. However, the total of applications for discounts is approaching fund availability, absent any policy intervention. Additionally, some organisations find the requirements for obtaining such funds to be onerous or contrary to their policies.

ROLE FOR LIBRARY REPRESENTATIVES IN NETWORK GOVERNANCE

The case study networks have widely varying governance and management structures.

For example:

- The Maine Public Utilities Commission (MPUC) governs MSLN.
- Wisconsin's Department of Administration manages BadgerNet.
- The West Virginia Library Commission administers SLN.

All of these networks are dependent on the network's information technology (IT) staff for ensuring the day-to-day management of network operations. But just as there are differences in network management (*e.g.*, some may be outsourced), there are also differences in overall network governance and how much input the library community has to make decisions or to set network policy.

For example, the OPLIN governing board in Ohio consists solely of member library representatives. Wisconsin's BadgerNet Advisory Council includes representatives of all network users including libraries, K-12 schools, higher education and state government. The Advisory Council advises the state Administration Department in areas like member bandwidth needs and planning for the next generation network. California's PLS allows the technical staff of member libraries to be involved with network issues through a committee structure.

INVOLVEMENT OF THE STATE LIBRARY

One common characteristic of the statewide networks is the active involvement of the State Library:

- The State Library of Ohio has strong influence over OPLIN.
- Operations and development as a result of its authority to appoint all of the network's board members.
- The State Library in West Virginia operates SLN.
- In Wisconsin, the State Library influences BadgerNet planning and operations through its seat on the BadgerNet Council.

Although MSLN's governing board is the Maine Public Utilities Commission (MPUC), the state librarian is responsible for suggesting policy and for representing the interests of libraries before the MPUC. Furthermore, the Maine State Library has staff members responsible for assessing the needs of MSLN members and for preparing an annual report that outlines the network's needs and presents an annual budget request.

THE OHIO PUBLIC LIBRARY INFORMATION NETWORK

HISTORY

The Ohio Public Library Information Network (OPLIN) began to take shape in 1994 when a small group of librarians from a suburban library system discussed the need for a statewide public library network similar to the networks used by academic libraries (OhioLink) and K-12 libraries (INFOhio). This group of librarians reached out to the Ohio Library Council (OLC, then known as the Ohio Library Association), which helped to develop a plan to create the network and lobbied state legislators for the funding to build it. Fran Haley, who had recently joined the OLC, was instrumental in bringing together experienced individuals to develop the network plan and in inviting the entire library community to participate in the process. Greg Byerly, who had previously directed OhioLink, was hired by the OLC to draft the initial plan for OPLIN.

He also worked to allow the state's public libraries to purchase telecommunications services from the statewide SOMACS (State of Ohio Multi-Agency Communications System) contract. The SOMACS contract provides postalised rates for its telecommunications circuits, so that the monthly price remains the same regardless of the length of the circuit or the location of the library.

OPLIN was created by state law in 1995. With the persistence of the OLC and the support of the legislature and then-Governor Voinovich, OPLIN was initially allocated $4.85 million. Before the state budget was passed in 1995, an additional $8 million was added to fund startup costs to network public libraries. The OPLIN board decided to provide funds for the initial installation connecting branch libraries to the network, but not to support recurring costs for these connections.

The board also decided to provide a telecommunications line for one library site (usually the main library) and to support its recurring costs in addition to purchasing computers so that each library would have two public workstations with which to access OPLIN. All but one of the 251 main library systems in Ohio joined OPLIN immediately. Local boards passed a resolution for each library system to join, and each established its own Internet access policy for the network. The library system pursued funding for the project at the right time, as the state budget was flush, and the overall economic situation in the state was favourable. Funds remained even after OPLIN had been built, allowing the libraries to purchase subscriptions to databases and other electronic materials.

SERVICES

OPLIN provides both broadband Internet connections and information services to Ohio public libraries. Its mission is to ensure that all Ohio residents have fast, free public Internet access through the state's local public library systems, as well as the use of highquality research and reference databases not available free of charge on the World Wide Web. OPLIN provides these services at no cost to the libraries.

Unlike the situation in many other states, OPLIN coordinates the acquisition and installation of the physical telecommunications circuits that connect the main libraries to the network's hub in Columbus. (Most other library networks deliver content and services primarily via a physical network provided by some other organisation.) OPLIN leases circuits for the main libraries under two contracts the state has with telecommunications service providers. Branch libraries, however, must obtain their own local broadband telecommunications connection to their main library. OPLIN also serves as the Internet service provider (ISP) for all public libraries in Ohio. It manages mail servers and provides the libraries with e-mail services. In addition, OPLIN provides web hosting services for those libraries with their own web site.

User Support and Communications

The OPLIN Support Center serves as the first line of defence for database problems and network troubleshooting. The center received 2,304 library technical service requests in fiscal year 2008, the majority of which related to e-mail issues. The OPLIN Support Center is open only during the workweek; after-hours and weekend calls are directed to the State of Ohio's Network Operations Center. OPLIN communicates with its members in a number of ways. It operates three e-mail lists: one for non-technical topics, one for the OPLIN office to announce new services and important changes to existing services, and one for technical topics. OPLIN also publishes a quarterly newsletter, participates on social networking web sites, publishes three blogs, and has a web site.

Telecommunications and Broadband Services

OPLIN obtains the local telecommunications circuits for all but one of the main libraries in the State of Ohio. These circuits connect the main library to the OPLIN hub in Columbus. As part of a state agency, OPLIN is authorised to lease these circuits under two state contracts: the SOMACS contract, serviced largely by AT&T and used to lease traditional T1 circuits that provide a capacity of 1.5 megabits per second (Mbps), and a separate contract for fibre-based Ethernet services.

OPLIN often transitions main libraries that need upgraded capacity to an Ethernet connection, but these Ethernet services are not available statewide. OPLIN also provides its members with continuous monitoring of broadband traffic. Every quarter, traffic statistics for each main library are reviewed to see whether traffic patterns warrant an upgrade to a fibrebased Ethernet circuit (or DS1 or DS3 if Ethernet is not available). The additional bandwidth and coordination for implementation are handled by OPLIN at no charge to the main library.

NETWORK STRUCTURE

In addition to the local circuits that connect the main libraries to the OPLIN hub, OPLIN maintains a high-capacity connection from its hub to the Internet over a shared, channelised DS3 connection that is managed by the Ohio Office of Information Technology (OIT). The OIT router manages traffic to OPLIN-provided resources, to the Internet, or back to other OPLIN member libraries.

The bandwidth charge for this connection to the Internet is the fastest-growing expense for OPLIN. Each main library receives a router provided by OPLIN to connect its circuit to the OPLIN hub. Management of this router is carried out collaboratively between OPLIN staff and the engineering group within OIT. The router represents the demarcation point between OPLIN services and the main library's local area network (LAN). Each main library is responsible for its own LAN management services. OPLIN offers each main library a subnet of 32 publicly routable Internet Protocol (IP) addresses. Each main library administers these addresses following its own policies.

As noted, OPLIN does not provide the local broadband connections for branch libraries. The branch libraries associated with each main library system can use a variety of options for connecting to the main library. In many cases, the SOMACS contract allows libraries to pay for a postalised T1, which is available statewide for only $400 per month. While the SOMACS contract is available to any branch library, occasionally less expensive options exist. Some branches choose to purchase a digital subscriber line (DSL) circuit to connect virtually to the main library through a virtual private network (VPN). On other occasions, the branch library is located close enough to the main library that a local telephone company can connect both locations with a DS1 for less than the $400 per month under the SOMACS contract.

Finally, in some communities, cable TV companies offering telecommunications services can provide a branch library with either a DS1 or an Ethernet connection. Fibre is another option that is gaining popularity among libraries in Ohio. The State of Ohio has signed a separate contract that includes AT&T's Optical Ethernet Metropolitan Area Network (OPT-E-MAN). OPT-E-MAN is typically provisioned via a fibre connection with bandwidth increments as low as 5 Mbps and scalable to 100 Mbps.

Libraries that can purchase fibre-based service are ideally positioned to add bandwidth quickly and less expensively than is the case with traditional telephone company services (*e.g.*, T1/DS1, T3/ DS3). Pricing for Ethernet services can vary significantly from location to location. The price for a 10 Mbps circuit can range from $600 per month to about $1,000 per month, not including router management fees and Internet access bandwidth.

GOVERNANCE

OPLIN is an independent state agency within the State Library of Ohio. It is governed by a board of eleven members selected by the State Library Board from the staffs of member public libraries and current or past trustees. The OPLIN Executive Director and the State Librarian or his/her designees serve as *ex officio* board members. Stephen Hedges has served as OPLIN's Executive Director since 2006 and supervises four staff members. OPLIN receives fiscal and logistical support services from the State Library of Ohio and contracts with OIT for assistance with network management. OPLIN is now defined in the Ohio Revised Code. Until recently, it was a line item in the State Library budget, meaning that it technically ceased to exist every 2 years. OPLIN is now part of the permanent law, which allows it to take advantage of longer service contracts.

FINANCE

The majority of OPLIN's budget—58 percent—is spent on purchasing Internet connections to public libraries, which it regards as its most important role. Another 30 percent is spent on databases, which make up about a third of the total cost of the Ohio Web Library database collection. About 2 percent of OPLIN's budget is allocated by the legislature for grant subsidies to local libraries to help defray the cost of filtering Internet content; another 1 percent funds conferences and other training for public librarians. The remaining 9 percent of the budget is used for all other costs—rent, salaries and benefits (for five staff), supplies, postage, office equipment, etc. Thus more than 90 percent of the OPLIN budget is spent on direct services to public libraries, and less than 10 percent on administrative costs. From the network's inception in the fiscal year (FY) 1995 budget bill through FY 2007, annual funding for OPLIN varied between $5 million and $8 million each year. Because of the state's recent fiscal problems, OPLIN's budget was reduced in 2008 and 2009, and additional reductions may occur in 2010. To make up for the loss of state revenue, OPLIN has entered into an agreement with eTech Ohio to manage its E-rate applications this year. OPLIN expects that eTech Ohio's E-rate expertise will lead to more federal E-rate discounts than in the past. Libraries can call on eTech Ohio for E-rate consulting, and eTech Ohio will also be conducting E-rate workshops.

WEST VIRGINIA'S STATEWIDE LIBRARY NETWORK

HISTORY

Many West Virginians depend on their public libraries for Internet access. The West Virginia Library Commission (WVLC) established the centralised Statewide Library Network (SLN) to meet this need. Beginning in the 1990s, the WVLC received a federal grant for a project to connect West Virginia public libraries with 56 kilobits per second (Kbps) frame relay lines leased from Bell Atlantic (now Verizon) and other providers. By 1999, all but 3 of West Virginia's 177 public libraries were connected.

The West Virginia Network (WVNET), the state's Internet service provider, was also instrumental in developing SLN. WVNET was established in 1975 to centralise the state's computing and data needs. It originally connected the colleges and universities in West Virginia to its central hub, and later grew to serve government offices, K-12 schools, and libraries. WVNET established a statewide intranet in 1994 and continues to provide Internet connectivity to libraries today. WVNET reports to the West Virginia Higher Education Policy Commission and is aided by a Computer Advisory Board, with representatives from higher education and other users of WVNET. Internet access spurred demand at libraries across the state for such resources as electronic journals, shared library resources, e-mail, and learning programmes.

Meeting this demand required more robust connections, so the Library Network 2000 plan was developed to upgrade and standardise the libraries' hardware and software. Technicians visited every library in the network and installed suitable cabling, reprogrammed equipment, issued new Internet Protocol (IP) addresses, and provided standardised Internet connections. The network staff received a Governor's Award and a National Association of State Information Resource Executives nomination for the planning and implementation of the Network 2000 project. In September 2002, Verizon provided a $1.6 million grant (over 2 years) for the Digital Bridge Project, designed to upgrade the 56 Kbps connections with DS1 (1.5 megabits per second) lines. As of summer 2009, all 177 libraries had been connected with a DS1 line.

Today, the success of this upgraded network is evident in libraries across West Virginia. At a March 2009 WVLC meeting, the Director of Weirton's Mary H. Weir Library, Rik Rekowski, reported that the library's Internet center had 16,000 visitors every year in a town with a population of only 18,748. Sandy Bumgardner, Director of the Upshur County Library, a service center for several libraries in very rural areas, said that many community residents lack access to highspeed Internet in their homes because dialup access is their only affordable choice. Furthermore, a number of residents who live in areas with affordable Internet access have cancelled their home subscriptions to save money.

These residents use the libraries' public-access computers to search the Internet, write résumés, and complete job applications. Further upgrades are planned for SLN. By 2012, the network will offer Ethernet connections that will operate approximately 10 times faster than T1.

SERVICES

SLN provides all the state's public libraries with Internet access, e-mail communication, data lines, hubs and switches, and technical support. Libraries may also receive funding and support for a shared integrated library system (ILS). In many other states, technical support for network services is the responsibility of the individual library.

West Virginia is different in that the libraries receive, at no charge, the following services:

- Wide area networking, local area networking, and wireless access support.
- Help desk services.
- Router installation and maintenance.
- PC software/hardware replacement and maintenance.
- UNIX hardware/software maintenance.
- ILS (if shared with other libraries).
- Hubs, switches, and associated cabling (both installation and maintenance).
- Equipment contract support.
- Data circuit installation and maintenance.
- Network monitoring.
- E-rate support.

West Virginia made the strategic decision to centralise technology support for its libraries at the state level. As a result, it achieves excellent statewide coverage with just 11 technicians. Each of the technicians directly supports libraries within an assigned region of the state, but he or she also provides support to neighbouring regions when the need arises. Most of West Virginia's public libraries had limited access to technical support before the WVLC filled this role. Libraries now have access to technology assistance for simple problems, such as printer jams, and more complex problems, such as router maintenance.

Network technicians also visit libraries to offer library staff members training on various topics, including using the Internet, e-mail, and online databases; establishing remote computer repair options; and completing E-rate applications. Network personnel also provide training sessions during annual library functions and offer classes throughout the year. For example, one SLN technician teaches simple troubleshooting measures to library staff so they can solve technical problems independently instead of calling a technician.

SLN's technical support takes a variety of other forms. A series of public service announcements provides basic information about computer viruses, how to perform software updates, and other troubleshooting tips. In addition, SLN maintains four regional desktop computer labs that allow library staff in those regions to access training without driving long distances or staying overnight. Two mobile laptop labs are available for on-site training in more remote libraries. Significant to this centralisation of technical support is the standardisation of the network equipment and configuration and deployment processes. Any member of the SLN staff, regardless of the region of assignment, can walk into any library and know what equipment and network configuration to expect.

In addition, technicians can implement upgrades to the network without having to customise each library's infrastructure. Mark Esslinger, Director of the Wayne County Libraries, "The main benefit of having a statewide network is that it eliminates the need for duplication of service if every county had to run its own network. The state is able to provide more qualified support than a county could. In the long run, it saves money. If there is a problem, there is one number the local library has to call for assistance. The state office always has somebody on staff qualified to assist with networking issues. Some of the counties may not have access to qualified technicians due to the rural nature of some areas of the state."

NETWORK STRUCTURE

The West Virginia Department of Administration manages a statewide contract for telecommunications services. All public libraries are connected to SLN by purchasing a DS1 from this contract; all of the state's 177 libraries now have a DS1 connection. Ordering and installation of the circuit are coordinated by the WVLC. Depending on the location of a library, the DS1 connects to either the northern data center in Morgantown or the state capital of Charleston in the south. Traffic destined for the Internet is handed off to WVNET, and the rest remains within SLN.

To comply with the Children's Internet Protection Act (CIPA), the WVLC provides Internet filtering using Netsweeper software hosted on the state backbone network. The WVLC shares this service with other state agencies that must filter Internet traffic, allowing the expense to be spread across a larger pool of members. An advantage of the design of SLN is that only Internet traffic is filtered through Netsweeper. Centralising the filtering tools has eliminated the need for individual libraries or systems to purchase their own filtering software. This large network requires careful bandwidth monitoring. The WVLC monitors the bandwidth use of individual libraries as well as the statewide network via a monitoring network operations center in Charleston. The monitoring software provides hourly/daily/ monthly bandwidth charts for each library, audible/visual outage reports, and battery temperatures.

GOVERNANCE

The WVLC, which established SLN, consists of seven members, all of whom are appointed by the governor and confirmed by the state senate. The WVLC appoints a secretary who serves as State Librarian and manages the WVLC Network Services department, one of the four departments within the commission's office. As noted earlier, the WVLC centralises support for libraries at the state level and achieves statewide coverage with only 11 staff members. A key to SLN's success is the uniform approach to network design and service, which lends itself to economies of scale. The WVLC has encouraged all libraries to join the network, giving it more power to aggregate demand and further upgrade connections. As discussed previously, the WVLC takes a similar approach to technology and E-rate support, centralising these services at the state level to derive benefits from the aggregation of service provision.

The WVLC developed and expanded SLN through a combination of advocacy and strong leadership. It directly recruited public libraries, which were added to the network as funds became available. At its inception, the network also included four academic libraries. As of 2009, there are two. One left the network as a result of a change in administration, and the other joined a private college consortium. The network includes other non-public library participants as well. The Archives and History Library, a department of the state's Division of Culture and History, shares a catalogue server with the WVLC. A few K-12 schools have also been added to SLN. Under state law, the WVLC cannot make direct grants to school libraries, so it pays for the cost of adding them as users of the integrated catalogue software.

FINANCE

SLN has enjoyed strong support from the West Virginia legislature and has tapped other funding sources as well. In 1996, the WVLC, WVNET, and the West Virginia Department of Education successfully implemented a $2.5

million grant from the U.S. Department of Education. The first libraries received Internet access under this grant. Additional funding through federal and state grants expanded the number of libraries in SLN. The final public libraries added to the network benefited from federal Library Services and Technology Act (LSTA) funds. Also in 1996, the legislature provided a onetime allocation of $1 million for upgrades and allocated $1 million for ongoing support. In March 1998, a $1.9 million grant from the Bill and Melinda Gates Foundation provided computers for the state's public libraries. A July 2002 grant of $991,281 from the State Telecommunications Users' Council allowed SLN to purchase servers.

In addition to state and foundation grant funding, the WVLC applies annually for E-rate discounts for SLN. The average E-rate discount rate in 2009 was 76 percent. State legislators cut SLN's fiscal year 2010 budget by 28 percent or $347,000 from its $1.1 million budget in fiscal year 2009. This reduction will most likely slow the upgrading of SLN libraries' local area networks, including evaluating and replacing wiring, switches, and other critical network components. The WVLC also plans to support SLN with some LSTA funds. This funding shift will reduce amounts available for other library programmes typically supported by LSTA funds, including direct grants to local libraries.

WISCONSIN'S BADGERNET NETWORK

HI$TORY

Since as early as the 1970s, Wisconsin has been one of the nation's leaders in creating long-haul video networks to provide distance learning to schools. In 1993, to build on this success, then-Governor Thompson established a Governor's Blue Ribbon Telecommunications Task Force.

The task force was charged to:

- Develop a vision for a statewide telecommunications network for educational institutions and government agencies; and
- Recommend changes in state statutes and policy to remove barriers to the realisation of this vision.

In its planning for the statewide infrastructure, the task force also was required to consider and integrate Wisconsin's existing K-12 video network—consisting of more than 8,000 miles of fibre throughout the state at the time—into the network plans. The Wisconsin Department of Public Instruction (DPI), which houses the State Library Agency, advocated for consideration of library needs in the network's development, and libraries played an active role in the planning effort. The State Library and several members of regional library systems participated in the task force and made their concerns and interests known to the task force participants and to legislators. The task force recommended the creation of BadgerNet in 1993, and the legislature adopted most of the task force's recommendations in 1995. Libraries were specifically included in the statute as eligible to access the BadgerNet network. Shortly thereafter, the legislature created the TEACH (Technology for Educational ACHievement) programme to help schools and libraries obtain and sustain their use of technology. BadgerNet was created at a time when the economy was stable and growing.

This economic stability allowed the state sufficient time to undertake the 3-year effort and engage many stakeholders in the development of the statewide network. Additionally, the positive economic climate and the growth of telecommunications services in the late 1990s allowed the legislature to add revenue to the state's universal service fund (which collects funds from in-state telecommunications providers) to fund the TEACH programme. Following another two-year planning process, in March 2005, the Wisconsin Department of Administration (DOA) entered into a new $116.7 million, 5-year agreement with the consortium of telecommunications providers that deliver BadgerNet services for a new converged, higher-capacity data and video network called the BadgerNet Converged Network (BCN). The transition to the new network was completed on September 1, 2006. The State Library Agency helped coordinate this transition. At that time, BCN was the largest state network of its type that AT&T, the prime vendor, had under contract.

SERVICES

Wisconsin's seventeen regional library systems are required to assist their member libraries in matters related to technology in exchange for state funding. In this regard, they play an important role in addressing local public library broadband and Internet connectivity needs.

Among the services they provide:

- The regional library systems manage wide area networks (WANs) for their member libraries. The WANs are part of the regional network infrastructure that ultimately connects to the BadgerNet backbone at four locations in the state. WANs are used primarily for shared integrated library system traffic and Internet access. Of the services offered through the BCN contract, the libraries most frequently use the WAN service, which links remote libraries to the headquarters of the regional library system in a hub-and-spoke network design.
- All seventeen systems provide consulting for the purchase of computer software and hardware.
- Many systems also offer centralised purchasing for software and hardware, which allows member libraries to obtain a lower price than they could negotiate individually.
- Sixteen of the seventeen regional systems make information technology (IT) staff available as the first point of contact to assist with troubleshooting and the installation of new software and hardware.

BadgerNet also offers high-resolution, real-time interactive video to approximately 350 K-12 schools. Included in these video services are a network scheduling function and specialised equipment that permits three or more locations to be joined together in a videoconference. Classes offered over the network are an integral part of instruction, with as many as thirtytwo separate conferences linking more than a hundred classrooms during a single hour. Finally, BadgerNet offers network support and help desk service around the clock.

NETWORK STRUCTURE

BadgerNet serves state government, some local governments, universities, technical colleges and tribal nations, and most of the state's K-12 school districts and public libraries. All state agencies are required to use BadgerNet; 900 state agency remote locations use the data network capability of the system to connect to their agency headquarters in Madison. In total, the network exceeds 2,400 end-points spread across each of the state's 72 counties. Although library participation is voluntary, about 97 percent of Wisconsin's public libraries have connected to the Internet via BadgerNet since the mid-1990s. As noted, the libraries generally use a WAN topology such that individual library circuits connect back to the headquarters of the regional library system. The regional system then aggregates the Internet traffic of its member libraries and provides a direct connection to the Internet service provider (ISP).

AT&T serves as BCN's prime contractor, although additional services are provisioned by a consortium of telecommunications providers that includes other local telephone companies. Fortunately for the regional public library systems, the BCN contract allows the local provider to provision service in a variety of ways while ensuring that each library's interface is always the same 10/100 Ethernet port. Routing of traffic through the aggregation and core layers of the network is always the same as well, regardless of the access layer technology. Without exception, Wisconsin's regional library systems have adopted the hub-and-spoke WAN design. Choosing one library, often the headquarters of the regional library system, to act as the hub provides equipment consolidation advantages as well as bandwidth and port access to the Internet.

Two aspects of BCN are somewhat unusual and particularly beneficial to Wisconsin's library connectivity. First, the BCN contract covers all three network layers (a local access connection, an aggregation point, and a core). Most statewide networks provide the backbone, but the library or library system must acquire the local access connection on its own. BCN, through the TEACH programme, subsidises the cost of the local connections in addition to maintaining the backbone. The network's comprehensive end-to-end service is one reason why almost every public library in the state uses BCN. Second,

BCN includes an Ethernet port as the end-user interface. An Ethernet port makes it extremely easy for the library to connect its equipment (such as a firewall, local switch, or router) to the network because the interface will always be an industry standard 10/100 Ethernet port. Because BCN uses Ethernet connections, the library can purchase flexible increments of bandwidth.

In other words, the library can increase its capacity to 3 megabits per second (Mbps), 5 Mbps, 10 Mbps, 15 Mbps, 20 Mbps, etc. (traditional telephone company offerings are limited to either 1.5 Mbps or 45 Mbps). Some of the larger telephone companies, such as AT&T and Verizon, and some larger independent phone companies deploy fibre optic cables to libraries requesting highspeed circuits. Typically, fibre is deployed for sites needing 10 Mbps or greater, but some companies deploy fibre to sites with as little as 3 Mbps in anticipation of future growth. The BCN portfolio of services does not, however, include asymmetrical services, such as digital subscriber line (DSL), microwave, and satellite technology alternatives, because it was too difficult to include every available technology and keep the service consistent. Even though these options are not available through BCN, some library systems purchase DSL services outside of the BCN contract; DSL is often used for patron wireless Internet access.

GOVERNANCE

BadgerNet is the state's telecommunications network; it does not provide Internet service. Most BadgerNet users (*e.g.*, state government, schools, and libraries) receive their Internet access via WiscNet. WiscNet is a not-for-profit association that operates under the auspices of the University of Wisconsin-Madison. It is governed by a board of directors representing member institutions. A representative from the State Library and a representative from the regional library systems are on the board. WiscNet started providing Internet access in 1991 to 26 colleges and universities in the state. When the first BadgerNet network was built in the mid-1990s, WiscNet expanded its services to include K-12 schools and public libraries. BadgerNet is administered by the network office in the DOA. The BadgerNet Advisory Council advises the DOA and the service provider on customer issues relating to the network contract, the operation of the network, and the process for developing timely solutions for services provided under the contract; it also provides a forum for planning. The council is made up of representatives from constituent groups, including one representative of a regional public library system and a representative of the State Library.

FINANCE

BadgerNet and its service vendor operate under a 5-year contract, and prices are stable for libraries within this contract period. Under the TEACH programme, schools, libraries, and other eligible institutions pay a reduced rate for their broadband connections; the remainder is paid by the TEACH programme. Schools and libraries pay $100 per month for a broadband connection up to 3 Mbps and $250 per month for a connection between 4 and 100 Mbps. The BCN contract ends in 2011, and the BadgerNet Advisory Council is actively planning for the network's future contract service requirements.

The BadgerNet contract charges the same rate to each library regardless of the distance between the library and the aggregation node. These postalised rates ensure that rural libraries pay the same monthly price for access to the BadgerNet network as urban and suburban libraries. For public libraries in the state, the average membership fee in WiscNet is about $450 per year. More than 90 percent of the libraries have this fee paid by their regional library system. From its inception, BadgerNet required its vendors to build in rural as well as urban areas and to offer postalised rates. While this helped reduce the price for rural libraries to connect to the network, it has caused problems in urban areas. Some urban libraries, especially in the Milwaukee area, are finding that they can save money by purchasing service from other providers instead of from BCN. The TEACH programme uses state universal service funds to subsidise local access connections to BadgerNet for K-12 schools, public libraries, and regional library systems. TEACH pays for equipment, the installation costs for the local data lines and video links to BadgerNet, and a portion of the monthly service costs.

TEACH receives its funding from the state's universal service fund and from the federal E-rate programme. On an annual basis, TEACH spends approximately $13.8 million to subsidise network costs for schools and libraries. The subsidy for public libraries and regional public library systems is approximately $3 million annually. TEACH received additional spending authority in the fiscal year 2007-2009 budget, which enabled more than 60 percent of the state's public libraries to increase their bandwidth at no direct cost to the library. Separate from the funding for the TEACH programme, the state's universal service fund also provides an increasing amount of state aid to regional library systems. In prior years, the state universal service fund has generated $5 million for state aid to library systems. The state's fiscal year 2009-2011 budget funds the regional library systems totally out of the state's universal service fund, increasing the contribution by $11 million annually.

THE MAINE SCHOOL AND LIBRARY NETWORK

HISTORY

The Maine School and Library Network (MSLN) was created after a coordinated 2-year planning effort led by Maine's library and education communities. In fall 1994, three organisations in the library community—the Maine Library Association, the Maine Educational Media Association (representing school librarians), and the Maine Library Commission—joined forces to represent the interests of public libraries before the Maine Public Utilities Commission (MPUC). The result of these efforts was the creation of MSLN, one of the earliest and most comprehensive state programmes to improve libraries' Internet connections. This advocacy effort focused on an investigation by the MPUC into allegations that NYNEX had overcharged its customers. After the libraries formally intervened and participated actively in the case, MPUC Chair Thomas Welch announced on May 1, 1995, that he wanted to permit NYNEX "to use up to $4 million of the rate reduction we require to provide rate reductions or other services to the libraries and schools of Maine."

It was left to NYNEX to work with others, including schools and libraries, to develop a plan for implementing this rate reduction. A group led by librarians and including schools, the MPUC, telecommunications carriers, the cable companies, and the University of Maine negotiated intensely over the summer of 1995. Ultimately, the group settled on a plan to provide 56 kilobits per second (Kbps) frame relay connections for all public schools and libraries in the state, with free Internet access, including equipment and free network support services. The Internet service provider (ISP) would be the University of Maine System Network (UNET). The MPUC adopted the plan proposed by the librarians and others on January 5, 1996. The initial MSLN plan called for an allocation of $20 million to connect more than a thousand public schools and libraries in Maine for 5 years. Maine's Supreme Court upheld the commission's decision on March 15, 1996, when it issued a decision refusing to consider an appeal of the ratepayer case. A parallel effort was undertaken in the state legislature to establish the legitimacy of the MPUC action. To guide this effort, the library organisations formed a Joint Legislative Committee to advocate for the expansion of the MPUC's authority to grant discounted rates and services for libraries. A few weeks after the Supreme Court decision, the Maine Legislature approved a bill that amended the MPUC's authority. In 1999, the Maine Legislature codified the programme and provided funding to continue MSLN beyond its initial 5-year period.

The legislation allowed the MPUC to collect a surcharge on intrastate telephone services and deposit the revenues into the Maine Telecommunications Education Access Fund (MTEAF). Once the legislature had authorised this new source of funding, MSLN became known as MSLN2. Maine is now considering how to upgrade MSLN to accommodate the growth in Internet usage. The bandwidth available through MSLN "is now at its practical limits and is no longer meeting current needs of schools and libraries; in its current structure, it cannot scale to meet future needs." The Department of Education and the Maine State Library are considering how to provide 100 Mbps capacity to all schools and libraries, but acknowledge that doing so will require a new strategy for procuring service and recognition that no single technology will best serve all regions of the state. Schools and libraries are consolidating traffic in central locations to reduce costs, but these central locations require more bandwidth than is currently available. As a result, some schools have opted out of MSLN and negotiated alternative connections from ISPs that can provide them greater bandwidth. This strategy may meet the individual school's needs, but it does not allow for economies of scale and cost efficiencies that come from a homogeneous network. The Department of Education believes that it should develop an upgrade strategy based on fibre optic technology. It believes this is a "future-proof" technology that can scale to very high data rates through upgrading of only the end equipment. The department also acknowledges that fibre may be too expensive in some areas. It notes that wireless service can be a practical solution for service to islands off the coast of Maine, as well as some very rural communities. To move forward on this approach, the department recommends engaging in a collaborative effort with the research and education communities— something several other states, particularly Connecticut, Rhode Island, Missouri, and Iowa, are doing.

SERVICES

MSLN is one of the first statewide networks to provide Internet connections for all schools and libraries. Participation in MSLN is voluntary, and 49 of Maine's 271 public libraries do not receive MSLN Internet services. These 49 libraries have other connections, often through their community's cable company contract; a few have no Internet connection. MSLN also offers technical support through a circuit rider service that provides advice and assistance by phone, e-mail, and in person to solve MSLN members' technical problems. Currently, MSLN funds a single circuit rider position. The circuit rider visits schools and libraries to assist them, assess their future broadband needs, and hear concerns. The circuit rider focuses on the sites with the most serious problems and with the fewest local resources to solve those problems. Because the circuit rider cannot address the needs of every library, the programme tries to train local libraries to develop their own sustainable uses of MSLN without ongoing technical dependence on a circuit rider, and to integrate circuit rider efforts with those of other training programmes through the State Library and the Department of Education.

Since 2007, the State Library has been a community partner in WebJunction, the webbased training service for the library community. In addition, Maine's three regional library systems offer workshops and other continuing education activities to member libraries. The State Library also offers limited training through its coordinator of learning and technology, who coordinates training efforts with the regional library systems. In addition, the Maine Association of School Libraries provides some training opportunities for school library media specialists.

NETWORK STRUCTURE

The network supporting Maine's libraries is an interesting case study since it defies the typical rules for the establishment of a network. Almost invariably, networks emerge from a need to access a resource or application. The need exists before the network is built or significantly modified because few have the vision or the resources to build it otherwise. The State of Maine took the unusual step of creating the network first, when libraries were only beginning to need access to the Internet. Maine thus developed a very simple design to serve its needs.

Two main characteristics of successful library networks are aggregation and centralisation. MSLN achieves both of those key characteristics, but in an unusual way. Rather than three distinct layers that aggregate traffic (a local access connection, an aggregation point, and a core), MSLN allows each school and library to use a local access circuit (56 Kbps or 1.544 megabits per second) to connect directly to UNET (the ISP) and the Internet. The flat MSLN network structure makes it easier for individual sites to connect directly to each other through the Internet, so that any library can host a resource that any or all MSLN libraries can access. (A hierarchal design does not necessarily prohibit direct connections between locations, but it often narrows the opportunities.) As noted earlier, the original plan called for each school and library to have a 56 Kbps frame relay circuit connecting the school/library to UNET. In 1998, the MPUC approved upgrading of schools and libraries to a T1 connection if they were exceeding the capacity of their 56 Kbps connection. The network aggregates library traffic to two UNET nodes within the state (located in Portland and Bangor) rather than a library system's main library. That design, coupled with standard, ubiquitous transport (T1), allows MSLN to offer consistent service across the state for any library to use. An additional benefit of aggregating all the library traffic is a lower monthly recurring expense for Internet access. The average cost of Internet access measured by the megabit always decreases as more traffic is aggregated. The downside of a flat network structure with only two aggregation points is that traffic destined for a centrally managed library resource (or for another library) must traverse the Internet to reach its destination. This route means that Internet traffic must travel a greater physical distance; the result is added delay, which may cause a potential drop in service. The Internet treats all traffic equally and will not recognise "high-priority" traffic even if marked as such by a library. Therefore, high-priority packets are not delivered over lowerpriority packets. While these can be genuine issues, they have not affected libraries using MSLN.

GOVERNANCE

The MPUC is the governing body of MSLN. The commission decided to retain ultimate responsibility and authority over the network since ratepayer monies were being used to support it. However, the commission created an advisory board with limited defined functions necessary to administer the fund and the network. In 2007, the legislature disbanded the MSLN advisory board. The state librarian and the commissioner of the State Department of Education are now responsible for policy and for representing the interests of libraries and schools before the MPUC. Each agency has staff members responsible for assessing the needs of libraries and schools and preparing an annual report to the MPUC that outlines the network's needs and a budget request for the next year.

The project manager provides day-to-day management of MSLN, including oversight of schools and libraries regarding the use of MSLN Internet bandwidth, development of recommendations to the Department of Education and Maine State Library on future bandwidth growth, coordination of circuit moves, and changes of circuits. The project manager also consults with school and library personnel on the impact on bandwidth of their technology initiatives.

FINANCE

Libraries that decide to participate in MSLN have the advantage of requesting service from a contract held jointly between the Maine Department of Education and the State Library. Compared with other library networks, Maine's is unique in many respects but not when it comes to aggregating its purchasing power. MSLN offers a significantly lower price for T1 service than an individual library could ever hope to obtain for the same service because the MSLN contract offers the telephone company the opportunity to provide the service on a statewide basis. Offering 900 T1s is more economical for a carrier than providing one T1, and the carrier's contract pricing reflects that cost savings. In Maine, T1 services are purchased from FairPoint for any location in the state, even if the provider is an independent telephone company. MSLN can offer a fixed price for T1 service to any library in the state regardless of the local provider.

This aggregation also relieves the individual library of the burden of requesting and evaluating proposals for connectivity to meet the federal E-rate requirements. Certainly one of the factors for success for libraries in Maine is the ability to purchase or upgrade standard service from an existing contract anywhere in the state. MSLN is funded by two surcharges on telecommunications services: the federal E-rate programme surcharge on interstate services and the Maine Telecommunications Education Access Fund (MTEAF) surcharge on intrastate services. E-rate discounts pay for approximately 60 percent of network costs, and the state programme funds the remaining 40 percent. No later than March 1 of each year, the Department of Education and the State Library file a joint proposal for support for the next fiscal year. After a prescribed comment period, the MPUC issues an order by May 1 that establishes the amount to be collected from contributing state telecommunications carriers and a level of funding for libraries that do not apply for the federal E-rate programme. MSLN funding should remain steady for the foreseeable future as the network's revenue is generated through the federal and state universal service funds and not through state appropriations. The MTEAF collection changes from year to year depending on MSLN needs. MSLN administrators are aware of the need to keep the assessment rate as low as possible, and they lowered the request rate for fiscal year 2008. In fiscal year 2007, the annual cost for MSLN was approximately $4.4 million. Funds from MTEAF pay for telecommunications services, Internet access, internal connections, computers, training, and content.

In addition, MTEAF funds:

- The circuit rider, who helps primarily small schools and libraries.
- A consultant to assist with the federal E-rate process.
- An administrator to collect the surcharges from telecommunications carriers.
- A project manager to work with schools and libraries and track needs.
- Free access to a variety of databases.

CALIFORNIA'S PENINSULA LIBRARIES AU TOMATED NETWORK

SERVICES

PLAN is responsible for the day-to-day operation of the network and provides PLS libraries with a variety of telecommunications and broadband services through a centralised information technology (IT) department. In addition to the IT director, PLAN staff members include a database administrator, systems engineer, network administrator, and assistant database administrator/project manager. These technicians supervise wide area network (WAN) services (network connectivity and network monitoring), local area network (LAN) services (switch and router hardware administration), and enterprise services (integrated library system, patron computer time management, e-mail, web hosting, and 24/7 help desk support). In addition, PLAN staff members organise training for member library staff and negotiate reduced costs for training and equipment purchases. The community college administers firewall services for the network.

NETWORK STRUCTURE

Until the recent network upgrade to fibre-based services, PLS relied on a traditional huband- spoke frame relay design provisioned by AT&T. San Mateo Community College served as the hub of the network, and the individual libraries (spokes) were served with DS1 connections. Today, patron and administrative workstations are placed in separate virtual local area networks (VLANs) within each library. The administrative VLAN is shown in red and the patron VLAN in blue. Creating separate VLANs for patrons and administrators reduces opportunities for security violations. Typically, each library has at least one wireless access point, and some of the larger libraries have as many as five. PLS created a VLAN for wireless users as well, thereby isolating them from administrative traffic.

Each library now has fibre inside the building connecting it to the network. The majority of the libraries connect at 5 Mbps, which is more than triple the 1.5 Mbps (frame relay DS1) they had previously. However, a number of larger libraries implemented 10 Mbps and have already seen usage peak at or near circuit capacity. The process for increasing bandwidth is simple, requiring only a request that specifies the bandwidth amount desired and the date by which the increase is needed. Each PLS library pays for an increase in bandwidth. In PLAN's current hub-and-spoke design, traffic entering AT&T's fibre-based Ethernet network is routed to the core of the PLAN network at San Mateo Community College. PLAN centralises services, such as e-mail, the integrated library system (ILS), and firewall services, at the college data center. Any traffic originating at a remote library and terminating at another remote library will travel to the network core and be redirected by the PLAN head-end router. However, most of the traffic originating from remote libraries travels to the Internet.

GOVERNANCE

PLS was one of fifteen statewide library systems authorised under the California Library Services Act. As a result of recent consolidation efforts spearheaded by the California State Library, library systems in California now number eight. In July 2009, PLS combined three library systems to form the Pacific Library Partnership (PLP). This new library system was established through a joint powers agreement; however, the four participating library systems, including PLS, retain a great deal of autonomy and maintain an independent system administrative council and their own joint powers agreement. The PLS Administrative Council, composed of library directors from PLS member libraries, is responsible for overseeing PLAN. PLAN currently serves only PLS, and PLS administrators have no immediate plans to expand it to serve other PLP members.

FINANCE

PLS supports 35 library branches. It is funded primarily by member libraries, which in turn are supported largely through local property tax revenue. PLS also receives support under the California Library Services Act, the federal Library Services and Technology Act (LSTA), and local contracts for special services. Member libraries share the up-front and ongoing maintenance costs of the central system, the connectivity costs of the transmission system, and the support staff that manage and operate the system. PLS created and maintains the network with funds from its general budget. PLS applies for federal E-rate discounts for eligible costs of operating PLAN, excluding Internet access and internal connection costs. PLS's discount rate is 50 percent.

CONCLUSION

Libraries are at the forefront of providing no-fee Internet access to the public. In 1994, just 8.2 percent of public libraries provided this service; as of 2009, 100 percent of libraries do so. While this is a vital role in every community, the library is the only source of no-fee public Internet access in 71 percent of communities. The core mission of libraries is to connect people with ideas and information. Internet access makes it possible for libraries to fulfill this mission through online resources that can, for example, help people find jobs, improve their skills, access government services, create small businesses, complete school homework, and conduct research. Libraries have reported high demand for Internet access; indeed, in the majority of libraries, the demand for publicaccess computers far outweighs the supply. As demand for public access to the Internet grows, so, too, does the need for higher bandwidth in the library.

In some communities, libraries play the important role of broadband anchor institution; in other words, by obtaining high-bandwidth connections, they drive the deployment of advanced technologies to communities that might be unable to obtain that level of service through residential demand alone. In short, libraries that are able to meet the demand for no-fee public Internet access play a vital role in serving both their users and their communities. To help libraries achieve this capability, the Bill and Melinda Gates Foundation initiated the Opportunity Online Broadband Grant Programme.

This programme provides funding and support to help State Library agencies in seven states—Massachusetts, New York, Virginia, Arkansas, Kansas, California, and Texas—develop leadership and improve library connectivity to the Internet. The American Library Association's Office for Information Technology Policy (OITP) is participating in this programme, providing research and consulting services to state libraries, as well as developing publications that address key issues salient to the program's goals. The purpose of this publication is to provide a snapshot of five different library networks that provide users with no-fee Internet access. Libraries can establish such networks in many different ways and with various leadership structures, so the case study sites were

6

Library Catalogue: The Special Problems of Serials

STANDARDS

In libraries have versions of the AACR2 and MARC standards for a long time been internationally accepted standards. In subject databases such as Chemical Abstracts, MEDLINE and PsycINFO is no standards, but the "Common Communication Format" (CCF) is ment to serve such databases. In archives and museums are other principles followed. Resource Description and Access is a recent attempt to make a standard that crosses the domains. It should be considered that all these standards differ from the standards used by authors to refer to their sources. All these standards represent alternative way of bibliographical recording.

COMMON COMMUNICATION FORMAT

"The users of the CCF on the other hand, coming from many different backgrounds (some indeed national libraries), would never consider aiming at such a level of homogeneity between records originating in different systems. They have been able to accept that there will be different practices in record creation resulting in records which, when merged into a database, will show their different origins."

"Early in its deliberations the Group undertook a comparison of all of the data elements in:

- The Reference Manual — ASIDIC/EUSIDIC/ICSU-AB/NFAIS Interchange Specifications, and — the USSR-US Common Communication Format.

With these six standard formats as a guide, the Group identified a small number of data elements which were used by virtually all information-handling communities, including both libraries and abstracting and indexing organisations. These commonly used data elements formed the core of the CCF. A technique was developed to show relationships between bibliographic records, and between elements within bibliographic records. The concept of the record segment was developed and refined, and a method for designating relationships between records, segments, and fields was accepted by the group. The first edition of CCF: The Common Communication Format was published in 1984."

DESCRIPTIVE CATALOGING

"Descriptive cataloging" is a well-established concept in the tradition of library cataloging in which a distinction is made between descriptive cataloging and subject cataloging, each applying a set of standards, different qualifications and often also different kinds of professionals. In the tradition of documentation and information science (*e.g.*, by commercial bibliographical databases) the concept document representation (also as verb: document representing) have mostly been used to cover both "descriptive" and "subject" representation.

Descriptive cataloging has been defined as:

- "The part of cataloging concerned with describing the physical details of a book, such as the form and choice of entries and the title page transcription."

SUBJECT CATALOGING

This is mostly known as classification and (subject) indexing. Classification is the assignment of a given document to a class in a classification system. Indexing is the assignment of characterising labels to the documents represented in a record. Classification is a kind of controlled vocabulary while indexing may use controlled vocabulary, free terms, or both.

CATALOGING TERMS

- Main entry or access point– generally refers to the first author named on the item. Additional authors are added as "added entries." In cases where no clear author is named, the title of the work is considered the main entry.

ONLINE PUBLIC ACCESS CATALOGUE (OPAC)

An Online Public Access Catalogue (often abbreviated as OPAC or simply Library Catalogue) is an online database of materials held by a library or group of libraries. Users search a library catalogue principally to locate books and other material physically located at a library.

HISTORY

Early online catalogs

Although a handful of experimental systems existed as early as the 1960s, the first large-scale online catalogs were developed at Ohio State University in 1975 and the Dallas Public Library in 1978. These and other early online catalogue systems tended to closely reflect the card catalogs that they were intended to replace. Using a dedicated terminal or telnet client, users could search a handful of pre-coordinate indexes and browse the resulting display in much the same way they had previously navigated the card catalogue. Throughout the 1980s, the number and sophistication of online catalogs grew. The first commercial systems appeared, and would by the end of the decade largely replace systems built by libraries themselves.

Library catalogs began providing improved search mechanisms, including Boolean and keyword searching, as well as ancillary functions, such as the ability to place holds on items that had been checked-out. At the same time, libraries began to develop applications to automate the purchase, cataloging, and circulation of books and other library materials. These applications, collectively known as an integrated library system (ILS) or library management system, included an online catalogue as the public interface to the system's inventory. Most library catalogs are closely tied to their underlying ILS system.

Stagnation and dissatisfaction

The 1990s saw a relative stagnation in the development of online catalogs. Although the earlier character-based interfaces were replaced with ones for the web, both the design and the underlying search technology of most systems did not advance much beyond that developed in the late 1980s. At the same time, organisations outside of libraries began developing more sophisticated information retrieval systems. Web search engines like Google and popular e-commerce web sites such as Amazon.com provided simpler to use (yet more powerful) systems that could provide relevancy ranked search results using probabilistic and vector-based queries. Prior to the widespread use of the Internet, the online catalogue was often the first information retrieval system library users ever encountered. Now accustomed to web search engines, newer generations of library users have grown increasingly dissatisfied with the complex (and often arcane) search mechanisms of older online catalogue systems. This has, in turn, led to vocal criticisms of these systems within the library community itself, and in recent years to the development of newer (often termed 'next-generation') catalogs.

Next-generation catalogs

The newest generation of library catalogue systems are distinguished from earlier OPACs by their use of more sophisticated search technologies, including relevancy ranking and faceted search, as well as features aimed at greater user interaction and participation with the system, including tagging and reviews. These newer systems are almost always independent of the library's integrated library system (ILS), instead providing drivers that allow for the synchronisation of data between the two systems. While older online catalogue systems were almost exclusively built by ILS vendors, libraries are increasingly turning to next generation catalogue systems built by enterprise search companies and open source projects, often led by libraries themselves. The costs associated with these new systems, however, have slowed their adoption, particularly at smaller institutions.

UNION CATALOGS

Although library catalogs typically reflect the holdings of a single library, they can also contain the holdings of a group or consortium of libraries. These systems, known as union catalogs, are usually designed to aid the borrowing of books and other materials among the member institutions via interlibrary loan. The largest such union catalogue is WorldCat, which includes the holdings of over 70,000 libraries worldwide.

RELATED SYSTEMS

There are a number of systems that share much in common with library catalogs, but have traditionally been distinguished from them. Libraries utilise these systems to search for items not traditionally covered by a library catalogue. These include bibliographic databases — such as Medline, ERIC, PsycINFO, and many others — which index journal articles and other research data. There are also a number of applications aimed at managing documents, photographs, and other digitised or born-digital items such as Digital Commons and DSpace. Particularly in academic libraries, these systems (often known as digital library systems or institutional repository systems) assist with efforts to preserve documents created by faculty and students.

CATALOGUING AND PROCESSING

LIBRARY ORGANISATION

Standards

Most small, private, or classroom library collections do not need a formal system of library organisation as the individual books can be easily located. As the collection becomes larger, access becomes problematic unless some method of grouping is devised. Many different systems address this problem. For most school libraries, the international standard is the Dewey Decimal Classification scheme and either Sears List of Subject Headings or the Library of Congress Subject Headings. Descriptive cataloguing is defined by rules outlined in the Anglo-American Cataloguing Rules (AACR2). Refer to the latest editions of these resources to obtain the most current practices in cataloguing.

Every item in the collection must be described using a standard format. The same basic components are contained in each description. Always cited in the same order, they must employ consistent punctuation. Such standardisation of procedures enhances the local, national, and international exchange of bibliographic data and is essential in computerised systems. To a computer, Hamlet and Shakespeare are just a string of characters. The machine will fail to recognise one as a title and the other as an author unless it is told where each is located in a descriptive record and how each will be introduced.

If schools intend to exchange bibliographic data on a local or provincial basis, they should conform to the standards outlined in this document. The exchange of bibliographic data or information can occur in a number of ways, one of which is participation in a union catalogue. Historically, union catalogues have progressed from manual card and thesis files to on-line shared databases to catalogue records electronically linked via Internet. Union catalogues form one of the main building blocks of resource sharing or shared services such as interlibrary loan, cooperative cataloguing, cooperative preservation, and cooperative collection development activities. Standards must be used by libraries and library systems to participate in union catalogues.

Educational Rationale

For students and staff to make the most effective use of the school's educational resources, the nature, extent, interrelationship, and location of these resources must be clearly identified. School libraries do not exist in an information vacuum but are part of a growing information network. Therefore, they should be provided with access to systems that are compatible with national and international standards.

The process of standardised cataloguing and classification results in the creation of a library catalogue.

In a school library, the catalogue is a tool to:

- List, the print and non-print resources available in the school.
- Describe print and non-print resources.
- Direct users to similar materials.
- Record purchasing and publishing history.
- Indicate the location of the resources.
- Assist students in obtaining the skills of information retrieval.

The catalogue enable users to:

- Retrieve information efficiently.
- Increase understanding by students and staff of information retrieval systems.
- Plan, order, and check resources efficiently.
- Develop information retrieval skills that are transferable from one school library to other school, public, college, university, and special libraries.

Non-Standard Systems

In-house devised methods of library organisation are to be discouraged.

These non-standards-based solutions result in the following:

- Students and staff requiring training in the specific use of the collection, the knowledge of which is not transferable to other libraries.
- Systems becoming inconsistent over time with changes in Personnel.
- Cataloguing becoming useless when an attempt is made to convert it to a standard machine readable format.

Methods of Implementing Standards

In applying these standards, school libraries and school divisions/districts which do not have centralised cataloguing have a number of options.

They may:

- Do their own original cataloguing;
- Obtain derived cataloguing;
- Purchase commercially produced cataloguing;
- Use any combination of the above.

Wherever possible, commercially produced cataloguing should be attained. No matter what options are used, consumers of cataloguing should be knowledgeable in terms of what to look and ask for about the standards. This recalls the importance of the training in cataloguing required to ensure consistency and accuracy. School libraries must be familiar with cataloguing standards and should establish local cataloguing policies.

Original Cataloguing

Original cataloguing refers to cataloguing an item by examining certain parts of it to obtain information needed to describe it. While original cataloguing allows for on-site, immediate, and locally applied cataloguing, there are some concerns.

These include:

- Original cataloguing is time-consuming for the cataloguer and the data processor/typist. The teacher-librarian's time can be much better spent working with teachers and students. In addition, library technician and library clerk time in school libraries is usually at a premium.
- Lack of library technician and library clerk time usually results in a backlog of materials which have not been catalogued or processed fully. These materials cannot be used by staff or students.
- Inexperienced cataloguers spend long hours misapplying rules. Thus, the advantages of using a standard system are often negated and re-cataloguing is often necessary at a future date.
- Cataloguing is an expensive process when done by unqualified personnel. If the hours spent by cataloguers and data processors/

typists were costed out, it would become apparent that commercial cataloguing is more economical.

Derived Cataloguing

Derived or copy cataloguing refers to the process of cataloguing items by using existing bibliographic records obtained from various sources and altering those records to conform to local cataloguing standards.

Cataloguing information may be found in:

- Cataloguing-in-publication (CIP) data found within the item.
- Book catalogues.
- Non-book catalogues (*e.g.*, microfiche and CD-ROMs).
- Electronic catalogues (*e.g.*, the Internet). An on-line directory known as Hytelnet provides a well-organised means by which to browse through library catalogues or databases worldwide. Two telnet addresses worthy of mention are:
  i. Telnet locis.loc.gov (Library of Congress, mainly books) and
  ii. Telnet dra.com (Library of Congress — Data Research Associates, Inc., mainly films and videos).

While derived cataloguing does result in definite cataloguing savings, both in terms of cost and time, it should be noted that catalogue cards still must be typed manually or cataloguing records must be entered manually into an automated library system. Furthermore, cataloguing standards and formats may vary from catalogue to catalogue. This will also affect the amount of editing required to meet locally established practices.

Commercial Cataloguing

Commercial cataloguing refers to cataloguing services now being offered by a number of firms. It may take the form of simplified cataloguing records for only certain titles to customised cataloguing for specialised collections. Care should be taken in choosing commercial cataloguing that follows national and local cataloguing standards.

The advantages to purchasing commercial cataloguing include:

- Requiring less expertise on the part of the teacher-librarian (the main task for the school library staff may be in filing the cards in a manual environment or loading MARC records in an automated environment).
- Converting a card catalogue to an electronic format enables the school to have it done by a commercial vendor.
- Improving consistency.
- Centralising cataloguing reduces time spent duplicating the cataloguing for the same titles

Many jobbers or wholesalers routinely offer cataloguing for a nominal fee. Libraries considering automation in the future will want to consider ordering

MARC catalogue records along with card sets. This investment in the future allows the school to stockpile MARC data for the automation project. It also greatly reduces the amount of time required to complete the recon, or retrospective conversion of the catalogue.

Combination

Most schools opt for a combination of commercial and original cataloguing, purchasing commercial cataloguing whenever possible, and doing original cataloguing for items in the collection for which commercial cataloguing is not available.

Union Catalogues

Centralised cataloguing in a divisional or district processing centre can result in a union catalogue where the print and audiovisual materials of that network of libraries are known. Union catalogues achieve uniformity throughout the system, avoiding duplication of effort and promoting resource sharing.

RULES AND AUTHORITIES

The set of rules that currently outlines international cataloguing standards in most English-speaking countries are in the Anglo- American Cataloguing Rules(AACR2). Because AACR2 contains provision for a number of options, and because the rules are open to various interpretations, this document has been compiled to suggest the minimum level which should be followed by schools cataloguing materials for use in Manitoba.

Anglo- American Cataloguing Rules Revised (Concise AACR2)

Descriptive cataloguing is defined by rules described in the American Library Association's Concise AACR2 — 1988 Revision.

An outline of these rules follows:

- The Description of Library Materials.
- General rule (0)*.
- Title and statement of responsibility area (1).
- Edition area (2).
- Special area for serials, computer files, maps, and other cartographic materials and music (3).
- Publication distribution, etc., area (4).
- Physical description area (5).
- Series area (6).
- Note(s) area (7).
- Standard number (8).
- Headings, Uniform Titles, and References.
- Choice of access points (21-29).
- Headings for persons (30-44).

- Geographic names (45-47).
- Headings for corporate bodies (48-56).
- Uniform titles (57-61).
- References (62-65).

Classification Authorities

All materials should be classified to the levels outlined in the most current edition of The Abridged Dewey Decimal Classification and Relative Index. This one volume edition contains the same basic numbers as the full edition but permits the possibility of expansion should there be a need.

Subject Heading Authorities

The individual library may choose between Sears List of Subject Headings and Library of Congress Subject Headin(gsese Bibliography). The Sears Listhas long been the standard for school and smaller libraries. For most school libraries it will suffice. The Library of Congress subject headings should be considered only for larger libraries. All other situations cannot support the cost. Changes in technology may justify the use of Library of Congress subject headings in the future. Commercial vendors will provide the opportunity to select one or the other or both. When cataloguing is purchased, both Sears and Library of Congress subject headings should be requested.

Then when the records are loaded, Sears would be used for the present time. The school library must update its edition of Sears regularly. Additional Canadian subject authorities may be derived from the National Library of Canada's Canadian Subject Headings and the Sears List of Subject Headings: Canadian Compani(osnee Bibliography).

The National Library of Canada's Canadian Subject Headings supplements the Library of Congress Subject Headin.g Ssears List of Subject Headings: Canadian Companiocnan be used in conjunction with the current edition of the Sears List of Subject Headings. Assistance in the selection of French language subject headings may be found in Répertoire des vedettes-matièreavailable on microfiche, revised every six months, from Laval University Press.

Services documentaires multimedia (SDM) in Montreal publish the CD-ROM version known as RVM. SDM also publishes Vedettes-matière jeunesse which is an adaptation and simplification of Répertoire des vedettes-matière for materials aimed at young people aged 4 to 12. This product is available in thesis, diskette, and on the Internet. The choice of subject authority is important in the construction of an automated catalogue. Sears, Library of Congres, sand National Library of Canada (NLC)subject headings are each flagged differently in an automated catalogue. MARC records often include both Sears and NLC headings. Any school library wishing to index its OPAC only with Sears headings would be required to set up the software to index only properly flagged fields.

Dictionaries

There is no single dictionary that has been designated as an authority for Canadian usage in cataloguing. This can create some difficulties in the creation of a MARC catalogue when the sources of MARC records may be using alternate spellings. A typical example is the American spelling of "labour" and the Canadian version "labour." The individual library must decide to accept American spelling or select any good Canadian dictionary and change. Consistency in spelling is a major factor in the production of a useful card catalogue or OPAC. The extra time and effort this requires may render the decision to convert American spellings to Canadian ones impractical.

ALA Filing Rules

ALA Filing Rules are the standard for manual card catalogues which should be followed. Automated catalogues result in filing and filing rules becoming redundant.

MARC Cataloguing Guides

The National Library of Canada's Canadian MARC Communications Format: Bibliographic Datnad the Library of Congress's USMARC Format for Bibliographic are useful tools for those working with MARC data. For the school library environment, it is recommended that a less technical guide such as Beaumont and Associates' Make Mine MARC (With Integrated Format) be used.

ORGANISING A SCHOOL LIBRARY

Organising a school library is challenging.

The following steps are designed to simplify the project:

- Assemble all library resources from all areas of the school. Library personnel should avoid including.
- Textbooks.
- Sets of supplementary texts and readers.
- Workbooks, lab manuals, or teacher's editions.
- Multiple copies (six or more) of any book used as a class set.
- Library personnel should weed resources that are.
- Worn and damaged items.
- Superseded editions.
- Uncirculated for the past three to five years.
- Unnecessary duplicates.
- Non-fiction with old copyright dates and/or with inaccurate, non-metric, condescending, stereotypical, or biased information.
- Mend books in need of minor repair.
- Sort four sections of resources (keeping duplicate copies of the same items together) into the following.

- Easy books (picture books and easy fiction for Grades K-3).
- Fiction books (novels and short stories).
- Non-fiction books (books of fact, fairy tales, and folklore).
- Audiovisual.
- Arrange easy books in alphabetical order by author on the shelves.
- Arrange fiction books in alphabetical order by author on the shelves.
- Divide the non-fiction books into broad groups using the 10 main Dewey classes as a guide. Remove any books that can be used as quick reference such as encyclopaedias, dictionaries, almanacs, and atlases. Place them in a separate pile. These items will form the core of the library's reference collection.
- Sort audiovisual resources according to media format. To summarise, the four major groups of resources are.
- Easy books (arranged alphabetically by author).
- Fiction books (arranged alphabetically by author).
- Non-fiction books (roughly sorted into 10 broad Dewey subject groups with an eleventh group for reference).
- Audiovisual.

AUTOMATION

The first significant change in the way a library delivers basic service is automation. All school libraries are expected to be automated in the future. Data is the necessary ingredient for any computer to perform at its optimum. No other field in education has a better application for current computer technology than the library. The library has always been a database. In its new format the card catalogue becomes an OPAC (Online Public Access Catalogue). Searches which once were time-consuming can be done in seconds on a well-designed OPAC.

In many ways, the traditional card catalogue has been as much a roadblock as an aid in education. The seldom understood innerworkings and cross-references of the card system are replaced by the far simpler keyword access of the modern OPAC. Students and staff, with some instruction, learn to manipulate large data files through the use of Boolean operators. By combining search terms such as author, title, subject, and abstract, the user is able to determine quickly where the appropriate information is to be found.

Getting Started

Even if there is little or no funding in the budget for library automation, the school can begin to prepare itself for that eventuality. MARC records can be purchased for new acquisitions along with catalogue card sets. For these items there will be no need to worry about recon as the MARC data will be ready to load into the cataloguing module of your chosen automated library system. Materials that are currently on the shelf present another challenge. Regardless of which library application software the library may eventually select, full MARC records are required.

There are many sources of MARC records but not all records are of a good quality. MARC records derived from the Library of Congress or the National Library of Canada databases are uniformly good. Records from these sources require little or no editing because they are full records. Records derived from other sources, including some of the major jobbers, are not as consistent. They often are not full MARC records and, invariably, they require some additional time and effort to raise them to the standard of the National Library of Canada or Library of Congress. Sometimes companies identify records as MARC when they are not (*e.g.*, Microlif records are not full MARC records).

Libraries can prepare to automate by reading Selection of Automated Systems: Criteria for School Libraries in Manitaonbda Selection of Resources: Policies and Procedures for Manitoba Schools. These two documents are available from the Instructional Resources Unit, Manitoba Education and Training. French versions are available from the Direction des ressources éducatives françaises.

Visitations

Many schools in the province have already converted their libraries to automated systems. Contact them and arrange a visit. The Instructional Resources Unit has a document available entitled Automated School Library Systems in Manitotbhat lists automated schools. Automated schools have learned a great deal and know how to avoid pitfalls.

Ask such questions as:

- Where to obtain MARC records?
- How much original cataloguing is necessary?
- How good is the data?
- How good is the application software?
- What were the difficulties encountered?
- Any vendor training? If so, is it useful?
- Is the vendor responsive to school needs?
- How much did the project cost?

Weeding

A library benefits from judicious weeding. The most expensive part of any library automation project is the conversion of the old catalogue into a MARC format. Old textbooks, teacher editions, dated scientific materials, worn, torn, and yellowed items should be discarded before the conversion process begins; otherwise, much time, effort, and money can be wasted doing recon on these materials. Note: The Instructional Resources Unit, Manitoba Education and

Training, has a collection of old approved Manitoba textbooks. Before discarding such material from your school library, please contact this Unit to see if your material is wanted.

Preparing the Shelf List

The next phase is preparing the shelf list. If the shelf list has been catalogued up to the level described in this resource, recon is much easier. The more complete the shelf list, the simpler the task of matching against an existing database. If the shelf list is not up to standard, then the task becomes more difficult. It may become necessary to recatalogue many books entirely.

The shelf list may be:

- Sent to a commercial jobber who attempts to match the information on the card with an existing bibliographic record such as one from A-G Canada Ltd. (formerly ISM Library Information Services), or another local resource, TKM in Brandon.
- Matched in-house using one of the compact disc MARC databases.
- Matched online against the holdings of a bibliographic vendor (*e.g.*, A-G Canada Ltd., and TKM).
- Entered partially in-house on diskette and sent off to a bibliographic vendor who attempts to match the "skeletal records" against their MARC database (TKM offers such a service).

If the shelf list does not include ISBN (International Standard Book Number) or Library of Congress numbers, arrange for volunteers to begin adding this data to the shelf list cards. The presence of this information greatly increases the chance of getting a "hit" and subsequently reduces the time and cost of deriving MARC records. Contact the Instructional Resources Unit, Manitoba Education and Training, for a copy of the publication Commercial Cataloguing and Processing Services for Books and Audio Visual Mater.

DESCRIPTIVE CATALOGUING

Cataloguing and classification are used to develop an index of the library collection to enable users to determine the availability of resources.

Create a card or manual system with two different files (using 3 x 5 inch cards) that have:

1. A shelf list file for staff use.
2. A dictionary catalogue for use by staff and students.

Shelf List

The shelf list is an inventory file and forms a complete record of the materials owned by the library. It should be housed separately from the regular catalogue. It is called a shelf list because its cards are arranged in the same order as the materials on the shelves.

Dictionary Catalogue

The dictionary catalogue, an index to the library collection, should be located in the main part of the library. The file is called a dictionary catalogue because its cards are arranged alphabetically. To create these files, information on each book or item in the collection has to be collected, assigned, and recorded. Four basic steps are involved that are similar either to creating a manual card catalogue or to gathering information for an automated system.

The steps are to:

- Record the bibliographic information for the item.
- Assign classification numbers.
- Assign subject headings.
- Determine other indexing terms.

Preparation For Cataloguing

As this information is collected or assigned, record it on 3 x 5 inch pieces of thesis. As the catalogue cards are typed from these slips, they are sometimes referred to as "Typing Slips" or "T-slips." A T-slip is required for each item. When completed, the cards are data processed/typed and filed. An alternative to this T-slip method is the use of one of the commercially-available systems that allows the user to generate complete card sets from the input of this initial shelf list information. The cataloguer may also choose to work directly from the item, by penciling in the Dewey number, underlining the main entry, and writing subject headings on the reverse of the title page. This avoids the use of T-slips.

SUBJECT HEADINGS

Subject headings consist of words, groups of words, or acronyms that are used to describe the subject of a work. As access points in the catalogue, these headings are extremely important in communicating the holdings of a library. Add subject headings to the T-slips to provide access to the intellectual content of the material. In selecting subject headings, the cataloguer decides what index terms appear in the dictionary catalogue for the book. The chosen headings are numbered with arabic numerals and are recorded. It is important to use consistently the same terminology to designate a particular subject. For this reason, libraries have developed standard lists of subject headings. The most commonly used lists in Canadian school libraries are the Sears List of Subject Headings and the Canadian Companion to the Searslist. A supplemental choice would be the most recent edition of the Library of Congress Subject Headings and the National Library of Canada's Canadian Subject Headings.

The latter two titles supply an expanded number of subject possibilities. Note that subject headings are never assigned from the Dewey Decimal Classification. Before assigning subject headings, the main subject or subjects of the book must be determined. This is done by examining the title, table of contents, description on the dust jacket, preface, text, and illustrations. The next step is to write down the subject and check to see if that choice is permitted in the standardised list. If the subject selected is not in the list, the related subjects must be consulted. It is possible, although not advisable, to add a local subject heading.

This should be done only when all other avenues have been exhausted. The standard subject lists represent a controlled vocabulary that has been carefully constructed over a number of years. Local subject creativity — if taken to excess — results in a garbled catalogue. If local headings are added to the catalogue, write them in your copy of Sears or LCSH for future reference. Typically, two subject headings per item is sufficient for most school libraries, although there are occasions when three or more may be required to cover the scope of the item. Select as specific a heading as possible. A book about bears should be given the subject heading BEARS rather than the general heading ANIMALS. For a book about several different animals, the more inclusive heading ANIMALS should be used rather than separate headings for each animal mentioned in the text. Determining whether to use a specific or a general subject entry can pose difficulties. The introduction to Sears describes how to designate them correctly. The subject heading is listed at the bottom of the T-slip preceded by an Arabic numeral. Such a notation is called a tracing and tells the cataloguer what other cards exist. School libraries often find it valuable to include subject headings for Fiction and Easy materials. This makes it easier to identify storybooks about a particular subject or theme. In general, add the word FICTION as a subdivision of other subjects to indicate that the item is a work of fiction.

CLASSIFICATION

A classification number now should be added to the T-slip. It appears in the upper left-hand corner opposite the author. In classifying library collections, numbers or letters are assigned to the books to represent the subject of the book. These notations, which are called "call numbers," are also used to arrange the books on the shelves. Generally library collections are separated into four major categories: Easy, Fiction, Non-Fiction, and Reference.

Non-Fiction

School libraries primarily use the Abridged Dewey Decimal Classification scheme to organise their non-fiction materials. It is a hierarchical classification scheme which uses the decimal principal for subdivision. There are ten main classes into which all areas of knowledge are subdivided. Each main class is broken down into 10 subdivisions and each subsequent division is further broken down into 10 more subdivisions.

Examples follow:

- 900 — History.
- 970 — North American History.
- 971 — Canadian History.
- 971.2 — Canadian Prairie History.
- 971.27 — Manitoba History.

The Abridged Dewey Decimal Classification is frequently misused and some formal instruction in classification should be undertaken before attempting its use. Contact Red River Community College or the University of Manitoba, Faculty of Education, regarding courses and programmes.

Number Building in Dewey

As a general rule, the Dewey classification number should be kept as brief as possible. Assignment of class numbers begins with determining the general subject of the book and the treatment it requires. Clues may be gathered from the title, the table of contents, the description on the dust jacket, the preface and the text. Titles can be misleading and classification by title alone is not recommended. If a book has two or more subjects try to determine which subject best describes the contents of the item. Then select the classification number accordingly. The Dewey Decimal Classification scheme classifies materials primarily by a disciplinary approach to the subject. The subject "corn" as a farm product goes under the number for farming. "Corn" as a grain may go in a number in the Pure Sciences, the 500s. "Corn" as a basis for designing decorative displays for fall goes in the 700s. Once the subject area of the book has been determined, a class number is assigned in the following manner.

Use the current unabridged or abridged edition of Dewey to:

- Turn to the outline of the ten main classes provided at the beginning of the classification scheme and determine in which main class the item belongs.
- Turn to the outline of the 100 divisions of the 10 main classes, (also provided at the start of the classification scheme) and determine in which division of the main class the item belongs.
- Turn to the schedules (*i.e.*, the detailed outline of the classification numbers) and select the most specific number for the item. For all but the very largest school collections, a maximum of three places beyond the decimal point, or the first logical break, should be sufficient.

AUDIOVISUAL MATERIALS

The cataloguing of audiovisual materials such as videorecordings, kits, computer software, and sound recordings follows the same general patterns as those for books. As with books, the cataloguer must still identify the title, the publisher, and date of production but many audiovisual items will not have identifiable authors.

In cataloguing audiovisual materials the number of frames, the components of the kit, or the duration of the recording are identified rather than the number of pages. Guidelines for the cataloguing of online information resources are being formulated. This includes numeric databases, computer forums, discussion groups, mailing list servers, online public access catalogues, and full-text databases.

General Material Designation [GMD]

The General Material Designation [GMD] is included to alert the user that the item in question is not a book. It is appended in square brackets [ ] after the title and indicates the precise format of the item. As with the subject headings, only certain terms are to be used as GMDs.

The most common ones which are likely to be used in a school library are:

- Activity card (see kit)
- Computer file (replacing
- Machine Readable model
- Data File, as the GMD for
- Computer software)
- Chart
- Filmstrip
- Game
- Globe

kit (2 more media)
map
model
picture
realia
sound recording
transparency
videorecording

The Specific Material Designation [SMD] is a term indicating a special format of material (usually the format of the physical object[s]) to which items belong (*e.g.*, videodiscs and videocassettes). These SMDs are used in the 300 field.

The procedures outlined in the chapters on classification and subject indexing are equally applicable to audiovisual materials. The following examples illustrate some of the most common types of audiovisual materials likely to be encountered in school libraries and may be used as guides in cataloguing. Further guidance and examples in cataloguing audiovisual materials may be found in Jean Weihs's Non-book Materials: The Organisation of Integrated Collections

TYPING CATALOGUE CARDS

Automatic card generating systems are available as an alternative to typing the cards. If you must type catalogue cards, they are to be typed on 3 x 5 inch card stock which is readily available from any library supply firm. Each card should follow a standard format.

The catalogue cards are to be single spaced throughout, with the following exceptions;

- Double-spacing before the beginning of the first note.
- Beginning the tracings at the bottom of the card but above the hole.

The typist should set up the typewriter in the following way:

- Margin 2 spaces from the left edge of the card
- 1st tab 9 spaces from left of card (1st indention), 11 spaces from left of card.
- 2nd tab 13 spaces from the left margin (2nd indention)

FILING CARDS

ALA (American Library Association Filing Rules)

For manual card catalogues, the ALA Filing Rules are the standard which are to be followed.

Shelf List

The shelf list file contains one card for each distinct item in the library and is arranged in the same order as the items on the shelves. Different shelf lists are created for materials in various locations such as Reference, AV and VTR.

To file shelf list cards for the main collection, group them first into main categories: one for Easy, one for Fiction, one for Non-Fiction, and one for Reference cards.

- *Easy:* Arrange the cards in alphabetical order by author (or by title in cases where there is no author). Sub-arrange the books by the same author alphabetically by title.
- *Fiction:* Arrange the fiction cards in alphabetical order by author (or by title in cases where there is no author.) Sub-arrange the books by the same author alphabetically by title.
- *Non-Fiction:* Arrange the non-fiction cards in numerical order by Dewey number, remembering that Dewey numbers are decimal numbers. The following is an example of a correct sequence 971 971.004 971.2 971.24 In cases where the library may have several different books by the same author, file first by Dewey number and then sub-arrange by main entry.

Dictionary Catalogue

- Interfile all author, subject and title cards in one alphabetical sequence.
- Alphabetise by the TOP line of the card. When the top lines are identical, sub-arrange by the next line on the card.
- Ignore the articles "a", "an" and "the" when they occur at the beginning of a title. These articles need only be considered in alphabetising when they occur in the middle of the heading. In French,

ignore the articles "le", "la", "les" and "l' " only. "Du", "de", "d' " and "un(e)" will be filed under those articles.

- Alphabetise character space by character space. Blank character spaces come before character spaces with letters. Thus, shorter words come before longer words beginning with the same letters.
- Numbers expressed as numerals (arabic or roman) are filed according to their numerical value; this file is before the first alphabetical file (*e.g.*, before "A").
- Numbers that are spelled out as words are filed as spelled.
- Abbreviations are filed exactly as written, not as if spelled out.
- Apostrophes are disregarded and the word containing the apostrophe is filed as one word.
- Proper names with prefixes are treated as a separate words unless joined to the rest of the name directly or by an apostrophe without a space.
- Subject cards with dates as subdivisions are subarranged chronologically with the earliest date first.

PROCESSING

Once the cards have been prepared and filed, prepare the items for circulation. Use the following as a guide.

Books

- Stamp the book with the school stamp in the following places.
- The fly leaf.
- The lower part of the title page.
- On the outside edges of the pages, with the book firmly closed.
- Type a book pocket and card for each item according to the example given on the next page. Note that the author's surname and the first name are both typed. The same tabs that are used for typing the catalogue cards may be used to type the book card and pocket.
- Type the call number for each book on a label and attach it to the book. Cover the label with a mylar label cover. Both spine labels and mylar label covers are available from any library supply company. Be consistent in the placement of the labels.
- Most libraries prefer to paste the pocket in the back of the book so as not to cover title information found in the front. It is important to be consistent in the location of the pocket. If a library does put the pockets in the front, a blank page can be introduced to put the card on. Again be consistent about the use of the front or back. If date due slips are being used, attach one to the pocket below the typed title.
- Books with thesis dust jackets should be covered with a plastic dust jacket for protection.

- If the item is to be circulated in an automated system the barcode should be affixed to the item and covered with mylar barcode tape. It is a good practice to write the barcode number on the inside cover in case the label becomes separated from the book. Systems typically employ portable barcode readers. Placement of the automated label on the cover, as opposed to the inside of the cover, offers the practical advantage of not requiring that every book be removed and opened during inventory.

Audiovisual Materials

Audiovisual materials come packaged in so many diverse ways that it is difficult to detail the various means of processing.

In general, follow these steps:

- Stamp the item with the school stamp.
- Prepare a book card and pocket as if for a book and attach it to the box or container. It is a good idea to label the component parts of the box so when the item is returned it is easy to verify nothing has been lost or misplaced.
- Prepare the call number label and attach it to the box. Cover the label with mylar tape.
- If the item is to be circulated in an automated system, affix the barcode label and cover it with mylar tape. Write the barcode number inside the box in case the label is removed from the box.
- For compact sound discs and CD-ROMs, book cards, pockets, and barcodes should be attached to the containers. Any library-specific identifying marks (*i.e.*, call number and institution name) may be written on the transparent centre of the disc as close to the hub and as clearly as possible. A fine point, permanent, silver metallic ink marker works well.

MARC CATALOGUING FOR MANITOBA SCHOOL LIBRARIES

MARC tapes, MARC format, MARC records and MARC compatible are terms which now dominate the lexicon of library literature. All school libraries and teacher-librarians who plan to automate will have to come to terms with MARC records. The purpose of this part of the guide is to explain what a MARC record is and to provide some guidelines for MARC cataloguing in the school libraries of Manitoba. The importance of following this standard cannot be overstated.

If school libraries are to share their cataloguing, and take advantage of the MARC databases available to assist in the recon task, it is essential to adhere to the following standards. The creation of MARC records would allow for the electronic access to bibliographic records, thus facilitating resource-sharing among school libraries.

What Does MARC Mean

A MARC record is a Machine Readable Cataloguing record. By "machine readable" is meant a record that a computer can read and interpret. The following parts will explain why MARC is important and how it is made possible. A cataloguing record is a bibliographic record, containing the information shown on the catalogue cards described earlier in this guide.

Typically a record includes:

- Describing the item.
- Adding entries.
- Arranging subject headings.
- Labelling call numbers and shelf list information as well as additional information.

Why is MARC Necessary

Because computers cannot think or reason they must be provided with guides that enable them to interpret the data which has been inputted into them. The MARC record contains directories or guideposts before each piece of bibliographic information to tell the cataloguer and the computer what type of data is to be found in a specific field. Author, title, and subject are examples of the various field types. Because the lengths of names and titles are usually different, the best library software allows for unlimited field lengths and an unlimited number of fields. Guidance on selection of automated library systems is found in a companion volume to this work. It is available from the Instructional Resources Unit, Manitoba Education and Training, and is entitled Selection of Automation Systems: Criteria for School Libraries in Manitoba

MARC Terms and Definitions

To understand what is being talked about when MARC records are being discussed one needs to be acquainted with the following terms: delimiters, fields, tags, indicators, subfields, and subfield codes.

Delimiters

With different kinds of keyboards, different keys are used to represent the delimiters. In some cases a $ is used, or (-) for Microlif records. For the sake of convenience, a $ will represent the delimiter in this document.

Fields

Bibliographical data is divided into a number of fields to facilitate retrieval: fields for authors, fields for titles, and so on. The fields are further subdivided into one or more subfields. For example, the place of publication, the publisher's name and the date of the publication are all included as part of the MARC field tagged "260."

Tags

A tag is a three-digit number which precedes each field in a MARC record. The tag identifies the field and the kind of data that follows to the computer.

The most frequently encountered tags for monograph and audiovisual resources are:

- TagField
- 010 LCCN
- 016 National Library of Canada control number
- 020 ISBN
- 040 Cataloguing Source
- 082 Dewey Decimal Classification number as assigned by Library of Congress (LC) or National Library of Canada (NLC)
- 090 Local Call Number
- 100 Author main entry field
- 110 Corporate main entry
- 111 Conference main entry
- 130 Uniform title main entry
- 245 Title field
- 246 Varying forms of the title
- 250 Edition field
- 260 Publication information
- 300 Physical description
- 440 Series statement — Title (traced)
- 500 General note area
- 504 Bibliographic note
- 505 Contents note
- 520 Summary or annotation
- 521 Audience level note
- 600 Personal name subject heading
- 610 Corporate subject heading
- 611 Conference subject heading
- 650 Topical subject heading
- 651 Geographical subject heading
- 690 Local subject heading
- 700 Personal name added entry
- 710 Corporate name added entry
- 740 Variant title
- 856 Uniform resource location (URL)
- 901 Local barcode number
- 903 Local price

A typical MARC field for the ISBN number would appear as:

- 020 $a0880223707

There are 999 fields which may be used in a MARC record, but only a fraction of the possible fields will ever be found in any single record. About 10 per cent of the tags are used over and over again and the MARC cataloguer will quickly become familiar with them.

Indicators

Two spaces follow each tag. One or both of these spaces may be used for indicators. In some fields, only the second space is used. Sometimes only the first is used and sometimes both are assigned. Consult the Canadian MARC Communication Format for details. Each indicator will be a number from 1 to 9. Each individual digit has a meaning. In the following example the first three digits are the tag (245 being the title field tag), and the next 2 digits "1" and "4" are indicators.

The "1" is the first indicator and the "4" is the second:

- *245 14:* $aThe trials of life $ba natural history of animal behaviour/ $cDavid Attenborough.

The first indicator of "1" in the title field indicates that there should be a separate title entry in the catalogue. In the card catalogue environment, this means a title card should be printed for this item. A "0" as a first indicator means that this is a main entry by title and the cards should be printed with the traditional hanging indention. The second indicator displays the number of non-filing characters at the beginning of the field. The trials of life, the second indicator is set at "4" so that the first 4 characters (the "T," the "h," the "e," and the space) will be skipped and the title will be filed under "trials." Indicators act as signals to the application software. They define how the software should treat the information within a specific field. Should the library ever consider having authority control work (*e.g.*, correct/consistent spelling) done on their database by a large commercial vendor, correct use of indicators is critical.

Subfields Are Marked by Subfield Codes

Most fields will contain several related pieces of data. Each type of data within a field is called a subfield, and each subfield is preceded by a subfield code. For example, the physical description field defined by the 300 tag typically contains a subfield for the number of pages, one for physical details such as illustration, and a further subfield for dimensions in centimetres.

- 300 $a234 p.:$bill.;$c24 cm.

Subfield Codes

Subfield codes are one lower-case letter preceded by a delimiter. Each subfield indicates what type of data follows it. The subfield codes are $a for extent, $b for other physical details and $c for dimensions.

Using This Publication

The following summary details the MARC tags most likely to be encountered by teacher-librarians during recon or original data entry. The list may appear intimidating at first but most MARC cataloguers will quickly become familiar with the meanings of the various tags. Not all fields will be found in every entry. Notes have been included indicating fields which are repeatable (R) or not repeatable (NR).

Examples are:

- Tags — Will be followed by the names of the fields they represent. Repeatable fields (those which can appear more than once in any given record) will be followed by an "R," non repeatable fields (those which can appear no more than once in any given record) by an "NR."
- Indicators — The use of the indicator is explained in the fields where they are used. Indicators are one digit numbers. Starting with the 010 field, two spaces are left for the indicators if required. Indicators are not required in all fields.
- Subfield Codes — All the data in each field is divided into subfields, each of which is preceded by a subfield code. In almost all cases the subfield will be followed by a delimiter followed by a letter or a number. The name of the subfield will follow the code.
- Examples — Examples will follow each field. In the examples a "0" = a blank space. For the sake of clarity one space will be left between the tag and the first indicator, one will be placed between the second indicator and the first subfield code, and one space between the subfield code and the subfield data.

MARC Leader

The MARC leader is the first block of data which appears at the top of a MARC record. The leader consists of a number of fixed fields and its primary importance is to provide information to the application software (*i.e.*, the OPAC) about how to process the record. It consists of 24 fields and by-and-large the cataloguer will not be concerned with this area at all. The application software will normally record a control number and the date of entry automatically. This, of course, will depend upon the type of application software involved. Individual users should consult their software guides as to how to deal with this particular area. For the purposes of clarity the MARC Leader will not be included in any of the examples in this document.

MARC Fields

010 LCCN Library of Congress Card Number (NR):

- Indicators: Undefined
- Subfield most commonly used: $a
- Example: 010 __ $a910988

016 National Library of Canada's Control Number (NR):

- Indicators: Undefined
- Subfield most commonly used: $a
- Example: 016 __ $a860937070

020 ISBN International Standard Book Number (R):

- This ten digit number is becoming the unique number by which books and their corresponding MARC records are identified. If the library should own both the hardback and the paperback edition of a book, the ISBN numbers may be repeated for this field. Typically a paperback edition will be indicated as (pbk) and noted after the ISBN.
- Indicators: Undefined
- Subfield most commonly used: $a ISBN
- Examples:
- 020 __ $a0771034356
- 020 __ $a0771013396 (pbk)

040 Cataloguing Source (NR):

- Indicators: Undefined
- Subfield most commonly used: $a Cataloguing source
- Example: 040 __ $aDLC

082 Dewey Decimal Classification Number (R):

- Indicator 1:
- Type of edition (*e.g.*, 12th)
- blank — no edition information recorded
- 0 — Full edition of Dewey
- 1 — Abridged edition
- Indicator 2:
- Source of DDC number
- blank — no information provided
- 0 — assigned by LC
- 4 — assigned by agency other than LC

Non-Fiction Number Building in Dewey

Note: In many cases the call number selected by the Library of Congress or other cataloguing agency will be far longer than the school library requires. Rarely will a school library find it necessary to build Dewey Numbers three or more places beyond the decimal point. In cases where extremely long Dewey numbers are encountered the cataloguer in a school situation should feel free to truncate at three places beyond the decimal point or at the first logical break.

The cataloguer may opt to truncate the call number at the slash or apostrophe as desired:

- Subfield most commonly used: $a
- Example:

- 082 04 $a960.4/31
- 082 04 $a960.4'31

Fiction

All fiction works in a school situation should be classed as F or FIC but not both. In many cases an 800 classification number will be encountered when deriving records from a MARC database. These items should be classed as F when encountered in a school library situation.

090 Local Call Number

The 090 field is used to indicate the local call number and if an item has a special location in the library. It is also used to alert users to copies of books which are located at other sites within the school division/district.

Local Call Number (R):

- Indicators: Undefined
- Subfields most commonly used:
- $a Local call number
- $b Special location within library
- $c Number of copies held
- $d Location within school division/district
- Examples:
- 090 $a971 BER $bREF
- 090 $a328 VIC $bOS
- 090 $a659.4 DAY $c 2 copies $d
- Crescentview School.

100 Level Fields

Be aware that many indicators have been eliminated as of January, 1995. These indicators are marked by an asterisk. The 100 level fields are reserved for author and uniform main entry by title. As there can only be one main entry, unlike many other MARC fields this one is not repeatable.

100 Personal Name Main Entry (NR)

(NR, as there can be only one main entry):

- Indicator 1: Type of personal name
- 0 — Forename only
- 1 — Single surname (most common)
- 2 — Multiple surname
- 3 — Name of family
- Indicator 2: Blank
- Subfields most commonly used:
- $a Name (surname and forenames)

- $c Titles and other words associated with name
- $d Date of birth and death
- $q Expansion of initials in parenthesis (*i.e.*, a qualification of the name in a fuller form)
- Examples:
- 100 1_ $aBerton, Pierre,$d1920-
- 100 1_ $aGiroux, Lionel,$d1878- 1967.

110 Corporate Main Entry (NR)

During a recon the cataloguer will encounter many examples of corporate main entries. A corporate body is an organisation or group of persons that is identified by a particular name (*e.g.*, an association, government, government agency, religious body, local church, conference).

- Indicator 1: Type of Corporate name
- 1 — Place or place and name
- 2 — Name direct order
- Indicator 2: Blank
- Subfield most commonly used: $a Name
- Example: 110 2_ $aManitoba Library Association

200 Level Fields

240 Uniform titles (NR):

- In the absence of adequate authority tools to verify alternatives properly, it is recommended that the 240 field not be used.

245 Title Statement (NR):

- This is a mandatory field in all MARC records:
- Indicator 1: Should the title be indexed as a title main entry?
- 0 — No added entry; No author is given
- 1 — Title added entry (most common; used when an author is present)
- Indicator 2: Number of filing characters
- 0-9 The number of filing characters, including spaces

E.g., for a title The Spanish Inquisition, the second indicator would be 4. The letters t, h, e, and the space following them are then ignored in alphabetising titles. The book would be alphabetised with the "S's."

Subfields most commonly used:

- $a Short title/title proper
- $b Remainder of title (subtitles)
- $c Remainder of title page transcription
- $h GMD (General Material Designation) used most often for media

246 (R) Varying Forms of Title

- Indicator 1: 0 —No title added entry
- 1 —Title added entry

- Indicator 2: Blank — no information provided
- 0 —Access for portions of title
- 1 —Parallel title
- 2 —Distinctive title
- 3 —Other title
- 4 —Cover title
- 5 —Added title page title
- 6 —Caption title
- 7 —Running title
- 8 —Title from spine
- Subfield Codes:
  - Short title/title proper
  - Number or designation (R)
  - Part or section (R)
  - General Material Designation
  - Other titles and other title information
  - Remainder of title page transcription
  - Designation of volume and issue and/or dates associated with the title
  - Miscellaneous information

Following are the types of titles which are included in this field — parallel, distinctive, cover, added title page, caption, running, spine, other.

Examples: Parallel Title; Title Statement —

- 245 00 $a Guide du camping au Québec = $bQuébec camping guide/ $c Association des terrains de camping et caravaning du Québec.
- 246 11 $aQuébec camping guide

250 Edition Statement (NR)

- Indicators: Undefined
- Subfields most commonly used $a Edition statement
- Examples: 250 $a6th ed.

260 Publication, Imprint/release (NR)

- Indicators: Undefined
- Subfields most commonly used
- $a Place
- $b Publisher
- $c Date of publication
- Example: 260 $aNew York:$bRandom House, $cc1991.

Note: For school libraries doing original cataloguing, it should be sufficient to record the first city listed on the title page and ignore subsequent cities listed. The same rule can be used in the case of multiple publishers. A "c" should precede the date in the entry if the date of publication is derived from the copyright date. The distributor should be added for all audiovisual materials as the source is often different from the producer. Describe the item in hand.

300 Level Fields

300 Level Physical Description or Collation (R):

- The physical format of the item being described is recorded in this area. The physical description includes: the pagination or extent of the item, its physical details and details of accompanying materials.
- Indicators: Undefined
- Subfields most commonly used
- $a Extent of item (number of pages)
- $b Other physical details (*e.g.*, illustrations, maps, ports, etc.)
- $c Dimensions (*e.g.*, 24 cm.)
- $e Accompanying material
- Examples:
- 300 __ $axii, 300 p.:$bcol. ill.;$c24 cm.
- 300 __ $a2 computer disks;$c3 1/2 in.
- 300 __ $a4 filmstrips (60 fr. each): $bcol. and b & w;$c35 mm.

400 Level Fields

- Series Statement/ Added Entry — Title (R): This field is used for series that are traced in the catalogue. The name of the series will be found on the title page or elsewhere in the book.
  - Indicator 1: Undefined
  - Indicator 2: Non-filing characters
  - 0-9 Number of non-filing characters (for initial articles, including spaces).
  - Subfields most commonly used
  - $a Series title
  - $v Volume or number in the series
  - Examples:
    a. 440 _4 $aThe history of modern Europe
    b. 440 _4 $aThe ship;$v29

500 Level Fields

- 500 General Notes (R): If a book has an index or the library desires to add some additional information it is recorded here.
  - Indicators: Undefined
  - Subfield most commonly used
  - $a General note (used when no specialised note field has been defined for the information)
  - Example: 500 __ $aIncludes index.

- 504 Bibliography Note (R): If a work has a bibliography, discography or filmography it should be recorded in this field.
  - Indicators: Undefined
  - Subfield most commonly used
  - $a Bibliography/discography note
  - Example: 504 __ $aIncludes bibliographical references and index.
- 505 Contents Notes (NR): This field is typically used to trace the contents of multi-volume works. It should be preceded by the label Contents.
  - Indicator 1:
    a. 0 — Contents (complete)
    b. 1 — Contents (incomplete)
    c. 2 — Partial contents (if items missing)
  - Indicator 2: Blank
  - Examples:
    a. 505 0_ $a1. The stars (24 min.). —2. The universe (25 min.)
    b. 505 1_ $av. 1. Report — v.3. DNA update.
    c. 505 2_ $av. 1. Claudius the god.
- 520 Summary Note, Abstract, or Annotation (R): This field is commonly found in MARC records derived from a source such as the Library of Congress. Summary notes are recommended in automated systems. A keyword search of a note field will greatly enhance the recovery of materials to meet the thematic approach often used by teachers. Summary notes should be kept concise.
  - Indicator 1: Usually blank
  - Indicator 2: Undefined
  - Subfield most commonly used $a Summary, abstract or annotation.
  - Example: 520 __ $aExplains the concepts of continental drift, vulcanism, and plate tectonics.
- 521 Audience Note (R): Reading levels or intended audience levels are placed in this field if the levels are specifically stated in the item itself. All other methods are marginally reliable and useful at best.
  - Indicators: Undefined
  - Subfields most commonly used: $a Audience level
  - Examples:
    a. 521 __ $aGrades 3, 4, 5.
    b. 521 __ $aEarly years.

600 Level Fields

- 600 Subject Added Entry — Personal Name (R): This field is used for any subject heading which is a personal name. The form to be followed will be the same as if entering a personal name in the 100 field. This field is commonly used for the subjects of biographies and literary criticism.

- Indicator 1:
  a. Type of personal name
  b. 0 — Forename
  c. 1 — Single surname (most common)
  d. 2 — Multiple surname
- Indicator 2: Source of the subject heading
  a. 0 — Library of Congress Subject Heading
  b. 5 — National Library of Canada (NLC) English Subject Heading
  c. 6 — National Library of Canada (NLC) French Subject Heading
  d. 7 — Source of Subject Heading or Term Specified in Subfield $2

• Note Regarding Sears Subject Headings: The National Library of Canada does not provide an assigned indicator for Sears headings. For libraries which change or edit records or do original cataloguing, an indicator of 7 is used. Subfield most commonly used
  - *$a:* Name (surname and forename)
  - *$q:* Expansion of initials in parenthesis
  - *$b:* Numeration (Roman numeral and name used with the entry element of a forename heading)
  - *$c:* Titles and other words associated with the name (R)
  - *$d:* Birth and death dates
  - *$t:* Title
  - *$x:* General subdivision (R)
  - *$y:* Chronological subdivision (R)
  - *$z:* Geographical subdivision (R)
  - *$2:* Source of subject heading or term
  - Examples:
    a. 600 10 $aShakespeare, William,$d1564- 1616$xComedies
    b. 600 10 $aNicholas$bII,$cEmperor of Russia,$d1868-1918.
    c. 600 10 $aDavidson, Donald,$d1917- $xCriticism and interpretation.

• 610 Subject Heading — Corporate Name (R): Corporate bodies, government agencies, or other organisations are placed in this field. The coding is similar to the 110 field used for Corporate Main entry.
  - Indicator 1: Type of Corporate name
    a. 0 — Surname (inverted)
    b. 1 — Place or place and name
    c. 2 — Name (direct order) most common

- Indicator 2: Source of subject heading
  a. 0 — Library of Congress Subject Heading
  b. 5 — National Library of Canada (NLC) English Subject Heading
  c. 6 — National Library of Canada (NLC) French Subject Heading
  d. 7 — Source of Subject Heading or Term Specified in Subfield $2
- Subfields most commonly used:
  a. *$a:* Name
  b. *$b:* Subheading (R)
  c. *$d:* Date of conference meeting, etc. (R)
  d. *$c:* Place of meeting, conference, etc.
  e. *$t:* Title
  f. *$x:* General subdivision (R)
  g. *$y:* Chronological subdivision (R)
  h. *$z:* Geographical subdivision (R)
  i. *$2:* Source of subject heading or term
- Examples:
  a. 610 10 $aUnited States.$bArmy $xHistory$yCivil War, 1861-1865.
  b. 610 20 $aCanadian Open Golf Championship Tournament$d (1968:$cToronto, Ont.).

• 611 Subject Heading — Conference or Meeting (R): If the conference itself is the subject of the book, then the established name of the conference should be placed in the 611 field.
- Indicator 1: Type of conference or name of meeting
  a. 1 — Place or place and name
  b. 2 — Name (direct order)
- Indicator 2: Source of subject heading
  a. 0 — LC Subject Heading
  b. 5 — NLC—English Subject Heading
  c. 6 — NLC—French Subject Heading
  d. 7 — Sears Subject Heading
- Subfields most commonly used
  a. *$a:* Name
  b. *$c:* Place of meeting
  c. *$d:* Date
  d. *$n:* Number of the conference
- Example: 611 20 $aConference on Library Technology$d

• 630 Subject Heading — Uniform Title Heading (R): The 630 field is not recommended for use by school library personnel unless they have had specialised training in it.

- 650 Subject Added Entry — Topical Heading (R): The bulk of all subject headings will be listed in this field. Topical headings include general subject terms, including the names of events or objects.
  - Indicator 1: Normally blank
  - Indicator 2: Source of subject heading or authority
    a. 0 — Library of Congress Subject Heading
    b. 5 — NLC — English Subject Heading
    c. 6 — NLC — French Subject Heading
    d. 7 — Subject Heading From Source Specified in Subfield $2
  - Subfields most commonly used:
    a. *$a:* Topical subject heading
    b. *$x:* General subdivision (R)
    c. *$y:* Chronological subdivision (R)
    d. *$z:* Geographical subdivision (R)
    e. *$2:* Source of subject heading or term
  - Examples:
    a. 650 _7 $aMagic$2Sears
    b. 650 _0 $aAnimals.
    c. 650 _0 $aTaxation$zCanada.
    d. 650 _0 $aChurch and state in Germany$y20th century.
    e. 650 _5 $aInuit$zCanada.
    f. 650 _6 $aTimbres-poste$zCanada.
- 651 Subject Added Entry — Geographic Name (R): Places, natural regions, sites, parks, and political jurisdictions are placed in this field.
  - Indicator 1: Undefined
  - Indicator 2: Denotes the subject heading authority from which the heading was derived
    a. 0 —LC Subject Heading
    b. 5 —NLC—English Subject Heading
    c. 6 —NLC—French Subject Heading
    d. 7 —Subject Heading From Source Specified in Subfield $2
  - Subfields most commonly used:
    a. *$a:* Geographic name (R)
    b. *$x:* General subdivision (R)
    c. *$y:* Chronological subdivision (R)
    d. *$z:* Geographical subdivision (R)
    e. *$2:* Source of subject heading or term
  - Examples:
    a. 651 _0 $aCanada$xBoundaries$z United States.
    b. 651 _0 $aUnited States$xHistory $xChronology.
    c. 651 _0 $aGermany$xPolitics and government$y1918-1933.
- *690 Local Subject Headings (R):* It is not recommended that schools

indulge in creating their own subject headings. As strange as many subject headings derived from Sears or the Library of Congress may seem they are the international standard. Cataloguers are strongly encouraged to use approved headings only. The 690 field is reserved for those rare situations where no suitable heading can be located in the standard list of subject terms. The indicators and subfields in the 690 area are identical to the other 600 fields.

700 Level Fields

- 700 Added Entry — Personal Name (R): Typically, tracings such as editors, illustrators, and joint authors are entered in this field.
  - Indicator 1: Type of personal name:
    a. 0 — Forename only
    b. 1 — Single surname (most common)
    c. 2 — Multiple surname
    d. 3 — Family name
  - Indicator 2: Type of added entry
    a. Blank — No information provided 2 — Analytical entry (used for someone involved with only a portion of the work)
  - Subfields most commonly used:
    a. *$a:* Name
    b. *$c:* Titles and other words associated with the name
    c. *$d:* Date
    d. *$q:* Qualification of the name (fuller form)
    e. *$t:* Title of the work
  - Examples:
    a. 700 1_ $aGal, Laszlo.
    b. 700 1_ $aBerton, Pierre,$d1920-
    c. 700 1_ $aMillar, Ken,$d1915 —$tMoving target.
- 710 Added Entry — Corporate Name (R): Most school libraries can skip this field. It is used to add any additional corporate name which may be associated with the work. Coding for the field is the same as for the 110 main entry for corporate names.
  - Indicator 1: Type of Corporate name
    a. 1 — Place or place and name
    b. 2 — Name direct order (most common)
  - Indicator 2: Type of entry:
    a. Blank — No information provided
    b. 2 —Analytical entry
  - Subfields most commonly used:
    a. $a: Name
    b. $b: Subheading (R)
    c. $c: Place

d. $d: Date (R)
e. $t: Title of work

– Examples:
a. 710 1_ $aUnited States.$bArmy Map Service.
b. 710 2_ $a Law Society of Upper Canada.
c. 710 2_ $aFoundation for Inner Peace.$tA course in miracles.

800 Level Fields

- 856 Uniform Resource Location: This field is used for electronic location and access and contains information needed to locate an electronic resource, such as electronic journals and books. Indicators and subfields are being developed.

900 Level Fields

The local holdings fields are added to assist patrons in finding the material they require. The fields vary depending on the application software. For example, MicroCAT uses 090 for the call number and 595 for the local notes. BiblioFile and ISM use the 090 to 099 fields.

CATALOGING RULES

Cataloging rules have been defined to allow for consistent cataloging of various library materials across several persons of a cataloging team and across time. Users can use them to clarify how to find an entry and how to interpret the data in an entry. Cataloging rules prescribe which information about a bibliographic item is included in the entry and how this information is presented for the user; It may also aid to sort the entries in printing the catalogue. The larger a collection, the more elaborate cataloging rules are needed. Users cannot and do not want to examine hundreds of catalogue entries or even dozens of library items to find the one item they need. Currently, most cataloging rules are similar to, or even based on, the International Standard Bibliographic Description (ISBD), a set of rules produced by the International Federation of Library Associations and Institutions (IFLA) to describe a wide range of library materials. These rules organise the bibliographic description of an item in the following areas: title and statement of responsibility (author or editor), edition, material specific details (for example, the scale of a map), publication and distribution, physical description (for example, number of pages), series, notes, and standard number (ISBN).

The most commonly used set of cataloging rules in the English-speaking world are the Anglo-American Cataloguing Rules, 2nd Edition, or AACR2 for short. AACR2 provides rules for *descriptive cataloging* only and does not touch upon *subject cataloging*. AACR2 has been translated into many languages, for use around the world. In the German-speaking world there is also the *Regeln für die alphabetische Katalogisierung* (RAK). Library items that are written in a foreign script are, in some cases, transliterated to the script of the catalogue.

7

Children Libraries and Serials Tasks

INTRODUCTION

As per the aims and objectives are taking into consideration, the ICDL is unparallel. They strictly follow the pre-defined policy. The ICDL always promote cross-cultural development among children, and therefore it intentionally not use the machine translation. But it mentions some volunteer translator for the same. Within a short period of time ICDL has flourished rapidly in wellorganised way. It maintains the list having date wise addition of books in the collection. The ICDL is very transparent in its each policy and function.

ICDL: FOUNDATION

- *Collection*: To create a collection of more than 10,000 books in at least 100 languages that is freely available to children, teachers, librarians, parents, and scholars throughout the world via the Internet. The materials included in the collection reflect similarities and differences in cultures, societies, interests, lifestyles, and priorities of peoples around the world. The collection's focus is on identifying materials that help children to understand the world around them and the global society in which they live.
- *Education*: To develop a greater understanding of the relationship between children's access to a digital collection of multicultural materials and children's attitudes towards books, libraries, reading, technology, and other countries and their cultures.
- *Technology*: To collaborate with children as design partners in the development of computer interface technologies that support children in searching, browsing, reading, and sharing books in electronic form.
- *Business*: To provide a platform for operational excellence that insures the Library grows in strict accordance with it strategic priorities and in a manner that leverages its outstanding human and intellectual resources to achieve the Library's mission of reaching as many children as possible with the best of children's literature.

CONTEXT OF EVALUATION

Digital libraries are complex social, institutional and technical systems. No evaluation can possibly address all of these aspects together. Thus, different approaches have been used for different evaluation goals.

Context includes selection of a goal, framework, viewpoint or level(s), basic approach or perspective of evaluation. There are different types of approaches of digital library evaluation on the basis of different aspects.

No single approach can exhaustively evaluate the all aspects of any digital library.

Here we try to incorporate most of the approaches as possible.

The approaches are:

- *System-centered approach*: Most prevalent. Involves study of some aspect of performance. Includes assessing effectiveness and/or efficiency of some feature or some specific design or some technological component. Applied in a number of studies with results that may inform specific choices in design or operations.
- *Human-centered approach*: Also widely applied. Involves study of behaviour in respect to given information needs, such as information seeking, browsing, searching including performance appraisal of given tasks, either predetermined or observed in natural settings. Used in a number of studies that illuminated human behaviour, requirements, needs, or difficulties encountered. Provides implications for design, but indirectly rather than directly.
- *Usability-centered approach*: Involves assessment of different features, particularly in respect to portals, by users. It is a bridge between systems- and human-centered approaches. Used in several studies with mixed, or self-evident results.
- *Ethnographic approach*: Involves study of life-ways, culture and customs in a digital library environment. Also involves study of impact of a digital library on a given community. Applied successfully in a few studies, with illuminating results, particularly as to impact.
- *Anthropological approach*: Involves study of different stakeholders or communities and their cultures in relation to a given digital library. Applied in one study with interesting results illuminating barriers between stakeholder communities.
- *Sociological approach*: Involves assessment of situated action or user communities in social setting of a digital library. Applied in one study with disappointing results.
- *Economic approach*: Involves study of costs, cost benefits, economic values and impacts. Strangely, it was applied at the outset of digital library history (*e.g.*, project PEAK) but now the approach is not really present at all.

CRITERIA FOR EVALUATION

Criteria reflecting performance as related to selected objectives. They include:

- What parameters of performance were concentrate on?
- What dimension or characteristic were evaluate?

  Criteria refer to chosen standard(s) to judge things by. Criteria are then used to develop measures. The importance of criteria follows from this truism: there can be no evaluation without explicitly or implicitly having some criterion or criteria first.Since, 1950's evaluation of IR systems uses relevance as the basic criterion for evaluation. Libraries use a variety of (more or less) standardised criteria for evaluation of components, such as a collection, or services, such as reference. Digital library efforts have not as yet developed anything similar as to evaluation criteria. A summary of most often used criteria follows.

USABILITY

Usability has been used widely in digital library evaluation, but there is no uniform definition of what does it cover in digital library context. Usability is a very general criterion that covers a lot of ground and includes many specific criteria – it is a meta term This was pretty much the umbrella under which usability was used in digital library evaluation. Here is a list of specific usability criteria applied in various studies:

- Content (of a portal or site):
  - Accessibly, availability
  - Clarity (as presented)
  - Complexity (organisation, structure)
  - Informativeness
  - Transparency
  - Understanding, effort to understand
  - Adequacy
  - Coverage, overlap,
  - Quality, accuracy
  - Validity, reliability
  - Authority
- *Process*: Carrying out tasks such as search, navigate, browse, find, evaluate or obtain a resource, etc.
  - learnability to carry out
  - Effort/time to carry out
  - Convenience, ease of use
  - Lostness (confusion)
  - Support for carrying out
  - Completion (achievement of task)

  - Interpretation difficulty
  - Sureness in results
  - Error rate
- Format:
  - Attractiveness
  - Sustaining efforts
  - Consistency
  - Representation of labels (how well are concepts Represented?)
  - communicativeness of messages
- Overall assessment:
  - Satisfaction
  - Success
  - Relevance, usefulness of results
  - Impact, value
  - Quality of experience
  - Barriers, irritability
  - Preferences
  - Learning

SYSTEMS FEATURES

As digital libraries are systems, many traditional systems evaluation criteria were used.

Some pertain to performance of technology others to performance of given processes or algorithms using technology.

- Technology performance:
  - Response time
  - Processing time,
  - Speed
  - Capacity
  - Load
- Process/algorithm performance:
  - Relevance (of obtained results)
  - Clustering
  - Similarity
  - Functionality
  - Flexibility
  - Comparison with human performance
  - Error rate
  - Optimisation
  - Logical decisions
  - Path length
  - Click throughs
  - Retrieval time

- Overall system:
  - Maintainability
  - Scalability
  - Interoperability
  - Sharability
  - Costs

USAGE

A number of studies concentrated on use of a digital library, considering this as evaluation.

Usage in itself is a criterion involving studies of:

- Usage patterns
- Use of materials
- Usage statistics
- Who uses what, when
- For what reasons/decisions

ETHNOGRAPHIC AND OTHER CRITERIA

Several ethnographic and anthropological studies used criteria derived from those fields. Among others, these involve determination of conceptions and misconceptions in and between different groups, their practices and environments, their culture, their language and frames of reference, priorities, learning, impacts and similar aspects that provide comparative evaluation in a broader context of a digital library..

ICDL: EVALUATION METHOD

The range of methods used in digital library evaluations is wide. It would be hard to find a scholarly evaluation method that was not used. It involves: What measures and measuring instruments were used? What samples were used? What procedures were used for data collection? What procedures were used for data analysis? In the present study involves mainly limited user study and systematic study of web site of ICDL with respect to Intel Pentium PCs with MS Windows having 14", 17" and 19" monitors.

Actually methodology includes:

- Surveys, including direct questionnaires and online surveys
- Structured interviews
- Focus groups
- Observations
- Task accomplishment
- Think aloud
- Case studies
- Transaction log analyses
- Experimentation

- Records analysis
- Usage analysis
- Documents, meeting, communication analysis (anthropology)
- Economic analysis

DATA COLLECTION

As the scope is very much little as per time span for evaluation and other constraints, only user survey and web site study were used for data collection.

ICDL: ANALYSIS AND EVALUATION

AUTHORITY

The ICDL was initially created by an interdisciplinary research team at the University of Maryland in cooperation with the Internet Archive. Members of the team include computer scientists, librarians, educational technologists, classroom teachers, graphic designers, and graduate students from the University of Maryland's (UMD) College of Information Studies (CLIS) and the UMD Human-Computer Interaction Lab (HCIL), a leader in children's interface design. The ICDL is now the principal activity of the independent not-for-profit ICDL Foundation, which continues to work closely with the University of Maryland by providing generous support for ICDL related research in the Human Computer Interaction Laboratory and the College of Information Studies. (The ICDL is a five year project funded primarily by the National Science Foundation (NSF) and the Institute for Museum and Library Services (IMLS) for creating a digital library of international children's books.

This five-year research project, created in collaboration with the Internet Archive and conducted by the University of Maryland, has five primary goals):

- To create a collection of more than 10,000 books in at least 100 languages that is freely available to children, teachers, librarians, parents, and scholars throughout the world via the Internet;
- To collaborate with children as design partners in the development of computer interface technologies that support children in searching, browsing, reading, and sharing books in electronic form;
- to better understand the concepts of rights management and "fair use" in a digital age;
- To evaluate the impact that access to digital materials may have on collection development and programming practices in school and public libraries;
- To develop a greater understanding of the relationship between children's access to a digital collection of multicultural materials and children's attitudes towards books, libraries, reading, technology, and other countries and cultures.

An initial prototype of the ICDL was introduced at a celebration at the Library of Congress in Washington, DC, in November 2002. At that time, the collection consisted of 181 books, which were provided by national libraries and other government agencies, public library systems, collaborating publishers, and individual authors and illustrators. Approximately half of the titles were within copyright protection and half were freely available in the public domain.

The materials selected for the prototype generally were in compliance with the selection criteria established for the collection by the National Advisory Board of Librarians; however, efforts were made to acquire and digitise as diverse a collection as possible to ensure that the functions of the ICDL interface could be effectively tested. Now International Children's Digital Library Foundation manages ICDL. From very beginning ICDL was developed and powered by well-reputed institutions. The ICDL Foundation has famous and scholar personalities in Foundation Directors and Board of Advisors.

AUTHENTI CITY

The information in the web site are very much authentic because the metadata regarding each item/book are explicitly stated with each and every book. Again authority and authenticity are correlated to each other.

COLLECTION/RESOURCES

The collection in the ICDL is comprised of different children books written in different languages. All books consisting of the scanned pages arranged serially. At the end of the initial research period, it is anticipated that the collection of the ICDL will consist of approximately 10,000 materials in at least 100 languages. Materials within the collection are made available through the Library over the Internet to all users without charge. The project does not support downloading, copying or printing of any materials in the collection.

The materials selected for inclusion in the ICDL are those that:

- Support the understanding of similarities and differences among and within countries, peoples, and cultures;
- Promote tolerance and acceptance;
- Are considered relevant to children in today's world;
- Have a high degree of appeal for children of an age between 3 and 13;
- Meet professionally accepted quality standards in terms of content, format, and presentation; and,
- Can be presented effectively in a digital format.

Relevance

Librarians, teachers, authors, illustrators, publishers, and children from all over the world suggest books that they think should be considered for our collection. Each book must be carefully evaluated before it can be added to the Library. In accordance with the goal of the ICDL, all information are relevant. Again as per the audience is concerned, the books included in the library are of basically children books. The metadata associated with the item are reasonable and relevant.

Formats

The formats of the books in the ICDL are of scanned image.
The digitised formats are obtained through:

- *Choosing books*: The ultimate selection of the books to be scanned.
- *Scanning books*: Books have to be scanned and saved TIFF image format into our database in order to get the book pages into our computers. Scanners take very detailed pictures of pages and save the images in a way that the computers of ICDL can recognise. Some of the books that are scanned for the ICDL are cut up and sucked into a scanner one page at a time to be automatically scanned. Other books are scanned one page at a time without destroying the books. Some of the really old books in the collection have to be repaired before they are scanned because the scanning process could cause them to fall apart. Sometimes the people who donate books scan them for ICDL. Other times the people who work at the ICDL scan them. Sometimes ICDL pay another company to scan books for the library. The technical specification including formats, naming convention and guidelines for scanning are enumerated below:
  - Technical Specifications:
    a. *File Format:* Uncompressed TIFF
    b. *Pixel depth*: 24 bit colour
    c. *Spatial resolution*: 300 dpi
    d. *Example*: Caralic-0001.tif (11.5 MB)
  - Naming Convention:
    a. Filenames should use the format <id>-####.tif where:
       i. <id>

Guidelines

- Scanning of the book cover to cover, including blank pages. Scan 0001 is assumed to be the front cover. If all pages are scanned, there should be an even number of scans.
- All scans should represent a single page, even if an image spans multiple pages.
- Cropping of the scan to the edge of the page. Clear direction is given to make all scans, including the cover page, the same size and dimensions (*i.e.,* number of pixels), or as close to the same size as possible.

- Scanning of pages with rotated images as they appear in the book.
- Provision of address for contact ICDL authority at icdl-rights@cs.umd.edu if senders have any questions.

Library Materials Selection

Selection Criteria for the ICDL

Materials selected for inclusion in the ICDL collection during the first five years of the project must support the research goals of the project and must be appropriate for one or both of the primary audiences identified as users of the Library.

The materials in the International Children's Digital Library, which are intended primarily to be used by children, parents, teachers, and school and public librarians, should:

- Support the understanding of similarities and differences among and within countries, peoples, and cultures;
- Promote tolerance and acceptance;
- Contribute to children's understanding of the diversity of the global society;
- Have a high degree of appeal for children of an age between 3 and 13;
- Meet professionally accepted quality standards in terms of content, format, and presentation;
- Be considered relevant to children in today's world;
- Be appropriate for the age levels of the intended audience for the collection;
- Be presented in their entirety and not adapted or abridged from their original published form; however, works originally published as abridgements or adaptations of other works may be included in the collection; and
- Be presented effectively in a digital format.
- Expand the scope and variety of cultures represented in the collection;
- Have achieved historical significance;
- Represent exemplary artistic, historic, and literary qualities, such as award winners; or
- Contribute to the project's research priorities.

Acquisitions Process

Materials included in the collection may be:

- Freely available in the public domain;
- Contributed by a National Library or another national agency that holds the rights to the materials;

- Acquired by the ICDL under a contractual agreement with the creator(s) or publisher(s) of the work or with another entity that has legal authority for its intellectual property rights; or
- Collaboratively acquired by the ICDL and other private or public special collections through a contractual agreement with the rights holders

Reconsideration of Materials

Objections to materials included in the collection will be considered by the ICDL National Advisory Board of Librarians and/or the International Advisory Board. The Board(s) will use the established selection criteria in determining whether the item is appropriate for the collection. The recommendation of the Board(s) will be given to the Director of Collection Development for the Library. The final decision concerning the retention or withdrawal of a work will be made by the Director of Collection Development.

USER INTERFACE

All web sites particularly a digital library is only as good as its interface. The interface is the entry point into the library. The user interface is the aggregate of means by which people (the users) interact with a particular machine, device, computer programme or other complex tool (the system). The user interface provides means of: Input - allowing the users to control the system, Output - allowing the system to inform. The junction between a user and a computer programme.

User interface design important for several reasons.

- First of all the more intuitive the user interface the easier it is to use, and the easier it is to use and the less expensive to use it.
- The better the user interface the easier it is to train people to use it, reducing your training costs.
- The better your user interface the less help people will need to use it, reducing your support costs.
- The better your user interface the more your users will like to use it, increasing their satisfaction with the work that you have done.

The ICDL uses Graphical User Interface (GUI) that takes advantage of the computer's graphics capabilities to make the programme easier to use. In ICDL, as maximum users are of 3-13 years age group, the GUI is appropriate.

The ICDL interface uses most of the basic components of GUI such as:

- *Pointing device*: The mouse that enables users to select objects on the display screen.
- *Icons*: Small pictures that represent commands, files, or windows. By moving the pointer to the icon and pressing a mouse button, users can execute a command or convert the icon into a window.

- *Desktop*: The area on the display screen where icons are grouped is often referred to as the desktop because the icons are intended to represent real objects on a real desktop. The ICDL interface is comprising of well-grouped desktop.
- *Windows*: In ICDL interface no such frames are used by dividing the screen into different areas where in each window user can run different programmes. But there is the possibility of opening separate window for certain purpose.
- *Menus*: Most graphical user interfaces let the users to execute commands by selecting a choice from a menu. The ICDL uses different menus and drop-down sub-menus in each menu for various information. The animated presentations of menus create a attracting and elegant effect.

Presentation

Overall presentation of web site is quite satisfactory in ICDL. It includes:

- *Information flow*: Information flow throughout the web site is very much impressive.
- *Navigation*: One can search or browse the required information directly by using different attributes that are relevant for the children. Different types of book reader are there for presenting the pages of the book. Again the options like next page, zoom in, zoom out etc are present for smooth navigation.
- *Visuals and icons*: Meaningful icons and graphics are used that create a pleasant flavour to the eye.
- *About texts*: Texts are legible and nicely looking.
- *Working with colour*: Colours used for the different components are really attractive and eye appealing mainly for the children.
- *Screen design and layout*: The ICDL uses tables for accommodating various elements of the web page.

Consistencey

Consistency must be acquired in many fields like visual appearance, control, and functionality, etc., for increasing the recall of the users. It includes:

- Different functions keys always have the same effects throughout the site.
- Prompt and help messages appear in the same way and the same place throughout
- Different colours used in the web site always have the same meaning
- Consistent use of headings
- Consistent use of terminologies and abbreviations throughout
- The main menus appeared on the top portion of the home page is absent in the other subsequent pages.

Organisation

The organisation of the information and different components of the web pages are very important for the users. The proper organisation may lead easy navigation of the relevant information the user needed.

It includes:

- Relative positions of different information in the page are nicely organised.
- Right linking of relevant information
- Well positioning of functional keys
- Inclusions of all relevant information in the small space mainly in case of advance search.
- Getting of information by minimal mouse clicking
- Systematic organisation of information so that users get the information they need by minimum scrolling of pages

Interactiveness

It includes dynamic nature of pages where web page cans response to the users. It is very much effective a informative web site like digital library. The ICDL has provisions of interactivity. In the searching mode, the Boolean search is very much interactive to the user's search query.

Attractiveness

It includes overall getup of the site.

It may comprising of:

- Use of proper colours in accordance with the children's liking and choice
- Use of different graphics instead of texts.
- Use of colorful cartoon-like icons
- In location search there is the provision of graphical search by using world map which is very attractive to the children

User Friendliness

User friendliness is the ultimate aims of user interface. The design should be synchronise with the user's needs and behaviours. The ICDL web site is very user friendly. The target audience, *i.e.,* children of different geographical and linguistic regions of the world, can easily find their relevant information through easy navigational tools.

There are various provisions of browsing and searching of books. In case of Boolean search, the search phrase formulation is shown in the page explicitly (e.g. Main collection AND Ten to thirteen AND Pink covers AND hobbies and crafts = 1 Books). In every searching and browsing mode there is the provision of language of the book, which is very much user friendly as per the children of diverse linguistic regions are concerned. Again country wise books are also useful for the wide range of children.

USE, USAGE AND USABILITY

The usage and usability of digital library is gaining the focal point of study. Actually the use of any digital object is the ultimate objective of any web site or digital library. Therefore the information must be uniform, consistent and well-organised, so that one can retrieve the relevant information by using navigational tools. The ICDL can be accessed through the commercial search engine like Yahoo, Google, etc.

The following search data are shown:

- Google search engine:
  - Search by the term 'ICDL' fetched 775000 listing in 0.12 seconds.
  - Search by 'international children's digital library' lists 3520000 sites in 0.11 seconds
  - Search by exact phrase "international children's digital library" through advanced search fetched 96800 listing in 0.14 seconds
- Yahoo Search Engine:
  - Search by the term 'ICDL' fetched 775000 listing in 0.12 seconds.
  - Search by 'international children's digital library' lists 3810000 sites in 0.02 seconds
  - Search by exact phrase "international children's digital library" through advanced search fetched 63500 listing in 0.31 seconds
- Use and users' statistics:
  - The ICDL has been visited by over a million unique visitors since, the launch in November, 2002.
  - Google is the number one Web site directing Internet users to the ICDL, followed by Farsibooksonline and Yahoo.
  - The users come from 166 different countries, most frequently from:
    a. United States (50%)
    b. South Africa (15%)
    c. China (7%)
    d. United Kingdom (6%)
    e. Canada (5%)
    f. Iran, Islamic Republic of (4%)
    g. Taiwan (4%)
    h. Philippines (4%)
    i. Australia (3%)
    j. Egypt (2%)
  - *Top books visited*: Our book preview pages have been visited over 650,000 times.

- *Book reader*: Our standard book reader is chosen most of the time to read books in the ICDL. The book readers receive the following use:a.Standard reader (52%) b.Adobe reader (23%) c.Comic reader (15%) d.Spiral reader (9%) e.Plus reader (1%)
- *Registered users*: On May 25, 2005, we launched a new interface that allows library users to log in with a user name and password. Currently, registered users can choose their preferred search interface and what language the library appears in. Kids can also choose a monster to guard their password. In the future, users will be able to personalise their search results, save favorite books on a bookshelf, and return to the last page they were reading. Here are some facts about our registered users:
    a. 1082 adults, 508 children -1031 females, 560 males,Preferred languages (of the nine languages the library is currently available in):
        i. English (72%)
        ii. Spanish (11%)
        iii. Chinese (5%)
        iv. Persian (4%)
        v. Arabic (4%)
        vi. Filipino (1%)
        vii. French (1%)
        viii. German (1%)
        ix. Hebrew (1%)
    b. Adults can choose their preferred search interface, and they choose Simple Search 73% of the time, followed by Advanced (24%), and Location (3%).
- Connectivity: The connection speed of our users breaks down to 17% dial-up, 40% high-speed, and 43% unknown.

From the data we can conclude that the library is used by varieties of users in all respect. We can say that the usability of ICDL is good as the aims of the Foundation is concerned. But still there are some scope of attaining the degree of usage and usability of the library.

Different usage and usability criteria used in ICDL and gaps if any are enumerated below.

- Graphics,
- Text,
- Content/Information
- Updates
- Layout/Space
- Presentation of information: It concerns the implications of using colours, fonts and display styles to present information. The colours

used in the ICDL pages are very much eye soothing and also attractive. The display styles for pages in the book are very lucrative in the spiral reader.

- Categorisation of Information
- Navigation,
- Colour,
- Visual Appearance,
- Advertisements/Pop-ups/Animation,
- *Downloading Time*: It includes factors in designing that impacts speed of downloading. As all pages of books in the library are of scanned images, it takes some amount of time to be downloaded.

SECURITY/PRIVACY

Security/privacy is the vital issue for any digital library. The ICDL states "Feel secure using the ICDL knowing that we protect the privacy of our members, especially children". The International Children's Digital Library (ICDL) is committed to protecting the safety and privacy of the users, especially children. The ICDL does not require anyone to provide any personal information to use the site and no one is excluded from the site for not providing personal information. The ICDL does allow users to create an optional profile that provides access to extra features such as selecting a preferred reading language. If a user chooses to create a profile, ICDL ask them to provide the following personal but not personally-identifiable information (only a user name and password, etc., are required):

- User name
- Password
- Age
- Gender
- Preferred reading language

users who register may choose to use their e-mail address as their user name. This information will only be used for two purposes. First, it allows the ICDL to send users a new password if they forget their old one. Second, adult users who register with their e-mail address may also opt to be on our mailing list to receive announcements about the ICDL

COST EFFECTIVENESS

As information are only accessed through network, the cost effectiveness is the vital issue when evaluating a digital library. The books can be accessed in ICDL without paying any money; it is absolutely free of cost.

SERVICES: REAL LIFE SITUATION

Services are comprised of searching and browsing of relevant information using the various tools provided in the web site. This is the ultimate objective of any digital library. The search statistics may help to develop better interface.

Between May 25, 2005 and August 31, 2005, ICDL looked at what the library users were searching for. This data helped to improve the search interfaces and understood what library users are looking for in a digital library and accordingly new interface was designed on March 22, 2006. Users overwhelming prefer the Simple search interface. The usage of the various search interfaces breaks down to the following:

- Simple search (71%)
- Advanced search (15%)
- Text or keyword search (10%)
- Location search (3%)
- Author search (1%).

Availability

Most of the books included in the ICDL are always available through the searching and browsing tools. Actually I tried for 100 books and no such false link is there. As the total collection is not verified I prefer to use the term 'most of the books'.

Searchability

Searchability basically includes effectiveness in searching and browsing so as to get required pages of the books. At first it is better to enumerate the provisions of searching and browsing in the ICDL site.

Searching

Simple Search

Various search facilities are there in the simple search. The menus/icons are arranged in four sides of the page. The provisions are: Location search

In location search there are two versions

- Graphical version using globe having world map and provision for turning the globe by clicking the arrow provided for the purpose. This is effective for little children who just learning the locations in the world map.
- Text version by using names of continents and countries.

Advanced Search

Advance search is composed of using various criteria for single search. Actually it is Boolean search using only AND operator.

The criteria are:

- Keywords
- Language
- Audience: Age, collection, etc.

- Appearance: Cover colour, format, length, shape, etc.
- Content: Continents, character, countries, time period
- Type: Feeling, rating, etc.
- Subject: Culture, history, science and nature, animals, etc.

The beauty of advance search is "unified search using more than one criteria used in the simple search at a time". The stating of search formulation statement is another effective feature in the advance search. The statement (e.g. Main collection AND Ten to thirteen AND Pink covers AND Hobbies and crafts= 1 Books) may increase the confidence of the users.

Keyword Search

As the pages of the books are of scanned image in TIFF format and no provision of using OCR technology, full text search is not possible. It only includes the meta-information about the books.

Directions:

- Typing the keywords into the search box
- Selecting the language user is searching in from the pull down menu
- Clicking the Search button to search for books with matching information

Browsing

Browsing of books will be done through four ways mentioned below:

- Recently added books
- Award-winning books
- Full book list
- Author and illustrator list

The browsing through Author and Illustrator list are effective but there are the oddness:

- No such indication element for author and illustrator; names are alphabetically arranged according to the surnames but no rendering of names are there which create confusion to some extent.

Referral

The ICDL provides referral service by mentioning link through which one can get the books. When we select any book, the metadata are listed in the right side to the cover/title image of the book. At the end of metadata, there are the provisions of links stating the addresses of the organisations from which one can purchase the same.

Links

The links in the web site are very much systematic and relevant. Not so false link is there in the page so far as my verification is concerned.. The links in the 'announcement' in the home page is not retrieved. After selecting a book to be retrieved there is the provision of link to the similar books available in the ICDL. No such external links are there for similar books the ICDL has. The links among the different pages are explicitly shown in the Sitemap menu.

POLICY

The policy of any digital library like ICDL, includes the written guidelines for attaining consistency and effectiveness in the web pages. The policy in the present study is comprised of collection development, copyright, privacy and link.

Collection Development Policy

Examination of the criteria used to select books that are appropriate for the ICDL collection. All works will be presented in their entirety and will not be adapted or abridged from their original published form; however, works originally published as abridgements or adaptations of other works may be included in the collection.

Materials included in the collection may be:

- Currently available in print and within copyright;
- Out of print but within the copyright protection of the country in which they were
- Published; or
- Freely available in the public domain.

Copyright Policy

Find out how ICDL protect the interests of rights holders while sharing their books with audiences throughout the world. The International Children's Digital Library respects the intellectual property rights and other proprietary rights of others. The ICDL has negotiated rights to include the books in the collection. These rights do not allow downloading, printing, or further distribution of the books in ICDL by the users. To obtain permission to download, print or distribute the books in ICDL, the user must be contacted to the rights holders directly.

The ICDL software does not support printing, emailing or saving of material accessible through the ICDL If any user believes that his copyright has been violated by material available through the ICDL, there is clear statement on behave of the ICDL Copyright Agent with the following information:

- Identification of the copyrighted work that user claim has been infringed;
- An exact description of where the material about which user complain is located within the ICDL collection;
- Users address, telephone number, and e-mail address;
- A statement by user that he has a good-faith belief that the disputed use is not authorised by the copyright owner, its agent, or the law;

- A statement by user, made under penalty of perjury, that the information in users notice is accurate and that the users are the owner of the copyright interest involved or are authorised to act on behalf of that owner;

Privacy Policy

ICDL is always trying to protect the privacy of the users/members, especially children. The privacy is maintained particularly for the personal information of the users. More provisions are already analysed in the Security/privacy section.

Links Policy

Links appearing on the ICDL web site must conform to the selection criteria for the books included in the collection. The sites linked should expand, enhance, and support books included in the collection. Sites linked to the ICDL must:1.Have a high degree of appeal for children from ages 3-13; 2.Support the understanding and use of books in the collection; 3.Be appropriate for the age levels of the intended audience for the collection; 4.Include content that is relevant and of interest to children ages 3-13; 5.Support the understanding of similarities and difference among and within countries, peoples, and cultures; 6.Contribute to children's understanding of the diversity of the global society; and, 7..Meet professionally accepted quality standards in terms of content, format, and presentation.

LEGAL ASPECTS

Some books are very old and others are just like those that user might find in school or public library. Most of the old books are out of copyright. This means that nobody owns these books so ICDL Foundation can put them on the ICDL without getting permission from anybody. For the newer books, the authority must get permission from the people or the company that owns the words and the pictures in the books. All of the books in the ICDL must meet the collection development standards. These standards are the rules that use to choose which books can go into the ICDL. The Advisory Board of Librarians and International Advisory Board created the rules for the purpose. Some of the legal aspects are included in the section 'Copyright policy'.

CONSTRAINS

- No main menus in the same fashion in the pages other than home page.
- No links in few places
- The ICDL software does not support printing, emailing or saving of material accessible through the ICDL

- No born digital objects are included in the ICDL
- External hyperlinks are few
- Some contradictory data exit
- The scanned pages need to remove noise
- No provisions of audio that are interesting to the intended audience
- No provision of machine translation

RECOMMENDATIONS

The ICDL has its strong objectives and planned policy. According to the aims and objectives of ICDL Foundation, the web site of International Children's Digital Library is very impressive in all respect.

Still some recommendations are given for the overall development of the ICDL.

- Some good animations may be inserted to the menus/icons to add the extra flavour
- Besides books, some non-book material like audio, video, animation, etc., may be included to instigate appetite of the children
- The scope will be given for inclusion of born digital books
- Digital noise in the scanned images have to be removed for better viewing the pages
- Some external links for similar information may be sited to the web page

CONCLUSION

The International Children's Digital Library (ICDL) was initially created by an interdisciplinary research team at the University of Maryland in cooperation with the Internet Archive. Members of the team include computer scientists, librarians, educational technologists, classroom teachers, graphic designers, and graduate students from the University of Maryland's (UMD) College of Information Studies (CLIS) and the UMD Human-Computer Interaction Lab (HCIL), a leader in children's interface design. The mission of the International Children's Digital Library Foundation (ICDL Foundation) is to support the world's children in becoming effective members of the global community - who exhibit tolerance and respect for diverse cultures, languages and ideas by making the best in children's literature available online free of charge.

8

Libraries Serials in the Digital Era

INTRODUCTION

By allowing users to search multiple databases simultaneously, federated search engines may save some steps in getting results from various library resources, and may also attain search results from databases users otherwise would not try without the federated search.

Even librarians at reference desks sometimes notice a good number of search results from databases they might not expect would have many good hits. But in no way can the federated search compete with Google in Google's strengths: speed, simplicity, ease of use, and convenience. Nor can the federated search truly serve as one-stop shopping for all library databases as people hoped, because some databases cannot be searched by the federated search for various reasons. The federated search probably cannot replace information literacy education or the learning process either, partly because it cannot make searching as easy as a Google search, as serious research may require selecting various information sources beyond Google results. In a certain sense, the federated search shifts the process of selecting a database from "before" performing searches to "after" performing searches.

Users still need to learn the functions of the library OPAC and periodicals indexes with names like ABI, CINAHL, ERIC, MLA, and CHICAGO, etc. It is also very helpful for users to learn other information literacy basics, such as the ability to interpret bibliography or to tell the difference between books, book chapters, and periodical articles, in order to make better use of the federated search engine offered by their libraries.

FEDERATED SEARCH

Federated search is the simultaneous search of multiple online databases and is an emerging feature of automated, Web-based library and information retrieval systems. It is also often referred to as a portal, as opposed to simply a Web-based search engine. It is sometime termed as broadcast search, parallel search, cross reference search, etc. Various terms are used to refer to these tools in the literature including: metasearchers, crosssearchers, cross-database searchers, portals, broadcast searchers or parallel searchers.

The term metasearcher is particularly prominent and is the term adopted by the United States National Information Standards Organisation (NISO), which has developed a Metasearch Initiative. However as Fryer explains, the term metasearcher can cause confusion due to its association with web Metasearch engines such as Metacrawler which function in a different way to federated search tools. The term federated searching is the function of search tools, which search a number of databases, particularly subscription databases, simultaneously with one interface. The content searched by federated search tools is content that could not normally be searched via a web search engine.

DEFINITIONS

Researcher defines federated search as, "Transforming a query and broadcasting it to a group of disparate databases with the appropriate syntax, merging the results collected from the databases, presenting them in a succinct and unified format with minimal duplication, and allowing the library patron to sort the merged result set by various criteria". In simple words, Federated searching will be defined as a search system using a common interface that enables the simultaneous searching of databases from a variety of vendors. Federated search technology enables users to search multiple information resources simultaneously through one search query. Users can then view search results in a single integrated list. In other words, users do no longer need to consult each information resource individually.

Instead, they can search multiple library catalogs (OPACs), Web sites (e.g. Amazon.com, Google, etc.), subscription and citation databases all at once. Federated search technology is an integral component of an Information Portal, which provides the interface to diverse information resources. Once the user enters his or her search query in the search box of the Information Portal, the system uses federated search technology to send the search string to each resource that is incorporated into the Portal.

The individual information resources then send the Information Portal a list of results from the search query. Users can view the number of documents retrieved in each resource and link directly to each search result. Metasearch, this word is synonymous to federated searching, people find no difference between federated searching but there is slight difference between federated and meta searching.

NEED AND PURPOSE OF FEDERATED SEARCH TOOLS

The need and purpose of the federated searching are as follows:

- The growth of different types of databases, produced by different suppliers, with numerous interfaces and logins means that library users can find it confusing when attempting to access information;

- Library OPACs and web-pages have been alienating users with their use of library terminology and by including long lists of databases that users find it difficult to select from and search;
- The needs and expectations of library users, particularly students using academic libraries. The growth of different types of databases, produced by different suppliers, with numerous interfaces and logins means that library users can find it confusing when attempting to access information.

There are certain purposes which can be served by the federated search are as follows:-

- Transforming a query and broadcasting it to a group of disparate databases with the appropriate syntax.
- Merging the results collected from the databases,
- Presenting them in a succinct and unified format with minimal duplication,
- Providing a means, performed either automatically or by the portal user, to sort the merged result set.

In traditional search engines such as Google, only sources that have been indexed by the search engine's crawler technology can be searched, retrieved and accessed. The large volume of documents housed in databases is not open to traditional Internet search engines because of limitations in crawler technology.

Federated searching resolves this issue by the technique described above and makes these deep Web documents searchable without having to visit each database individually.

ADVANTAGES OF FEDERATED SEARCH

There are certain advantages of using Federated Searches. Some of them are as follows:

- The reduced time it takes to do a basic search is benefit enough.
- Unified access to diverse content sources.
- Simultaneous searching across all sources.
- Ability to Simple search as well as advanced search.
- Integrated results which are easy to view and use.
- Direct links to the native source for further searching.
- Ability to filter, sort, save, print, export and e-mail search results

SEARCH MODELS

Search on data bases starts with simple search formulation using single keyterm and combinations of terms. The search results thus obtained can be listed in simple predefined format or using user customised format to get desired information. Various search models indicate the interactions of users search formulations and its interface with databases in a Library or online web access to aggregated databases.

OLD SEARCH MODEL

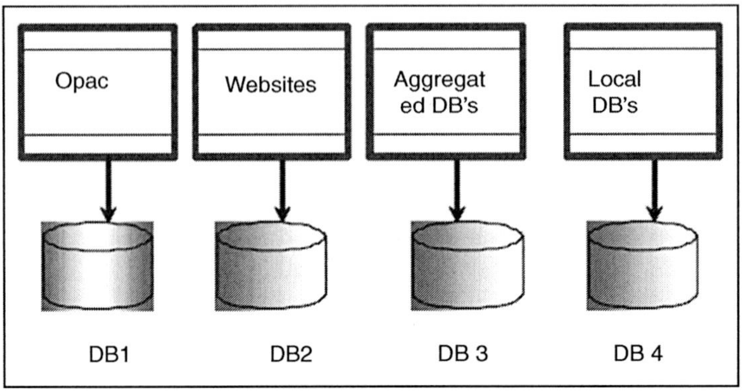

Fig. Old Srearch Model.

Without a federated search tool, each database requires its own unique search tool - significantly complicating and slowing the search process for patrons. In this kind of search model user submit their search query to individual database or search engines etc and individually they get their required information. This kind of search tools are very time consuming and most of the time user didn't get their desired information.

FEDERATED SEARCH MODEL

Using federated search, a single tool searches and accesses all databases with one, easy to use interface.

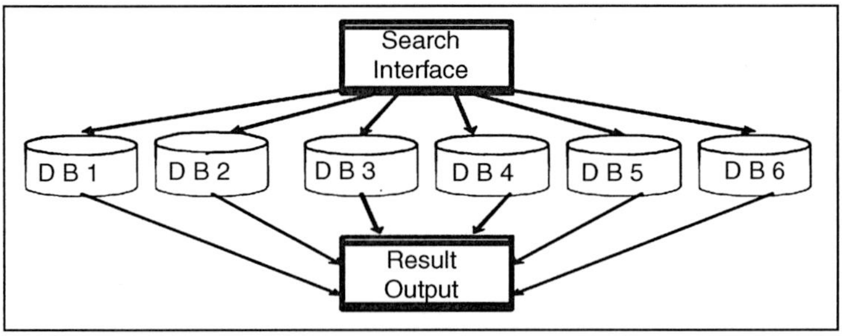

Fig. Federated Search Model.

It provides opportunity to the users that they get their desired information from various databases, search engines, etc.

FEDERATED SEARCH TECHNOLOGIES

There are mainly four technologies used for federated searching.

- Screen scraping or HTTP
- Z39.50 protocol

- ZING - SRW protocol
- XML gateway

SCREEN SCRAPPING OR HTTP

"Hyper Text Transport Protocol" - HTTP is the single most important technology that drives the web and yet remains virtually transparent. Without this protocol HTML and XML via the web would not be able to perform the myriad of tasks that we put them to daily.

The Hypertext Transfer Protocol (HTTP) is an application-level protocol for distributed, collaborative, hypermedia information systems. HTTP has been in use by the World-Wide Web global information initiative since, 1990. The HTTP protocol is a request/response protocol.

A client sends a request to the server in the form of a request method, URI, and protocol version, followed by a MIME-like message containing request modifiers, client information, and possible body content over a connection with a server.

HTTP communication usually takes place over TCP/IP connections. TCP guarantees that packets arriving to and from the web server are error free and in the right order. It doesn't however guarantee that packets arrive no matter what the network conditions are. When communications are congested or unavailable web page delivery is slow and can time-out.

Z39.50 PROTOCOL

Z39.50 is an American national standard for information retrieval. It is formally known as ANSI/NISO Z39.50-1995 - Information Retrieval (Z39.50): Application Service Definition and Protocol Specification.

This document specifies a set of rules and procedures for the behaviour of two systems communicating for the purposes of database searching and information retrieval. As a network application standard, Z39.50 is an open standard that enables communication between systems that run on different hardware and use different software The Z39.50 standard was developed to overcome the problems associated with multiple databases searching such as having to know the unique menus, command language, and search procedures of each system accessed.

Z39.50 simplifies the search process by making it possible for a searcher to use the familiar user interface of the local system to search both the local library catalogue as well as any remote database system that support the standard. In libraries, the Z39.50 protocol is most often used for searching OPAC sources.

The important facilities offered by Z39.50 are as follows:

- *Browse*: Allows the client to scan the contents of wordlists or indexes on the server. This can be particularly useful in the case of controlled keyword lists or facets.

- *Access and resource control*: Allows authentication of users, and cost control and online charging for commercial services.
- *Sort*: Allows the client to request different orderings of query results, eg. relevance ranking, sorting by date or version number, etc.
- *Explain*: Allows the client to interrogate the server about a number of details about its contents and its level of support for the application profile.
- *Item Order*: Allows offline ordering of materials in cases where they cannot be delivered electronically, or where per-unit charging (eg. online charging) is required. Such services are being supplied in an ad-hoc fashion by online Web-based component repositories such as ASSET. The item order service provides a ready-made and semantically standardised version of this service.
- *Item Update*: Permits an authorised client to update the contents of the remote database.

SRW (SEARCH/RETRIEVE WEB SERVICE)

Search/Retrieve Web Service is a new HTTP-based information retrieval protocol providing broadly the same facilities as Z39.50, but by means of very different technology. SRW is designed to be a low barrier to entry solution to performing searches and other information retrieval operations across the internet. It uses existing, well tested and easily available technologies such as SOAP and XPath in order to perform what has been done in the past using proprietary solutions. The protocol has two ways that it can be carried, either via SOAP or as parameters in aURL.

This second form is called SRU – Search Retrieve by URL. Other transports would also be possible, for example simple XML over HTTP, but these are not defined by the current standard. The primary function of SRW is to allow a user to search a remote database of records. This is done via the search Retrieve operation, in which the client sends a search Retreive Request and the server responds with a search Retrieve Response. The request has several parameters, most of which are optional. The response is primarily a list of XML records which matched the search, along with the full count of how many records were matched.

XML (EXTENSIBLE MARKUP LANGUAGE)

XML stands for EXtensible Markup Language. XML is a markup language much like HTML and was designed to carry data, not to display data. XML tags are not predefined. You must define your own tags. XML is designed to be self-descriptive and it is is recommended by the World Wide Web Consortium. It is a fee-free open standard. XML is not a replacement for HTML. HTML is about displaying information, while XML is about carrying information. In simple words, XML is a software and hardware independent tool for carrying information. It is used both to encode documents and serialise data.

It supports Unicode, allowing almost any information in any written human language to be communicated. XML is now as important for the Web as HTML was to the foundation of the Web. XML is everywhere. It is the most common tool for data transmissions between all sorts of applications, and becomes more and more popular in the area of storing and describing information. XML simplifies data sharing as in the real world; computer systems and databases contain data in incompatible formats. XML data is stored in plain text format. This provides a software- and hardware-independent way of storing data. This makes it much easier to create data that different applications can share.

SELECTION OF FEDERATED SEARCH ENGINE

In selecting a Federated search engine, one needs to bear in mind the following:

- The maximum number of resources the software can include
- The ease of setting up resource targets
- Availability of simple search options
- Speed of search results
- Limiting and refining searches
- Ranking results by relevance
- Export options, *i.e.,* print, e-mail, download
- Adequate statistics and reporting features

STANDARDS AND DEVELOPMENT

NISO – (US) National Information Standards Organisation launched and continue to develop initiatives in order to develop and adopt standard search and retrieval protocols for federated searching. XML – Web protocol and SOAP (Single Object Access Protocol)

ACCESS ISSUES WITH FEDERATED SEARCH

Verification, authentication and certification can be difficult for the federated search vendor. Since, federated search engines don't hold the data locally, *i.e.,* the engines perform the search, and send the results back to the portal. The federated search engine must be able to access multiple passwordprotected databases behind the scenes, or IP validate all at the one time, and show users their results in one easy navigable interface.The challenge for federated search vendors is to provide only licensed users access to databases, as specified for each license agreement that is in place for the organisation.

AUTHENTICATION

Authentication sets federated search engines apart form other expensive and highly sophisticated search software such as Verity and Autonomy. The latter usually restricts searches to internally generated information, ignoring subscription databases that enterprises have bought in-house. All the user needs with federated searching is ID, password or IP validation along with files to be searched, and the federated search engine do the rest..

THE SET–UP PROCESS

The set up process is lengthy and time consuming for both the Library and the vendor. This is not the end of the process either! It continually evolves as databases change, or new resources are acquired and links are added to the federated search portal.

INTERFACE ISSUES

We need to decide how much time is to be devoted to design, who is the audience and should this audience be able to perform multiple searches, without having to do more than input their ID and password or IP authenticate, and type in the search query.

REMOVING DUPLICATES (DE-DUPING)

Most federated search engines will de-dupe some only when requested. However this opens up a Pandora's Box about how the results are returned. User habits indicate that the end user views only the first ten hits or results. How do the vendor and the interface designer ensure that the highest hits are returned? This area is continually evolving, and it is up to the federated search engine provider, to provide what they can, to the best of their technological ability in this regard.

HOW FEDERATED SEARCH WORKS

Federated search computer programmes allow users to search multiple data sources with a single query from a single user interface. The user enters a search query in the portal interface's search box and the query is sent to every individual database in the portal or federated search list. Access details for the individual databases must be preset in the portal by its owner.

Federated search systems either rely upon vendors to create commercial portal systems, or they rely upon government or other organisations to provide open access portals. How federated search is implemented depends upon which of the two types of organisations is providing the portal. Federated search portals, either commercial or open access, generally search public access bibliographic databases; public access Web-based library catalogues (OPACs), Web-based search engines like Google and/or open-access, government-operated or corporate data collections.

These individual data sources send back to the portal's interface a list of results from the search query. The user can review this hit list. Some portals will merely screen scrape the actual database results and not directly allow a user to enter the data source's application. More sophisticated ones will de-dupe the results list by merging and removing duplicates. There are additional features available in many portals, but the basic idea is the same: to improve the accuracy and relevance of individual searches as well as reduce the amount of time required to search for resources.

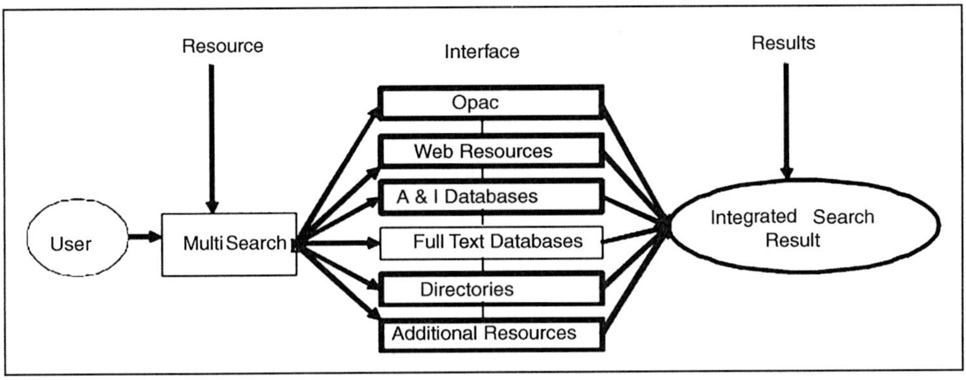

Fig. Diagrammatic Representation of Federated Searching.

In federated searching, a wealth of information is incorporated into a single repository that can be searched. In this model, the information is processed prior to the user's search. From the enduser's point of view, federated searching and metasearching may seem similar, because both provide a single interface to multiple resources, but they actually differ in many respects.

The pre-processing taking place in a federated searching environment, which we can describe as just-in-case processing, offers new opportunities regarding search methodologies and the presentation of results. For example, a ranking algorithm can be applied to each data element stored in the repository, unrelated to any future user query. Such an algorithm can take into account the number of times that an article has been cited, the number of articles that the author has published, the number of times that a book has been borrowed, a journal's impact factor, and other parameters.

A federated searching system can use the calculated rank to better evaluate the relevance of the specific item once it has been retrieved as the result of a query.

The system searches a local repository that was created earlier through the accumulation of data from numerous resources. Looking back a few years, we can see that the need for a single search interface to multiple resources arose some time ago, and, in fact, metasearching and federated searching have been available for quite some time.Such systems originated in a variety of environments; for example, Elsevier, a publisher offering numerous journals, created a federated search mechanism enabling its users to search all its e-journals through its ScienceDirect service.

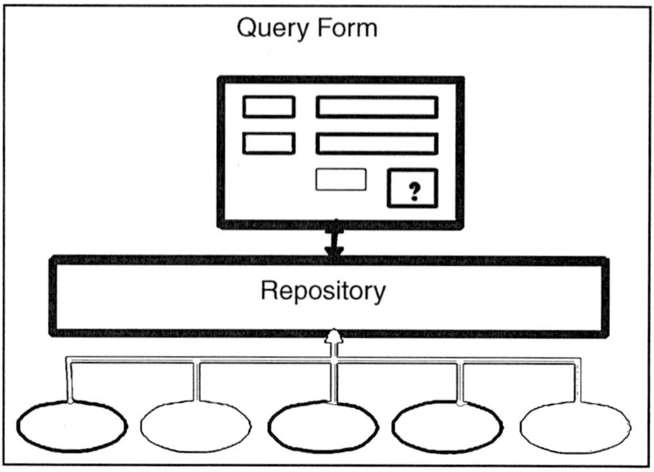

Fig. Diverse in Form Mation Resources.

As Elsevier acquired other publishers, it was able to add their journals to the same platform. Database vendors developed similar mechanisms. For example, Ovid provides a single interface to a few hundred databases that it publishes, and still retains them as separate databases.

Commercial organisations were not the only ones that addressed the need for a single search interface; several large research institutions created a local environment based on federation.

For example, the Los Alamos National Laboratory and the Ohio Link consortium in the United States, the University of Toronto in Canada, the Technical Knowledge Center of Denmark (DTV), and the Max Planck Society in Germany all offer large, diverse collections of e-journals that they store locally. These institutions have implemented federated searching to provide a single search interface across their electronic collections. However, not all organisations have the resources to adopt this just-in-case approach.

Furthermore, with the rapid increase in the number of heterogeneous resources that institutions offer their users, a single federated searching system can serve only as a partial solution.

IMPLEMENTATION

When a federated search engine is implemented at a particular library, it then becomes a unique service. Federated-searching software allows customisation, so no two implementations are exactly the same. For example, a library may choose to include all of its online resources as targets for a federated search engine or it may choose to create subject groupings first, each of which leads to a federated search service for a narrow topic.

Gerrity, Lyman, and Tallent discuss implementing a federated search system at Boston College, where they promoted the new service as "MetaQuest".

One application of federated searching is the metasearch engine; however, this is not a complete solution as many documents are not currently indexed.

This is known as the deep Web or invisible Web. Many more information sources are not yet stored in electronic form.

'Google Scholar' is an example of a project trying to address this.When the search vocabulary or data model of the search system is different from the data model of one or more of the foreign target systems the query must be translated into the each of the foreign target systems.

This can be done using simple dataelement translation or may require semantic translation.

FEDERATED SEARCH PROVIDERS

Individual institutions have their in-house Federated option and other institutions uses global federated search options, following are the popular federated search providers:

- Google Scholar
- Scopus
- Liberty

GOOGLE SCHOLAR

Google Scholar is seen as the competition for both campus institutional repository systems (at least in terms of search and discovery) and academic library federated searching. Google Scholar provides a simple way to broadly search for scholarly literature.

From one place, you can search across many disciplines and sources: peer-reviewed papers, theses, books, abstracts and articles, from academic publishers, professional societies, preprint repositories, universities and other scholarly organisations. Google Scholar helps you identify the most relevant research across the world of scholarly research.

FEATURES OF GOOGLE SCHOLAR

- Search diverse sources from one convenient place
- Find papers, abstracts and citations
- Locate the complete paper through your library or on the web
- Learn about key papers in any area of research

Google Scholar gives various option to the user so that they can search according to their equirements, such as time period, author wise search, subject wise, publication, institution wise etc and after giving the key term by the user, it searches that key term to various databases, search engines, journals etc and display the result on interface with name of author along with its full bibliographical description and it also provide citation information.

SCOPUS

Scopus is the largest abstract and citation database of research literature and quality web sources. It's designed to find the information scientists need. Quick, easy and comprehensive, Scopus provides superior support of the literature research process.Scopus is updated daily and it offers 15,000 peer-reviewed journals from more than 4,000 international publishers, over 1000 Open access journals, 500 Conference proceedings, over 600 trade publications and over 125 Book series. It also covers 33 million records, out of which, 16 million records include references going back to 1996 and 17 million pre-1996 records go back as far as 1869.

LIBERTY: QUEST

Liberty is a total web based library automation software which allows federated searching. In Liberty federated searching refers as "Quest" it capitalises our investment in online databases by providing library users with a single search point from with in Liberty.

Benefits of Quest:

- *Single Search Point for Multiple Databases*: Include databases that your organisation subscribes to in your Liberty3 search. Quest simplifies searching and access for your users.
- *Easy to Use*: Quest offers basic or advanced searching options, interleaves search results, and represents search results graphically. Quest allows a number of refine and sort options including sort by relevancy.
- *De-duplicate Searches*: Easily remove duplicates from search results by title or URL.
- *Customisable*: Quest offers you the option to include the library catalogue in the federated search. You can also select the databases you wish to search in your federated search.
- *Local Soft link Support and Service*: Quest is supported locally and hosted on Soft link servers. There is no need for you to worry about installation or maintenance.
- *The biggest players* in the federated searching industry are MuseGlobal (Muse Search), Fretwell- Downing (Zportal), and Webfeat (Knowledge Prism). These product offerings allow a user, regardless of vendor, to access multiple databases through one search interface. Endeavor (ENCompass) and ExLibris (MetaLib) are also in the federated search engine.
- Scirus, Wikipiedia, Pub med central, these are public domain site which provide federated searching.
- Publishers offering numerous journals created a federated search mechanism so that users are able to search their all journals. A

good example is Elsivers Science Direct. As Elsivers acquired other publishers, it was able to add their journals at the same platform.

- Database vendor develop the same mechanism such as Sliver Platter provide a single interface for more than 300 databases that they published SCOPUS, etc.
- Proquest, Ebsco, Gale Cengage and Elsevier etc are such databases who offer federated search. In Gale Cengage "federated search" refers as "Power Search".
- The NISO Metasearch Initiative seeks to develop industry standards for one-search access to multiple resources that will allow libraries to offer portal environments for library users offering the same easy searching found in Webbased services like Google.
- Many public and academic libraries also utilise Auto-Graphics' federated search solution AGent Search.

DRAWBACKS OF FEDERATED SEARCH

Limitations of the current generation of federated search engines. These include:

- The lack of a uniform authentication standard means that some databases are inaccessible to federated search engines.
- True, full, deduplication is impossible because databases download results in small sets and metadata standards vary by resource.
- Relevancy ranking is limited by the quality of the metadata, which usually does not include abstracts or full-text information.
- Although federated search systems are fundamentally software, they must be implemented and managed as a service, which takes a great deal of resources.
- Federated search engines cannot improve on the native interface in terms of search accuracy and precision.
- Federated searching is not for power searching needs. Just as with searching metasearch engines, only basic Boolean commands can be used.

The federated search has some other issues as well. First, it cannot cover all online library resources. The goal of one-stop shopping cannot be achieved completely by any federated search.

There are various reasons for this:

- Some databases do not work with any federated search at all, such as SciFinder Scholar. SciFinder Scholar does not use a web browser but rather requires its own internet client. Neither MetaLib nor WebFeat can cover SciFinder Scholar.
- If databases require a login, they will not work with the federated search.

- Some databases work with one federated search product but do not work with the other. MetaLib cannot search LexisNexis databases because LexisNexis does not allow Z39.50 or XML gateway access. WebFeat cannot search databases that do not have a search box on their front page because WebFeat counts on the search box on the native interface to search.
- Many libraries have databases on a pay-per-search basis, and libraries normally do not want them to be searched by a federated search for budgetary reasons.
- Some databases have a limited number of concurrent users, and if these databases are included in a federated search, the limited seat(s) is/are taken immediately whenever someone logs into the federated search, and no other users can use these databases. Libraries normally do not want to include databases with a very limited number of concurrent users in the federated search.

It may not make sense to add to a federated search menu the very specialised databases that most general users would not be interested in, or the databases that require special software. One example is Inter-university Consortium for Political and Social Research (ICPSR) that requires statistics software such as SPSS to view data.

CONCLUSION

In the electronic information environment one of the responses to the problem of bringing large amounts of information together has been for libraries to introduce portals. A portal is a gateway, or a point where users can start their search for information on the web. There are a number of different types of portals, for example universities have been introducing "institutional portals", which can be described as "a layer which aggregates, integrates, personalises and presents information, transactions and applications to the user according to their role and preferences".

A second type of portal is a "subject portals". A third type of portal is a "federated search tool" which brings together the resources to a library subscribes and allows cross-searching of these resources. They work using the Z39.50 protocol used by database suppliers to enable communication between computers. This protocol is not always effective because database suppliers have not always adopted it consistently so other protocols are also used such as HTML, XML and SQL. Since, these tools access resources that the library pays for, some type of authentication is required to ensure. Well before the launch of the World Wide Web, librarians recognised the need for establishing a common interface to search multiple sources. The ANSI/NISO gives the international search-andretrieval protocol, Z39.50, which was originally proposed in 1984 as a standard means of interrogating bibliographic databases. Since, then it has gone through three versions, the latest of which was issued in 1995. Federated search compliments the Z39.50 facility, it offers the ability to extend search beyond the online catalog virtually to any electronic resources that can be authenticated at the point of access. This means that users no longer need to jump from one search interface to another.

Information integration over distributed sources is an urgent problem to be solved for providing access to a variety of Digital Libraries through a common search interface and portal. Federated or cross-database search tools now available on the market are the correct solution for unifying access to a variety of information resources.

These tools can search not only library catalogs but also commercial abstracting and indexing databases, web search engines, and a variety of other databases, while often merging and de-duplicating results. Federated searching started in 1998 when Webfeat Team took the initiative to connect any or all of their databases at the same time through a simple, common user interface and turned this idea into a product called Webfeat.

WebFeat, the original federated search engine, used by over 15,000 leading public, academic, government and Global 1000 libraries and information centers — including over a third of the largest 100 U.S., public libraries, 18 statewide library systems, and 2 out of every 10 Association of Research Libraries (ARL) institutions, brings you the next frontier in federated search technology.

Originally founded in 1992 as an information technology consultancy. The WebFeat concept is simple: search any or all of your library's databases simultaneously with a single intuitive interface. WebFeat can search any database, including licensed databases, free databases, catalogs, Z39.50, Telnet, proprietary databases, anything! And with SMART, WebFeat's next generation usage tracker, you can report detailed database usage within your library with just a few mouse clicks.

9

Automation Software

INTRODUCTION

Electronic spread-sheets crunch numbers. Word processing programmes crunch words. Library automation and information storage and retrieval programmes crunch information. They help to deal effectively with information explosion. The purpose is important. If the selected software cannot retrieve right information at right time in right format for the right user, the sophistication and decor of the package is worthless. The categories of software explained before help in fixing the appropriate category of the software for the purpose of library automation. Based on what one has in terms of physical environment (computer) and social environment (users, staff) and what one can afford, suitable software has to be selected. There are many options and a large variety of software packages. It is suggested to acquire a commercially available software package. These are developed for use by a variety of customers. A great amount of skill and effort is put in their development. They are expected to be reliable, easy to use, well documented and they are available for a wide range of applications. Even then the selection of suitable software is difficult because of their availability in large number, over choice, tall claims, varied cost, technicalities involved, etc. It is necessary to know the various criteria that could be applied in selecting the suitable software. The four selected studies, by Glossbrenner, Library Systems Evaluation Guide, Rowley and Grosch provide a variety of selection criteria. This wider perspective of such criteria with be helpful and provide better pitch and outfield to play the serious game of selecting the suitable player-that is, the required software package.

CATEGORIES OF SOFTWARE

Computerisation of Library and information services, involves non-numeric data processing, text retrieval, manipulation of strings of characters and information retrieval, etc. Some general purpose software packages can be used for these purposes and for specific needs, special purpose software are also available in the market.

The various categories of such software and their features are:

- Basic software for data entry, validation, sorting and merging of files, and editing of data
- Word processing software to manipulate text-storage, recall, use and modify; alignment of margins, addition and deletion of string of characters, manipulate paragraphs, etc.
- Database management systems (DBMS) for creation and management of databases, file management systems, relational database management systems (RDBMS), network and hierarchical DBMS
- Text-Retrieval Packages for storage and retrieval 'of non-numeric records (tabular or even graphics). These are self-contained software, require minimum involvement of computer specialists, records are independent of variable length for natural language text, have access to data by context, inverted file access, user interfaces which makes them simple and easy to use. Search and indexing facilities are other important features
- Software Associated with Searching Online Retrieval System and CD-ROM Databases. Major online systems have their own software usually written in command language, provide access to external databases, private or personal file facility, and permit editing of search files on micros
- *Library House Keeping Software*: These have provision for acquisition, cataloguing, circulation control, serials control and statistical report generation.

Library automation software or computer based information storage and retrieval systems cover two major functional areas, namely:

- Control and management of library resources, and
- Access to documents and information.

These two areas deal with library house-keeping systems and text retrieval systems respectively. Gradually, the distinction between them is vanishing. In latest software packages there is provision for both library house-keeping operations as well as public access for information retrieval. In addition, there are software packages for re-organising and presenting information in desired format, producing publications, arid to control and manipulate statistical and financial data.

Library automation software packages can also be grouped in four categories:

- Word processing,
- Library house-keeping operations,
- Management communications and support, and
- Text retrieval.

The type of software can be categorised based on the hardware or computer systems used. For example,

- Microcomputer-based software
- Mini computer-based software
- Large mainframe-based software

Each of these categories of software may be either In-house software that is owned and operated by the library, or shared with other libraries through a consortium arrangement-through a bibliographic information network.

OPTIONS FOR SELECTION

In recent times, libraries are not encouraged to develop the software for its use. In other words, libraries are advised not to waste efforts, time and money in developing in-house programmes for library house-keeping operations and public access information storage and retrieval. Software development is a costly, time consuming and risky job whose results may be uncertain. However, the options available for selection of library automation software are summarised below:

- Acquire a prewritten, off-the-shelf software package (e.g. LIBSYS),
- Acquire a turnkey package incorporating both hardware and software (e.g. MINISIS, TULIS),
- Write in-house programmes,
- Commission writing of programmes, and
- Participate in the formation of, or join a cooperative that offers access to software and/or hardware and/or databases.

Rowley discusses the advantages and disadvantages of commercially available software packages. She concludes, "It is sensible to choose a commercially available package, -since, it is too costly to write a local software package or to commission someone to do this, even though a tailor-made package designed specifically for a given application is most likely to fit all the requirements of that application."

GUIDES TO COMMERCIALLY AVAILABLE SOFTWARE

There are a large number of commercially available library automation software packages. Studies that enumerate, compare and highlight the salient features of these software packages are also in abundance. An effort is made here to review some such selected studies to enable one to fathom the length, breadth and depth of the problem of selecting a suitable software for one's use. Clossbrenner in his book How to buy software: The master guide to picking the right programme describes much general and specific application software but does not mention the library housekeeping or information storage and retrieval software packages. A number of software packages are mentioned which could be used for general applications and other areas related to library automation. These include packages for word processing, database management, statistical manipulation, online searching of databases, etc. The book is a comprehensive, user friendly master guide for selecting suitable software for specific purposes. Hansen in Microcomputer user's guide to information online lists more than 100 sources of information, and their access software. Rowley lists some text retrieval software for microcomputer and for mainframe/ microcomputer systems. Further, She adds a list of library house-keeping software, their features and suppliers. Mahajan surveys some 40 software packages.

SOFTWARE WITH CD-ROM DATABASES

The CD-ROM databases are usually provided with information retrieval and public access software. Valas gives a comparison of some well known CD-ROM information retrieval software packages. There are not many publications dealing with the comparison of different CD-ROM information retrieval software packages. Richards and Robinson suggest a model for evaluating CD-ROM software whereas, Harry and Oppenheim discuss the various criteiia for evaluating electronic databases. jacso describes the evaluation, selection and installation of CD-ROM software, data ware and hardware. Jasco searches for skeletons in the database cupboard to find errors of omission and commission.

McFaul comes out with a final report on consistent interface guidelines. Tian-Zhu limits his' formal analysis to searching capabilities and ease of use of CD-ROM user interfaces. Sieverts and others give additional programmes for testing, evaluating and comparing software for information storage and retrieval. Most of these studies are confined to user interfaces as the principle of comparison of software packages. They usually give rules on how to rank the CD-ROM publications, how to give marks for the CD-ROM databases in addition to the software. In many cases the performance factors that are most important for professional searchers are usually missing from these collection of rules. Valas emphasises the performance factors that are considered to be the most important viewpoints for a professional searcher. "A retrieval system may be as user friendly as you wish; but you will not like it if one single e search step in an intricate query may take two hours and displaying the hits may take another two; or if complicated search strategies are not possible at all."

INDIAN SCENARIO

Chowdhury and Chowdhury discuss the automated text retrieval and library management software in India. A number of software packages have been released recently by government and private agencies. The authors provides a list of 20 and a brief overview of 10 selected Indian packages released upto 1994, namely, CATMAN, CDS/ISIS, LIBRARIAN, LIBSYS, MAITRAYEE, MECSYS, NIRMALS, SANJAY, TULIPS and WILISYS. Considering the cost aspect, it is concluded that CDS/ISIS along with SANJAY (with a few modifications) might prove to be the most suitable package for most Indian libraries. The authors compare the common features such as cataloguing, OPAC, online help, acquisition, circulation and serials control of the selected packages. However, the criteria to evaluate such packages are not discussed.

Major problem areas of library automation in India are as follows:

- Funds, manpower and retrospective conversion
- Facilities for entering data in desired format
- Downloading facilities for data
- Facilities for data exchange
- Problems in creating files in packages based on DBMS due to long fields for longer data fields (*e.g.,* in Oracle), and use of repeatable fields which are common in bibliographic and text database (e.g. SANJAY, LIBSYS, CDS/ISIS)

WHY IS SELECTION DIFFICULT

Selection of suitable software for library automation is always what Grosch calls, a case of "fud" where 'f' stands for fear, 'u' for uncertainty and 'd' for doubt.

This is because of the technical parameters associated with the selection of the software, such as the shape of network, computing platform, type of operating systems and various standards. Since, today's software investments are likely to be for longer term than those made some three decades ago, the overall system architecture may now play a stronger role in such selection.

The problems are:

- *A large number of software packages*: A conservative estimate shows more than 80,000 separate software packages for a variety of purposes-not all are for library house-keeping operations but a large number may include information storage and retrieval. The number of such packages is multiplying like 'coat hangers in a darkened closet'.
- *Over choice*: A large number of software packages give not only choice but over choice to select one that is suitable for the purpose.
- *Tall claims*: Advertisements for each software package tries to claim that it is one up and better than others. There is plenty of material to confuse the selector-journal articles, product brochures, direct mail solicitations and catalogues. The software producers generously distribute lot of advertising material.
- *Documentation*: Often the product manual supplied with the software does not provide adequate information for the installation and for using the software by the user on his own.
- *Cost*: At times, the software is costlier than the hardware on which it is to be used. Further, the software package is normally purchased as a one time investment.

Other common problems that make the selection of software difficult, relate to:

- Understanding the exact purpose for which it is to be acquired
- Knowing the physical and social environment in which it is to be used
- Understanding the educational and professional level, and aptitude of the persons who are going to use the software
- Knowing the compatibility, simplicity and ease of use of the software.

CRITERIA TO SELECT LIBRARY AUTOMATION SOFTWARE

To evaluate a particular software package, a simple procedure is to read the literature supplied by the manufacturer, look at the reviews and advertisements published in various computer magazines and to ask the salesperson for a demonstration of the programme. What is often found to be missing in this procedure is the basic conceptual understanding of what a computer does on a physical level and how the software works. It is not necessary to know the details of computer components, such as accumulators, registers, clock signals, instruction set of 380 microprocessors or computer programming, etc. But, when deciding on the best suitable software, more computer knowledge is required than just how to insert a disc into the slot and press a key.

However, the following general guidelines may be useful in selecting a programme.

- Locate and evaluate a knowledgeable dealer or sales person
- Thoroughly examine the documentation for the software you are considering
- Arrange for a demonstration of the software
- Prepare yourself before the demonstration
- Put the programme through its paces
- Evaluate the quality of support you can expect from the dealer or vendor.

CRITERIA FOR SELECTION: STUDY NO. 1

Glossbrener has given the following twelve sure-fire rules for selecting software.

- *Rule* 1: Do not take anything for granted: There is more hidden in the advertisements than it is revealed.
- *Rule 2:* You are not the stupid one: Don't ever let yourself feel foolish when looking at, reading about, using, or otherwise dealing with a computer programme. If its creators haven't lived up to their responsibility, it is their fault, not yours.
- *Rule* 3: How many and how long?: How many author names can you

put in that file? How long can each name be? Nothing brings a program's limitations to the surface faster than these questions.

- *Rule* 4: Forget about the sizzle and focus on the steak: Ask, what the programme can to do and how well it can do it? The advertisement may say, "This programme contains all the standard word processing features". Note, there are no widely agreed 'standard' features of any programme. In short, concentrate on performance and forget the decoration
- *Rule 5:* Whenever possible, make an effort to visualise yourself using the programme: Visualise, how much work will be involved putting all of your books, records, or magazines into database management files? Will you be able to enter each new book record? The more accurately you visualise the steps involved in accomplishing a task.the more you know about how a given programme will deal with those steps.
- *Rule* 6: Read at least two reviews of any programme before you buy.
- *Rule* 7: Get a demonstration on the identical computer, configured exactly as the one you will be using.
- *Rule* 8: Life will be easier if you stick with proven products offered by major hardware and software firms.
- *Rule* 9: Buy only the four 'building block': programmes to start with. It is easy to master a programme faster and comprehensively, if you concentrate on just one at a time. The four building block programmes are communications, word processing, electronic spreadsheet and personal filing or database management.
- *Rule 10:* Don't drive yourself crazy trying to get something to work. Ask.
- *Rule 11*: Nothing is impossible. But the game may not be worth the candle. Computers and software are so versatile that you can accomplish just about anything you want. But these will not save the time, effort and money.
- *Rule 12:* Whenever you can-WAIT! Make sure the rapidly changing software market place works for you.

CRITERIA FOR SELECTION: STUDY NP.2

There is another monumental work discussing various criteria to evaluate and select library automation software, particularly for the housekeeping operations. The eight volume series publication entitled Library Systems Evaluation Guide, is brought out by Jera.

Since, it was published in 1983, the Guide may be a little outdated. However, the principle evaluation criteria discussed are still valid. The coverage in eight volumes of the Guide is indicated in the table.

Table. Indication of Coverage in Library Systems Evaluation Guide.

Vol. No.	Title	No. of Pages	No. of Reference
1.	Serial Control	194	60
2.	Circulation Control	261	97
3.	Public Service	267	117
4.	Acquisitions	252	96
5.	Management Services	234	88
6.	Interlibrary loan	248	98
7.	Cataloguing	261	168
8.	System integration	278	198
	Total	**1995**	**922***

Note: * No effort is made to identify the unique references. The total number of references includes a number of multiple citations.

The Guide presents basic information on the requirements and techniques of evaluation of automated library applications in a concise and easily usable format. The Guide considers 'evaluation' as 'relative in nature'. Therefore, to determine the ability of various systems to meet a library's requirements, the systems must be compared with each other or to some reference model. The latter approach to evaluation is both easier and more objective, provided a reference model is available. The Guide provides such a reference model, which could suitably be adjusted to represent the requirements of a given library and then this model may be used to evaluate one or more number of library automation software packages.

The Guide suggests an eight-phase evaluation methodology.

- *Phase 1:* Setting objectives.
- *Phase 2:* Fine tuning of components of the methodology to agree with objectives.
- *Phase* 3: Selection of candidate systems for evaluation.
- *Phase* 4: Examination of accompanying system literature and documentation.
- *Phase* 5: Comparison of candidate systems with the functions and features table, and with the checklist of data elements.
- *Phase* 6: On-site evaluation of candidate systems.
- *Phase* 7: System selection and acquisition.
- *Phase* 8: Post installation evaluation.

CRITERIA FOR SELECTION: STUDY NO.3

Rowley emphasises the need to identify systems requirements before the selection of either software or hardware. The functional requirements are important. Therefore in the evaluation of any package for a given application, priority must be given to establish whether the software is capable of performing the tasks for which it is to be acquired.

General Criteria

- *Other's experiences*: Useful in indicating the potential and problems of a software package; some users may offer help and advice in implementing the package.
- *Cost*: Comparisons of prices of packages be made. What is included in the price of the package and what is excluded should be understood. Cost of hardware and database creation are additional costs.
- *Originator*: The originator's reputation, and experience in developing software is helpful. An established software house is more likely to be able to offer continuing support.
- *Supplier*: Sometimes the supplier is the same as the originator, if the supplier is a separate agency acting as an intermediary between the user and the originator, it may hinder direct communication between the user and the originator.

Technical Criteria

In addition to the general criteria of the selection, the following technical criteria should be considered, both when selecting between packages and also in assessing whether any specific package is suitable for a given purpose.

- *Language*: The programming language in which the software is written. Whether a compiler or interpreter is available on the given system to run it efficiently in terms of machine time and storage requirements.
- *Operating System*: The package must be suitable for running under the operating system on the hardware being used. Whether it is a single user or multi-user operating system that will function on a network.
- *Hardware*: Compatibility with software, its various versions and also ability to run other necessary or useful software on the computer system.
- *Ease-in-use*: The quality of the operator - machine interface, menus, commands, screen displays, documentation, etc. will enhance ease in use of the software.
- *Supplied format*: Software must be supplied on disks, tapes, etc., that can be run on the system and when required transferred to another medium such as hard disk.

Support Criteria

It is an important criteria for using the software and to fully exploit the various features of the software.

- *Documentation*: It includes both printed documentation and online help facility. The documentation should cover introductory exploration of the basic features, a full account of all features, a list of commands, an online help system, additional tutorial support, choice to interface at different levels depending on user's experience, etc.

- *Advice to setting up*: Assistance in installing and implementing the package must be provided. This may cover creation of databases, input formats, report formats, initialisation, etc.
- Training in the use of software package.
- *Maintenance*: This may include removing any bugs or errors that might become evident in the software as it is used for a greater variety of applications and improving the software so that it incorporates new facilities and concepts (*e.g.,* mouse, windows, popup menus).
- *User groups*: Many of the larger and well-established software packages (*e.g.,* CDS/ISIS, LIBSYS) have user groups or user clubs. These groups share expertise and experience in application of the software, discuss problems and limitations in using the software and present a concerted front to the software supplier for solving problems and asking for improvements.

CRITERIA FOR SELECTION: STUDY NO.4

Grosch discusses some procurement and evaluation factors together market trends that may affect the future of library systems. The major system evaluation and selection according to Grosch is the availability of the capabilities and product enhancements of the application software at the time of its installation. The other criteria include examining hardware platform options, operating system requirements, directions of the system developers towards open systems, conversion support, training, ongoing software support, record of old and new versions of the software, ease-of-use, etc. The advice is: 'Setting realistic goals that are attainable in your selection of a system, biting off only what can now afford but providing a goal enhancement base for future years, will result in an easier systems transition'.

CONCLUSION

Software is a computer programme for using computers and other such hardware to their optimum capabilities. As computers do only what they are told to do and therefore, the instructions given to computer should be unambiguous. Writing step by step instructions without any ambiguity to solve a particular problem is called programming. A software package can have one or more computer programmes to solve a specific problem. A programming language provides a special type of grammar and syntax to the programmer to enable him to give instructions in a simple and understandable way. Writing programmes and developing software packages involves special training, hardwork, time and money. For developing in-house software to solve complex problems, these requirements become severe and unmanageable.

Due to these limitations, the practicing librarians or information scientists should be exposed to some commercially available software packages. Software packages are generally available as commercial products which typically provide solutions to particular application problems. Since, they are developed on a commercial scale in a competitive market for use by a variety of customers, a great amount of skill and effort is put in their development. Therefore, they are reliable, easy to use and in many instances, well-documented. Ready-made software packages are now available for a wide range of applications such as management information systems (MIS), industrial support systems, office automation systems, library automation and information retrieval operations.

10

Art Serials: Indexes and Abstracts

INDEXING

According to the British indexing standard, an *index* is a systematic arrangement of entries designed to enable users to locate information in a document. The process of creating an index is called *indexing*, and a person who does it is called an *indexer*. There are many types of indexes, from cumulative indexes for journals to computer database indexes. This discussion concentrates on the back-of-the-book index, found in non-fiction books. Indexes are among those necessary but never spectacular products of hard as well as skilled work that can sometimes make the difference between a book and a good book. index review in *Books Ireland*, February 1994.

The chief purpose of an index is distillation, and in performing that task it can manage to suggest a life's incongruities with a concision that the most powerful biographical stylist will have trouble matching. Thomas Mallon, *New York Times*, 10 March 1991 the ocean flows of online information are all streaming together, and the access tools are becoming absolutely critical. If you don't index it, it doesn't exist. It's out there but you can't find it, so it might as well not be there. Barbara Quint, ASI San Diego Conference, 1994.

WHO DOES INDEXING

In the United States, according to tradition, the index for a non-fiction book is the responsibility of the author. Most authors don't actually do it. While a few publishers have in-house indexers, most indexing is done by freelancers, often working from home, hired by authors, publishers or packagers. More often, the indexer is hired by the publisher, and the fee is deducted from the money due the author.

If a packager hires the indexer directly, various payment arrangements can be made. Indexing work is not recommended to those who lack an orderly mind and a capacity for taking pains. A good index is a minor work of art but it is also the product of clear thought and meticulous care.

HOW IS INDEXING DONE

The indexer usually receives a set of *page proofs* for the book, often at the same time as final proofreading is being done by someone else. The indexer reads the page proofs, making a list of *headings* and *subheadings* and the location of each pertinent reference. After completing the rough index the indexer edits it for structure, clarity and consistency, formats it to specifications, proofreads it and submits it to the client in hard-copy form, on disk, by modem, or by e-mail. Since, the indexer is very late in the production process, there can be unreasonable time pressure. As to *how* to index, what goes on between the ear, that's a subject for books, courses, workshops and lifelong learning from experience?

Less time is available for the preparation of the index than for almost any other step in the bookmaking process. For obvious reasons, most indexes cannot be completed until page proofs are available. Typesetters are anxious for those few final pages of copy; printers want to get the job on the press; binders are waiting; salesmen are clamouring for finished books *surely* you can get that index done over the weekend? *Chicago Manual of Style*, 14th ed. Indexers are in effect trying to provide answers to a host of unasked questions.

Indexers therefore need to work as if their audience is present. But there are two snags: *first*, in most cases they do not know who this audience will be; *second*, in most cases they do not receive any feedback as to whether their judgements have been successful. From a communicative point of view, there is probably no more isolated intellectual task than indexing. The twilight howl of the indexer might well be Is there anybody there? David Crystal, editorial, *The Indexer*, April 1995

CAN'T A COMPUTER DO THE INDEXING

The short answer is no. Computers can easily construct a *concordance* but this is not an index, and is not very useful to someone looking for information. The so-called automatic indexing software programmes now appearing on the market are simply not up to the task of indexing a book. Book indexing involves a little bit of manipulating words appearing in a text, which computers can do, and a lot of understanding and organising the ideas and information in the text, which computers cannot do and will not do for many years to come. An example of the difference is that a book on protective gloves for occupational use might have a chapter discussing surgical gloves, how they get punctured and how they are tested for integrity, but might never use the word *holes*.

Yet a user of the book would expect to find this word in the index and be directed to the appropriate chapter. The indexer handles dozens or hundreds of such issues in every book. Where the text is already on computer disk, the indexing features of word processing programmes can ease the handling of page numbers and sorting, but the real indexing work is still done by the human.

Powerful dedicated software is also available for personal computers to aid the professional indexer in constructing, sorting, editing and formatting the index, whether from hard-copy text or computer files. Many indexers use one of the programmes listed on the Indexing Software page. Automated indexing was never intended to produce back-of-the-book indexes. As Indexicon demonstrates so well, back-of-the-book indexes cannot be automatically generated.

WHAT SKILLS OR EDUCATION DO INDEXERS NEED

Many publishers and packagers don't ask for specific degrees or credentials unless they are looking for someone with subject matter expertise for a technical book. Skills needed to learn indexing include excellent language skills, high clerical aptitude, accuracy and attention to detail. Once you are indexing professionally, you will find that self-discipline, curiosity, tolerance of isolation and love of books are necessary to keep going.

In addition to all this, of course, there are the business and marketing skills needed to succeed as a self- employed professional. Clients take their cue from you: if you behave in a professional manner, most of them treat you accordingly. Whoever the indexer is, he or she should be intelligent, widely read, and well acquainted with publishing practices also levelheaded, patient, scrupulous in handling detail, and analytically minded. This rare bird must while being intelligent, levelheaded, patient, accurate, and analytical work at top speed to meet an almost impossible deadline. *Chicago Manual of Style*, 13th ed. I wonder whether there is any profession in which a knowledge of one's tongue is of the slightest use.

HOW DO INDEXERS GET CLIENTS

Most people start by sending letters and resumes to publishers. Find their addresses in *Literary Marketplace*, *Writer's Market* and *Books in Print*, available in your library. It may take hundreds of letters to get a first indexing job. Experienced indexers say they get most jobs through recommendations from satisfied clients and networking, although some still come from marketing efforts. Now, many people interested in indexing are pursuing the apprenticeship model, working with an established indexer to build skills and experience. The three best ways to get work? Network, network, network.

HOW MUCH ARE INDEXERS PAID

That's the wrong question. A freelance indexer is running a small business; as a businessperson, you are not *paid*, you set prices and charge for a service. You are not an employee; you are an independent contractor. This is an important distinction because of how it changes your thinking. It's also very important for tax purposes, but that's off the subject.

HOW DO INDEXERS PRICE THEIR SERVICES

The two most common ways of quoting book index prices are per page and per entry. Different publishers prefer different methods, and indexes for different media also are priced differently. All the different ways of quoting prices can be reduced to a fee per hour. While experienced indexers come to know what rates per page or per entry they can afford to accept, beginning indexers would be well-advised to focus on the hourly fee when figuring their bids. This enables new indexers to decide what kinds of work are best for them, and to track improvements in skill, efficiency and income as they become experienced.

If you are starting out as a freelance indexer, you won't be able to get the same fee as an indexer with 10 years of experience. This does not mean inviting exploitation by unscrupulous clients. Remember, if you are qualified as an indexer, you are producing a professional product, and you should be fairly compensated. Set yourself a rock-bottom hourly fee for run-of-the-mill indexing, the lowest figure you should ever accept, and stick to it. Remember, no one says you have to take what the prospective client is offering. No one says the client has to pay what you charge. Both parties are free to negotiate or go elsewhere. It is your responsibility to set the fee you charge for indexing, and negotiate to get it. Indexers need to charge for their services according to the time they expect to spend on the work.

On the other hand, many clients want a predictable price since, they are under budget constraints. These clients will not pay by the hour, especially if they don't know your work. How do you quote your prices to get your hourly fee? If the client opens the discussion by saying she wants the index done for $1,200, or for a certain amount per indexable page, a fixed bid is called for. Fixed bids are good for the client but risky for the indexer.

The indexer must be familiar with the book before a reasonable bid can be given, because of wide variations in words per page and complexity of material. The expected number of entries per page or in the whole index should also be specified, since, this is a key factor in the time spent doing the index. Publishers in some fields want to ensure a detailed index, so they use pricing by the entry.

As long as both parties are clear on exactly what constitutes an entry and how they are counted, this has the advantage of compensating the indexer for extra time spent on complex material. Again, the expected number of entries per page should be specified. No matter how the bid is to be figured, start with the hourly fee to make sure you are being compensated according to your set rate.

First, estimate how many hours it will take you to do the index, including editing, proofing and preparing final copy. This estimate is crucial. Actually indexing a representative sample of the book is helpful here, and estimating skills should improve with experience. Then multiply by your hourly fee to get the total amount you expect for indexing the book. If the client wants a lump sum bid, you are done. To prepare a bid or price quote for a client who uses per-page pricing, divide your total estimate by the page count. To prepare a price quote on a per-entry basis, figure the total number of entries in the book and divide this into the total estimate.

In summary, use one of the following methods, where $FEE is the total fee, PAGES the indexable page count of the book, and ENTRIES the total number of entries in the book:

- Fixed price = $FEE
- Per-page rate = $FEE/ PAGES
- Per-entry rate = $FEE/ ENTRIES

If the client has a price or rate in mind, work the numbers backward to figure the hourly fee resulting from the client's number before deciding whether you can afford to accept it. When someone offers you an indexing assignment at $12 per hour, take note of the advice from Dr. Wellisch in the next quote; you could do almost as well at McDonald's! An hourly indexing fee should always be at least four times the wage one can earn by flipping hamburgers at a fast-food emporium.

WHAT KIND OF ANNUAL INCOME CAN I EXPECT FROM INDEXING

Here are some important factors which affect your income from indexing or any other independent service business:

- How you set your prices.
- How much you want to work.
- How skilled you are at finding enough good clients to keep busy.
- How skilled, and fast, you are at indexing.
- How much your business expenses are.

In short, your income depends on your motivation and your business skills as well as your indexing skills. There are indexers who treat it as a relaxing, part-time business; there are indexers who work long hours and support themselves in nice middle-class style as a result. Most probably fall in between. You have to decide what you are looking for. You need to spend time learning how to start and run a business as well as learning to index. Books and magazines on home-based business and entrepreneurship have lots of ideas and advice applicable to freelance indexers.

Seminars and workshops on business skills and sales technique can be quite useful, but be careful with your money. Talk to graduates before signing up. Suppose we look ahead to the future, finding that after gaining some experience, you reach a speed and skill level where the combination of rates paid by clients and the time you spend doing the work results in a good hourly rate. What hourly rate might you expect? ASI regularly surveys freelance and in-house indexers to find out what salaries and fees are being paid.

The latest survey is available on this web site, in the Members Area. If you are an ASI member, you may view and download the survey. In case you don't have access to this information, bear with me as I discuss the mechanics of estimating your self-employment income without using a specific rate. To estimate your annual income from indexing, multiply your hourly rate by the average number of work hours in a year.

Forty hours per week times 52 weeks a year is 2,080. Wait! If you want to index full-time, you need to consider all the time your business takes besides actual indexing. Writing letters and making calls to get work, rushing to the FedEx office before they close, billing, doing your tax return, shopping for supplies, backing up your computer files, meal breaks and occasional holidays and vacations are all unpaid time. Don't forget idle time between jobs; it takes several years of building a client base for most indexers to get full-time work. If you plan to put 40 hours per week into your business, then allowing for all the above within the 40 hours results in a rule of thumb of about 1,200 hours per year of actual paid indexing work. OK, multiply your hourly fee by 1,200. That's your gross revenue. But remember, this is a business; your actual income is much less.

To figure hourly income, self-employment taxes and federal, state and local income taxes come off the top, plus the cost of your supplies, utilities, ASI membership dues and the amortised cost of your office equipment. A good rule of thumb is to take at least 50 per cent off the rate. So, multiply your hourly income by how many hours you can work per year. If this is not enough for you to live on, don't quit the day job yet. Most indexers start indexing as a part-time moonlighting effort, supporting themselves with another job. Once they are sure they want to do this kind of work full-time, and clients are paying well and keeping them so busy it is hard to get everything done, they can make the decision to try full-time indexing.

Once you are well-established, idle periods and time spent marketing diminish, resulting in more paid work hours. You can eventually reach 2,000 hours per year, if you are willing to work more than 40 hours per week. In addition, a very good indexer who works fast can make a higher hourly rate for a given page rate, because it takes fewer hours to do the work. *Money* magazine recently published an article on successful homebased businesses which quoted one experienced freelance indexer who says he averages $50,000 per year. Some indexers are skeptical; others say this is possible after a few years if you work hard and find the right clients. Wealth... is more accurately measured in what you enjoy than in what you possess. Jean Aspen, *Arctic Son*

HOW CAN I LEARN TO INDEX

A local college or university with a Library Science or Information Science department may offer indexing courses. Many people take the indexing correspondence courses offered by the US Department of Agriculture. Assignments are graded by indexing professionals and a certificate of completion can be provided. If you are considering ASI membership, take note of the excellent self-paced course offered to ASI members. Available on interactive CD-ROM, this comprehensive course includes many practical exercises and self-assessments.

A certificate of completion can be obtained by taking the optional exams. Look at the Indexing Courses and Workshops web page for more information about all these options. Before you invest money in an expensive course, check out some books on the subject to gauge your interest and aptitude. Indexing cannot be reduced to a set of steps that can be followed! It is not a mechanical process. Indexing books is a form of writing. Like other types of writing, it is a mixture of art and craft, judgement and selection. With practice and experience, indexers develop their own style as do other writers. The best we can do as teachers of indexing is to present the rules and offer guidance.

DEFINITION OF ABSTRACT

Abstracts, like all summaries, cover the main points of a piece of writing. Unlike executive summaries written for non-specialist audiences, abstracts use the same level of technical language and expertise found in the article itself. And unlike general summaries which can be adapted in many ways to meet various readers' and writers' needs, abstracts are typically 150 to 250 words and follow set patterns. Because readers use abstracts for set purposes, these purposes further define abstracts.

PURPOSES FOR ABSTRACTS

Abstracts typically serve five main goals:

- *Help Readers Decide if they should Read an Entire Article*: Readers use abstracts to see if a piece of writing interests them or relates to a topic they're working on. Rather than tracking down hundreds of articles, readers rely on abstracts to decide quickly if an article is pertinent. Equally important, readers use abstracts to help them gauge the sophistication or complexity of a piece of writing. If the abstract is too technical or too simplistic, readers know that the article will also be too technical or too simplistic.
- *Help Readers and Researchers Remember Key Findings on a Topic*: Even after reading an article, readers often keep abstracts to remind them of which sources support conclusions. Because abstracts include complete bibliographic citations, they are helpful when readers begin writing up their research and citing sources.
- *Help Readers Understand a Text by Acting as a Pre-reading Outline of Key Points*: Like other pre-reading strategies, reading an abstract

before reading an article helps readers anticipate what's coming in the text itself. Using an abstract to get an overview of the text makes reading the text easier and more efficient.

- *Index Articles for Quick Recovery and Cross-referencing*: Even before computers made indexing easier, abstracts helped librarians and researchers find information more easily. With so many indexes now available electronically, abstracts with their keywords are even more important because readers can review hundreds of abstracts quickly to find the ones most useful for their research. Moreover, cross-referencing through abstracts opens up new areas of research that readers might not have known about when they started researching a topic.
- *Allow Supervisors to Review Technical Work without becoming Bogged Down in Details*: Although many managers and supervisors will prefer the less technical executive summary, some managers need to keep abreast of technical work. Research shows that only 15 per cent of managers read the complete text of reports or articles. Most managers, then, rely on the executive summary or abstract as the clearest overview of employees' work.

TYPES OF ABSTRACTS

Although you'll see two types of abstracts—informative and descriptive—most writersnow provide informative abstracts of their work.

DESCRIPTIVE ABSTRACT

A descriptive abstract outlines the topics covered in a piece of writing so the reader can decide whether to read the entire document. In many ways, the descriptive abstract is like a table of contents in paragraph form. Unlike reading an informative abstract, reading a descriptive abstract cannot substitute for reading the document because it does not capture the content of the piece. Nor does a descriptive abstract fulfill the other main goals of abstracts as well as informative abstracts do. For all these reasons, descriptive abstracts are less and less common.

SAMPLE DESCRIPTIVE ABSTRACT

We continue to document all major climatic variables in the uplands and floodplains at Bonanza Creek. In addition, we have documented the successional changes in microclimate in 9 successional upland and floodplain stands at Bonanza Creek (BNZ) and in four elevational locations at Caribou-Poker Creek (CPCRW). A sun photometer is operated cooperatively with NASA to estimate high-latitude atmospheric extinction coefficients for remote-sensing images. Electronic data are collected monthly and loaded into a database which produces monthly summaries. The data are checked for errors, documented, and placed on-line on the BNZ Web page. Climate data for the entire state have been summarised for the period of station records and krieged to produce maps of climate zones for Alaska based on growing-season and annual temperature and precipitation.

INFORMATIVE ABSTRACT

An informative abstract provides detail about the substance of a piece of writing because readers will sometimes rely on the abstract alone for information.

Informative abstracts typically follow this format:

- Identifying information;
- Concise restatement of the main point, including the initial problem or other background;
- Methodology and key findings;
- Major conclusions.

Informative abstracts usually appear in indexes like *Dissertation Abstracts International*.

SAMPLE INFORMATIVE ABSTRACT BASED ON NON-EXPERIMENTAL WORK

Environmental Impact Statement. Federal Register: December 11, 1997. "Endangered and Threatened Wildlife and Plants; Proposed Revision of Special Regulations for the Gray Wolf." Fish and Wildlife Service, Department of the Interior. On November 22, 1994, the U.S. Fish and Wildlife Service published special rules to establish non-essential experimental populations of gray wolves in Yellowstone National Park and central Idaho. The non-essential experimental population areas include all of Wyoming, most of Idaho, and much of central and southern Montana.

A close reading of the special regulations indicates that, unintentionally, the language reads as though wolf control measures apply only outside of the experimental population area. This proposed revision is intended to amend language in the special regulations so that it clearly applies within the Yellowstone non-essential experimental population area and the central Idaho non-essential experimental population area. This proposed change will not affect any of the assumptions and earlier analysis made in the environmental impact statement or other portions of the special rules.

SAMPLE INFORMATIVE ABSTRACT BASED ON EXPERIMENTAL WORK

Research reported by Daly, Miller, and their colleagues suggests that writing apprehension is related to a number of factors we do not yet fully understand. This study suggests that included among those factors should be the belief that writing ability is a gift. Giftedness, as it is referred to in the study, is roughly equivalent to the Romantic notion of original genius. Results from a survey of 247 postsecondary students enrolled in introductory writing courses at two institutions indicate that higher levels of belief in giftedness are correlated with higher levels of writing apprehension, lower self-assessments of writing ability, lower levels of confidence in achieving proficiency in certain writing activities and genres, and lower self-assessments of prior experience with writing instructors.

Significant differences in levels of belief in giftedness were also found among students who differed in their perceptions of the most important purpose for writing, with students who identified 'to express your own feelings about something' as the most important purpose for writing having the highest mean level of belief in giftedness. Although the validity of the notion that writing ability is a special gift is not directly addressed, the results suggest that belief in giftedness may have deleterious effects on student writers.

A MORE DETAILED COMPARISON OF DESCRIPTIVE *VS.* INFORMATIVE

The typical distinction between descriptive and informative is that the descriptive abstract is like a table of contents whereas the informative abstract lays out the content of the document.

To show the differences as clearly as possible, we compare a shortened Table of Contents for a 100-page legal argument presented by the FDA and an informative abstract of the judge's decision in the case:

- Descriptive Table of Contents of the Argument.
- Informative Abstract of the Decision.

Table of Contents of the Argument

Court Brief Filed Dec. 2, 1996, by the Department of Justice in defence of FDA's determination of jurisdiction over cigarettes and smokeless tobacco products and its regulations restricting those products to protect children and adolescents.

Statement of the matter before the court; statement of material facts:

- The health effects of cigarettes and smokeless tobacco.
- The basis for the assertion of jurisdiction.
  - The evidence that nicotine in cigarettes and smokeless tobacco "affect[s] the structure or any function of the body"
  - The evidence that the pharmacological effects of nicotine in cigarettes and smokeless tobacco are 'intended'.
  - The evidence that cigarettes and smokeless tobacco are 'combination products'.

- The rule.
  - Cigarettes and smokeless tobacco as combination products.
  - The regulatory goal.
  - Youth access restrictions.
  - Advertising and promotion restrictions.

Informative Abstract of the Decision

On April 25, 1997, Judge William Osteen of the Federal District Court in Greensboro, North Carolina, ruled that FDA has jurisdiction under the Federal Food, Drug, and Cosmetic Act to regulate nicotine-containing cigarettes and smokeless tobacco.

The Court held that "tobacco products fit within the FDCA's definitions of 'drug' and 'device,'' and that FDA can regulate cigarettes and smokeless tobacco products as drug delivery devices under the combination product and restricted device provisions of the Act.

With respect to the tobacco rule, the Court upheld all restrictions involving youth access and labeling, including two access provisions that went into effect Feb. 28:

- The prohibition on sales of cigarettes and smokeless tobacco products to children and adolescents under 18; and
- The requirement that retailers check photo identifi-cation of customers who are under 27 years of age.

The Court also upheld additional access and labeling restrictions originally scheduled to go into effect Aug. 28, 1997, including a prohibition on self-service displays and the placement of vending machines where children have access to them. The Court also upheld the ban on distribution of free samples, the sale of so-called kiddie packs of less than 20 cigarettes, and the sale of individual cigarettes. However, the Court delayed implementation of the provisions that have not yet gone into effect pending further action by the Court.

The Court invalidated on statutory grounds FDA's restrictions on the advertising and promotion of cigarettes and smokeless tobacco. Judge Osteen found that the statutory provision relied on by FDA, section 520(e) of the Act (21 U.S.C. 360j(e)), does not provide FDA with authority to regulate the advertising and promotion of tobacco products. Specifically, the Court found that the authority in that section to set 'such other conditions' on the sale, distribution, or use of a restricted device does not encompass advertising restrictions.

Because Judge Osteen based his ruling on the advertising provisions on purely statutory grounds, he declined to consider the First Amendment challenge to those parts of the rule. The government is appealing the advertising portion of the ruling.

BIBLIOGRAPHIC CITATION OR IDENTIFICATION

As more and more databases are stored and accessed electronically, abstracts are more frequently reproduced apart from the entire article or document. In a large corporation or government entity, for instance, an abstract of a progress report might be circulated and stored in a dozen offices or on multiple computers even though the report itself is filed in only one location. Clear identification is crucial so that readers who want to review the entire text can locate it from the information given with the abstract.

Depending on where your writing is printed and stored, you'll need to include different kinds of identifying infor-mation with your abstract:

- Bibliographic Citation
- Organisational Identification
- Internet Citation

BIBLIOGRAPHIC CITATION

If your writing will be printed and disseminated as a book, part of a book, or an article in a journal or magazine, give a full bibliographic citation that includes all the publication information so that readers can find print copies of the article.

ORGANISATIONAL IDENTIFICATION

If your abstract is part of a corporate or government document that will not be printed or disseminated outside the organisation, you need only include your name, the title of the document, its completion date, a project name, and an authorisation or organisational number. If your abstract will be circulated outside your organisation: your company or organisation name, the name of the organisation that commissioned the document, a contract number, a security classification, and key words to help in cataloguing your abstract.

INTERNET CITATION

If you're 'publishing' your own work on the World Wide Web or if your writing will appear on the Internet as part of a full-text electronic database, you can save readers time by citing the Internet address for the full text. Typically, writers note both print publication information and the URL —the *http* or *www* address—with the abstract.

PROCESSES FOR WRITING ABSTRACTS

Unless you work for an abstracting service, you'll usually write abstracts of your own finished work. This part explores some strategies for drafting your abstract. Strategies and advice on revising and editing are located in Key Issues in Preparing Abstracts.

CUT AND PASTE METHOD

Beginning with reading may seem odd since, you wrote the paper, but it can frequently be the fastest way to write an abstract because it allows you to 'lift' as much of the abstract from your original paper as possible:

- Guidelines for Using the Cut and Paste Method:
  - As you read through your own paper, highlight or copy sentences which summarise the entire paper or individual sections or sub-points of your main argument.
  - Write a sentence that summarises the main point.
  - Add sentences that summarise sections.
  - If you're writing a descriptive abstract, you're ready to begin revising.
  - If you're writing an informative abstract, look through your paper for details, particularly of key findings or major supporting arguments and major conclusions. Paste these into your abstract and proceed to editing for consistency and length—frequently in the original 'cuts' you will still have more detail than is necessary in an abstract.

OUTLINING METHOD

Frequently, the best place to start writing an abstract is to first make an outline of the paper to serve as a rough draft of your abstract. The most efficient way to do this is to write what Kenneth Bruffee calls a descriptive or 'backwards' outline.

Backwards Outline Instructions

- Read through each paragraph of your paper and write one phrase or sentence that answers the question 'what does this paragraph do?'.
- Take your list of descriptions for each paragraph and look for connections: *i.e.,* do these 3 or 5 paragraphs do something similar? What is it?.
- When you've reduced your outline to 4 or 5 accurate generalisations, you most likely have a descriptive abstract.
- If you're writing an informative abstract, fill in key details about your content.

Detailed Backwards Outline

Because informative abstracts need more detail, the regular backwards outline may not be as useful a strategy for this type of abstract. Instead, do a backwards outline on the lefthand side of a piece of paper. Then, on the right-hand side, answer the question 'what does this paragraph *say?*' for each paragraph in the paper.

Then complete the steps below:

- Take your first column and generalise down to 4-5 sentences about what the paper *does.*
- Use these sentences as topic sentences for the paragraphs in your abstract.
- Now, go to your second column and choose appropriate content for each section you outlined in #2. In other words, use the right-hand column to fill in details about what your paper says on each point outlined in #2.

KEY ISSUES IN PREPARING ABSTRACTS

These are some of the key issues in writing an abstract:

- Concise, Accurate Statement of the Main Idea.
- Organisation of Subpoints.
- Use of Details.
- Revising and Editing.

CONCISE, ACCURATE STATEMENT OF THE MAIN IDEA

Abstracts begin with a one-sentence summary of the main point of your paper and often introduce the problem the paper explores. Especially for papers based on research, the first sentence of the abstract announces the subject and scope of the research as well as the problem and your thesis. That's quite a bit of information to condense into a sentence or two, and so the concise statement of the main idea often takes careful revision.

Choose from these options to read more about preparing a concise statement of the main idea:

- Condensing Information for Non-research Papers
- Condensing Information for Research Papers
- Beware of Focusing too Narrowly
- Test Your Ability to Judge Conciseness

Condensing Information for Non-research Papers

Most non-research papers can be summed up in a nutshell statement—a single sentence that boils down a paper to its essential main point and doesn't aim to capture details, supporting arguments, or types of proof.

One-sentence Summaries for Different Types of Papers

Each of these non-research papers summarises its main point based on its overall purpose:

- This paper argues that the 'saving democracy' rhetoric surrounding the Gulf War was merely a mask for the U.S.'s interest in keeping oil prices down.

- Ethnography and ethnology are the preferred research methods of many anthropologists.

Condensing Information for Research Papers

In addition to stating the main point of the paper, research-based papers often need to set up the context and scope of the research as well. Setting the context includes stating the subject of your work as well as the problem that prompted your research. You might also refer to major researchers who have already done work on your topic as a way of setting the context. Remember, too, that your abstract must always include the main point of your paper, so don't neglect that focus as you work on stating the problem and context.

Example:

- In this example, note that the writer uses the names of key researchers to set the context and then focuses on what researchers don't yet know. After setting up the problem he's addressing in the research, the writer then announces the scope and focus of the paper in the second sentence:
  - Research reported by Daly, Miller, and their colleagues suggests that writing apprehension is related to a number of factors we do not yet fully understand. This study suggests that included among those factors should be the belief that writing ability is a gift....
- In this example, the writer announces the subject and scope of the research although he doesn't set context or suggest the problem that prompted the research. Depending on your ultimate goals for the abstract, you may be more successful with this approach that states the main point of your research paper even without setting context:
  - This report examines the changes in photo-synthesis with an energyproducing carnivorous plants, specifically the Venus Fly Trap.

Beware of Focussing Too Narrowly

No one who has ever written a concise restatement of a complex point will claim that the work was easy or straightforward. Usually, a writer needs to work back and forth between revising the restatement and re-reading the paper to be sure the main idea is stated accurately and clearly. Having worked so hard on that point, though, don't assume that you don't need to revise other parts of your abstract. In this example, the writer restates only the main point and dismisses key information from the 15-page document that should be included in the abstract.

Sample Abstract with Overly Narrow Focus

EPA is denying a petition to delete phosphoric acid from the reporting requirements under section 313 of the Emergency Planning and Community

Right-to-Know Act of 1986 (EPCRA) and section 6607 of the Pollution Prevention Act of 1990 (PPA).

This action is based on EPA's conclusion that phosphoric acid does not meet the deletion criteria of EPCRA section 313(d)(3). Specifically, EPA is denying this petition because EPA's review of the petition and available information resulted in the conclusion that phosphoric acid meets the listing criterion in EPCRA section 313(d)(2)(C) in that the phosphates that result from the neutralisation of phosphoric acid may cause algal blooms.

Algal blooms result in deoxygenation of the water and other effects that may ultimately lead to a number of serious adverse effects on ecosystems, including fish kills and changes in the composition of animal and plant life.

Test your Ability to Judge Conciseness

The biggest problem writers run into when beginning an abstract is providing enough accurate information to convey an article's main idea without providing more detail than is needed.

A DETAILED SUMMARY

A summary of: Jaime O'Neill, No Allusions in the Classroom, *Newsweek*, September 23, 1985. Author Jaime O'Neill's article, 'No Allusions in the Classroom,' emphasises the communication problem between teachers and students due to the students' lack of basic knowledge. The author supports this assertion by using a combination of personal experience, evidence obtained from recent polls, other professors' opinions, and the results of an experiment he conducted in his own classroom.

The experiment O'Neill conducted was an ungraded eighty-six question 'general knowledge' test issued to students on the first day of classes. On this test, "most students answered incorrectly far more often than they answered correctly."

Incorrect answers included fallacies such as: 'Darwin invented gravity' and 'Leningrad was in Jamaica.' Compounding the problem, students don't ask questions. This means that their teachers assume they know things that they do not.

O'Neill shows the scope of this problem by showing that, according to their teachers, this seems to be a typical problem across the United States. O'Neill feels that common knowledge in a society is essential to communicate. Without this common knowledge, learning is made much more difficult because teacher and student do not have a common body of knowledge from which to draw. The author shows the deterioration of common knowledge through poll results, personal experience, other teachers' opinions, and his own experiment's results.

SAMPLE RESTATEMENTS OF MAIN IDEA

To test your ability to find a balance between insufficient/inaccurate information and too much information, judge these sample restatements of the main idea of Jaime O'Neill's article:

- In 'No Allusions in the Classroom,' professor Jaime M. O'Neill discusses thefrustrations he had with his students not understanding his allusions. Is this a concise statement of the article's main idea?
  - Yes.
  - No.
- In the article 'No Allusions in the Classroom,' a teacher of 15 years, Jaime M. O'Neill exposes the overall lack of basic knowledge of college students in areas of history, geography, and politics. Is this a concise statement of the article's main idea?
  - Yes.
  - No.
- In the article 'No Allusions in the Classroom,' the author, Jaime M. O'Neill relays his frustrations resulting from what he finds to be a lack of basic or common knowledge of the American student. He is a professor who has taught at several different colleges in the United States. Through his experiences in the classroom he noticed the fact that students were not catching on to his allusions. He states in the article that this miscommunication is causing a problem in the education process. Is this a concise statement of the article's main idea?
  - Yes.
  - No.
- In 'No Allusion in the Classroom,' by Jaime M. O'Neill, the problem of ignorance is discussed. Jaime O'Neill says that college students lack common knowledge and it is interfering with education. Is this a concise statement of the article's main idea?
  - Yes.
  - No.
- Author Jaime O'Neill's article 'No Allusions in the Classroom', emphasised the communication problem between teachers and students due to the students' lack of basic knowledge. Is this a concise statement of the article's main idea?
  - Yes.
  - No.

ORGANISATION OF SUBPOINTS

After a summary of the main topic/problem/point of your paper or report, the abstract provides some detail on how you reached this point. The information provided in the abstract should follow the organisation of the paper/report itself, almost like providing an outline for the reader in text form.

ABSTRACTS OF PAPERS WITHOUT HEADINGS

When abstracting a paper that doesn't have headings and sub-headings, you must depend on your sense of major 'chunks' in the text.

Note

The numbers in this abstract are for illustration purposes only. Number 1 designates a concise statement of the main point. Number 2 designates a summary statement of the first major argument and its support.

Number 3 corresponds to a summary of the second major argument, and Number 4 corresponds to the second argument's support:

- This paper argues that the 'saving democracy' rhetoric surrounding the Gulf War was merely a mask for the U.S.'s interest in keeping oil prices down.
- Such an argument is made by *first* describing the ways in which OPEC controlled oil prices by limiting sales, pointing specifically to how Kuwait was producing more oil than allowed by current OPEC agreements.
- *Second*, the paper examines why the U.S., was invested in keeping good relations with the only two OPEC nations—Kuwait and Saudi Arabia—which frequently made trade agreements that benefited the U.S.
- *Finally*, the paper does a close reading of the newspaper coverage of the Gulf War, examining how an early recognition of the monetary incentive changed to a democratic one when Bush ordered troops to Saudi Arabia.

ABSTRACTS OF PAPERS WITH SUB-HEADINGS

When abstracting a paper that has headings and sub-headings, use those to help you identify key parts of the paper for your abstract. The following sample abstract, based on a research paper, uses the introduction, subjects, methods, results, and discussion headings from the original paper.

Note

The numbers in this abstract are for illustration purposes only. Number 1 designates a concise statement of the main point and 'problem' prompting the research. Number 2 designates a summary of the selection of research subjects.

Numbers 3 and 4 correspond to summaries of research methods and results, respectively, and Number 5 designates a summary of conclusions:

- 'Students in networked classrooms' examines the question of whether students in a computer classroom are more likely to engage in peer review than students in traditional classrooms.

- To test this question, two classes in each environment were studied.
- An observer participated in all four classes for the duration of a semester, noting the nature of the interaction between students. Further, the observer interviewed both students and teachers about the nature of peer interaction and review.
- Based on this sample, the study finds that students in computer classrooms are more likely, by a ratio of 2:1, to engage in peer review.
- As a result of this finding, the paper concludes that for this one variable, computer classrooms are a more effective environment in which to teach writing.

USE OF DETAILS

Details should be used judiciously in abstracts. Determining the amount of detail to provide depends a great deal on what type of abstract you are writing, the complexity of the paper, the word limit for the abstract, and the purposes you imagine readers of your abstract have for reading.

COMPLEXITY OF THE PAPER

An abstract of a five-page progress report is likely to be shorter than an abstract for a 100-page Master's thesis, mainly because a long paper will include more main ideas, not just details. Keep in mind your readers and their reasons for reading your abstract. Focus your abstract on main ideas and provide only those details that are crucial for readers to understand your main points.

WORD LIMIT FOR THE ABSTRACT

Some publications limit the length of abstracts to no more than 75 words. Others allow abstracts of complex documents to run up to 350 words. Be sure to check the publication's guidelines. If it has a low word limit, concentrate on capturing only main ideas from your paper. Don't try to cut a 200-word abstract down to 125 words by simply cutting connecting words, articles, etc. Even the shortest abstracts need to be readable, not telegraphic.

REVISING AND EDITING

When you work from your own texts, abstracts are usually easy to draft. After all, most writers begin by cutting and pasting from the text itself. But abstracts can be tricky to revise and edit, particularly if you need to reach a low word count. In this section, we offer some advice on strategies for moving from a first draft of an abstract to a polished finished version.

BEING CONCISE

When you cut and paste parts of your paper into your draft abstract, you may find that you initially include words and phrases that clarify the meaning in the paper but that simply add extra words in the abstract. Read your drafts carefully to cut unnecessary words. Note that the italicised words in the example can be cut without any loss of meaning in the abstract. 'Students in networked classrooms' examines *the question of* whether students in a computer classroom are more likely to engage in peer review than students in traditional classrooms.

To test this question, two classes in each environment were studied. An observer participated in all four classes for the *duration of a* semester, noting *the nature of the* interaction between students. Further, the observer interviewed both students and teachers about *the nature of* peer interaction and review. *Based on this sample*, the study finds that students in computer classrooms are more likely, by a ratio of 2:1, to engage in peer review. *As a result of this finding*, the paper concludes that, for this one variable, computer classrooms are a more effective environment in which to teach writing.

SMOOTHING OUT CONNECTIONS

After you revise for conciseness, you will also want to be sure that each sentence in your abstract leads smoothly into the next. Sometimes you need to add or change transitional words and phrases. Sometimes you need to repeat key words.

And sometimes, you need to combine sentences so that the connections between ideas are logically clear. In our example, we combine what were sentences 2 and 3 and the last two sentences:

- This paper examines whether students in a computer classroom are more likely to engage in peer review than students in a traditional classroom. Two classes in each environment were observed, with the participant observer noting interactions between students. Further, the observer interviewed both students and teachers about peer interaction and review. The study finds that students in computer classrooms are twice as likely to engage in peer review and concludes that, for this one variable, computer classrooms are a more effective environment in which to teach writing.

AVOIDING TELEGRAPHIC ABSTRACTS

A highly condensed style can save money when you send a telegram but can make abstracts too dense. Don't cut articles or connecting words that show relationships among ideas. Do repeat key words that show the content of your paper. Abstracts may be short, but they are meant to be readable.

POLISHING STYLE

A reader looks at a summary for the sole purpose of getting a quick glimpse of the article. As a result, she doesn't want to waste time with a lot of phrases and words that do not further the meaning, nor is she interested in the summary writer's opinion. Accounting for audience needs, there are three generalisable principles about the style of summaries:

USE OF 'I'

Although use of 'I' or 'we' is acceptable in some disciplines, many frown on its use in abstracts. Read several abstracts in the publication you're submitting to or the databases you expect to include your abstract. When in doubt, do not use 'I.' Instead, use the following strategies:

Substitute for 'I'

Most abstracts make the paper/report/study the focus of the abstract and the grammatical subject of sentences in the abstract.

Try these sentence openers:

- This paper explores...
- This study suggests...
- The report investigates....

Passive Voice

In combination with substitutes for 'I,' passive voice helps writers focus on the paper/report/study. Instead of, 'I propose that ethnography is a better research method than case study', the abstract might use: "Ethnography is proposed as a better research method than case study." Be sure to combine substitutes for 'I' with passive voice to avoid overusing the passive.

USE OF QUOTES

When using your own sentences, you don't need to put them in quotation marks. For example, if your methods section begins with "Three methods were used to investigate this question: case study, surveys, and observational research," feel free to repeat the sentence in its entirety in the abstract.

Remember, however, the following points:

- Revise the sentence so it makes sense in the abstract.
- Do not 'lift' sentences which are not your own.

USE OF LITERARY PRESENT TENSE

Abstracts use the present tense because we assume texts speak to the present even if their authors are dead and/or wrote the words in the past. As a result, write about the text and/or author as if they were composing the words at the moment.

For example:

- Hemingway describes Paris as......
- The Declaration of Independence states that all men are created equal.

Caution: This rule varies from discipline to discipline.

SOME DO'S AND DON'TS FOR ABSTRACTOR

DO's	Don'ts
1. Scan the document purpose fully for key facts.	1. Repeat words of the title.
2. Slant the abstract to the original.	2. Change the meaning of the audience.
3. Tell what was found.	3. Comment on or interpret the document. Do not use adjectives.
4. Tell why the work was done.	4. Mention earlier work.
5. Tell how the work was done.	5. Include detailed experimental results.
6. Place findings early in the apparatus.	6. Discuss details of conventional topical sentence.
7. Put details in succeeding sentence.	7. Mention future work.
8. Place general statements last.	8. Begin abstract with stock phrases.
9. Separate relatively independent subjects.	9. Use uncommon or rare phraseology.
10. Differentiat eexperiment from hypothesis.	10. Use questionable jargon.
11. Be informative but brief.	11. Waste words by stating the obvious.
12. Be exact, concise and unambiguous.	12. Say the samethings in two days.
13. Use short, complete sentences.	13. Use noun forms of verbs.
14. Use short, simple familiar words.	14. Over use synonyms.
15. Avoid unnecessary words.	15. Use a choppy, telegraphic style.
16. Employ normal technical English.	16. It should not be a mere recital of subjects covered. Expressions such as 'is discussed' and 'is described' should never be included!
17. Use direct statements.	17. The abstract should be a condensation and concentration of the *essential information* in the paper.
18. Describe conclusions in the present tense.	
19. Use abbreviations sparingly.	
20. Avoid using unusual words or phrases.	
21. Cite bibliographic data completely.	

INDEXING LANGUAGES

Analogously with natural languages, artificial languages with which the mediation between a collection of documents and its potential users takes place are also made up, as Elaine Svenonius has often explained, of four necessary components:

- Vocabulary, that is, all the elementary expressions used to define individual entities, attributes and relationships semantics, that regards the meaning for which a determined expression is included in the vocabulary and used in the language, that is, the relationships which are derived a priori from that meaning and which define it syntax, that regards the composition, by means of the structure of individual elements taken from the vocabulary, of more complex expressions pragmatics, which concerns the conditions and modalities for language application.

Authority control, or with the term vocabulary control, which Elaine Svenonius considers to be equivalent, involves the first component, vocabulary, and comes about in the second, semantics. This analytical approach to linguistic systems of 'cataloguing' mediation provides the most correct theoretical reference for a series of considerations, from which the properties and functions of authority control should result easier to recognise and consequently once clarified the relationships between authority control and the different cataloguing languages, to mark the subject indexing languages.

- Authority control can not be identified, nor is it advisable that it be identified, with a particular cataloguing language, since, syntax and pragmatic components are extraneous to authority control, which vice versa more than the vocabulary and semantic components characterise and diversify the single languages. This independence in relation to single cataloguing languages, or to particular types of language, constitutes a fundamental property and strong element of authority control. Its efficiency must be preserved and widely extended, with the punctual exclusion of the procedures of vocabulary control of those elements and aspects which, being distinctive of single languages, result reciprocally incompatible and thus do not lead to a process of unitary control. The origins of authority control are easy to locate in the paragraphs of the rules for bibliographic cataloguing by author and title, but it is now time to completely abandon the idea that authority control is a phase in the application of a particular cataloguing language, in order to project and realise a system of an unique and general authority control, which satisfies not only the needs of systems of truly bibliographic mediation, but also of systems of, among others, archival and museum mediation. The more it is general and international, the more vocabulary control is efficient, since, it permits the reduction of the waste of resources produced by the repetition of the same operations of control in different places, times and contexts. That is something particularly appreciated in an epoch in which everything is aimed at economising even on intellectual work. Especially, however, the more it is unique and general, the more authority control is efficient, since, it furnishes the unifying element between different cataloguing systems, indispensable for the realisation of instruments, logicians and informatics, which facilitate, and make coherent to the utmost, the research for information in documentary spheres which are traditionally separated, as for example, that of collections in libraries, archives, museums and those in digital formats accessible only by telematic means.

- Cataloguing languages are different, first of all, because of diverse pragmatics, that is because they are destined for use in distinct circumstances with distinct functions and modalities. But, authority control does not concern pragmatics. This means that the conditions and relationships which depend upon the material, formal and substantial characteristics of the single objects to describe and index, the various contexts in which such objects are described and indexed, the particular purposes for their description and indexing, and which determine the use of specific cataloguing languages, at any rate do not determine a diversification of authority control, either regarding the process or the product of such a process, which will be an univocal normalised expression inserted in a web of relationships. Inserting this consideration into the specific theme of this paper, it is impossible not to observe that the conviction that authority control is distinguishable, and must be distinguished, without ulterior specifications is still widespread, and that it is commonly held regarding 'authors'. This conviction, which is certainly involuntary, and thus not justified, in the normative activity of the IFLA, which on this subject published two distinctive guidelines, one which was formally presented as relating to the 'authority records' and one which was formally presented as relating to the 'subject authority entries' Moreover it is also easy to establish that such a persistent conviction has determined, although with non-identical consequences, the same organisation of two of the most important national systems of vocabulary control, that of the Library of Congress and that of the Bibliothèque Nationale de France. In the search screens the Library of Congress authorities are divided into subject authority headings, name authority headings, title authority headings and name/title authority headings; nevertheless, searching for the same expression either as name, title or name/title or as subject the authority record is retrieved. This demonstrates that the authority file is unique, that the control operations relating to the same expression are carried out only once, and that it is simply considered necessary to adjust the appearance of the control system to the conviction held above, making the 'subjects' seem separate from the rest of the entries. The *Notices d'autorité* of the BNF are analogically presented separated into *personnes physiques*, *collectivités*, *titres uniformes* and RAMEAU effectively divided. This means that at the BNF all the management and control operations for the same expression are duplicated, with a waste of resources which does not correspond to an increase of visible efficiency in the system, and which would be sad if it were motivated only by the obligation to conserve some, slightly justifiable formal differences between expressions which are equivalent the most evident case is that of the dates of birth and death, not normally stated in the terms given in the *fichier d'autorité personnes physiques*—which proposes, for example, the preferred form Dante Alighieri—but are present in the RAMEAU *vedettes*—where the preferred form is Dante Alighieri. These solution differences and uncertainties in the authority control systems, from which can be derived only problems and waste, beginning with the error of considering the 'subjects' as semantically distinguishable entities, on the same level as persons, corporate bodies and works. It is therefore indispensable to clarify that it is impossible to identify an entity as a subject if not in relation to the to pragmatics, that is, to the concrete circumstances which have implied in such a case the use of a subject indexing language in the cataloguing record of a document. However since, authority control does not regard those circumstances, it is not theoretically correct, nor practically useful, to perceive and practice a subject authority control as a process in itself. In the FRBR model, which in reality is also reflected in the *Guidelines for authority records and references*, are the classes of entities *work, expression, manifestation, item, person, corporate body, concept, object, event* and *place*. These entities "represents the key objects of interest to users of bibliographic data", and each one having a formal expression as the primary necessary attribute which designates it can be subjected, and it is potentially opportune that they all be subjected, to the authority control procedures. The 'subject' is not an entity in the FRBR model, it is a relationship, which does not rigidly correspond to single classes of entities, but which can involve vice versa entities belonging to each of the classes proposed in the model. It was certainly not indispensable that FRBR remind cataloguers that the name of a person, the corporate body name or the title of a work can be inserted in a cataloguing record in order to realise different functions. However, FRBR goes further since, it suggests the possibility that even the terms which represent these entities for which only the subject function is indicated can be linked to a cataloguing record with a diverse function. If in fact "typically the user will formulate a search query using one or more attributes of the entity for which he or she is searching, and it is through the attribute that the user finds the entity sought", and if, for example, the second and most important attribute of the work, after the title, is the 'form', that is "the class to which the work belongs', how is it possible to allow an efficient search, using this attribute, of a work concretely expressed in a manifestation if not designating this attribute with a controlled term, which cannot but be the same used, in the context of other cataloguing records, for subject access? Putting it very simply, if Walter Scott's *Ivanhoe* is an historic novel, how is it possible to retrieve, by literary genre, the various manifestations of this novel if not directly or indirectly linking the relative cataloguing records to the term 'Historical novel', thus inserting into the search mechanisms of the editions of a work a term presumably also used in the subject indexes, but which in this case does not express the subject of the work? It is true that above all in our catalogues until now, we did not bother to activate retrieval requirements for 'genre' too much, but this has been only a convenient default, seeing as how Cutter already, over a century before the FRBR, had indicated the search by literary genre as one of the requisites of the catalogue. If we then move from the bibliographic context to other cataloguing contexts, the use of potentially expressive subject descriptors in order to indicate something else becomes quite prevalent. 'Etruscan Ceramics' for example, is a term for which the function of a subject is typical in a bibliography, but probably is to be excluded in the catalogue of a museum collection, in which 'Etruscan ceramics' will indicate what the indexed object is, not its theme. That of the 'form of the work' in FRBR is the most relevant, but not the only case of the potential use of an entity *concept, object, event or place* for the purpose of indicating not the subject, but another characteristic of the indexed and described document. Absolutely nothing in the form and the meaning of a term can predetermine the function that the term will play in the single cataloguing record and consequently in a particular index, above all if from the bibliographic context we widen the field to other cataloguing contexts. On the other hand however, to be efficient, unique and general, authority control must leave that function out of this consideration. This further confirms that there is no theoretical or practical justification for continuing to distinguish a subject authority control in the general activity of vocabulary control. It is not by chance that IFLA, having produced the two guidelines on authority records quoted, has nevertheless produced an inevitably unique guideline for the codification of authority records in a readable format for the machine, that is to say *Unimarc. Authorities* in which a specific field for all subject entries alone as such do not exist.

- Semantics is pertinent in authority control, in the three forms described by Elaine Svenonius: referential, relational, category. Referential semantics concerns the uniqueness of meaning of each of the elementary expressions included in the vocabulary: it is the task of authority control to guarantee this uniqueness, supplying each strictly indispensable and sufficient expression of all the formal elements to impede any misunderstanding in use and interpretation. The potential polysemy of an expression is a frequent phenomenon in natural languages, which has no effect on communication, since, normally pragmatic circumstances clarify the meaning for which the polysemic expression is effectively used. But a general authority control, although it is functional in most cataloguing contexts, cannot delegate the referential semantics to the clarifying properties of a single context, nor be conditioned by those properties, and must rather satisfy completely and alone the needs of unambiguousness of the expressions of the vocabulary in all the cataloguing contexts. In this regard, the case that immediately comes to mind is that of those proper names, often called 'geographic', which, in common use, can indicate both a territory and the population of that territory, as well as the corporate body that holds sovereignty over that territory. In some contexts these proper names do not result poysemic: in the context of the author cataloguing 'Italy' is not effectively polysemic, since, the meanings of the territory and of the population are not pertinent to the context; while, certainly but not alone in other contexts, of the subject indexing, those proper names are very polysemic, to the point of sometimes making syntactic relationships ambiguous and the compre-hensive meaning of the entries in which they are inserted doubtful, as well as often making the search and selection of the cataloguing information fastidiously heavy. To be efficient, general authority control must resolve the problems of real polysemy even when not common to all the cataloguing context, and must guarantee the unambiguousness of the expressions in any context in which they are used. The relational semantics concerns the relationship of meaning between all the expressions included in the vocabulary. Among these relationships one is unquestionably considered pertinent to any form of authority control, and that is the equivalence relationship: if in various cataloguing contexts two or more expressions can be used with the same meaning, that is if they indicate the same entity, these two or more expressions are correlated in the authority file, in such a way to guarantee the individualisation of that entity by means of any of these expressions. Traditionally the principle of uniformity was applied to the equivalence relationship, for which one of the expressions was designated as preferred, and became the only one effectively present in the cataloguing records. The informatics management of authority control can offer alternatives to this solution, which allow us to realise a unique and general authority control without imposing the use of the same expression in all contexts, but it must be kept in mind that uniformity has its value as an element of coherence and of predictability in catalogues, and that thus it is opportune to give it up only in the presence of real and fundamental cataloguing needs. The control of equivalence relationships, however, does not exhaust the needs of semantic correlation of any cataloguing language. Author and title bibliographic cataloguing imposes control of some cases of associative relationships in point and of hierarchical relationships. The opportunity of controlling this type of relationship can only increase with the application of the FRBR model. Extended to all categories of entities, the control of associative and hierarchical relationships represents a fundamental need for the subject indexing languages, but it is presumable that it is indispensable or useful for any other cataloguing language too, and certainly advantageous for the interconnection between different languages. It is thus appropriate carried out on the level of general authority control. Obviously on this level of control only hierarchical and associative relationships of universal validity may be expressed, that is those explainable by the typical and essential definition of the entity submitted to authority control, and which thus cannot be contradicted in any particular context. Any entity can then be involved in semantic relationships that are not universally valid, but inherent to the context of application of a determined language. Such relationships must not be expressed on the level of general authority control, but in specific and sectorial vocabulary and classification control instruments, for the elaboration of which the existence of a general semantic control instrument does not necessarily constitute an obstacle, rather a facilitation. Substantially a semantic relationship structure is a classification structure, and thus needs a primary general criteria of subdivision, upon which ulterior articulations can be based. General bibliographic classifications are based upon a primary articulation by subject, which implies the possibility that the same concept, if pertinent to more than one subject, belongs to several classes. This does not correspond to the needs of characteristic semantic structuring of authority control, since, as has been repeated several times in this paper, such a process must leave out of consideration the single context, even when disciplinary, in which the single entities are concretely quoted. With a view to authority control it is therefore necessary to adopt another general criterion of classification which is independent of single contexts, but is valid and useful in all of them and has a secure application. More than a century of studies and of practice in indexing has shown that the criterion of categorical analysis which consists, as regards semantics in the individuation of a limited number of general and universal semantic categories answers these requisites, so that each entity can belong to only one category and in the assigning of each entity, for the single attributes which constitute the typical definition, to one of the individuated categories. The individuation of semantic categories is necessary to avoid incongruities and contradictions in the identification and expression of semantic relationships, but it is also more generally necessary for the normalisation and the informatics management of authority control. It is certainly not a case that upon the citation of general semantic categories is based all of the mentioned *Guidelines for subject authority and reference entries*, nor is it a case that every field of *Unimarc. Authorities*, excluding those of the notes and equipment information, correspond to a semantic category. In the exercise of this general categorial semantics the authority control is however not alone. Even in the FRBR model, in order to control other types of cataloguing relationships, some general semantic categories have been individuated principally usable even in authority control. This shows a convergence of needs and solutions which induce one to hypothesise that the full actuation of the FRBR model make a unique and general authority control realisable, but that even a unique and general authority control is indispensable for the full actuation of the FRBR model.

- Authority control is applied to the single units of vocabulary regarding a priori their characteristics and relationships, those which are constantly valid and for which the single unit is admitted in the comprehensively understood linguistic system. That is, authority control concerns the paradigmatic, not the syntagmatic, side of linguistic communication, and does not thus a posteriori regard the relationships which depend upon connotations of objects to describe and index, and which exist between the unit of vocabulary only when and since, both are present together in a determined statement. Thus the syntax which is the representation of these relationships through the ordering in sequence of correlated units, and which is one of the most distinctive elements between diverse languages cannot be object of a real authority control, but can be object, when necessary, of only a correction verification and of substantial uniformity in the area of the application of a particular cataloguing language. Understanding the syntax of authority control involves a series of inconveniences, which do not appear to be compensated for by any particular advantage. It impedes the realisation of a unique and general vocabulary control which is a connecting factor between different cataloguing languages. This is because syntax is the element for which less compatibility is shown not only between typologically distinct languages, but also between kindred languages which could easily share the same vocabulary. The cases of subject indexing languages are seen as emblematic. The differences between various languages which express a theme in pre-coordinated form, and of those with post coordinated languages, are not so many differences in terminology, but are rather differences in the grade and form of expression of the syntactic relationships, which sometimes makes it impossible to establish the equivalencies not only between index entries expressed by languages which draw from different natural languages, as the MACS project has shown, but even between entries expressed by languages which draw from the same natural language. As an inevitably ulterior consequence, the authority control pretext of syntactic constructions adds a notable heaviness to the entire process to this contraction of its own area of efficiency, with a very useless increase. It does not determine a major expressive-ness, since, it is virtually uncontainable of the whole of the forms submitted to control, which contradicts the first requisite of controlled vocabulary which is to be such even regarding its growth. The constant expansion of the vocabulary is a need of cataloguing languages, but it has the condition that the gathering of new forms is always motivated by the need to express new unitary concepts as a general limit, not new concept correlations which can easily be expressed through the combination of pre-existing forms. To create a new authority record for the string Hospitals—Administration—Data processing—Evaluation—Computer programmes, when authority records already exist for each of the single terms that compose it, it is not in any way useful to the expressiveness of the language, but obliges us, at least in theory, to the fulfillment for this entry of all the procedures of control and of semantic correlation. Being in this case particularly articulated and heavy, such procedures were not in the least way effected, which confirms the complete uselessness of this authority record, the creation and measurement of which has nevertheless absorbed resources. And here is one of the motives, certainly the most concrete and practical, for which the authority control of syntactically constructed entries must be avoided. The creation of authority records for this type of entry determines a waste of resources, which are subtracted from the more qualifying aspects of authority control, making the realisation more difficult, if not impossible. Moreover, the problem is noticed even in the Library of Congress and the Bibliothèque Nationale de France since, both institutions, in order to avoid the collapse of their vocabulary control systems, are activating a review of the procedures aimed at limiting the application of authority control to only elementary expressions, at least to the extent that they are compatible with the use of indexing languages which remain substantially enumerative. Inverting the preceding procedure at the Library of Congress a new one has been established to avoid the creation of new phrase headings and the progressive transformation of many pre-existing phrase headings in entries with subdivisions is in course. At the same time the list of free-floating subdivisions has been notably amplified, with the attribution of the qualification of free-floating to many subdivisions which were not previously free-floating, which has offered the eventuality that for a new entry constructed combining pre-existing expressions it will be quite rare that a new authority record will be produced. Analogous interventions are also taking place in RAMEAU, although it is a more recent language conception and thus less enumerative that LCSH. When improperly extended to expressions constructed for syntax authority control results quite weakened and inefficient in its semantic component, which loses the necessary rigour both in individuali-sation of relationships and in categorial analysis. To give a simple example, what is the entry immediately above, the BT of Hospitals—Administration? Hospitals? Administration? Health facilities—Administration? Health facilities—Organisation? Hospitals—Organisation? And what is the category to which the entry belongs? Is it the category of Hospitals given in the entry in the first position or that of Administration, which is the focus of the corresponding syntax? But above all, can such uncertain semantics ever satisfy the general needs of authority control? Or again, to ask a final question, does it make sense to corrupt to such a point authority control only to extend partially and occasionally syntax to an aspect of cataloguing languages, which is not pertinent to it?

In the articulation of preceding considerations, the sense of the relation between authority control and subject indexing languages is given, but almost hidden behind the closer examination of the single problems. It is well to reassume them here. The existence of subject indexing languages certainly does not call for or imply the existence of a particular authority control exclusively dedicated to subjects. Authority control, being an interconnecting element between different cataloguing languages, must concern all the categories of entities, and in such a way satisfy even the lexical needs of subject indexing languages.

The use of subject indexing languages, as for other cataloguing languages, contributes to the individuation of new expressions to be submitted to authority control, expressions whose ordinary use can not predetermine their possible successive uses, and that thus, once completed the control procedures, can be used in any cataloguing context, either for indicating a subject or for indicating something else. Cataloguing languages, which include among others subject indexing languages, necessitate a verification of the expressions used which are not merely formal, but in addition more completely semantic. Such a verification, since, it sticks to meanings and relationships of universal validity, is appropriate that it be effected at the level of general authority control.

On the other hand, it is not opportune to extend authority control to syntactic constructions, because this reduces the rigour and efficiency of the control process, weighing it down until it becomes unfeasible, and impeding its function of unifying element between diverse cataloguing languages. Each cataloguing language, and thus each subject indexing language, possesses its own syntax and the verification of the correctness of its syntax can only be effected in the circum-scribed context of the application of each language. This conception of relationship between authority control and subject indexing languages is born from the meeting, already fertile, but which can become even more so, between technological progress and theoretic reflection.

Informatics has made telematic interconnection between different documentary contexts, virtually simultaneous access to several contexts and deriving of data from one context to another not only possible but technologically easy. However a common logical linguistic instrument is lacking, and this is evident to everyone, but it is not the duty of informatics to furnish it. As concerns subject indexing languages the theoretic reflection has already individuated the principles which are functional in the elaboration of that instrument. Principles which in Italy have already been adapted, diffused and often clearly defined by the Gruppo di ricerca sull'indicizzazione per soggetto, and which can now find application in the project for renewing the *Soggettario*, promoted by the Biblioteca Nazionale Centrale di Firenze.

Among the most important are: the principle of the subject as relationship property, a factor of coherence and pertinence in a text and no longer as a pre-existing entity supplied with a name; the principle of the separation between semantics and syntax, with the control of the first which can leave the proper formal structures out of consideration of the single languages, and thus be potentially unique and general, and the control of the second which is rather the actuation of those structures; the principle of the definable relationship, for which the semantic correlation of the vocabulary unity is exclusively founded on the essential definition of each unity which is universally valid. Authority control being unique and general, and thus adequate for the situation created by technological progress, must make use of the most advanced theoretic reflection on subject indexing languages, and at the same time must satisfy the needs of subject indexing languages much more than it has until now.

EVALUATION OF INDEXING LANGUAGE USED IN COLLECTIVE CATALOGUES OF UNIVERSITY LIBRARIES

It is a fact that the interactivity between thematic representation, indexing language and information retrieval is conducive to continuous evaluations of language perfor-mance during search strategies, guiding their refinement and use in the indexing of documents. The studies of Henzler, Betts and Marrable, Fidel and Gil Urdiciain demonstrated this relevance when they evaluated the performance of indexing language and of natural language in automated systems such as online catalogues and specialised databases.

The results obtained revealed that the combination in the use of terms of indexing language and natural language proves to be ideal when devising strategies, affording quality in the retrieval by subject carried out and expected by the user. In addition, Gil Urdiciain observes an increase in relevance in information retrieval with the use of indexing language, inserted in a context of high subject specialisation, placing the precision of database systems before recall.

The indexing languages, characterised as knowledge organisation systems that correspond to the lists of subject headings and thesauruses, are controlled languages built from the principles and meanings stemming from terms that are part of specialised language and natural language, representing the set of terms to recover the indexing information. They should be structured in a multidimensional plan, crossing cultural and geographical boundaries of access and representation, without disregarding the main functions which include eliminating ambiguity, controlling synonyms and establishing semantic relationships.

The primary function of indexing languages is to represent the content of documents in an information retrieval system, according to content, and its second function is to mediate information retrieval by representing the users questions, according to use, hence, playing a key role in the indexing and information retrieval processes and enabling the represen-tation of documented contents, thus facilitating user-search by topic whenever information needs to be accessed quickly and accurately. The considerations of Zeng and Boccato lay out the need for constantly updating the indexing languages used by online catalogues of university libraries, in line with the innate characteristic of scientific progress and the plethora of dynamic and progressive knowledge generated by universities.

The views and comments of librarians and users are collaborative to consolidate these processes, in light of the fact that they should be seen as individuals who interact, understand and interpret their environment and at the same time, share their knowledge with a community of interpreters. On this matter, Hjørland reports that the socio-cognitive views are interested in individual cognition, however, approaching it from a social context. Accordingly, the process of individual knowledge is associated with the historical, social and cultural context of units and information systems responsible for organising and retrieving information. Thus, the objective of this study is to evaluate the use of alphabetical indexing language of online collective catalogues, focusing on technologies of representation and information retrieval from the standpoint of university libraries and within the socio-cognitive context of librarians and users.

THE ALPHABETICAL INDEXING LANGUAGES OF UNIVERSITY LIBRARIES' ONLINE CATALOGUES

Indexing languages are support tools for indexing and information retrieval, which are a fundamental component of automated information systems for organising and disseminating information in specialised scientific areas that require a greater control of terminology. Fernández Molina and Moya Anegón consider online catalogues as automated retrieval systems of information that are more generally available and which are the first to be used by any user when there is a need for information.

In the First Meeting of Experts on an International Cataloguing Code, held in 2003, also known as 'Principles of Frankfurt', the functions of the catalogue were organised, corresponding to the environment of online catalogues, hence, the Paris principles were expanded to the field of bibliographic description by subject and to the conceptual models established by IFLA—International Federation of Library Associations. The evolution of representation and information retrieval, made possible by technological advances, can also be evidenced by the agility of the description activity, through cooperative cataloging that enables importing standard records in other retrieval information systems from various libraries, in accordance with international standards, aiming to interchange them, hence, contributing to the formation of online Bibliographic Database. This process offers advantages in terms of time, as the cataloging of a specific work will be much faster and easier, resulting in a lower cost.

Cooperative cataloging must be carried out carefully and specifically, regarding the thematic processing of the information and considering the guiding principles to conduct quality indexing. This is a result of developing the indexation during cataloguing, according to a defined indexing policy adopted by the system and with the proper use of alphabetical indexing languages as knowledge organisation systems. It can be concluded that the proper use of indexing language is necessary to ensure the implementation of quality indexing and information retrieval processes used by indexers and by users.

The shifts in paradigms within the scope of indexing as a representation process of information for constructing online catalogues, from the proposed use of *FRBRs,* are collaborative in these processes. The construction of online catalogues focused on users and on social context that involves the processing of information must be performed by multidisciplinary and integrated teams: Librarians, users, authors, catalogue designers, systems analysts, among others, valorised by the presence of librarians as promoters in the design of access points, exemplified also by the analytical access of subjects, authors and titles and other resources applicable to the representation and information retrieval. From this perspective, it is important to use relevant indexing language that portrays not only the profile of the catalogue, but also its user communities and, therefore, the evaluation studies of indexing languages to assist in choosing the more suitable knowledge organisation system to meet such purposes.

EVALUATION STUDIES OF INDEXING LANGUAGES IN INFORMATION RETRIEVAL SYSTEMS—METHODOLOGICAL APPROACHES

When discussing the research work and evaluation methods of indexing languages in information retrieval systems, we verify a correlation between these themes and the epistemology of science information that includes independent outlooks to consolidate this scientific field. Several aspects influenced the development of this area, defining different epistemological paradigms, yet interrelated and comple-mentary. They are characterised by the existence of physical views, cognitive views and socio-cognitive views in the process of information retrieval.

The physical paradigm values the information retrieval system and the message transmitting process, and inserted in this context, we consider the online collective catalogue as 'physical' and the bibliographic record as the transmitter, which transmits the information to the user that receives the message. This information will be encoded to be transmitted as a message by the indexing language, which is then decoded by the user, sharing the same code of the bibliographic record. The communication design enables the feedback of the process, which may cause noise or silence in the recovery process of the information recorded on index supports. In contrast, the evaluation studies with a quantitative approach, from the 1970s, illustrate a shift from the physical view to the cognitive view, signaling the development of evaluation studies focussed on the user.

In the cognitive paradigm, the user is placed in an active position to elaborate ideas, concepts, etc. within an individual context. This scenario is viewed through the human dimension outlook, that is, the perspective focussed on the user, because the information retrieval systems should be modelled according to the user, in the framework of their information needs and their behaviour patterns in the search and use of information. However, since, the 1990s, the cognitive approaches have been analysed and criticised by many researchers which, in addition to divulging the cognitive processes of individuals to carry out indexing processes and designing building systems for information retrieval, aggregate 'context' as an important element, emphasising a social-cognitive view, hence, rendering this process effective.

Our view, supported by Capurro, leads us to presume that the construction of a retrieval information system holds users and their information needs as its focal point. The users, in turn, playing an active role in the socio-cultural context, enable the storage and perform the recovery and interpretation of the available bibliographic records. Consequently, the individual is seen as a part of a society and thus, the studies developed from the socio-cognitive approach regard the phenomena as embedded in a social context.

In the research development of information science, especially in the evaluation of indexing language thematic, we see that the theories about the quantitative and qualitative methods are part of this important scientific-theoretical scenario depicted by the physical and cognitive paradigms. This demonstrates the applicability of these approaches in the evaluation studies focussed on the system and on the user and not considering evaluation studies of indexing languages by the socio-cognitive approach based on epistemological ideas resulting from the social paradigm.

The quantitative methodology, representative of the physical paradigm, enables gathering information from a larger number of respondents, statistical analyses and, usually, the comparison and generalisation of results. From this perspective, we emphasise the classical indexing language evaluation studies; the Cranfield I and Cranfield II Projects, which were developed in 1957 and 1963, respectively,; the Lancaster study, which established the parameters and quantitative indices of precision and recall, which are applicable to assessing information retrieval systems exemplified by the MEDLARS system and the Aberystwyth Test.

These were developed in 1970 inscribing the issue of specificity as a substantially important matter in the development of alphabetical indexing languages, in addition to the research of Torres and of Oliveira, the object of whose empirical study was the Subject Headings List of the BIBLIODATA network, the particular interest of our study. The qualitative methodology works with a plethora of interpretations, meanings, beliefs, values and attitudes, establishing close relationships with the theoretical and conceptual foundations arising from the cognitive paradigm in the Information Science area, showing the change from physical view to the cognitive view, and characterising the elaboration of evaluation studies guided by the user.

Qualitative evaluation studies on indexing languages developed by Owens and Cochrane and Toews are examples of this methodology scenario, depicting the importance of using international guidelines and standards in the construction of knowledge organisation systems that are compatible with the users search needs. Qualitative methodology provides direct involvement with individuals, places and interactive processes; starting a descriptive collection guided the accuracy that must exist during the analysis of data interpretation.

It should be noted that in the context of qualitative methodology, the cognitive approach is present in the area of information science when conducting searches on thematic processing and information retrieval, showing the actions undertaken by librarians and users during the development of these processes. Thus, studies using the qualitative-cognitive methodology show the subjectivity of the librarians and users mental activity during their professional activity. This is seen from actions that intend to reveal the implicit aspects in the knowledge structures of these professionals and users.

The studies of Dervin on the sense-making approach, initially applied to the communication sciences area, contributed to developing cognitive approaches. The data collection technique called Focus group was also used in qualitative-cognitive research work, initially in the marketing area and then in social sciences, ergonomics, health sciences, information science, and others. In the field of information science, the research work of Connaway applied the focus group technique to analyse the performance of the online catalogue of the University of Wisconsin-Madison, with emphasis on the evaluation of indexing language adopted by the system from the users perspective.

The introspective technique of the Verbal Protocol or 'Think Aloud' is applied to qualitative evaluation studies where the individuals express, aloud, what they think and what goes on in their minds while performing a task. These statements are recorded, and the individuals behaviour, such as facial expressions are also recorded. Thus, the language of thought performs many cognitive processes such as perception and reasoning. In Brazil, the pioneer research work using the technique, developed by Fujita and Fujita, in observing indexed reading, shows excellent results in the use of the verbal protocol, illustrating new aspects of indexed reading, among other contributions.

By using the verbal protocol technique, users can 'think aloud' by producing opinions and comments about the object being evaluated, hence, carrying out a cooperative and participatory evaluation: The users participate by identifying and understanding problems of information retrieval and by using the system in their own work environment. Thus, Boccato and Fujita developed a research work to evaluate, from the users perspective, indexing language DeCS-Descriptors in Health Sciences, used for information retrieval in the LILACS system produced by BIREME, in order to obtain indicators to outline language improvement strategies in the area of speech and language therapy. The study led to the consideration of the statements issued by the four participants and the results of the analysis revealed that the DeCS language in speech therapy demonstrated the search had unsatisfactory results on information retrieval.

In summary, regarding research development in the information science area, especially the thematic evaluation of indexing languages, we saw that the quantitative and qualitative methods are part of this important scientific-theoretical scenario portrayed by the physical and cognitive paradigms. This demonstrated the applicability of these approaches in evaluation studies focussed on the system and the user, not considering evaluation studies of indexing languages by the socio-cognitive approach based on the epistemological ideas resulting from the social paradigm that regards users inserted into their social environment.

THE SOCIO-COGNITIVE CONTEXT OF INDEXERS AND USERS IN UNIVERSITY LIBRARIES

The socio-cognitive context concerns representation and information retrieval from the perspective of individuals in their socio-cultural-historical context, on the assumption that the users information needs are constructed from outside to inside, that is, the users environment influence and contribute to constructing this need, which will be represented by their mental models associated with their conception of the world, reflected on their real information interest. Boccato and Fujita The context performs the mediation between the real situation in the library, guided by the analysis concepts used by the indexers, and the linguistic system, the indexed language adopted by the system, characterised by the representation of the indexed documents.

The socio-cognitive context of indexers refers to " a prior knowledge that such professionals have their working tools and the real needs of users". The activity of indexing leads to the indexer adopting a conception of the matter which should be intimately related to their established institutional objectives and to the information retrieval system itself, detailed in the indexing policy. These conceptions of subject analysis, which we believe affect the performance of the indexer, are classified according to Albrechtsen in simplist conception, content-oriented conception and requirements-oriented conception. The users previous knowledge is characterised by the university, by the research groups and by the online collective catalogue, elements that guide and influence the expression of their need for information, concomitant with the cognitive processes to meet this need.

Thus, the socio-cognitive context is a factor to be considered in the indexing process development, from indexing reading, aimed at the analysis and representation of information consistent with the users search needs. Associated with the socio-cognitive aspect, the physical aspects, to which the institution and/or the information system are linked through the mission, objectives, the strategic plans and philosophy, and the psychological aspects are fundamental to form the indexers context, as very significant variables in the construction of this process.

The indexing language seen as the indexers expertise and prior knowledge, should enable highly accurate content matching of the documents and the users information needs expressed by their repertoire, resulting from prior knowledge constituted by the university, the research groups, the curriculum classification of scientific and academic disciplines and by the information retrieval system itself. In this case, the holistic and collective views of indexers and users are favoured, as they contribute to the definition of a thematic processing of information and to the modelling and construction of information retrieval systems.

Based on this concept, the information science area turns to a theoretical dimension brought into focus by interpretive approaches, focused on the semantic factors and the information social context of indexers and users. In this sense, our research work is contextualised between the shift of cognitive paradigm to the social paradigm, which puts the context of indexers and users in the center of the informational processes, characterised by the representation and information retrieval and knowledge. Therefore, this research focuses on the socio-cognitive context of indexers and users, based on the theoretical perspectives of Hjørland, which approves a 'methodological collectivistic approach' for the proposal of conducting an assessment study on the use of indexing language in online catalogues of specialised scientific areas of university libraries, focusing on technologies of representation and information retrieval, using the verbal protocol as a data collection technique.

The verbal protocol technique, viewed by the socio-cognitive approach, focuses on the individual when performing a particular activity and its cognition related to its production context. With regards to the indexers, the interest is the thematic processing of information, specifically the indexing and the use it will make of indexing language when representing the information. From the users perspective, the focus is on information retrieval by subject, by using language to search for information and interacting with their environment.

MATERIALS AND METHODS

The data collections were performed on a sample of nine libraries of the UNESP in the three knowledge areas, exact sciences, humanities and biological sciences, of the civil engineering, education, and dentistry courses. The empirical study objective was the Subject Headings List of the Bibliodata Network used in the processes of indexing and information retrieval in the online collective catalogue ATHENA is demons-trated in table.

The methodology consisted of a three-part diagnostic study:

- Operation and procedures in the processing of indexed information in the UNESP Libraries Network based on the perspective of the General Coordinator of Libraries;

- Operation and procedures in the processing of information in the UNESP Network of Libraries from the cataloguers outlook;
- The users evaluation on access and retrieval of online information.

Table. Selection of UNESP University Libraries and their Tespective Identifications

Course	Area	Libraries/Brazilian City	Identification
Civil engineering	Exact sciences	Bauru	E1
		Guaratinguetá	E2
		Ilha Solteira	E3
Education	Humanities	Presidente Prudente	H1
		Rio Claro	H2
		São José do Rio Preto	H3
Dentistry	Biological sciences	Araçatuba	B1
		Araraquara	B2
		São José dos Campos	B3

To perform the first part, organisational diagnostic questionnaires were administered to the directors of university libraries. The preparation of the questionnaire was essential for the organisational diagnosis, consisting of a total of twenty-six open, closed and mixed questions.

In the second part, for the operation and procedures for the processing of information in the UNESP Network of Libraries from the cataloguers outlook, we used the cognitive approach with the verbal protocol introspection technique, as follows:

- *Group Verbal Protocol* (GVP) with the heads of libraries, cataloguers, reference librarians, faculty staff users, head researchers and research group staff, and student body users for accessing the participants knowledge on the processing of indexing content of university libraries as a source of qualified data collection in the diagnosis.
- Individual Verbal Protocol was conducted with by Cataloguers to identify the procedures of subject analysis and representation in cataloguing books, as well as to identify the difficulties and restrictions.

In the third part, regarding the evaluation of user access and retrieval of online information, Individual Verbal Protocols were performed with undergraduate freshmen and senior Users, of the aforementioned courses. In the introspective technique of verbal protocol " the individuals, talk aloud, and express what occurs in their minds during the execution of a task". These statements are recorded and transcribed verbatim to be analysed later through the establishment of categories. In the context of this study, the verbal protocol, seen from the socio-cognitive approach, focuses on the individual at the moment of undertaking a specific activity and his cognition in relation to his context of production.

In addition to this, it should be pointed out that the participation of the cataloguer is evidenced in the development of the indexing in the cataloguing via the use he makes of indexing language during this activity. With respect to the user, the focus is centred on the search and retrieval by subject, by means of the use of language in the satisfaction of his research needs integrated with his environment consisting of the university, research group, syllabus and catalogue.

Individual verbal protocol consists of the recording of the 'think aloud' of a single individual during the undertaking of a task, and group verbal protocol itemises the discussion of a copy-text on the subject that involves the task to be observed and, consequently, collected from the utterances of the individuals and from their cognitions of the theme being dealt with and evaluated. The different modalities of verbal protocols follow similar procedures in their application:

Procedures that Anticipated Application of Verbal Protocol

Definition of the universe of the research:
- *GVP and IVP*: University libraries of the UNESP Library Network Brazil.

Selection of copy-text:
- *GVP*: Passage between pages 205 and 208 of the following article: Dias, EW, Naves, MML, Moura, MA. The information-seeking behaviour of researchers and subject analysis.
- *IVP-C*: The bibliographical record itself to be catalogued for inclusion in the ATHENA catalogue of the UNESP Library Network.
- *IVP-U*: The bibliographical record itself retrieved from the ATHENA catalogue of the UNESP Library Network.

Definition of the task:
- *GVP*: Discussion of the copy-text previously referenced.
- *IVP-C*: Undertaking of the by cataloguers of the indexing for the cataloguing of books on dentistry, civil engineering and education, highlighting the use of the LCARB in the process of the representation of information.
- *IVP-U*: Undertaking by the users of information retrieval on topics determined by them in dentistry, civil engineering and education, in the collective Athena catalogue, by subject field, using the LCARB indexing language.

Selection of the individuals:
- *GVP*: Three librarians, one teacher and one student.
- *IVP-C*: Population of by cataloguers from the three knowledge areas, biological, exact and human sciences, respectively, dentistry, civil

engineering and education, amounting to nine individuals from UNESP libraries.

- *IVP-U*: Population of undergraduate users from the first and last year of the dentistry, civil engineering and education courses in nine libraries of UNESP, totaling eighteen participants.

Informal Conversation with the Individuals

In this conversation, the researchers contacted the individuals through the General Coordination of Libraries explaining the objectives of the research, the methodology used and agreeing a date for the collection of data. The anonymity of all the participants was protected.

Procedures Adopted During the Application of Verbal Protocol

- *GVP*: After the reading of the copy-text, a discussion was initiated, in which the researcher made the necessary interventions so as to prompt the participants. The entire discussion was recorded and transcribed verbatim.
- *IVP-C*: Every expression of thought uttered by the cataloguer during the execution of indexing in the cataloguing task and recorded with the aid of an MP3 device.
- *IVP-U*: Every expression of thought uttered by the user during the development of indexing in the bibliographic search and recorded with the aid of an MP3 device.

Procedures Following the Application of the Verbal Protocol

Transcription of the recordings:

- *GVP*: After the recording of the discussion of the text by the individuals, a literal transcription was made with the identification of the sources of the individual statements. This identification was made in the following way: Head of Library, reference librarian, cataloguer, Faculty Staff Users/teachers, Student Body Users.
- *IVP-C*: After the recording of the 'think aloud' during the indexing in the cataloguing, a literal transcription was made of the recordings of the individuals statements.
- *IVP-U*: After the recording of the 'think aloud' during the information retrieval, a literal transcri-ption was made of the recordings of the individuals statements.

Analysis of the Transcriptions

- With the transcriptions ready, a detailed reading of the data was undertaken in search of significant and recurring phenomena for the construction of the categories. Following the construction of the categories, we returned again to the data to extract passages from the transcription that exemplified each category. Thus, the procedures adopted for the organisation diagnosis applications in university libraries, and the individual and group verbal protocols were conducted in order to characterise the organisational/academic context in the UNESP Library Network and to observe the views of cataloguers and users to analyse the actions and opinions of the participating individuals regarding indexing during cataloguing and information retrieval. Thirty-six data collections were held for nine groups of verbal protocols, nine individual verbal protocols with cataloguers and eighteen individual verbal protocols with student body users. The total number of individuals participating in this research was seventy-two persons, with forty five in the group of verbal protocol; nine cataloguers and eighteen students. The collections began in May 2006 and concluded in September 2007; they were conducted in the individuals work or study environments, namely the premises of the nine UNESP Library Networks that were previously scheduled to participate in our study. In addition, we should highlight the difficulty of bringing all the participants together in the same place on the same day and at the same time, since, the execution of the data collection was possible only when all of them were in the same field of observation. The transcripts of the data collection generated a substantial amount of data. Considering the socio-cognitive approach to the interaction of the organisational environment and the different perspectives arising from the different participants involved in the data collection indicated the complexity in analysing these transcripts, thus, the reading in full of the verbal protocols were performed, since, the language used by the individuals is not always the same used in the literature. For the collected data analysis procedures and to meet our study proposals, twelve categories were elaborated based on the theoretical frameworks, the research objectives and the statements made by the participants who contributed to exemplifying each phenomenon; each category was systematised into three themes:

- Indexing language by content: indexing procedures:
  a. Procedures for indexing representation;
  b. Language selection;
  c. Choosing terms;
  d. Performance of language in the indexing representation process;
  e. Indexing language by usage: knowledge/importance of language;

f. search strategy;
g. performance of language in the information retrieval process;
h. system precision and recall ability;
i. evaluation of the information retrieval system;
j. Indexing language by form: procedures for construction, upgrading and maintenance of language;
k. the role of the librarian in the construction, upgrading and maintenance of language.

RESULTS AND DISCUSSION

The results presented aim to demonstrate the vision of the context in which the by cataloguers and the users are inserted and, consequently, of the use that is made of indexing language in the indexing in the cataloguing and in the information retrieval. To this effect, we analysed the organisational diagnostics questionnaires completed by the heads of libraries and the individual and group verbal protocols.

The analysis of the organisational diagnostics question-naires revealed a picture of administratively consolidated university libraries, promoting a participative management, many involving the users in the process of the planning of products and services. With regard to the activity of indexing in cataloguing, it was confirmed that the libraries are aware that the LCARB is an instrument of terminological control adopted for the representation and information retrieval in the ATHENA catalogue. In addition, when asked whether the referred indexing language meets the needs of representation, the replies varied between 'does not meet' or 'partially meets'.

In the information retrieval process, almost all the libraries concurred in responding that the language does not meet the needs of users searches by subject, although all of them provide formal and informal training of users which includes the use of the ATHENA catalogue in the information retrieval process by subject field. The qualitative analyses of the data collected with the application of the verbal protocol technique, in the individual and group modalities, were undertaken on the basis of the selection of the statements uttered by the individuals in this study in the choice of twelve categories, systematised in three thematic axes regarding the use of the Subject Headings List of the BIBLIODATA Network.

The indexing language has been widely discussed by cataloguers and users, teachers and students, in group and individual verbal protocols in the three knowledge areas and has given rise to many questions and concerns about the performance and importance of this mediation and communication instrument between indexing and information retrieval in online collective catalogues of the specialised scientific areas of university libraries.

The socio-cognitive context of UNESP Library Network cataloguers, comprised by the university, library, UNESP quality standard for bibliographic records, Subject Headings List of the BIBLIODATA Network, parallel indexing languages, ATHENA catalogue and the teachers and undergraduate students of specialised scientific areas influenced the indexing, which provided us important results on the use of LCARB for the information representation in the online collective catalogue ATHENA.

Such results arrived from the declarations uttered by the participating individuals in the Group (PVG) and Individual (PVI) Verbal Protocols may also be verified, in their entirety, identified in the following way: Heads of Libraries (HL), by Cataloguer participant in the group verbal protocol (C), by Cataloguer participant in the Individual verbal protocol (C-I), Reference Librarians (RL), Faculty Staff Users/teachers (FS-U) and Student Body Users (SB-U) and accompanied also by the identification of the respective libraries.

In a synthetic analysis, the use of LCARB proved to be a 'required' instrument in the UNESP Network, which was used for confirmation and validation of subject headings to be described in field 650. This important finding is associated with some aspects, also explicit by the obtained results.

As a first aspect, due to the fact that LCARB does not have a specialised and updated vocabulary and as it does not provide a consistent syntactic and semantic structure, it was observed that the use of parallel knowledge organisation systems was a frequent practice in the search for specificity that is required by the thematic processing of information in scientific areas, through the description in field 690, reflecting the plethora of knowledge in which the university library is inserted.

NATURAL-LANGUAGE PROCESSING AND AUTOMATIC INDEXING

Indexed books represent the most common example of a subject information retrieval system. Problems associ ated with both the quality and cost of human intellectual indexing have made automatic indexing an attractive goal. During the 1950s and early 1960s there was great optimism that this goal would be readily achieved. However, many of the ideas proposed for text analysis, indexing, and machine translation have proved to be simplistic; the complexity and richness of natural langu age defeated these workers. The indexing problem can be stated quite simply. It requires a content analysis of documents followed by characterisation of such content by descriptive labels.

This requires the following steps:

- Conceptual analysis of the significant content of a document.
- Expressing the analysis by a set of words or phrases to represent the subject.
- Translating the relevant subject descriptions into standard language.
- Arranging the standardised subject descriptions according to the syntax of the indexing language used in the information system.

The ease with which the problem can be expressed does not imply ease of solution. For example, a human indexer reads a section of text and can determine its subject content without conscious thought—reading the text normally involves understanding, which implies that content analysis has been accomplished. This can best be seen when the smooth flow of this process is interrupted, as may happen when the subject matter of text is both complex and unfamiliar. The indexer then has repeatedly to re read and examine text until understanding is acquired.

Then subject analysis is the relatively easy matter of selecting the most appropriate indexing phrase. For this solution to be a model for a computational approach to indexing, however, it must be expressed in algorithmic form: a major problem. To investigate how it has been tackled, a brief look at some applications of statistical indexing techniques will be followed by a more extensive survey of Natural Language Processing (NLP). No attempt will be made to survey the areas involved in expert systems and of knowledge representation; Walker's Knowledge Systems and Prolog provides a useful introduction to these areas.

DATABASE INDEXING

At present the literature dealing with indexing topics and concepts is mainly concerned with retrieving infor mation from texts stored in databases, whose function is usually to inform the user of some easily quantifiable fact and also to point the user to some relevant document. The pointing function may be either an abstract, or keywords removed from either the orig inal text or the abstract itself. In neither case is the text manipulated by the system similar to a book. Dealing with such texts is essentially easier than dealing with a book, for the following reasons: the texts normally involve only several sentences as opposed to tens or hundreds of thousands of words; they are usually in the form of abstracted data; and large num bers of significantly different texts are present in the database, and measures of dissimilarity and similarity between texts are thus normally easier to quantify than for a book. Comparisons between manual and automatic indexing systems show further data on the difficulties of indexing books.

Cleverdon noted that:

- 'If two people or groups of people construct thesauri in a given subject area, only 60 per cent of the index terms may be common to both;
- If two experienced indcxers index a given docu ment using a given thesaurus, only 30 per cent of the index terms may be common to the two sets;
- If two intermediaries search the same question on the same database on the same host, only 40 per cent of the output may be common to both searches;

- If two scientists or engineers are asked to judge the relevance of a given set of documents to a given question, the area of agreement may not exceed 60 per cent.'

Although these are generalisations, and there are likely to be areas where the performance will exceed these figures, in others it will be considerably worse. Cleverdon suggested that many of these problems could be solved by eliminating the thesaurus and using instead the title or abstract of the article in free-text form; an approach which has had some success, and results from the work of Salton seem to show that performance exceeding that of manual indexing can regularly be achieved for many users, though Blair and Marron come to very different conclusions with the same data, claiming that fewer than 20 per cent of relevant documents are being retrieved.

ARTIFICIAL INTELLIGENCE (AT) APPROACHES TO INDEXING

Much of this work has been shown to be adequate for abstracts, particularly scientific or technical. Indeed, all current automated text-indexing systems are based largely on such statistical work, and hardly show even moderate sophistication in attempting any form of con tent analysis.

These techniques are less useful when applied to longer texts where keywords may form poor identifiers for the subject matter" and recourse still has to be made to the intellectual indexing process to identify correctly the 'aboutness' of a particular section of text, though even this may prove inadequate for research purposes. For example, when it is necessary to determine whether a particular idea has been put forward by a given researcher it is often found that indexes, to books or to databases, form poor tools for solving this problem."

CONTENT ANALYSIS

Despite the incursions of a variety of non-textual forms requiring indexing, the bulk of the material that indexers are likely to deal with is the precursor of books—galleys and paste-ups. To mimic human intellectual analysis of these texts it is necessary to determine their content by attempting con tent analysis that implies comprehension by the pro gram. It may seem curious that so little progress appears to have been made in content analysis of texts, when human indexers do such analysis with no apparent effort—syntax analysis; semantic analysis; and discourse analysis.

SYNTAX ANALYSIS

If the overall objective is to determine the intellectual content of tne text, then a sub-problem presents itself when we have to determine the meaning of a sentence. In most systems this means that sentence structure must be determined and possibly regularised in order to simplify the subsequent semantic analysis, which can now be designed to work with less rich forms of words—and therefore those that are more amenable to computational processing.

Syntax analysis performs two main functions in analysing natural language input:

- *Determining the Structure of the Input*: Syntax analysis should identify the subject and objects of each verb and determine what each modifying word or phrase modifies. This is most often done by assigning a tree structure to the input, in a process referred to as parsing;
- *Regularising the Syntactic Structure*:4 Subsequent processing can be simplified if we map the large number of possible input structures into a whatsoever, despite the amusing/apocryphal stories of the results of com puterised content analysis—for example, 'the editors of the new Macmillan Guide to Britain's Nature Reserves do realise the mammoth is extinct, even though it appears in the book's index. An over-zealous computer, working though the text, seised upon a sentence beginning: 'This guide is a mammoth work..."

This apparent lack of progress implies lack neither of effort nor of desire to attend to needs expressed by those involved in the literary field. Many of the problems are well known, if not well understood, for it is the challenge of natural-language processing that a text in its entirety may be less ambiguous than its individual parts. So a natural-language processor must resolve this ambiguity by applying context to select from the various possibili ties available, which are governed by the lexicon and grammar. This is hard because the text may contain the information required to resolve ambiguities, or it may be implicit in the shared background of the author and the reader.

To see more clearly the problems that arise when we look for meaning in text, three stages of text analysis will be examined. These are smaller number of structures. Some material in sentences can be, and usually is, omitted without changing the meaning: *e.g.*, 'She earns less than Mary1. By restoring the omitted text, the sentence structure can be regularised. Other transformations can relate sentences with normal word order to passive and cleft constructions: these will allow subsequent processing to concern itself with a much smaller number of structures. Thus, although there is no absolute need for regularisation, its absence will require usage of more complex semantic rules.

To determine whether regularisation, or even syn tactic analysis prior to semantic analysis, is required, computational linguists have looked at the work of psychologists interested in the way people deal with unusual or abnormal sentences, because such sentences may produce errors giving some understanding of how people deal with sentences in real life. It may be argued that people can use syntactically correct material which lacks any meaning; for example: 'Twas brillig, and the slithy toves'. Here syntax is the only factor giving an appearance of intelligibility. This shows that sentence parsing by humans can take place on the syntactic level with no need for semantics.

Sentences which are ungrammatical, but clear in their intended meaning, for instance 'She like go holiday.', show that semantics may drive an adequate interpretation of a sentence when syntax is poor. Thus we have two strategies used to give meaning to sentences: a syntactic-driven strategy which may be used when semantics are weak or non-existent; and a semantic-driven strategy when syntax is weak. Both methods may be used to extract meaning from a sentence if sections are not clear on the first reading.

In other attempts to explore ways of dealing with sentences in real life, psychologists have been interested in sentences where the reader is 'led up the garden path' in assuming that the sentence means one thing, then when the last word or two is read, sees that his assump tions were erroneous.

An example of this is: 'The horse raced past the barn fell.', where the reader thinks the horse was racing past the barn—until the last word is met, then backtracking occurs in an attempt to re analyse the meaning of the sentence, which is interpreted in the sense, 'The horse raced past the barn fell.' Marcus attempts computer-simulation of the human approach to this problem, and hopes to obtain insights into strategies used for sentence parsing. This should give not only an understanding of how people interpret the written word, but also possible strategies to be adopted by a computer/parsing program.

PARSERS

Historically, parsing algorithms can be divided into three sections: context-free parsers; transformational parsers; and augmented context-free parsers such as the augmented transition network.

CONTEXT-FREE PARSERS

A context-free parser attempts to decompose a sentence by successively applying a series of derivations such as:

- Sentence (S) = noun phrase (NP) + verb phrase (VP).
- Noun phrase = article (T) + noun (N).
- Verb phrase = verb (V) + noun phrase.

With 'The girl had a lamb' the mapping would result in:

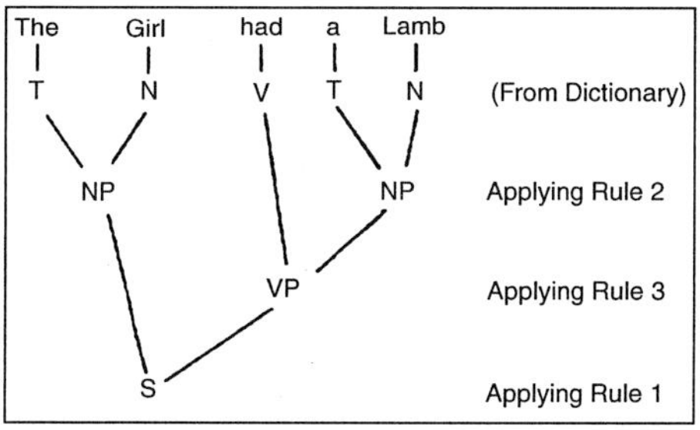

This type of parsing is known as bottom-up; the parse is started at the lowest level, that of individual words, and then built up towards a more complex construction. It could, however, start at the top of the tree and attempt to fit the structure to the sentence. Thus the task is to find a set of rules in the grammar of the language, which, correctly applied, produces the sentence being parsed. This is the top-down approach, always implemented with backtracking as a large number of possible parses at one level of the analysis turn out to be unsuccessful when the next level is attempted. The program must be able to retrace its steps to a previous stage and re-commence an alternative parse. There are advantages and disadvantages in both approaches.

A top-down approach tends to be a poor choice for ambiguous sentences; a bottom-up approach reduces the possible number of interpretations the pro gram has to consider. Thus, if ambiguities arc not a feature of the document, a top-down approach would give a more efficient program. Already many difficulties are manifest in this system; the grammar rules given are too simple for any real life situation, and extensions have to allow for more complex and variable sentence constructions. This may result in an unacceptable number of possible parses: for example, the sentence: 'Gravely concerned with spreading racial violence. President Kennedy used his press conference to issue counsel to both sides in the struggle' produced 136 possible analyses. An excessive number of pos sible solutions leads to the abandonment of this par sing strategy and the adoption of transformational grammars.

TRANSFORMATIONAL PARSERS

Harris proposed the theory of linguistic transformation, elaborated by his pupil Chomsky, which attempts to generate the deep structure of a sentence, representing its syntactic and semantic interpretation. Thus a sentence such as 'The boy broke the window' can have a number of transformations:

- The window was broken by the boy (passive transformation);
- It was the boy who broke the window (cleft transformation);
- Was it the boy who broke the window? (question transformation).

All these sentences have constituents in common. If this underlying structure—the deep structure—can be uncovered, the difficulty of ascertaining the meaning may be reduced. In the case of the sentence, 'The boy broke the window', deep structure might be represented as:

However, though the process of sentence generation from deep to surface structure can be accomplished using only a small number of transformations to produce an acceptable output, the converse does not hold. Hundreds of different reverse transformations apply to each given structure at the analysis step, making this a very ineffi cient process unless extra information is present to guide transformations into paths with a high likelihood of producing the correct deep structure.

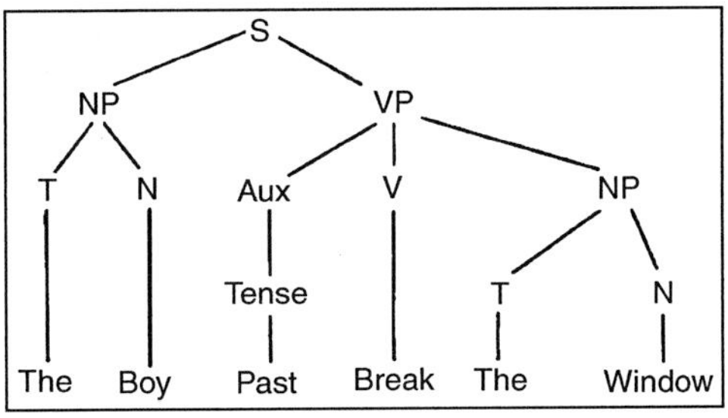

Examples of systems which apply a series of reverse transformations may be seen in Petrick "and work by the MITRE group, all done in the 1960s. However, these types of parsers are no longer in common use, as not only were they found computationally inefficient, but a considerable amount of linguistic development has taken place since, the mid-1960s which is reflected in the greater sophistication in both concept and software. Many critiques of transformational grammar are available, but Wilks also postulates the alternative strategy of Preference Semantics," whose core is a system of preferential choice between deep semantic patterns with no conventional grammar analysis or generation.

Wilks argues that transformational grammar was devised independent of considerations of meaning, context and inference, and goes on to 'consider such an even apparently structural-grammatical matter as the ambiguity of prepositions; 'out of', for example, is highly ambiguous, which can be seen from any reflection on such sentences as: I live out of town. I hit her out of anger. I threw the ball out of the window. The statue is made out of marble.... Transformational grammar makes no suggestions whatever as to how the choice should be made.' Preference Semantics, oriented very much towards processing complex sentences, is suggested as a more plausible way of tackling this problem.

AUGMENTED TRANSITION NETWORK (ATM)

The last syntax analyser to be examined is the Aug mented transition network, which has the same power as a transformational grammar, but is considerably more straight forward. In a simple transition network (TN) the grammar is composed of states interconnected by branches specifying transitions between states. Thus a sentence could be represented by: that is, a sentence consists of a sequence of: noun phrase, verb, noun phrase. And a noun phrase consists of: article, adjective, noun.

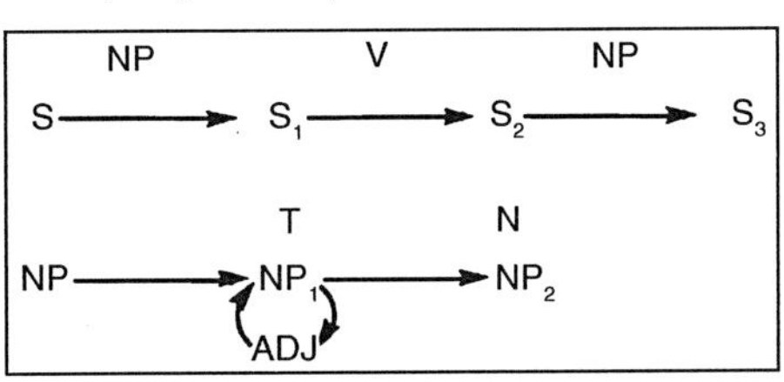

This style of transition network is recursive; thus, repetitive patterns, for example a series of adjectives immediately preceding and modifying a noun, are catered for without recursion having to be implemented over the whole network. The TN can perform tests that govern the transition from one state to the next and can be programmed to query sentences where grammar might be suspect. So far, this is simply another variant on a regular grammar, but it has the advantage of recursion and of being represented in the form of a digraph, or directed graph, consisting of nodes joined by arcs.

The arcs are labelled by words or word categories; for example, noun (N) or noun phrase (NP), and it is the task of the parser to traverse the graph from node to node. In this example it can only move from node S, to S2 if the next item in the parse can be identified as a verb. Representing a gram mar as a digraph enables formal mathematical opera tions to be performed on the graph, as well as defining its properties. An augmented transition network (ATN) consists of this system with the addition of a system for generating deep structure and allowing grammatical constraints to be imposed, so that it has the important property of performing both surface and deep analysis simultaneously.

Generally, an ATN parser works in a similar way to the top-down context-free parser and uses the conventional backtracking routines to escape from possible parses which proved untenable. Examples of working grammars based on the ATN model include the Linguistic String Parser, - DIAGRAM, Proto-RELADES, and LAS. A com parison between an ATN and a two-stage parser—known as the sausage machine—may be found in the work of Wanner.

CONTEXT-SENSITIVITY

Despite considerable progress in parsing many major problems still remain, at least a proportion of them requiring context-sensitive grammars for their probable resolution in terms both of parsing and semantic pro cessing. An example of the type of difficulties which have proved hard to resolve can be gained by studying prob lems associated with parsing compound nouns.

The following closely follows Sparck Jones who states that three processes apply to compound nominals: they have to be:

- *Bracketed*: Wicker (bread basket) *vs* (wholemeal bread) basket;
- *Lexically disambiguated*: Bread = loaf vs bread = money;
- *Given a meaning characterisation*: Basket for bread *vs* basket with bread.

She states, 'various strategies, or rather non-strategies, have been adopted to deal with compound nouns. One, for example, is to put compound nouns in the lexicon. A second is to assume that restrictions on the possible interpretations of the constituents, for a specific universe of discourse, will force an appropriate interpretation on the whole. A third is not to attempt a full characteriza tion of the whole. And a fourth is to disregard elements which cannot be processed. These are all unsatisfactory, for obvious reasons. We cannot put all the compounds, even for a limited domain, in the lexicon. We cannot rely on sense restrictions to give us an acceptable interpreta tion. We cannot assume that an explicit characterisation is unnecessary. And we cannot throw parts of the input away.'

Furthermore, even with a considerable quantity of domain-specific knowledge, there must be differences in interpretation of:

- 'These border plants are expensive'—implying that the set of plants being considered are those normally found in a border; and
- These border plants have to be replaced'—that is, these plants in the border have to be replaced. The location of the plants is under consideration irrespective of the actual type of plant found there.

At present no system can cope with such nuances of meaning. We could take the matter still further. If we were to use the same core of words, but applied to a different domain: The IRA have done so much bombing that all the border plants have to be replaced' we have a situation where 'border plants' could apply to plants which grow, but is more likely to apply to factories (= plants) located at the Eire/N Ireland border. Disam biguation here would be a far from straightforward task.

The problem lies in parsing having been syntax-driven; most parsers are based on context-free grammar, whilst the underlying problems of ambiguous structures essen tially need semantic guidance not only from the context but also by using referents from domains of personal experience of the reader. However, any conclusions formed from considering these facts can only be tentative, and influenced by the domain of discourse of any particular text. For example, much work has been done on the automatic indexing of chemical texts.

M The interest for many potential readers in this field is likely to be bound up with chemical structures, physical processes and chemical reactions. By their nature these are domain-restricted, and, due to the logical way chemical names are built up, eminently suitable for the application of stemming techniques— which in the process of stripping off prefixes and suffixes will be able to identify the structure, elements or con stituent groups of the compound under discussion—followed by statistical analysis. Few other subjects will be so amenable to this type of analysis.

INDEXING QUALITY

One also needs to ask 'How good an index do we need?' These ambiguities may simply be ignored, and reliance placed on other, clearer, sections of the text to fill in the doubtful areas, and/or human intervention for disambiguation. This crucial question could only be answered according to individual needs. Factors to con sider include the costs of checking entries manually for possible errors; of running a program that produces fewer errors than the one currently in use; and of errors—if the error rate is low enough users are likely to be satisfied with the performance. At present, linguistic analysis of text by computer is not far enough advanced for such questions to be answered, but if we draw on results obtained from statistical, non-linguistic, indexing systems, we can surmise that 100 per cent accuracy is not needed for acceptable performance.' The caveat should be added that, as with most research on indexing, these results apply to large databases, and may well be inapplicable to texts such as books.

SEMANTIC AND DISCOURSE ANALYSIS

The object of parsing a sentence is only the first stage in a strategy to attempt to find some way in which the meaning of a sentence and the meanings inherent in a series of sentences could be represented in a computer with the aim of manipu-lating concepts and ideas inherent in the text with the same facility as the computer can manipulate characters.

It is only when text can be understood by a computer that we can hope to simulate the intellectual actions of a human indexer. As in the case of syntactic analysis, a realistic solution to the problem of semantic analysis must imply simplifi cation—in which case we need to specify a formal language on which to map natural language. Furthermore, in the case of indexing, we must decide also whether any other specialised needs must be met cither in the form of extra semantic information, or, conversely, whether all the information obtained from a full seman tic analysis would be required for our purposes.

It has been suggested that the task is to examine the semantic component of:

- Methods of identifying meaningful units in the input document;
- The derivation of document descriptions from these;
- The construction and use of classifications and other forms of index language organisation.

Unfortunately none of these aims is achievable without the addition of substantial quantities of outside knowledge. Part of this may come from the text itself, but many more assumptions of knowledge common to the author and the intended audience are made than may initially be obvious. Difficulties arising here may be illustrated by reference to a straightforward description: 'Just before dawn, the Valiant sighted the Zwiebel and fired two torpedoes. It sank swiftly, leaving few survivors."

Understanding this simple story is more than under standing the sum of its parts. We have to consider what the 'it' refers to. There are four possible antecedents: dawn; Valiant; Zwiebel; torpedoes. Straightforward syntactic analysis enables us to exclude torpedoes and semantic analysis excludes dawn, but only general world knowledge enables us to surmise that Valiant and Zwiebel must both be ships, and there is a causal relationship between firing torpedoes and sinking another ship. This type of implicit information, inherent in all texts, must be recovered to enable an automated indexing system to make an intelligent assessment of the suit ability of particular phrases or concepts as index entries. This search for meaning is at the root of both semantic analysis and discourse analysis and this aspect of computational linguistics has so far proved intractable.

Most attempts to solve the prob lem have been restricted in their domain as a conse quence of the method used to overcome the problem, which is attempting to assemble all the knowledge needed to answer any particular problem. This knowl edge could be used at the syntactic analysis stage by removing some syntactically plausible but semantically unlikely parses. The organisation of such quantities of knowledge is no trivial undertaking, though it has been attempted. One notable method was that of frames, ' based on the observation that new knowledge tends to be assimilated by identifying at least a portion of it with patterns inherent in pre-existing information.

These frames may be:

- Prototypes, describing classes of objects, actions, or situations: *e.g.*, chairs, running, attending the theatre. They form a general framework of expectations—so whether one goes to a theatre in Edinburgh or Vienna, the general outlines of what one does, how one behaves, and the point of the visit remain broadly the same. Consequently the 'going to the theatre' frame is likely to remain valid;
- Instance frames, describing particular instances of action, etc., *e.g.*, yesterday's visit to the theatre.

There are obvious similarities between frames and context-free grammar: prototype frames correspond to the rules of the grammar itself and instance frames to detailed grammatical knowledge. The concept of frames may also be considered as a context-free description of world knowledge. Some frame-based knowledge representation langu ages have been developed and this type of work has lead to the development of scripts that attempt to contain the meta-knowledge needed to understand a given simple narrative. Thus, if a computer program has the appropriate script for a particular scene, it is possible to arrange for it to query anomalous situations, ask apparently intelligent questions and make responses to queries that involve concepts not directly mentioned in the text.

The classic example of a script is that of a restaurant where information is present about the characters, scene and typical actions. Anaphoric resolution thus becomes easier. For example: 'The customer told the waiter that he would like some wine.' We know that waiters serve food and drink, and customers order it, so it is clear that he must refer to the customer, not the waiter; whereas 'The customer told the waiter that he should bring the wine list' would result in he applying to the waiter, as it is the job of the waiter to bring this and similar items. This example shows that scripts cannot be used in novel situations: for these plans can be used, with attempts made to construct a causal chain.

This is no trivial problem: many of the required connections may be implicit, rather than directly stated, in the text. However, a system has been implemented by Wilensky as PAM (plan applier module) and as a simplified system called micro-PAM. These systems produce a complex series of inferences that raise the problem of which inference should be followed. The database of rules and scripts needed is very large even for what would normally be considered as fairly trivial situations, such as the restaurant scenario. A system requires considerable development effort to 'understand' even those episodes which consist of a relatively low number of sentences, even only one sen tence.

Avoiding generalisation, it can be seen that if a large number of sentences deal with essentially the same concept, then processing of the information becomes easier than if rapid changes of content in the sentences necessitated the implementation of a large number of plans in the system. A natural-language indexing system might use semantic analysis of text to produce suitable index entries, but only if the domain of discourse was very restricted. Unfortunately, this is also the area where statistical analysis and word stemming techniques can be quite successfully applied; the more diffuse areas prove intractable both for statistical analysis and discourse analysis.

The former is unsuited to this work, as keyword extraction may have little relevance to the production of useful index entries, and the very vastness of the domain in the latter poses difficult problems despite efforts to produce generalisations of text. One way of dealing with this problem is to develop a system, goal subsumption, which tries to plan for the satisfaction of several goals at the same time. In spite of all these strategies, however, the problem has in essence remained unsolved, particularly in attempts to transfer laboratory results to the domain of ordinary texts.

CONTROLLED VOCABULARY

- An essential process is the joining together of subcultures when a wider common language is needed. Often two groups independently develop very similar concepts, and describing the relation between them brings great benefits... The Semantic Web, in naming every concept simply by a URI, lets anyone express new concepts that they invent with minimal effort. Its unifying logical language will enable these concepts to be progressively linked into a universal Web.

Thus concludes Tim Berners-Lee's seminal 2001 *Scientific American* article on the Semantic Web. The concepts established here are strong ones, and the vision of a thoroughly inter-connected Web of data that these concepts suggest, could prove a catalyst for the way we research, develop, interact with, and build upon ideas, culture and knowledge. The idea presented here, of independent groups working with similar concepts, is applicable to the very technologies that can serve as the Semantic Web's underpinnings.

The Semantic Web communities and library communities have both been working towards the same set of goals: naming concepts, naming entities, and bringing different forms of those names together. Semantic Web efforts towards this end are relatively new, whereas libraries have been doing work in this area for hundreds of years. The tools and vocabularies developed in libraries, particularly those developed by the Library of Congress, are sophisticated and advanced. When translated into Semantic Web technologies they will help to realise Berners-Lee's vision.

Semantic Web technologies are now, in their own right, starting to reach a state of maturity. Berners-Lee, the director of the World Wide Web Consortium (W3C) and Eric Miller, W3C Semantic Web Activity Lead, frequently describe these technologies in terms of the Semantic Web Stack. Many of the components depicted as layers in the Semantic Web Stack are already in place, although not nearly as widely implemented as most Semantic Web proselytisers would like.

Development on the various levels depicted in this graphic has been a long time in the making. In a recent interview with Andrew Updegrove in the *Consortium Standards Bulletin*, Berners-Lee identifies one cause of the slow rate of development, implying that each layer is dependant on the layers below it. "We were asked to hold up the query and rules work because people didn't want to start on it until the ontology work had finished, so for some we were in danger of going too fast".

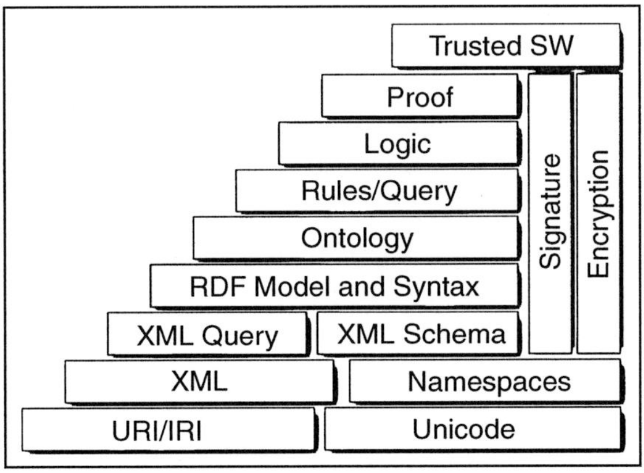

Fig. W3C Semantic Web Stack Taken from W3C Web Site, Licenced Under CC Attribution 2.5 Licence

As the technologies represented by the Semantic Web Stack continue to mature, there is a tremendous potential for the library community to play a significant role in realising Berners-Lee's vision. In a presentation at Dublin Core 2004, as well as in a number of other presentations over the years, Eric Miller implored the library community to become active in Semantic Web development.

Miller outlines the role of libraries in the Semantic Web as follows:

- "Exposing collections—use Semantic Web techno-logies to make content available;
- Web'ifying Thesaurus/ Mappings/ Services;
- Sharing lessons learned;
- Persistence".

While all of these roles are significant, the idea of moving thesauri, controlled vocabularies, and related services into formats that are better able to work with other Web services and software applications is particularly significant. Converting these tools and vocabularies to Semantic Web standards, such as the Web Ontology Language (OWL), will provide limitless potential for putting them to use in myriad new ways. This will enable the integration of research functionality—such as searching and browsing diverse resources, verifying the identity of a particular resource's author, or browsing sets of topics related to a particular concept—into all sorts of tools, from online reference sources and library catalogues to authoring tools like those found in Microsoft's Office Suite.

Miller also emphasises the role that libraries can play in helping to realise the trust layer in the Semantic Web Stack, stating, "Libraries have long standing trusted position that is applicable on the Web". The Semantic Web has a lot to gain by recruiting libraries and librarians and involving them in the development process. The W^{3}C's stated mission is "to lead the World Wide Web to its full potential by developing protocols and guidelines that ensure long-term growth for the Web". This focus on protocols and guidelines helps explain why the Semantic Web Stack includes little to no mention of content. For example, it includes an ontology layer, which is primarily represented by OWL—a Web Ontology *Language*—a specification for adding Semantic Web enabling functionality to existing ontologies.

More recently, another Semantic Web technology—Simple Knowledge Organisation System (SKOS) Core—has been designed for the encoding of the contents of thesauri. The W^{3}C's emphasis has been on how to encode ontologies, which fits with their stated mission. The source of ontologies and vocabularies is outside the scope of the W^{3}C's concerns, although the usefulness of such ontologies is certainly dependant on their validity and trustworthiness. This is where Miller's thoughts on the role of libraries seem most relevant.

Libraries have a long-standing history of developing, implementing, and providing tools and services that make use of numerous controlled vocabularies. Presumably, part of the process of 'web'ifying thesaurus, mappings and services' involves converting existing tools into Semantic Web standards, such as OWL and SKOS. Miller, and other vocabulary experts recognise that this would be of tremendous value to Semantic Web initiatives. Taking these steps would reduce the need for Semantic Web development to revisit decisions made over the centuries that libraries have been organising and describing content, which ties into the related idea of 'sharing lessons learned'.

INCREMENTAL PROGRESS —INITIAL DEVELOPMENTS

Progress on bridging the gap between the Semantic Web community and the library community has been underway for some time. A variety of projects are in progress, or completed, that will help to bring more of the tools that libraries develop into the Semantic Web and more general Web Services spheres. Many of these projects are being developed within the Dublin Core Metadata Initiative (DCMI), which draws heavily on both the Semantic Web and library communities, as well as a variety of other information architecture and metadata communities. One example of such collaboration is the expression of a sub-set of MARC Relator Terms in RDF for use as refinements of the DC contributor element.

Relator terms allow a cataloguer to specify the role that an individual played in the creation of a resource, such as illustrator, calligrapher, or editor. Allowing some of these terms to be used as refinements of contributor allows the expression of much more specific relationships between individuals and the resources they create. An example of the use of MARC Relator Terms, both in a MARC record and in Dublin Core, can be seen in figure. Figure depicts a mnemonic MARC record with personal name added entries for correspondents.

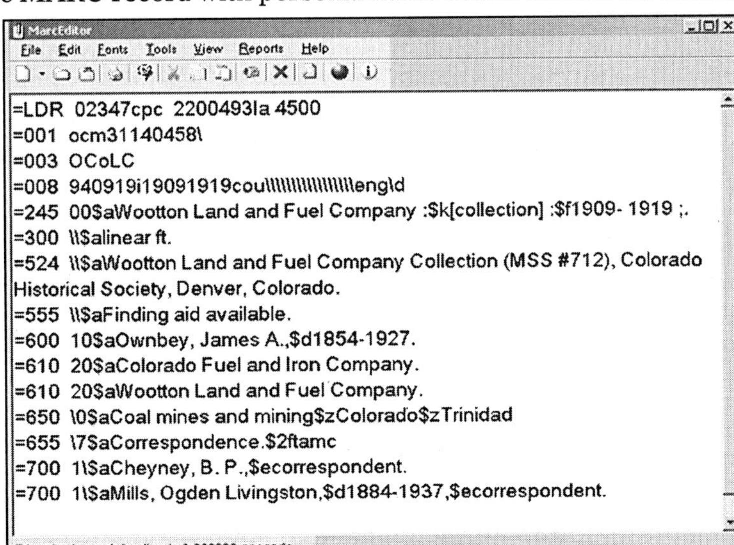

Fig 2.2. Relator Terms in and MARC

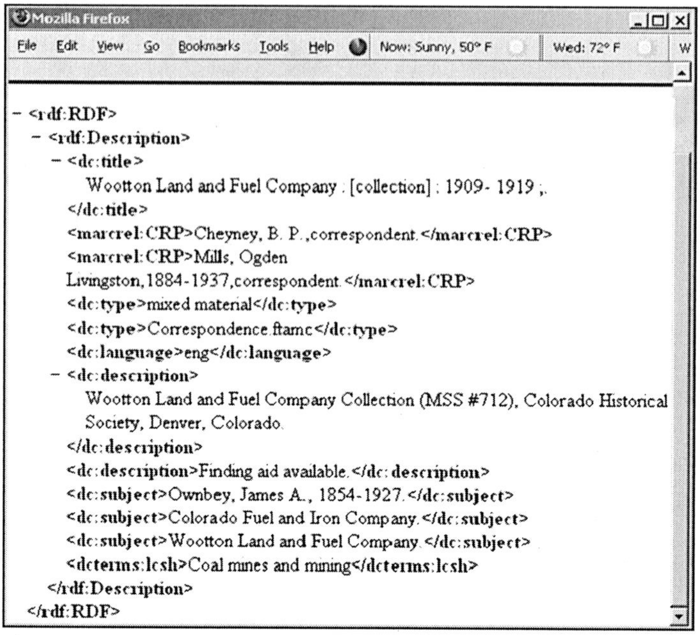

```
- <rdf:RDF>
  - <rdf:Description>
    - <dc:title>
        Wootton Land and Fuel Company : [collection] : 1909- 1919 ;.
      </dc:title>
      <marcrel:CRP>Cheyney, B. P.,correspondent.</marcrel:CRP>
      <marcrel:CRP>Mills, Ogden
      Livingston,1884-1937,correspondent.</marcrel:CRP>
      <dc:type>mixed material</dc:type>
      <dc:type>Correspondence.ftamc</dc:type>
      <dc:language>eng</dc:language>
    - <dc:description>
        Wootton Land and Fuel Company Collection (MSS #712), Colorado Historical
        Society, Denver, Colorado.
      </dc:description>
      <dc:description>Finding aid available.</dc:description>
      <dc:subject>Ownbey, James A., 1854-1927.</dc:subject>
      <dc:subject>Colorado Fuel and Iron Company.</dc:subject>
      <dc:subject>Wootton Land and Fuel Company.</dc:subject>
      <dcterms:lcsh>Coal mines and mining</dcterms:lcsh>
    </rdf:Description>
  </rdf:RDF>
```

Fig 2.3. MARC Relator Terms in and DC

The 700 tags at the end of this record each include a subfield e, which contains a MARC Relator term identifying the role of these individuals. The corresponding Dublin Core Record in 2b represents this same information using the 'marcrel' namespace with the Relator code 'CRP', which corresponds to the term 'correspondent.' The concept of author added entry, represented by MARC tag 700 in 2a, is implicit in the Dublin Core example because the Relator terms are all element refinements of dc:contributor.

Another example of collaboration can be seen in the ongoing work to bind the Metadata Object Description Schema (MODS) metadata element set to RDF and to the DC Abstract Model so that MODS terms, or alternately new DC properties derived from or related to these MODS terms, could be available to Dublin Core Application Profiles. Similar collaborations between the Institute of Electrical and Electronics Engineers Learning Object Metadata group and DCMI resulted in an RDF binding of IEEE-LOM, which essentially serves to make IEEE-LOM metadata statements and records useable within the context of the Semantic Web. A summary of this process was reported at the Ariadne Conference in 2003. This presentation resulted in a joint-task force between the IEEE and DCMI communities to formally map the IEEE-LOM Schema to the DCMI Abstract Model as well.

Progress on this process can be tracked on the DC Education Working Group's Wiki. However, both of these examples apply to metadata elements and resource descriptions themselves. The progress that has been made on bringing tools from the library world into the Semantic Web has, thus far, been entirely focussed on the idea of exposing library collections. Incorporating elements used in library resource descriptions into the sets of resource properties that are used to enable the Semantic Web is a large step, and enables library metadata to interoperate with Dublin Core and other RDF encoded metadata. Authority records, library thesauri, and library controlled vocabularies, if converted into formats that support Semantic Web technologies, have an even greater potential for revolutionising the way users—and machines—interact with information on the Internet.

AUTHORITY CONTROL—CORE PRINCIPLES

The benefits and virtues of authority control have been debated and restated for decades. When we apply authority control, we are reminded how it brings precision to searches, how the syndetic structure of references enables navigation and provides explanations for variations and inconsistencies, how the controlled forms of names, titles, and subjects help collocate works in displays, how we can actually link to the authorised forms of names, titles, and subjects that are used in various tools, like directories, biographies, abstracting and indexing services, and so on. We can use the linking capability to include library catalogues in the mix of various tools that are available on the Web. In order to enable these capabilities in a Web-based environment, it will be necessary to move the records that facilitate linking and aggregating in the library into more universal and generalised encoding. The Library of Congress is taking steps in this direction, particularly through work on MARCXML for Authority Records and the Metadata Authority Description Schema (MADS), along with crosswalks to go between them. A next logical step is to begin work on translating this data into the Resource Description Framework (RDF), which is not a trivial task.

SUBJECT AND GENRE VOCABULARIES FOR THE SEMANTIC WEB

There are a vast number of controlled vocabularies for various forms of subject access to library materials. Some of these vocabularies are classification schemes, such as *Dewey Decimal Classification* (DDC) and *Library of Congress Classification* (LCC).

Others are controlled lists of subject headings or terms, which adhere to national and international guidelines for thesaurus construction, like the Library of Congress Subject Headings (LCSH), the two Thesauri for Graphic Materials: Subject Terms (TGM I) and Genre and Physical Characteristic Terms (TGM II), Guidelines on Subject Access to Individual Works of Fiction, Drama, Etc. (GSAFD), and the Ethnographic Thesaurus. Some of the subject thesauri published by The Getty, such as The Getty Thesaurus of Geographic Names (TGN) and The Art and Architecture Thesaurus (AAT) are truly hierarchical thesauri. Many of these controlled vocabularies are registered as DCMI Encoding Schemes in the DCMI Terms namespace.

Registered Encoding Schemes qualifying the DC Subject element include:

- Dewey Decimal Classification (DDC),
- Library of Congress Classification (LCC),
- Library of Congress Subject Headings (LCSH),
- Medical Subject Headings (MeSH),
- National Library of Medicine Classification (NLM),
- The Getty Thesaurus of Geographic Names (TGN),
- Universal Decimal Classification (UDC).

However, when these vocabularies are used as values of DC Subject in metadata records outside of the library context, the syndetic structure of the source vocabulary is all but lost. There is no way for search tools or other applications to make use of information about related terms and variant forms as part of the entry vocabulary. In some cases, item metadata for Dublin Core records is included within a larger system that relies heavily on MARC data, such as OCLC WorldCat. When this is true, many of the Library of Congress controlled vocabularies are indirectly linked to these Dublin Core records by virtue of the availability of MARC authority records for the controlled vocabularies in those systems.

Systems outside of these application environments need to be able to retrieve and translate or otherwise make use of MARC authority record data to make effective use of the hierarchies, equivalency relationships, and structures in the content of controlled vocabularies. These vocabularies present tremendous potential for improving access to web resources and Semantic Web data, as well as enhancing networked applications.

Search engine results could be dramatically improved, both in terms of precision and recall. Different subject vocabularies covering the same concept space could be merged together or associated, providing an environment where differences in terminology between different communities would provide less of a barrier to effective browsing of resources. Front-end interfaces could be built for a variety of online reference tools that take advantage of the rich structure of relationships between topics that is provided by controlled vocabularies. In some regards, libraries are only now realising the full potential of catalogue records to provide innovative and new browsing interfaces.

An example can be seen in North Carolina State Library's new, Endeca powered, catalogue interface, which is presently built entirely on the structure of bibliographic records. This new catalogue interface allows users to refine a search by navigating through record clusters that share a particular property. Drawing on the idea of faceted classification, clusters can be grouped by subtopic, genre, language, time-period, geographic region, and in a variety of other ways. These facets are derived from information in various access points, subject headings and subdivisions in a particular bibliographic result set. It is easy to envision a similar technique being used to broaden searches and even to present initial browse interfaces to specific collections of information resources. When interfaces start to leverage the power of authority control in new and interesting ways, the benefit to users will be immense. Another example of initiatives to leverage authority control is OCLC Research's Terminology Services project to 'offer accessible, modular, Web-based terminology services'.

The Terminologies Pilot Project in October 2005 explored techniques for encoding sample vocabularies, means of mapping between them to help users identify relationships, and methods for incorporating the resulting services into other applications and tools. These services are the beginning of a rich tapestry of semantics that can be delivered within a user's current context, whatever that context is. In some cases, the services may be entirely carried out by server-side applications.

Almost any application that serves content dynamically could include a navigation system that draws on the hierarchies and relationships between terms in LCSH, and could provide search interfaces that draw on term equivalencies to retrieve a broader set of resources when doing keyword searches. Additionally, there could be services that exist within client side applications, pulling vocabulary structures from the network and integrating them into authoring tools.

One such service component prototyped for the OCLC pilot uses the Microsoft Office 2003 Research Services Pane to access genre terms. "... if a college student wishes to categorise a reading list of fiction titles based on genre, he could copy the titles into a Microsoft Excel 2003 workbook, open the Research services pane, send a search to the OCLC Research GSAFD vocabulary service, and then place the results into his document". This provides the user with the ability to browse and search genre categorisations without having to leave the application in which the search results will be used.

Additionally, the more sources of data are made available in this way, the more automated the process can be. If the Research Services Pane had access to bibliographic records, genre or subject categorisation could be fully automated and available at the touch of a button. A cataloguer could use a similar tool to suggest appropriate terms from a controlled vocabulary, which will lead to lots of cost saving opportunities. Similar applications could be developed as browser plug-ins or extensions.

A sidebar application could be built for FireFox that could harness the power of controlled vocabularies when browsing Web resource that provide some degree of keyword tagging or folksonomy support. Imagine browsing a resource like Flickr and being able to query LCSH for relationships that may be defined between subject terms through the tags labelling the subject of a particular photographic image and tags for various related concepts. The sidebar could include hyper-linked broader, narrower, equivalent, and associative terms that would pull together additional photographs tagged with those related terms. In a different context, such an application could attempt to scan html source code for word frequency and try to guess the primary topics, returning related terms from a controlled vocabulary, and perhaps linking to search engine results for the concepts represented. Additionally, a similar service could be provided using a word highlighted by the user. The possibilities are endless.

NAME AUTHORITY FOR THE SEMANTIC WEB

The benefits of authority control—search precision, more powerful navigation, collocation, and linking between various tools and resources—apply to metadata about the creators of resources as well as to subject access. The library community is well positioned to play a significant role in these developments. Libraries have been dealing with identification, disambiguation, and collocation of names of content creators since, the beginning of cataloguing. The different forms of name used by the same creator in various print publications and other types of resources have always led to some degree of difficulty in grouping works together.

The syndetic structure of name authority files has proven itself a very useful tool to help collocate works by an author regardless of the form of name on a particular item. The proliferation of resources on the Web extends the scope of the collocation problem. Initiatives are appearing in the Web community to help provide better mechanisms for identifying persons, families, and corporate entities that have a role with respect to information resources.

InterParty is a European Commission funded project exploring the interoperation of 'party identifiers,' which would provide standard identification numbers to serve the same purpose that authorised forms of names serve in library applications: to help collocate and disambiguate individual content creators. More recently, some of the InterParty members and others submitted a similar proposal for International Standard Party Identifiers (ISPI) as an ISO standard. More directly related to Semantic Web Development is the Friend Of A Friend (FOAF) project. FOAF is about "creating a Web of machine-readable homepages describing people, the links between them and the things they create and do". Finding ways to integrate these initiatives with existing mechanisms for name authority control in libraries can help to bring library catalogues into the mix of tools available on the Web.

Additionally, the availability of library authority data in a more Web-friendly format has the potential to positively influence the organisation of the broad spectrum of Web content already available. The development of a Virtual International Authority File (VIAF) has been a key idea moving forward this initiative.

Virtual International Authority File (VIAF)

Presently, authority files are maintained and developed by a large range of national bibliographic agencies. To make the most of this potential, it is useful to first integrate the somewhat disparate sources of authority data that exist even within the library community. These agencies develop files that are generally focused on the creators of content relevant to a particular national and cultural identity. As geographic boundaries become more and more porous, and culture becomes much more international, there is increasingly overlap between the authority files maintained by these agencies.

The concept of a Virtual International Authority File (VIAF) has been discussed since, the 1970's within the International Federation of Library Associations and Institutions (IFLA). Initially, IFLA envisioned a single shared file; more recently the concept has evolved into one of linking existing national and regional authority files. The primary objective of this vision is to facilitate sharing the workload and reducing cataloguing costs within the library community. The community is expanding, especially in Europe, where libraries are viewed as one of many 'memory institutions', along with archives, museums, and rights management agencies.

Ideally, authority files can be freely shared among all of these communities. A shared file would reduce the cost of doing authority work by avoiding repetition of effort while combining various forms of names that are particular to resource published within the context of a particular region, culture, or nation. Combining or clustering the forms of name will result in a much richer set of authority information, enabling users to access information in the language, scripts, and form they prefer.

Additionally, a single international authority file system will be far more useful when integrated into various Web retrieval tools and Web content descriptions. Such a tool could be used by a wide range of Web systems to improve the precision of user's searches and to provide the user's preferred display of the language and script of names. Authority records are used to collocate resources that utilise varying forms of name, but collocation does not need to dictate the script or language used by the end user display.

Figure shows how a single entity—whether it is a concept, person, place, or thing—has a variety of labels that identify it in different languages and scripts. Traditionally, library systems have relied on a preferred label for all entities, although the preference would vary depending on the geographic context of the system.

Merging or linking records that utilise different languages and scripts allows the end-user to select the language and script used to display information about entities irrespective of system's default preference. This is appropriate in a truly global Web, where geographic and national boundaries are considerably less significant.

A variety of projects have sought to address this language challenge in recent years, exploring mechanisms to combine individual authority files. One such project, the European Commission funded Author project converted a sample of authority records from five European bibliographic agencies in France, England, Belgium, Spain, and Portugal into the UNIMARC format and made them available as a searchable file. "The challenge was that each library has its own language, cataloguing rules, bibliographic record format and local system for its online authority file". Combining these records into a single UNIMARC file required a large amount of record normalisation. No attempt was made to link the records for the same entity.

More recently, OCLC Online Computer Library Center Inc., the Library of Congress, and Die Deutsche Biblioteck (DDB) began a joint project to test the idea of a VIAF. OCLC used matching algorithms to link name authority records of these two national bibliographic agencies and built a server to store the combined records. Additional phases of the project will involve ongoing maintenance to update the central file when either source is updated and possibly the development of a multilingual end user interface. Following the evaluation of the project, the addition of new partners will be explored, particularly those potential partners with non-roman authority records.

LEVERAGING A VIAF ON THE SEMANTIC WEB

When combined with developments in the broader metadata, Web-design, and Semantic Web communities, the power and utility of VIAF outside of libraries becomes clear. Authority record data can be associated more easily with a variety of Web resources, allowing users and potentially machines to immediately start to evaluate the information they are looking at. A quick search of bibliographic data related to a given resource author allows the retrieval of her dissertation, which could be mined for data about the degree granting institution.

Other bibliographic records could be retrieved to help evaluate the original Web resource and related works could offer pathways to additional relevant resources. As other resources start including metadata that uses identifiers or headings to link to a VIAF, the opportunity to connect more interesting bits of information can add significant value to any Web-based information resource. Wikipedia entries, journal articles, Who's Who biographical info, an individual's blog, their homepage, or the homepage of their place of work can all be interconnected, as well as linked to journal articles, bibliographic records in catalogues and in e-commerce sites, and a variety of other scholarly resources. These interconnections have extensive implications for research.

Once there is a corpus of biographical information combined into a data store that is connected to authority data, the information can be used to make inferences about any document, article, Web page, or blog entry that turns up when searching for information. For example, imagine a blog post that includes information about its author's identity. This information could be referenced against available biographical data and used to make inferences about the veracity and objectivity of the post's content.

If the author were affiliated with the Recording Industry Association of America (RIAA) a trade group representing the U.S recording industry, or the Electronic Frontier Foundation (EFF), a non-profit legal organisation focused on defending 'digital rights', heavily involved in fighting bad uses of Digital Rights Management technology, and opposing limitations on fair use, the statement is likely to be much less objective than content posted by a Harvard law professor. While an agent or search tool couldn't necessarily flag such resources as potentially biased without additional information about the affiliate organisation, it would still be very useful to present these additional facts to the user when returning search results.

The metadata community has a number of initiatives underway for describing people, both as agents of resource creation and for the utility of describing relationships between people, describing connections between people and organisations, and for capturing other contact information and other descriptive information about individuals and groups. Examples of such initiatives include the Dublin Core Agents Working Group's work on defining a metadata standard for agent description and identification. Ultimately, this work should result in the development of an Application Profile for agent description.

Also, work has been completed on 'Reference Models for Digital Libraries: Actors and Roles' within the DELOS/NSF Working Group. This work culminated in Final Report, issued in July 2003. Interestingly, this work goes well beyond the scope of authors and content creators; instead the DELOS/NSF model categorises Actors as Users, Professionals, and Agents. In this context, agents are the traditional content creators that help populate a digital library and professionals are the developers of the digital library itself and the providers of digital library services.

The scope of their work may be much deeper than is necessarily relevant to discussions of authority control on the Semantic Web, although the models used and conclusions drawn may prove to play an important role in future discussions about authority control for names. Another initiative, the Friend Of A Friend (FOAF) project described earlier, is of particular use to the Semantic Web community, because it was conceived with the Semantic Web in mind and is built upon the RDF data model.

FOAF expresses identity through any property value pair, allowing you to aggregate data about individuals using any unique property, such as an e-mail address or the URL for a home page. FOAF is primarily designed for community building, but when the possible privacy issues of sharing personal data are resolved there is much potential for FOAF to help aggregate public information about individuals. FOAF could be used to aggregate all sorts of resources, both by and about individuals—Again, resources such as, Wikipedia entries, journal articles, Who's Who biographical info, the individual's homepage, their blog, or their place of work. This information could be glommed into a program like Piggy Bank—a FireFox extension for viewing, collecting and merging RDF encoded data, developed by the Simile project —or any other Semantic Web enabled tool, and processed along with other local or remote data stores. For example, a local data store of vcards and/or FOAF data might include private data, such as phone number, calendaring system, and e-mail address. The very presence of that particular identifier in a local store of RDF data about people might change the context of any information interaction with a Wikipedia or Who's Who entry.

Using any 'unique' property to identify entities will certainly help to aggregate most of them, but it would miss entities that are not described using a particular piece of identifying information. Inferences about which descriptions represent the same entity will only go so far in establishing a positive match. The ability to completely aggregate such data becomes even more powerful when the identifying properties can be referenced against the VIAF to determine alternate forms of name and representations in alternate scripts. This allows a query of available RDF data to be much more comprehensive when deciding what pieces of data should be aggregated.

MARKUP AND ENCODING OF AUTHORITY DATA

One of the most valuable activities that libraries and librarians can engage in, both to help realise the Semantic Web and to generally increase the findability of electronic resources in general, is the process of creating versions of vocabularies in machine-readable format. Thesauri, authority files, classifications schemes, and subject heading lists—collectively referred to as Knowledge Organisation Systems—have enormous potential for enhancing the discoverability and organisation of resources in a networked environment.

The potential only increases when such systems are provided in formats designed for emerging Web technology, such as OWL and SKOS—two of the ontology schema of the Semantic Web.

- Knowledge organisation systems can enhance the digital library in a number of ways. They can be used to connect a digital library resource to a related resource. The related information may reside within the KOS itself or the KOS may be used as an intermediary file to retrieve the key needed to access it in another resource. A KOS can make digital library materials accessible to disparate communities. This may be done by providing alternate subject access, by adding access by different modes, by providing multilingual access, and by using the KOS to support free text searching.

The perceived benefits of knowledge organisation systems are of particular importance, and apply to networked resources beyond the scope of digital library materials. The availability of machine-readable representations of various thesauri and other controlled vocabulary enables more effective search and retrieval, better browse functionality and general organisation of materials online, and the automatic creation of context sensitive linkages between available resources and data sets.

Additionally, and most importantly for Semantic Web development, providing controlled vocabularies outside of traditional library systems enables a variety of applications to more effectively merge and manipulate data and information from disparate sources. There are many steps that need to be taken to realise this set of goals. Firstly, the library and Semantic Web communities must agree on how best to encode these vocabularies.

Many of the subject schemes already exist in one or more machine-readable representations. Much of LCSH exists in MARC records in library catalogues and the databases of cataloging services such as OCLC's WorldCat and RLIN 21. All of the LC controlled vocabularies are available as complete files of MARC 21 or MARCXML formatted authority records through the Cataloguing Distribution Service of the Library of Congress.

The Getty provides licenced access to its vocabularies in three formats: XML, relational tables and MARC, and provides sample data from each vocabulary for free. At first glance, these formats do not appear to be of much use in the context of RDF, but the standardisation and global use of MARC makes it possible to convert these into RDF-friendly data. One approach is the creation of URIs to identify each terminal node on the source XML structure as a unique concept that can be used as a property in the RDF and DC Abstract Model sense. This prospect has the potential to retain as much of the detail available in the source format as possible, but may prove unnecessary and undesirable due to the complexity of the resultant sets of properties.

On the other hand, the information from MARC records may in fact be useful for automatic processes and machine activities. The richness of MARC authority data, and the time and effort invested in developing, encoding, and sharing this data, provides a unique and powerful set of vocabularies. However, it remains to be seen whether the complexity of the resulting XML records would be an impediment to intero-perability. An alternative approach involves simply cross-walking the XML data into an already defined RDF-friendly form.

Along the way, detail about relationships between terms will likely be lost, but the end product will probably be much simpler to work with. One possible target RDF vocabulary, the Simple Knowledge Organisation System (SKOS) Core has much potential in this context. SKOS Core provides a model for expressing the structure of what they refer to as a 'Concept Scheme'. "Thesauri, classification schemes, subject heading lists, taxonomies, terminologies, glossaries and other types of controlled vocabulary are all examples of concept schemes". SKOS Core provides a means of expressing most of the semantic relationships included in most library subject vocabularies. For example, 'prefLabel' and 'altLabel' represent 'use' and 'use for' references, while 'broader' and 'narrower' are used to identify hierarchical relationships. SKOS allows for the creation of new labels and the encoding of more specific types of relationships as well. Additionally, SKOS provides mechanisms for various types of notes—scopeNote, definition, example and note.

The SKOS Core community has drafted documentation on 'Publishing a Thesaurus on the Semantic Web," which provides a guide for using SKOS to both describe and encode vocabularies in RDF. Converting large controlled vocabularies into RDF data is certainly a good way to get sample data sets to use to build prototype services. However, the long-term maintenance of such data stores may be problematic. As changes are made to the source vocabulary, those changes need to be propagated through to all the various formats that the vocabulary is made available in.

In the context of SKOS, this is a manageable task. SKOS extensions have been proposed to allow for versioning and the tracking of changes made to controlled vocabularies over time.

However, in cases where vocabularies are likely to be managed in a variety of different formats, the SKOS extensions are less helpful. Another approach is to harvest the source data in its native format and translate it into a variety of output formats either as nightly batch processes or on-the-fly as data is requested.

Progress is being made in this area, such as OCLC's work on exposing vocabularies in a variety of delivery formats, including MARCXML and SKOS. It doesn't matter whether the data store is MADS, MARC, RDF, or some arbitrary flavour of XML, it can be transformed into another format either on-the-fly or as a batch process. A centralised name authority database could be created from the national authority files available in various library communities and stored as normalised MARC 21.

If this data store is deemed useful to the Friend of a Friend (FOAF) community, the data can be turned into RDF. Similarly, Web services like Flickr could convert and makes use of Library of Congress Subject headings to augment both the searching and development of their folksonomies.

THE ART OF INDEXING

The Producer Price Index (PPI) has one of the longest histories of any economic statistic. The first PPI under its previous title of Wholesale Price Index (WPI) was published by the Board of Trade in 1903 in a parliamentary paper on Wholesale and Retail Prices. The series ran from 1871, and represented the weighted arithmetic mean of price relatives of 45 commodities, mainly basic materials and foodstuffs. Prices were largely derived from the average values recorded at the time of import or export.

In 1935, indices were rebased on 1930=100 and continued to be published until 1955. These earlier indices were rather crude and did not attempt to measure prices of finished goods at all. A description of these early statistics is contained in *Stafford*, while the indices are shown in *Mitchell*. The present structure of the PPI largely derives from the mid 1950s. An article published in 1956 effectively sets out the concepts underlying the present set of indices. Since, that time, there have been seven rebasings but the basic concepts have remained unchanged.

BASIC CONCEPTS

The two main sets of indices which are published for the home PPI are: *Output indices*—the prices of goods produced by manufacturers in the United Kingdom for sale in this country, and *Input indices*—the materials and fuel purchased by UK manufacturing industry as part of their current expenditure. These include imports of raw materials and semi-manufactured goods as well as home-produced inputs of materials, fuel and semi-manufactured goods. The latter are generally represented by the output price indices of the appropriate industry. Output PPIs are commonly known as 'factory gate' prices to reflect the fact that they measure prices of goods before they are transferred to the distribution or retail sectors. This is a crucial difference between the PPI and the Retail Price Index (RPI), also produced by ONS, which measures prices of goods and services paid by households. Other important points are that PPIs reflect prices at the time of order rather than delivery and should reflect actual prices achieved rather than any notional list price. An article comparing movements in the RPI and PPI over the period 1990 to 1994 was published in Economic Trends in August 1998.

USES OF PPI

The PPI has three main categories of customers:

- Other parts of the Office for National Statistics, which use the data for deflating the national accounts, particularly the index of production, capital expenditure and stockbuilding;
- Economists at the Treasury, the Bank of England, and City institutions, who regard the PPI as a measure of current inflationary processes in the overall economy. The DTI, MAFF and industrial economists also use PPIs for monitoring price pressures on sub-sectors of UK industry; and
- Commercial customers, including MOD and its suppliers, who use the indices as an impartial measure of prices for contractual purposes, and for comparing with their own patterns of purchases and sales.

EXPORT PRICES

Export price indices (EPIs) have been collected since, 1993. These are collected in a broadly similar way to PPIs but prices for export rather than the UK market are requested. EPIs have been used to deflate the export component of the Index of Production, as well as the value of exports of manufactured goods recorded in the Balance of Payments, since, the publication of the 1996 National Accounts.

The rationale for developing EPIs to deflate these flows within the national accounts is set out in *Williamson and Ruffles.* At present, EPIs cover around half of manufactured goods, and it is planned to steadily increase their coverage over the next few years.

IMPORT PRICES

Import prices covering raw materials and semi-manufactured products have always been collected as part of the material and fuel input indices. The categories covered are divisions 00 to 68 of the Standard International Trade Classification (SITC). A recruitment exercise is currently under way to develop import price indices (IPIs) covering capital goods as well as finished intermediate products.

RESOURCES USED

The present numbers of suppliers and items for the main PPI enquiries are:

	Suppliers	Items
PPI (home sales)	4,000	9,000
Import Prices	400	900
Export Prices	1,000	2,500

The number of export price items is presently being extended and may increase to a maximum of 5,000. The estimated total government costs of conducting the PPI, including export, import and service sector prices were £2.0 million in 1997/98, and involved 52.2 staff years. Compliance costs for industry—that is the estimated cost of the time spent by contributors in providing the data—were £200,000 in 1996/97.

STANDARD INDUSTRIAL CLASSIFICATION

Since, 1995, the Standard Industrial Classification (SIC) used in the PPI system has been the 1992 version. More detailed information was published in the Official Journal of the European Community *OJEC*, which also allows comparison with the Combined Nomenclature used by Customs and Excise. SIC(92) is consistent with EUROSTAT and United Nations recommendations and allows consistent comparisons between European countries.

Earlier classifications have been

- 1980 SIC from 1983 to 1995.
- 1968 SIC from 1973 to 1983.

In terms of all manufacturing industry, the main differences between the most recent SICs have been:

- 1968 SIC to 1980 SIC Petroleum refining was excluded from all manufacturing, while output of slaughterhouses was included in all manufacturing.
- 1980 SIC to 1992 SIC Petroleum refining was included in all manufacturing.

A reasonable length of time-series is shown at the time of reclassification.

PUBLICATION

High-level PPIs are published first in a monthly PPI First Release. More detailed figures are published in Business Monitor MM22—around 900 PPIs are produced each month. Results are also published in the Current Cost Accounting Monitor and in the Aerospace and Electronics Cost Indices Monitor.

PRICE COLLECTION

STATUTORY BASIS

The collection of producer price indices, which had previously been voluntary, was moved to a statutory basis in 1991. The move was to improve the quality of the overall and component indices and ensured a greater response to recruitment forms, particularly in areas such as aerospace and shipbuilding, where companies were previously reluctant to provide data because of the complicated nature of their industries. Price collection in Great Britain is statutory under the Statistics of Trade Act 1947; and since, 1993 has also been statutory in Northern Ireland under Article 5 of the Statistics of Trade and Employment Order 1988.

PRICES REQUESTED

At the time of recruitment to the home PPI, ONS request that companies supply price quotations for items which have the following attributes:

- Are representative of the company's production in the relevant heading which is a six-digit code within the 1992 Standard Industrial Classification.
- Are manufactured and sold within the UK. The definition of UK manufacture is that the nature of the good must be changed within the UK. As examples, assembly of imported parts within this country would be included, but not a simple repackaging of an imported good.

Prices are then requested on a monthly basis:

- The prices quoted should represent a price which would be achieved in a significant proportion of UK sales, after discounts and excluding VAT.
- The product must be quoted on the same basis each month - *i.e.,* the same product and same terms of sale.
- The product and terms of sale must be described in enough detail to ensure consistency each month.
- The price must be recorded at the time at which the product is ordered. PPIs are published on this basis but for such purposes as deflating turnover in certain industries, PPIs are lagged so that they relate to time of delivery.
- Prices are ex-works price, *i.e.,* excluding any delivery charge outside the factory.

The most recent price history is returned to the contributor. Prices should be recorded as well as the date of any change. A contributor may choose to supply data in the form of a price index. Prices may be supplied up to three months ahead. The price averaged over the month as a whole is then calculated by the ONS.

Excise Duties

The headline PPI includes excise duties on such items as tobacco, petroleum products and alcoholic drinks. For analytical purposes, an additional all manufacturing PPI excluding excise duties is published in the PPI First Release, so manufacturers in these industries are asked to provide prices both including and excluding excise duties, and indices are published on both bases. Since, 1998, the series excluding duty have been used for deflation in the national accounts, in line with international guidelines.

Average Prices

Generally, contributors are discouraged from simply providing average prices covering all transactions in a particular month. Experience has indicated that such average prices tend to be very volatile and can be affected by an occasional very large order. Such fluctuations reflect changes in customer mix rather than genuine changes in prices. For this reason, contributors are asked to quote prices for a similar transaction each month, though there are industries such as the manufacture of construction materials, *e.g.,* bricks or cement, where average prices are accepted as a preferable alternative to unrealistic list prices.

Charge-out Rates

It is difficult for contributors in particular industries such as ship-building and repair, to provide quotes as so much of their work is one-off in nature which means it is difficult to quote for the same product over a period of time. In such cases, hourly charge-out rates give an approximation to the trends for the product or service itself, whilst keeping the compliance costs to a minimum.

However, they can lead to distortions in not allowing for productivity increases over time and excluding any price movements in the raw materials involved. There are exceptions but this method of pricing is generally best avoided if possible.

Where labour charge-out rates are used, ONS staff are advised to:

- Ensure they cover one specific type of a constant mix of labour.
- Avoid industries where productivity gains or development are likely to be rapid.
- Avoid industries where the materials element in prices is high.
- Ensure the quoted rate reflects what the customer actually pays.

Rates per tonne of material are more likely to be satisfactory than labour charge-out rates, but ONS staff are asked to:

- Ensure the rate is what the customer pays after discount.
- Include the cost of the material and ensure this is specified precisely.
- Ensure quotes cover specific products or product types.
- Ensure the working of the material is the predominant element in the product being quoted for. Design charges should be excluded.

Import Price Collection

Prices of imported raw materials and semi-manufactured goods are also collected as part of the PPI system. Contributors are selected from a list of importers supplied by Customs and Excise. They can either be manufacturers in their own right or may operate as importers who then sell on to manufacturers; in the former case they should represent the price they typically pay for the product quoted, in the latter case they should record the price they would charge to a UK manufacturing company. They can either be manufacturers in their own right or may operate as importers who then sell on to manufacturers; in the former case they should represent the price they typically pay for the product quoted, in the latter case they should record the price they would charge to a UK manufacturing company.

Export Price Collection

Export prices are collected on a separate form from the home PPI.

The crucial differences are:

- Goods must be manufactured in the UK and destined for export.
- Quotes are requested for both EC and non-EC destinations
- Prices should be supplied in the currency which their overseas customer pays.
- The ideal definition is FOB but other terms are acceptable, on the

grounds that trends on the various definitions should be similar. Prices should be provided on a consistent basis—*i.e.,* the same good to the same destination. Prices to another part of the same company are generally avoided, but will be accepted if necessary. In such a case, export prices as quoted on the company's INTRASTAT form or Customs documentation are acceptable.

Field Officers

A recent innovation is the use of a field officer to liase with contributors to ensure that the prices they provide meet the specified criteria. Such field officers have been used successfully in other countries, particularly the USA and France, and it is planned to increase their use in this country as resources permit over the next few years.

Published Sources

A few price quotations are obtained from published sources rather than direct from companies. Examples are prices for imported metals, which are obtained from the London Metal Exchange and for meat which come from the Meat and Livestock Commission.

CALCULATION OF INDICES

Price Relatives

The next stage after collecting prices for a specific good from companies is to derive a price relative, which is the pure price for an item divided by its price in a base year, currently 1995. Algebraically, the price relative at time t is equivalent to $\frac{P_i * 100}{P_b}$. The price relative in general follows the same movements as the price of the item but allowance is made for changes in specification. Around 2,400 specification changes were undertaken in the home PPI during 1996.

Laspeyres Indices

Producer price indices are base-weighted indices—that is to say they are weighted according to the sales or purchases in the base year, currently 1995.

The simplest form of a Laspeyres index is:

$$\frac{100 * \sum Q_b P_t}{\sum Q_b P_b}$$

where Q and P are the quantities and prices respectively of products—the subscript b denotes 'in the base period' and the subscript *t* denotes 'in the current period'. The base year is updated every five years, so that 1995 = 100 PPIs were published for the first time in October 1998. Until recently, the base year underlying the PPI was actually one year earlier than the reference year, *e.g.*, the PPI for 1985=100 was based on weights relating to 1984. However, the base year and reference year have coincided from 1995 when the indices based on 1990=100 were reclassified from the 1980 SIC onto the 1992 SIC.

Gross and Net Sector

PPIs are measured on two different bases—gross and net of inter-sector sales. As an example of the concepts, the motor industry is comprised of many companies supplying parts to a few car manufacturers who then produce the final product for sale to the customer. The gross sector output of Division 34 would include both the sales of the parts and the sale of the finished cars. The net sector output of Division 34 would measure only the finished product and exclude the intervening stages.

All sales of capital goods are regarded as final products, and so are not netted out. Most countries calculate PPIs on a gross basis, and the UK supplies PPIs on this basis to EUROSTAT. However, the high-level output price indices given prominence in the First Release are on a net basis. The argument for the latter presentation is that this is the measure which best reflects manufacturing inflation on the rest of the economy.

Since, inflation affecting the output prices of intermediate goods will implicitly be factored into the output prices of finished products, the gross sector approach can be seen as duplicating the contribution of the manufacture of intermediate goods. Gross sector indices, however, also contain valuable information, and are used to deflate the total turnover of industries, which by definition are on a gross basis. Apart from the highest-level indices in the First Release and tables of Business Monitor MM22, the rest of the indices published since, October 1998 have been on a gross sector basis.

Level of Detail Collected

Contributors are initially asked to select a representative quote at the 6-digit SIC(92) level. PPIs are calculated at the 6-digit SIC (92) level and are grossed to the 4-digit class and higher levels. Items are numbered within the 6-digit heading they are recorded, so that for example a washing machine would come within SIC (92) code 297113 with the ten-digit code of the form 2971130001.

Export Price Indices

EPIs are collected at the 6-digit Combined Nomenclature (CN) level published annually by HM Customs and Excise. This is also known as the Harmonised System (HS). For publication purposes and for deflation in the national accounts, the indices are aggregated to a three-digit CN level. For the purposes of deflating turnover for export, EPIs are converted to SIC(92) by the Balance of Payments branch of ONS, who forward them on for deflation of the export component of the Index of Production.

Import Price Indices

IPIs are collected using the 6-digit CN, but published according to the Standard International Trade Classification (SITC). The detailed relationship between CN and SITC is shown in *Guide to the classification for Overseas trade Statistics* published annually by HM Customs and Excise.

Reconstitution of Indices

A reconstitution of an index occurs when an item is to be deleted or added to an index. This is distinct from a specification change, where a contributor changes the specification of an item for which prices are supplied, but the weights of the item are unchanged. In a 'recon', the weights of an item are changed, together with other changes to ensure weights continue to add up to 100 per cent. A multiplication factor is applied to ensure that the value of the reconstituted index four months prior to the most recent calculated month are unchanged.

Derivation of Weights

The PPI is at present re-weighted every five years. The most recent results were first published in October 1998 with 1995=100. The weights used in the PPI system have two main sources:

PRODCOM

The value of sales in the base year is extracted from the PRODCOM enquiry. PRODCOM, an acronym for Products of the European Community, collects data on sales from some 25,000 contributors annually under a EUROSTAT directive. An attempt is made to exclude the value of exports from the weight at index level. However, due to the lack of data, total sales including exports are used to calculate each contributor's weight at item level.

To reduce variability at index level, sales from two years are used to derive weights. It is important to note that the weights within the PPI are product-based, while the turnover figures underlying the Index of Production (IOP) are based on the main industrial products of particular companies. For IOP purposes, adjustments are made to the PPIs to allow for this difference in coverage and also the fact that PPIs relate to time of order while IOP relate to time of delivery.

Purchasing Data

Data on manufacturing companies' purchases of materials and fuel were obtained from quinquennial Purchases Enquiries, until recently. The last of these was collected in respect of 1989. To minimise contributors' costs, information on purchases is now collected as part of the Annual Business Enquiry (ABI). Particular industries are targeted on a rotating basis so that all industries are covered in a five-year period.

Input-Output Tables

Input indices are calculated from ONS's Input-Output Tables, which use ABI and PRODCOM data as sources. As a result, input indices shown in table of Business Monitor MM22 are calculated no lower than Input-Output Group level. To derive weights for the high-level net sector indices, it is necessary to exclude transactions between industrial groupings. These are also derived from the Input-Output tables. A methodological manual explaining these tables was published in 1997.

Import Price Indices

A contributor's weight in the import price index system is derived from the value of a company's imports in particular 6-digit CN tariff headings as obtained directly from the company. Weights at tariff code heading and above are derived from the total imports recorded in the Customs and Excise Returns in the base year.

Export Price Indices

A contributor's weight in the export price index system is derived from the value of the company's exports at a six-digit CN heading for EU and non-EU destinations separately. This is in general taken from the Customs and Excise returns in the base year confirmed by the company if necessary. Weights for EPIs above 6-digit headings are taken from the Overseas Trade Statistics for the base year.

Seasonal Adjustment

To assist economic analysis, four high-level PPIs are published in seasonally adjusted form. On the output side, these are the indices for all manufacturing excluding excise duties, and manufacturing excluding the food, beverages, tobacco and petroleum industries.

On the input side, the indices for all manufacturing and manufacturing excluding food, beverages, tobacco and petroleum industries are seasonally adjusted to take account of volatile seasonal movements, especially in electricity and food input prices.

The US Bureau of the Census seasonal adjustment package is used. Once a year, full results are taken on board for the most recent three months, but otherwise only the most recent two months figures and the month a year before the current month are revised.

SAMPLE RECRUITMENT

Home PPIs

The sampling frame of companies for domestic PPIs is the production survey in the base year at the time at which recruitment takes place. For 1990, it was the Quarterly and Annual Sales Enquiries (QSI/ASI) while it has been the PRODCOM enquiry for 1995, which will continue in future base years. Until recently, sampling has been on a cut-off basis—so that only the largest firms in each industry are selected for new recruitment, though in the past, when recruitment was on a voluntary basis some small firms were selected, some of whom are still in the sample. The contributor coverage at the all manufacturing level amounts to some 44 per cent of production.

Import Price Indices

Importers of raw materials and semi-manufactures are recruited to the IPI panel by selection of the largest importers in specific headings recorded on Customs and Excise returns.

Export Price Indices

Exporters are recruited to EPIs by selection of the largest exporters in specific 6-digit CN. So whilst agents can be recruited for the IPIs, they are not recruited for the EPIs; only exporters who are also manufacturers are included in the panel.

Prices Supplied by other Government Departments

Other government departments provide indices for a few industries, as follows:

- *Department of Trade and Industry (DTI)* provides indices for energy industries, including electricity, gas and petroleum, based on DTI's monthly surveys to companies in those industries.
- *The Ministry of Agriculture, Fisheries and Food (MAFF)* provides monthly prices on many of the outputs from UK agriculture purchased by UK manufac-turing industry. These prices are either taken from MAFF surveys or from the Meat and Livestock Commission, the Home-Grown Cereals Authority or the National Farmers Union.
- *The Department of the Environment, Transport and the Regions* calculates price indices for output of construction.

Trade Associations

In the past, when the PPI was a voluntary survey, data for certain industries, such as brewing, were provided by trade associations. In recent years, the trend has been to move away from such quotes and to recruit data directly from companies. Very few quotes are now collected from trade associations.

New Price Quotes

The base price for an item is the price in the base year, currently 1995. If a new item is recruited after the base year, a notional base price is set so that the initial price relative for the item is calculated to be the same as its parent index. For instance, suppose a new manufacturer of washing machine is recruited in January 1999. If the value of the item's first stage parent index 'cloth washing and drying machines' - 2971130000 under SIC (92) -stands at 120.0 at that time, and the price of the washing machine is £300, then the base price will be assumed to have been £250 in 1995, so that a price relative of (300/250)*100 =120.0 in January 1999 is calculated—the same as its parent index. From that point on the price relatives for the new item will be calculated relative to a notional base price for that item of £250 in 1995.

NEW SAMPLING SCHEME FOR HOME PPIS

The methodology used to calculate the PPI has been reviewed and between 1999 and 2000 a new sample design is being introduced. Once this design has been fully phased in a new estimator will be introduced. This will require an extended parallel run and is not likely to be introduced until late 2001.

The main elements of the new sampling scheme are:

- Sampling from Prodcom;
- Using an optimal allocation; and
- Sample rotation.

Sampling from Prodcom

The new PPI sample will be chosen from those companies selected for Prodcom. This will ensure that the most up-to-date information for products and sales will be available for the sample. The sampling units for the PPI sample are contributor product pairs, which are created by matching contributors to the products they produce. For instance if a Prodcom contributor made five products then five contributor-product-pairs would be created.

Optimal Allocation

To ensure that the PPI sample gives the best results possible within its limit of 9,000 price quotes a month an optimal allocation has been calculated using data from 1996 Prodcom.

The objectives in calculating the allocation of price quotes between six digits were:

- Minimising the sampling error of the all manufac-turing index;
- A maximum of 9,000 price quotes in total;
- Providing the highest quality four digit indices possible;
- Each six digit index to have at least three contributor product pairs;
- Each four digit index to have at least five contributor product pairs;

- Broadly the same resources should be needed for monthly calculation of the PPI.

The allocation calculations were statistically complex. In very simple terms the allocation of price quotes for a stratum within a six digit was related to:

- The squared value of sales;
- The number of contributor product pairs; and
- The variance of the prices for the product.

The higher the relative value of any of these, then the higher the allocation. To minimise the sampling error for the overall index, each contributor provides only one price quote per product. The only exception to this is where the optimal allocation was greater than the number of contributor product pairs available from the Prodcom sample. In these instances contributors were asked to provide two or three price quotes for a product.

Effect of New Sample

Using the optimal allocation to select a sample from the contributors to the 1996 Prodcom survey showed two main effects on the sample. The first was that it increased the number of contributors from 3,700 to just under 7,000 but with the same total of 9,000 price quotes. As a consequence, more of the contributors were providing fewer price quotes. 70 per cent of the new sample provide just one price quote in total compared to 38 per cent of the present sample. The sample has also been re-balanced to better reflect current production.

The total number of price quotes for most products has remained fairly stable, but there are a few indices that have gained or lost a large number of price quotes. These include a large decrease in price quotes for navigation instruments and large gains for computers, motor vehicles and aircraft. Comparing the sample selected from 1996 Prodcom with the current panel showed that out of the present 9,000 price quotes from around 3,700 contributors, 2,000 price quotes were retained.

Phasing in the New Sample

The 7,000 new price quotes to be recruited to the PPI sample are too many to obtain in one exercise.

Recruitment of new price quotes will therefore be done in three 'waves', each comprising of a set of four digits:

- The first wave requires about 3,000 new price quotes to be recruited between June and December 1998. The new quotes will be run in parallel with the current sample from February 1999 for a few months during which time the PPI will be published using the current sample. Once the impact of the new sample has been assessed it will be linked into the PPI. The length of time the parallel run can be carried out may be limited by the resources available;

- The second wave of 1,000 new price quotes will be recruited between January and June 1999, and will be linked into the PPI indices after July 1999, depending on the results of the parallel run in the first wave. This wave will be selected from 1997 Prodcom;
- The third wave of 3,000 new price quotes will be recruited between June and December 1999, and will be linked into the PPI indices after February 2000, depending on the results of the parallel run in the first wave.

This wave will probably be selected from 1997 Prodcom, although there is a chance that 1998 Prodcom might be used if the timing of Prodcom results and PPI selection can be brought closer together. It is important to note that the updating of the sample will have no impact on back data.

Sample Rotation

The proposed method of rotation for the PPI is to select the sample afresh from each year's Prodcom sample. Contributors who have been dropped from the Prodcom sample will no longer be available for the PPI, but their replacements will be available. Selecting a new sample each year will retain a large proportion of the contributor product pairs in the PPI sample, but will allow rotation for the smaller contributors. It is proposed to introduce rotation for the PPI once the new sample has been fully introduced.

The main benefits of rotation for the PPI are that it will:

- Pick up new products and new contributors;
- Pick up existing companies making a product for the first time;
- Update company structures once a year only, and provide sales figures if structures have changed;
- Fill in gaps in the sample caused by contributors dropping out; and spread the burden of completing forms between smaller contributors.

PROCESSING AND DATA VALIDATION

Contributors return price movements by means of a pre-printed form containing the most recent details provided to the ONS. These are sent to contributors at the beginning of each month. They return their latest prices, and may provide future prices if they know the position for the three months ahead. The form asks contributors to check if the specifications are still up-todate and representative and to amend accordingly. Forms for companies in Northern Ireland are despatched via the Department of Economic Development in Belfast.

Data Validation

There are two tests which staff use to check price movements on the home PPI with contributors:

- *Monthly Movements Outside the Range -2.5 to +5 per cent*: These are known as 'dubious' price movements and are only input after checking with the contri-butors. Any information given by the contributor is included on the computer system. For the more volatile export and import price indices wider gates of -7.5 to +7.5 per cent are used.

- *Monthly Movements Outside the Range -25 to +25 per cent*: These are known as 'incredible' price move-ments. These are also queried with contributors. Unlike 'dubious' price movements, these must be specifically confirmed on the computer system with an explanation—otherwise they will be rejected.

As well as these checks before returns are input, there are also the following checks at later stages. Indices which move by more than 5 per cent are highlighted in prints following the two monthly calculation runs. Reasons for such movements must be shown on the printouts and circulated to internal users of the data. 'Too stable' letters are sent to contributors whose prices are recorded as not having moved for a set period, currently around eighteen months.

Data Collection by Telephone

Telephone Data Entry (TDE) is a means by which contributors return prices by inputting prices via their telephones. This was pilot tested largely successfully with service sector prices and was extended to the main PPI during 1997 and 1998.

Imputation

The PPI computer programmes impute for non-response in the most recent few months.

The rules for the home PPI are:

- If response in the lowest level index is over 50 per cent, the computer imputes based on a simple average of the observed movements in the received returns within the relevant sub-category.
- If response in the class is under 50 per cent, the computer imputes based on the simple average of movements at division level.

Imputation for EPI and IPI are similar, though if response at the first stage is below 50 per cent, imputation is based on movements for EC exports, non-EC exports or total imports as appropriate.

Treasury Targets

Targets are agreed with HM Treasury for response rates and revisions to ONS's key economic statistics.

The PPI is subject to two Treasury targets:

- Response in the all manufacturing output index at the first time of publication should exceed 82 per cent, with response weighted according to sales, and

- The revision in the estimate of the year to year all manufacturing output price index should not exceed 0.125 per cent between time of first publication and the first 'firm' estimate published two months later.

Allowances for Quality Changes

Care must be taken when a the specification of an item changes to ensure that only the 'pure' price change is recorded as such for PPI purposes. As well as changes of good, specification changes take place for alterations in terms of terms or units of sale. There are three types of specification changes in the PPI system:

Revisions Policy

The policy is to show significant revisions, but to suppress minor changes to avoid unnecessary inconvenience to users of the PPI. Indices for the most recent two months are shown as provisional and can be changed as later data are received the following month. Indices published for the third month are made firm as long as response is 95 per cent or more. Indices are always made firm after five months. Once an index is made firm it is only changed if there is a revision of 0.2 or more. Only the most recent five months indices are recalculated normally but earlier data will be revised if the revision in the first stage index is over 1 per cent or 5 per cent. Higher level indices are only changed if the revision is 0.2 per cent or more.

Linking between Base Years

The general policy for linking PPIs between different base years is as follows:

- To link earlier data onto the present base year, users may either link onto the earliest month published on the present base year—which is January 1991 for the 1995=100 database, or follow the national accounts practice of linking on at January 1994.
- To link later data onto an earlier base year—link later data onto the latest month published as firm—say July 1998 for the 1990 = 100 database.

Confidentiality

Under the Statistics of Trade Act 1947, criminal sanctions are in place to prevent the unauthorised release of company data by ONS staff. Depending on the circumstances either the Office or individual members of staff would be liable for fines and/or imprisonment for unauthorised release. In addition, because of the confidentiality of the data, company price information is not released outside the division responsible, apart from direct line managers. An index is only published if it is felt it would not disclose company information either to a member of the public or another company in the industry, though confidential indices can be used by other parts of the Government Statistical Service for national accounts purposes or for the calculation of other inflation measures as long as the publication of these other outputs is at a sufficiently aggregated level not to disclose the levels of these confidential indices.

Ad hoc Indices

ONS offers the facility to produce *ad hoc* indices to customers specification. For instance, an oil company may supply the weighting details of the various components that go into making an oil rig. For a fee, the ONS will calculate an index with monthly updates.

SUBJECT ANALYSIS

This review updates the 1986 *ARIST* chapter on subject analysis by SCHWARTZ and EISENMANN. The aim is a global approach. Thus, efforts were made to locate and include studies beyond those performed or published in the United States. Although the items reviewed come mainly from the period 1986-1988, earlier works not covered by the previous *ARIST* chapter have occasionally been included. Some much earlier items are referred to when necessary for purposes of comparison or context.

Subject analysis here means the presence, identification, and expression of subject matter in document texts, databases, controlled and natural languages, information requests, and search strategies. From the user's viewpoint, subject analysis is tightly bound to subject access. Therefore, the means by which information on a subject can be retrieved from various sources is also pertinent.

The literature reviewed is grouped into six broad categories:

- Indexing theory and practice;
- Controlled vocabularies;
- Search strategies and searching methods;
- Natural-language searching;
- Automatic indexing and related procedures; and
- The use of citation relationships in information retrieval.

Clearly these categories are not mutually exclusive, and some of the items reviewed could legitimately belong to more than one category.

INDEXING THEORY AND PRACTICE

General Discussions

Much has been written on various aspects of indexing over the years, but no really comprehensive book on the subject seems to have been produced, and those texts that do exist are now somewhat out of date. WEINBERG has compiled a volume of papers that, she claims, covers the 'state of our knowledge and the state of our ignorance' on the subject of indexing. Because her book is based solely on papers presented at a 1988 conference of the American Society of Indexers, the individual chapters vary in quality.

Topics covered include book indexing, automatic indexing, indexing software, database design, and the literature of indexing. Ironically, the outstanding chapter is about searching rather than indexing and is authored by SARACEVIC, who summarises the results of the comprehensive study described elsewhere in this review. He correctly points out that 'people who do research on searching rarely, if ever, cite literature on indexing research and *vice versa*. Yet there is an obvious connection, and perhaps more bridges need to be built between the research and practice of indexing and that of searching."

This observation coincides closely with one of the conclusions made by LANCASTER 20 years ago as a result of the evaluation of MEDLARS—namely, it is highly desirable that the indexers also be the searchers. Elsewhere, WEINBERG hypothesises that indexing fails the researcher because it deals only in a general way with what a document is 'about' and does not focus on what the document offers that is 'new' concerning a topic. She suggests that this distinction is reflected in the difference between 'aboutness' and 'aspect,' between 'topic' and 'comment,' or between 'theme' and 'rheme' but she fails to convince that these distinctions are really useful in the context of indexing or that it might be possible for indexers to maintain them.

A related study is the doctoral dissertation by CROWE, who discusses the feasibility of indexing the 'subjective viewpoint' of an author. She suggests that the indexer focus on the "problem situation' addressed by the author, including the questions addressed in the author's work. Aboutness is a slippery concept. The subject content of a document is sometimes referred to as intrinsic aboutness. What the document may be used for, why it was acquired, and other variable external' considerations are referred' to as extrinsic aboutness.

GORDON looks at indexing not in the context of aboutness as used by BEGHTOL and KHANZHIN but in relation to the interdependencies of the document descriptions, queries, and matching algorithms of the information retrieval system in use. He argues that a change in any of the three parts of the system mandates alterations in the other two if the system is to operate effectively. COCHRANE also reflects this holistic point of view. GRUNBERGER tested the assumptions that the frequency of a term on a page and the location of that term within a paragraph are good indicators that such a term would be selected in indexing. Neither of the hypotheses was supported.

AZUBUIKE and UMOH advocate maximum indexing, a concept that calls for exhaustively indexing a document using a variety of indexing strategies. While some would maintain that exhaustively indexing a document from both general and specific aspects leads to low precision in retrieval, the authors argue against this view. CHANG refers to the limitations associated with permuted title indexing and citation indexing and concludes that intellectual effort in indexing is still necessary. Based on the idea that knowledge is symbolic, VICKERY provides a review of methods whereby knowledge can be represented.

The review includes discussion of the use of symbols and symbol structures, semantics, and roles, categories, and relations present in subject statements. The arrangement and representation of knowledge as reflected in classification schemes and thesauri are also touched on. In addition, work in the area of 'semantic primitives' or 'semantic factoring' is reviewed and leads to a brief discussion of several means of representing knowledge for reasoning, including symbolic equations, frames, and semantic nets.

The review closes with a short description of a prototype reference and referral expert system developed by the author and his colleagues that uses many of the knowledge representation techniques reviewed. The continual problem of the interaction of the subjective and objective in the organisation and retrieval of information is addressed by NEILL through a review of the works of Brenda Dervin and Karl Popper as well as other writers whose works were influenced by or amplify Dervin and/or Popper.

The effect of the subjective in classificati6h and in indexing is discussed along with its impact on information retrieval, leading to a description of an information system called Projekt INSTRAT, which utilises some of Popper's concepts. The review concludes that although subjective and objective viewpoints follow different paths, their final solutions are similar. BLAIR looks at indeterminacy in indexing — *i.e.,* the probability that a term the user chooses will be in the set of potential terms available to the indexer *and* in the set of terms used by the indexer.

Increasing the number of terms assigned to a document increases the chances of a hit, but success is not guaranteed. Blair suggests that the user should always identify a highly relevant document as a model for further searching. CROFT outlines some areas of research in artificial intelligence, such as the development of expert systems, that should be fruitful in solving the problems of indeterminacy in both indexing and term selection for retrieval. Expert systems are designed to assist the user in query formulation and selection of relevant documents.

Predominantly non-verbal fields of knowledge present special difficulties in indexing. Geographical and geological mapping are two primarily visual fields that are not served well by verbal systems. GRANDE explores the ideograph as a model for database design, indexing, and retrieval of geological information, while MARKEY discusses consistency aspects in the indexing of visual materials.

The requirements for indexing in videotex and related systems are addressed by YEATES, with special reference to the British Prestel system.

Prestel's indexing approaches include: menu-controlled reference frames, alphabetical name and subject indexes, keyword indexes, gateway indexing to other systems, online and print indexes, user-controlled indexes, mnemonic page numbers, and Pagemarker—a 'bookmark' feature that allows users to tag specific pages for later rapid recall. ASRIBEKOV deals with the broad subject of textual compression in information systems. Conversion of primary text to alternative forms and to secondary represen-tations are both covered.

Precoordinate Indexes

It is a curious anomaly that in an age in which the online searching of databases is commonplace, greater interest exists than ever before in the characteristics of precoordinate indexes in printed form. Moreover, literature on this subject continues to pour out. The reason, of course, is that computer processing provides an efficient means for generating multiple entries systematically from a single input supplied by an indexer. A book by CRAVEN gives a useful overview of the subject, although its value is reduced by the fact that some of the approaches included are not described clearly or illustrated with sufficient examples.

Elsewhere CRAVEN describes a coding scheme for expressing relationships among terms within a string used as input to index-generation programmes. He also examines the possibility of extending the concept of string indexing from index display to the provision of descriptor phrases for proximity searching. One of the most sophisticated approaches to precoordinate indexing was developed by Jason Farradane more than 30 years ago. Termed 'relational indexing,' the method involves the use of role indicators to express precise relationships among terms.

Farradane's work is described by BROOKES. SCHNELLING points out the limitations of alphabetical subject catalogues based on a controlled vocabulary of subject headings. He proposes a method combining standardised and free terms. For each broad area covered by a catalogue it is necessary to derive a 'pattern'—a set of categories into which the literature seems to fall naturally. These categories can then be adapted as standardised subject headings or subheadings.

However, within the general framework provided by this pattern, it will be necessary to index in more detail by the use of free terms. He illustrates the approach advocated by a discussion of indexing requirements in the field of literary scholarship in general and Shakespeare in particular. The somewhat grandiose title applied to this approach—'pattern indexing'—suggests something quite new.

In fact, the only thing claimed is that while a broad terminological structure can be pre-established for any field, the fine details of indexing will always require the use of free terms. While this is eminently sensible, it is hardly original. This fact is recognised by HARRIS, who refers to the process of indexing with a combination of controlled and uncontrolled terms as use of a 'part-controlled vocabulary.' He suggests that this technique is "probably widely used in various kinds of information service, but has not been formally recognised as a design option for librarians". The string indexing system that has generated the most literature, of course, is PRECIS and it continues to do so.

DYKSTRA contributes a primer on the subject. MAHAPATRA and BISWAS study the interrelationships of the role operators used in PRECIS indexing, and DYKSTRA suggests that PRECIS'S clear rules lend themselves to use in automatic indexing. Somewhat related to PRECIS is POPSI. BISWAS and SMITH describe a variation of POPSI that they refer to as a computerised deep structure indexing system. One of the oldest and most respected of the printed indexes is that produced by Chemical Abstracts Service (CAS). The indexing policies of CAS are discussed by ROWLETT, and the history of subject indexing at CAS is covered by ZAYE *ET AL.* On the international front, BIELICKA and SCIBOR review indexing trends in Poland and compare them with international trends. GHANI explores the potentialities and problems of using uniterm indexing in the Arabic language. Many of the problems outlined center around problems of standardisation in the language itself.

Quality of Indexing

It is difficult to look at the quality of indexing in isolation—*i.e.,* without evaluating some information retrieval 'system' in which the indexing is only one of several factors affecting overall performance. Indeed, more work may have been done on consistency of indexing than on quality. Recently, however, some interesting approaches to the evaluation of indexing have been introduced. WHITE and GRIFFITH use methods external to the indexing system being studied to establish a set of documents judged to be 'similar in content.'

Using sets of this kind as the basis for evaluation, they look at three characteristics of the index terms assigned to items in the set within a particular database:

- The extent to which terms link related items. The obvious measure of this is the number of terms that have been applied to all or most items in the set. The items can be considered closely linked if several subject terms apply to all of them.
- The extent to which terms discriminate among these sets within the database. The most obvious measure of this is the frequency with which terms that apply to most documents in the set occur in the database as a whole. Very common terms are not good discriminators. For example, in MEDLINE the term 'human' may apply to every item in a set but is of little value in separating this set from others since, it applies to so many items in the database. On the other hand,

terms that occur rarely in the database will be useful in highly specific searches but of little use in identifying somewhat larger sets.

- The extent to which terms discriminate finely among individual documents. Rarity is an applicable measure here also. So is the exhaustivity of the indexing: a term may apply to all items in a set, but cannot discriminate among its members; the more additional terms that are assigned to each member, the more individual differences can be identified.

To look at quality in this way, one must first establish the test sets, retrieve records from a database for the members of each set, and study the characteristics of the terms assigned. White and Griffith used the technique to compare the indexing of their test sets in different databases: MEDLINE was compared with PsycINFO, BIOSIS Previews, and Excerpta Medica. A comparison of databases in this way is a check on the assumption that test-set items are in fact similar in content. White and Griffith used co-citation as the basis for establishing their test sets, although other methods, including bibliographic coupling, could be used.

The value of this work is limited by the fact that only very small clusters were used. Moreover, the validity of the method as a test of human indexing depends entirely on one's willingness to accept a co-citation cluster as being a legitimate standard. One could make a persuasive argument that it makes more sense to use expert indexers as a standard for judging the legitimacy of the co-citation cluster. WHITE and GRIFFITH claim that the method is useful to a database producer as a check on the quality of indexing, and they present examples of terms that should perhaps have been used by MEDLINE indexers or added to the controlled vocabulary. However, such 'quality' checks can be done more simply. Sets of items defined by a particular term or terms can be retrieved from several databases and their indexing compared without the use of co-citation as a standard. In fact, this type of study has also been done by the same group of investigators. For 11 requests posed by specialists in the medical behavioural sciences, comparative searches were performed in MEDLINE, Excerpta Medica, PsycINFO, SciSearch, and Social SciSearch.

In the first three databases the searches were performed on:

- Controlled terms; and
- Natural language.

In the citation databases, searches were performed:

- Using the natural language of titles; and
- Using citations to known relevant items as entry points.

While the purpose of the investigation was to study the quality of MEDLINE indexing, little was discovered that could be posed as recommendations to the National Library of Medicine (NLM) on indexing practice, although some recommendations on indexing coverage could be made.

The most important findings of the study were that:

- The incorporation of natural-language approaches into search strategies resulted in significant improvements in recall compared with the use of controlled terms only;
- Citation retrieval should be considered an important adjunct to term-based retrieval because additional relevant items can be found using the citation approach; and
- No single database is likely to provide complete coverage of a complex multidisciplinary literature.

The work reported by White and Griffith and by McCain *et al.* forms part of a series of investigations done at the College of Information Studies, Drexel University, to evaluate various aspects of NLM's coverage and handling of the literature of the medical behavioural sciences. GRIFFITH *ET AL.* present an overview of all the studies, including the coverage of the databases, the quality of the indexing, and the results of searches in the medical behavioural sciences.

AJIFERUKE and CHU are critical of the 'discriminating index' for terms used by White and Griffith, which takes into account how many times a term is used within a database but not the size of the database. They propose a new measure that does. HRAŠOVA and JANÁKOVÁ conclude that consistency in keyword indexing is greatest when very few or very many keywords are chosen. This makes sense. It is relatively easy to agree on the two or three most important terms. Consistency will begin to decline after this but is likely to increase again when virtually all terms that could possibly be assigned to a document have been assigned.

One factor that might have some influence on the quality of indexing is the availability to the indexer of appropriate reference tools. BAKEWELL gives details on almost 200 books of possible value to indexers. To improve indexing and classification procedures, to make them more responsive to user needs, it is necessary to understand the bases on which people categorise or group documents in everyday life. KWASNIK, for example, is looking at the categories into which people sort their mail. She presents some preliminary results based on her observations of eight members of a university faculty.

The average number of terms assigned to a document in indexing tends to have a significant effect on the performance of a retrieval system. CLEVELAND and CLEVELAND studied the effect of indexing depth on retrieval performance for conventional Boolean searching methods and for the 'indirect method' of retrieval devised by GOFFMAN. They concluded that the latter, unlike the former, is relatively insensitive to indexing depth.

The indirect method involves the matching of a query against document clusters, which are established on the basis of term co-occurrence, the identification of the cluster that best matches the query, and the identification of the cluster member closest to the query. This document can then be used to locate other related items. CLEVELAND *ET AL.* also tested the hypothesis that when the indirect method is used for searching, indexing from full text is not essential to optimum retrieval. They conclude that optimum retrieval results can be achieved with less than full text when the indirect method is used.

CONTROLLED VOCABULARIES

General Discussions

The term 'index language devices,' which can be traced back more than 20 years, is somewhat misleading in that some of the 'devices' referred to are legitimate components of index languages while others, such as term weighting, are outside the index language *per se* and are more correctly referred to as 'indexing devices.' A detailed analysis of two important devices—weighting and relational indicators—is provided by KÖRNER. Role and relational indicators, various approaches to the linking of terms, facets, human and automatic weighting are all included in his review. KRISTALÑYI *et al.* suggest the use of the universal facets of time and space as a way to increase compatibility in various automated systems in the Soviet Union.

CHANDRASEKHARAN *et al.* apply graph-theoretic techniques to solve the 'minimum vocabulary problem' for a dictionary—*i.e.,* to identify the smallest set of words needed to define all the words in the dictionary. They claim that the minimum vocabulary principle can be applied to reduce the size of a controlled index language but fail to elaborate on this application. EASTMAN reports on a preliminary study of the extent to which overlap in postings occurs among hierarchically related terms in a controlled vocabulary, using data from MEDLINE and Medical Subject Headings, and she considers the implications of the overlap phenomenon for searches involving negations.

NELSON and TAGUE discuss the distribution of index terms over a collection of documents. They point out that a rank-frequency distribution well describes the distribution of terms of high frequency, while a frequency-size distribution provides a better picture of the distribution pattern for low frequency terms. They describe a 'split model,' using a rank function for the high frequency terms and a size function for the low frequency terms, the point of transition between the two being determined empirically or by rule. On a more practical level, NELSON found that users of an online public access catalogue (OPAC) at the University of Western Ontario tend to employ terms that occur very frequently in the catalogue. The construction of controlled vocabularies involves the establishment of relationships among 'subjects.' JOHANSEN makes a distinction between relationships established on 'linguistic' and 'non-linguistic' levels and attempts to present a 'method of disclosing the structure of a subject by examining its constituent elements and their mutual relationships.'

SUOMINEN deals with the subject of syntactic relations in index languages. STIEG and ATKINSON compare indexing and indexing languages in the ERIC,

LISA, and Library Literature databases as one aspect of a broader comparison of these three sources. Bibliographic classification schemes, lists of subject headings, and thesauri are all examples of index languages—*i.e.,* vocabularies that can be used to represent the subject matter of documents and of information needs. BIELICKA *et al.* and JABRZEMSKA and SCIBOR review the types of index languages in use in Poland, and STANCIKOVA presents a similar review for Czechoslovakia.

Information retrieval in the humanities is generally considered to be more difficult than it is in the sciences because the terminology used by humanists is less precise. WIBERLEY explores this situation by studying the entry terms used in leading encyclopaedias and dictionaries in the humanities. He concludes that although some of the terms are imprecise, most of them are quite precise and consist of names of individuals or of creative works; this finding suggests that subject access in the humanities may be less of a problem than previously supposed.

SANTAVICCA points out the crucial role that a knowledge of languages plays in the selection of terms for indexing, thesaurus control, cross-references, and access points. He suggests that the manipulation of text in international databases requires a kind of trilingualism: a knowledge of the user's native language, a knowledge of the foreign language in question, and a knowledge of the system's operating language. An inability to exploit any of these will result in diminished system performance. He concludes that the importance of studying foreign languages must be recognised if users are to be well served.

Classification Schemes

In a brief overview, ROMAN provides an introduction to classification, which is seen as the adaptation of prevalent philosophical views to library materials. She examines recent changes in thinking that have influenced current views of classification. BEGHTOL discusses classification in terms of the underlying justification of the system.

In the past, classification systems have been based on literary, scientific, philosophical, or educational warrant. She suggests that more investigations will occur in the future in the area of 'enquiry warrant' systems built as direct responses to user demands. While she seems to trace the idea back only to 1984, it was discussed as 'user warrant' by LANCASTER in 1972. In a comparison of five classification schemes for physics and chemistry, SNOER considers the impact of online catalogues on classification systems.

The schemes examined are the Library of Congress Classification system (LCC), the Dewey Decimal Classification system (DDC), the Universal Decimal Classification system (UDC), and the former and present systems of the University of Copenhagen. The author stresses the value of using UDC's Common Auxiliary for Place in existing call numbers to enhance retrieval. She concludes that radical revision of classification to suit the online environment is not necessary but that improvements can be made to existing schemes.

In a more global view than is often encountered, HOLLEY examines the impact of electronic technology on classification and subject cataloging and speculates on how this might affect third world countries. He fears that changes occurring in approaches to subject access and subject analysis in the developed countries will not take the needs of the third world into consideration. The International Federation of Library Associations (IFLA) is encouraged to provide a forum for the third world to cope with this situation.

The value to users of an index to a classification scheme is observed by NAKAMURA, who points out that even though such indexes are often rejected on the grounds of inflexibility, the very nature of such a fixed system is helpful for the user who is unfamiliar with a particular scheme. However helpful an index may be, it cannot fully compensate for the difficulty in using classification as a search tool. The author suggests a number of approaches to concept classification as possible remedies.

Since, its controversial entrance into American public libraries over a century ago, fiction has remained something of a stepchild in terms of access. BAKER, BAKER and SHEPHERD, and SHEPHERD and BAKER examine the application of classification to fiction in American public libraries. Their survey of the literature indicates that patrons find classification a useful tool in locating the types of books they want. Suggestions for further study are included. On the same topic, SAPP describes four classification schemes for fiction: LCC system, DDC system, Frank Haigh's fiction classification scheme of 1933 (HAIGH), and L. A. Burgess's scheme of 1936 (BURGESS). These are evaluated along with discussions of shelving schemes, subject headings, and topical access to fiction through standard print indexes.

Mention is also made of experiments by the Danish librarian Annelise Mark Pejtersen in online subject indexing for fiction. SAPP recognises the difficulties in classifying fiction and recommends further study to determine if the need for classification here justifies the effort. New systems, and modifications to older ones, are evolving in response to demands for more effective subject retrieval. LIU-LENGYEL describes the development of the Chinese Classification System over 2,000 years and notes the problems that lack of standardisation has caused in Chinese libraries. This may have been somewhat remedied by the adoption of the new Chinese Book Classification system as a standard in 1981.

SUKIASYAN examines trends in classification in the Soviet Union. Several projects have explored the value of classification schemes for retrieval in OPACs. Some researchers are looking at the LCC system and the DDC system for this purpose. Using OCLC MARC records as a research base, MARKEY and MARKEY and DEMEYER have tested the potential of the DDC system for retrieval. They demonstrate that, used in combination with Library of Congress Subject Headings (LCSH) and keywords in title, DDC can increase recall and retrieve relevant items not retrievable by any of the other fields on the record.

CHAN has examined theoretical issues related to whether or not the LCC can be used to enhance subject retrieval in an online catalogue, while WILLIAMSON is also working on a project to test the potential of using LCC for subject retrieval. HUESTIS reviews strategies for overcoming the major problems involved in the use of LCC in OPACs. KHOSH-KHUI has looked at the relationship between length of class numbers in LCC and DDC and subject specificity.

Although the length of number in both schemes does increase with specificity, it is not in itself a good indicator of specificity of subject headings assigned to items or of the number of headings assigned. GOPINATH discusses the use of classification schemes and thesauri in a symbiotic relationship that can improve information retrieval. The concept of a 'thesaurofacet' or 'classaurus'—a device that incorporates features of a faceted hierarchical scheme with those of a thesaurus—is a practical application of this symbiotic relationship.

AITCHISON looks at two thesauri that have used the H. E. Bliss classification as a source for construction and considers the merits of using the second edition of Bliss for this purpose. O'NEILL *et al.* look at the problems involved in mapping from one classification scheme to another, with particular reference to the LCC and the DDC systems. They introduce the notion of 'class dispersion' as a measure of the ease with which a class in one scheme can be mapped to another scheme. DUNAYEV and POLYAKOV describe the problems involved in deriving a mathematical description of classification schemes.

Subject Headings

The emergence of OPACs has also caused a revival of interest in subject headings, as they are traditionally used in libraries, and the limitations of these vocabularies for effective subject access in the online environment. WYKOFF provides a brief overview of the history of the use of subject headings in online access. MASSICOTTE describes how displays of subject headings in OPACs can be made more browsable, while MARKEY discusses the integration of Library of Congress Subject Headings (LCSH) in machine-readable form into online catalogues. Over the years LCSH has been the subject of much criticism.

COCHRANE groups the criticisms into four categories of needs:

- The need to improve the form of headings and to add more scope notes;
- The need to improve the cross-reference structure;
- The need to improve subdivision access; and

- The need to improve the syndetic structure of the system by use of classification.

She examines suggestions for improvements and discusses how these fit into the online environment. In an article that begins by reiterating the criticisms of Anglo/Western bias in LCSH and the inability of the Library of Congress (LC) to keep the vocabulary up to date, HENIGE presents a further concern that headings are not being changed to reflect current scholarly consensus. To be effective in reference work, he says that headings must be accurate and in step with current scholarly thought. LC, however, has always taken the position that LCSH should reflect the content of published literature rather than the cutting edge of scholarly research.

DYKSTRA points out that the 11th edition of LCSH adopts the very precisely defined terminology of thesaurus construction, but she argues that its use of 'broader term,' 'narrower term,' and 'related term' is misleading because LCSH does not maintain the precise logical relationships implied by these terms in a carefully constructed thesaurus. LCSH can only be considered as a list of accepted subject terms used in LC; it is not a true thesaurus. It has always been difficult to determine the policies and practices that LC adopts *vis- à-vis* LCSH.

With the exception of Haykin's guide published in 1951, there has been very little explanation available. The revised edition of LC's *Subject Headings Manual* and the second edition of *Library of Congress Subject Headings: Principles and Application* provide two excellent sources to guide the librarian in using the subject headings for items in a collection. Knowing how headings are interpreted and used by LC will help promote consistency among libraries in their application. FROST and DEDE have studied the compatibility between LCSH and the use of subject headings by one large research library.

Methods by which a controlled vocabulary is updated are another matter of general interest. A study by BACKUS *et al.* tested two hypotheses concerning the annual revision of the National Library of Medicine's (NLM) MeSH vocabulary. It was hypothesised that new terms are added to the vocabulary when their broader terms have increased in number of postings and that the distribution of terms in the hierarchical 'trees' of the vocabulary would reflect the distribution of terms in search requests made to the system.

Neither hypothesis was supported. MCCARTHY discusses the extent to which consistency occurs in the assignment of headings in order to bring like works together. She concludes that consistency is not as high as it should be and proposes an increase in the number both of headings assigned to an item, as well as cross-references, as possible remedies. She also recommends that cataloguers examine the literature on the subject in question to see what headings have been applied in the past. She believes that the use of online catalogues increases the importance of consistency in assigning subject headings and also simplifies its achievement. MILLER presents a very brief outline of the application of automation to the production of LCSH and points out the advantages and disadvantages of the program. Many libraries have made it a standard policy to review and revise the subject headings assigned to catalogue records by member libraries of OCLC, Inc. SALAS-TULL and HALVERSON evaluate this practice in light of the time and expense involved in comparison with the number of changes libraries actually make to the OCLC records.

They examined revisions made by research, academic, and public libraries and found that there was little difference in the number of revisions among the three types of libraries and that the total number of revisions was lower than expected. They conclude with several suggestions for cataloging departments that use subject heading review policies. Since, the 1940s there has been interest in a uniform code for subject headings. With the general adoption of the *Anglo-American Cataloguing Rules,* 2nd edition *(AACR2),* interest in a similarly uniform guide for subject access has been renewed.

STUDWELL and ROLLAND-THOMAS suggest a form for such a code and urge an international effort to develop a standard code. In the same spirit, STREBI offers examples of revision and retrospective conversion of subject headings performed by the Austrian National Library as models for other libraries to consider. The use and effectiveness of subject headings for biomedical materials have also been the subject of recent research.

MASARIE and MILLER compare terms used by health professionals with the standardised vocabulary found in MeSH. Fifty hospital charts were randomly selected and subjected to a computer analysis that matched terms with two MeSH-based vocabularies; the first consisted of MeSH terms, and the second consisted of MeSH terms plus cross-references. Approximately 50 per cent of the words used in the charts matched the MeSH-related vocabularies, with about 40 per cent of these proving to be exact MeSH terms or entry terms. Also working with MeSH, RADA *et al.* evaluated entry terms and tested a method for producing new entry terms.

Documents indexed by MeSH terms were compared with documents indexed automatically to see if the automatic indexer could map from title words to controlled terms through the use of entry terms better than it could without using entry terms.

Some entry terms were found to be ambiguous. In a method for producing new entry terms, the authors present an algorithm to map terms from the *Systematised Nomenclature of Medicine* to MeSH. While the new *SNOMED* terms were not helpful in indexing, they did suggest how MeSH might be improved. A new algorithm was formulated to join the two sets of terms, and the combined *SNOMED*/MeSH vocabulary was judged to permit improved indexing over the MeSH terms alone.

Thesauri

WEINBERG and CUNNINGHAM provide a brief comparison of online thesauri with print versions. The interfaces for a number of different vendor systems are evaluated, and the article includes recommendations for improving online thesauri. CHAN and POLLARD provide an annotated directory of thesauri used in online databases. The linking and evaluation of thesauri are necessary tasks in improving retrieval systems. RADA presents a number of considerations in connecting and evaluating thesauri. Experimental linkings of MeSH with the *SNOMED,* CMIT (Current Medical Information and Terminology), and PDQ thesauri are discussed.

In these experiments, similarities are identified and differences are exploited to generate better thesauri. MILI and RADA also report on efforts to merge thesauri to create more powerful vocabularies, and MANDEL reviews the problems involved in integrating thesauri and other forms of controlled vocabulary within an online bibliographic network. SCHONDORF presents a study utilising the Thesaurus Database developed by the Gesellschaft fur Information und Dokumentation in Frankfurt, which examines unconventional relationships among thesaurus terms.

The study presents examples of how these relationships provide orientation support within the thesaurus's vocabulary for indexing and retrieval. ROSTEK and FISCHER describe the computer 'modelling' of a thesaurus within a frame system with a graphical interface. BELLAMY and BICKHAM deal with the development of a thesaurus for the subject cataloging of books in a special library in biomedicine.

SEARCH STRATEGIES AND SEARCHING METHODS

General Discussions

An enormous study of factors affecting the performance of online searches was undertaken over a period of several years at the now defunct Matthew A. Baxter School of Library and Information Science at Case Western Reserve University. The methodology and results for the final phase of this project are presented by SARACEVIC *et al.* The study involved 40 users, each providing one question, and 39 searchers. Interviews with the users were tape recorded. For each question, nine searches were performed, four by project staff and five by outside searchers, for a total of 360 different searches.

A related experiment was also undertaken, involving the classification of user questions by 21 judges. The results of the searches were evaluated by the users in terms of relevance and utility. The bewildering variety of data collected during the project makes effective summarisation virtually impossible. Perhaps the most significant finding was that different searchers were likely to have quite different interpretations of a question and, thus, used different search approaches and retrieved different items. Moreover, each searcher tended to find some relevant items not found by the others, although the chance that an item would be judged relevant increased with the number of searchers retrieving it. The investigators suggest that these results argue the need for multiple searches for the same question by different searchers, but an alternative conclusion might be that a team approach to the analysis of a question and a consensus approach to an initial search strategy might be the preferred mode of operation.

Earlier FIDEL had also discovered that experienced searchers show little agreement in the selection of terms, and even earlier studies consistently revealed that users of card catalogues also tend not to agree much on what terms to use in searching for items on a particular topic. HARTER looks at problem-solving attitudes and abilities of searchers as factors affecting search success. FAIRHALL categorises the various skills associated with searching performance, while SCHIFFMANN reminds us of the value of 'hedges' in the handling of repeated search requests.

VIGIL contributes a major monograph on the searching of online databases, including psychological factors in searching. Over the past 25 years a number of attempts have been made to measure unobtrusively the quality of reference services offered by libraries. Such studies have focussed on the ability of libraries to answer factual questions. MCCUE has now pioneered the unobtrusive evaluation of online searching in libraries.

Twenty-one public libraries throughout the United States were each asked to perform the same search in two different databases; the searchers did not know that they were being tested. Two 'outside expert database searchers' evaluated the results. Using a point system, each search was scored on strategy, general techniques, and results. General techniques covered such aspects as searcher mistakes in entering terms or use of incorrect procedures. Results were also given numerical scores; a worthless citation earned no points, an excellent one earned.

The library scores ranged from 419 to 155. McCue concludes from her statistical analysis that the only variable that correlated positively with high search scores was the number of items retrieved. This is hardly surprising. In effect the scoring method takes recall into account since, it gives positive scores to 'useful' items but not precision. The entire method of scoring, however, is of dubious quality. In the long run it is the results that matter, so it seems pointless to devise a scoring method that takes not only results but search strategy and search technique as well into account.

HANSEN compares the results of a group of inexperienced subjects who performed manual searches followed by online searches with the results achieved by a matched group of subjects who performed online searches followed by manual ones. The differences in the results were not statistically significant. Nevertheless, she concludes that inexperienced searchers may get the best results when performing a manual search after an online search, at least in the case of 'a large and complex topic with an expanding literature," a conclusion that receives very weak support from her data.

In a doctoral dissertation, DALRYMPLE compares the searching of card catalogues with the searching of online catalogues, looking at the activity as essentially a problem-solving task. Within her experimental setting, users found more relevant items and were more satisfied with their results from the card catalogue. Users spent more time and reformulated their strategies more often when using the online catalogue. The search patterns of users of the CATLINE database of NLM are analysed by TOLLE and HAH and compared with the search patterns of MEDLINE users.

FIDEL discusses how analysis of the search behaviour of human intermediaries can be used to identify rules by which such experts select 'search keys'—descriptors from a controlled vocabulary or free-text terms. She claims that when more research has been performed on expert search behaviour, it should be possible to build a knowledge base for use in an intermediary expert system for online searching. By observing 47 searchers in action, FIDEL concludes that free-text terms and descriptors are selected with about the same frequency.

However, those who prefer the free-text approach and avoid controlled vocabularies are more likely to be searchers on science topics who search several databases for each request. The evaluation of the results of a search involves some criterion for judging the relevance of retrieved items. EISENBERG and SCHAMBER review various approaches to the definition of 'relevance' used by earlier writers and propose a 'user-centric-cognitive model' that views the user as the 'central and active determinant of the dimensions of relevance.'

In a related paper, HALPERN and NILAN discuss the subject of relevance in terms of 'source evaluation,' the weight that a person places on a source of information beyond its substantive content—authority or expertise represented, uniqueness, and so on. After using judges to rate documents on both relevance and utility, REGAZZI claims that no operational difference exists between relevance-theoretic and utility-theoretic models of evaluation.

WAGNER examines the cause of 'false drops' in online searching. They are less prevalent in searches that use only controlled vocabulary terms, but in any case they account for only a small percentage of errors, and that retrieval error is, to some degree, unavoidable, especially in searches seeking high recall. The author stresses awareness of the causes of false drops and advises that the professional be able to explain their occurrence to the user.

BLACKSHAW and FISCHHOFF view online searching as a decision-making process. Volunteer searchers were observed while performing author, title, or subject searches in an online catalogue in a public library. The authors report that searcher performance resembles that revealed in studies of decision making in other contexts.

BELLARDO looked at variables that might affect the performance of online searchers, using two test searches with students from six different library schools. Findings suggest that differences in performance can be attributed to general verbal and quantitative aptitude, artistic creativity, and an inclination towards critical and analytical creative thinking, but the associations are all very weak. High intelligence and other factors often cited as important attributes may not be *necessary* for high performance.

Bellardo claims that searching performance may not be predictable on the basis of cognitive and personality traits. End-user searching has become increasingly common with the growth of home computers, favourable searching rates for the home user and, most particularly, the emergence of more and more databases on CD-ROM. OJALA looks at who end users are, where they are, and why they are searching and makes some projections for the future. SEWELL and TEITELBAUM report the results of investigations of end-user searching of NLM databases over 11 years through transaction logs, interviews, and questionnaires.

SULLIVAN *et al.* compared end-user searching with delegated searching and discovered that the end users were no less satisfied with their results, retrieved fewer items, and achieved a high precision. All aspects of end-user searching are reviewed in a compilation by KESSELMAN and WATSTEIN. End-user searching, in some environments at least, may require a user-friendly interface to make the search process as simple as possible.

POLLITT describes one approach, based on use of a menu, that has been developed at NLM. Called Men USE, it is an improved version of an earlier prototype, CANSEARCH. Pollitt claims that it "provides inexpensive, high-quality, subject-specific browsing and searching of the MEDLINE database for users who have no training or experience in information retrieval". The interface described by BATES is intended to help users develop their own search strategies rather than to be an automatic 'transparent' aid to the user.

WILLIAMS discusses the wider issues involved in the design of transparent systems and describes a number of approaches, which she categorises as gateways, front ends, intermediaries, and interfaces. However, her article is tangential to this chapter because it deals more with interface technology than with interface content. INGWERSEN emphasises the importance of browsing facilities in solving search problems.

Information retrieval studies have increasingly taken the viewpoint that computer-human interfaces can be better designed if they are based on the concept of an adaptive, cognitive model. A review of cognitive models in information retrieval by DANIELS examines recent literature in this area, mainly from the standpoint of the user. A number of natural-language and controlled-vocabulary information retrieval systems that use cognitive models are discussed. The review concludes that cognitive models in the various systems work reasonably well because they function in constrained environments.

Suggestions for further incorporation of cognitive models in future systems designs are offered. VECCIA describes nine online systems that can be used to search the *Washington Post.* She compares the various types of searches the systems permit and notes items excluded from indexing. The downloading of bibliographic records from online searches has become increasingly common. LARGE discusses the subject, including downloading from CD-ROM databases, and looks at the reuse of downloaded records in local databases. JAMESON treats downloading and uploading in greater detail, including legal aspects.

Searching in Online Library Catalogues

Traditionally library catalogues have provided somewhat limited capabilities for searching by subject. The replacement of the card catalogue by online public access catalogues has brought about a great resurgence of interest throughout the library profession in all aspects of subject access. For one thing, it has been found that the proportion of catalogue searches that are subject searches has tended to increase considerably as OPACs fall into place. LIPETZ and PAULSON confirm this trend in a 'before and after' study at the New York State Library.

FROST studied catalogue users at the University of Houston and concluded that students search more often by subject than do faculty. However, on the basis of a study at the City University prior to the automating of their catalogue, HANCOCK suggests that subject searching of manual catalogues may have been more prevalent than previously thought. KASKE has found great variability in the proportion of OPAC searches that are subject searches—by hour of day, day of week, and week of semester. In discussions of online catalogue development in libraries two approaches are particularly evident.

One is to improve the interface between user and system, and the other is to enhance or augment the system itself. An analysis of online subject searches led one group of librarians and information specialists to conclude that an online catalogue must compensate for a user's inability to match his or her subject headings exactly with those of LCSH, must provide more than one searching option, and should permit users to refine large retrieval sets. HILDRETH also argues for a more interactive interface between the user and the system.

One essential feature is to provide the user with information concerning the status of the search as it progresses. The Subject Access Project performed at Syracuse University in the late 1970s determined that augmenting subject headings of traditional bibliographic records with terms from tables of contents and back-of-the-book indexes may be an efficient and relatively inexpensive way to improve subject access in the catalogue. BYRNE and MICCO describe a study in which an average of 21 multiword terms, drawn from indexes or tables of contents, were added to MARC records for 6,000 books.

Results of their studies indicate that searches of these augmented records achieved much improved recall compared with searches on titles or subject headings. DIODATO considers the same issue from a slightly different point of view when he studies readers' descriptions of books to determine if the descriptions match terms from the tables of contents and indexes. He concludes that tables of contents and indexes are two sources of terms that are likely to reflect terms that the user would use in searching for the books.

JAMIESON *et al.* have compared the searching of uncontrolled keywords occurring in bibliographic records with the searching of controlled terms in the records. In recognition of the millions of bibliographic records presently in MARC format in libraries and information centers, CHITTY argues that the issue is not how to improve the information on the record but how best to use the information already present. In actuality, the approaches to improving online catalogues are not a choice between whether the content is enhanced or the interface is improved. The content, the system/user interface, and the user are all integral parts of the system.

DWYER points out that many developments in the bibliographic organisation of libraries over the years have resulted in split files; he proposes that a total retrospective conversion be implemented as one means towards building better catalogues. Quality cataloging is a necessity because the accuracy of a system's content ultimately determines the success of retrieval. Because any transition to an online catalogue involves choices and trade-offs, Dwyer stresses the importance of understanding the true costs involved and of understanding the users' requirements in order to make intelligent choices in questions of design.

LAWRY raises the question, 'Can online catalogues be too easy'? The question indicates a concern that a system that appears to 'think' for the user, by assisting the user in query formulation, search strategy selection, and evaluation of retrieved titles, is unintentionally misleading the user. Lawry stresses the importance of user education to make effective use of all the tools available in the library.

BATES presents a model of subject access in online catalogues based on three design principles:

- Uncertainty;
- Variety; and
- Complexity.

Bates argues that because indexing is characterised by variety, searching should no longer be based on the exact matching of terms but, instead, should help the searcher by displaying and 'making it easier to explore' a variety of terms. Two tools proposed for improving search performance are an end-user thesaurus and a 'front-end system mind'; the former is basically a vast entry vocabulary, and the latter is a semantic network, incorporating the entry terms, that allows a searcher to select from a variety of methods for generating semantic associations.

The design approach proposed is intended to be implemented in existing catalogues based on LCSH without the need for any reindexing. Bates seems optimistic about the future of subject access in online catalogues. Not so BORGMAN, her colleague at UCLA. Based on studies of user behaviour in subject searching—whether in library catalogues or in broader bibliographic databases—she concludes that "we do not yet have sufficient knowledge of user behaviour to make improvements in system design".

Using the OKAPI (Online Keyword Access to Public Information) system, WALKER and WALKER and JONES investigated possible methods for improving subject searches. Automatic word stemming, synonym and cross-reference tables, and techniques for the approximate matching of words were all studied. They concluded that weak stemming is beneficial but that strong stemming is of doubtful utility, that semiautomatic spelling correction should be used in online catalogues, and that cross-reference lists to allow automatic cross-referencing should be compiled using input from cooperating libraries.

The cross-reference lists investigated were extremely simple, incorporating abbreviations, noun-adjective pairs, alternative terminology, alternative spellings, irregular plurals, related terms, numbers, and phrases. The phrases category is a little different from the others in that it consists of word combinations that should not be split up by searching algorithms because the meaning of the individual words is quite different from that of their combination.

A much more comprehensive study was the doctoral research project of LESTER. Her objective was to determine what features would be needed in online catalogues to increase the success of users in matching their search terms with LCSH. Random samples of user subject terms, selected from the transaction logs associated with the NOTIS/LUIS online catalogue at Northwestern University were compared with LCSH. For user terms that failed to match the headings, 22 different strategies for achieving a match were investigated.

Strategies that did *not* improve matching significantly were: use of a spelling checker, singular/plural conflation, phonetic spelling, exact matching in either subject or personal name authority files, and any process involving geographic name authority files. The strategies of right truncation, string searching with adjacency, and searching of keywords with Boolean operators significantly improved the matching whether or not the database were augmented by the inclusion of subject and name authority files and/or the ability to search all fields of a bibliographic record. It is interesting to compare Lester's finding on authority files—that they would have little effect on subject retrieval—with the finding of VAN PULIS and LUDY—that subject authority files are little used even when made available online. MICCO *et al.* report on a project at Chatham College to develop an expert system capable of searching for and providing access to knowledge at the same level as a skilled reference librarian. The project proposes a system that will develop a user profile and diagnose information need, then connect the user to the information through a network interface that will include the use of CD-ROM technologies. The system is envisioned as using a Macintosh-style interface with windows and a mouse. It would have a three-tiered structure: the first level providing access tools, the second providing access to monographs, and the third providing access to periodicals. As currently projected, the system will use the same types of heuristics employed by expert human searchers rather than the textual keyword searching approach frequently used in computer-based systems. Several projects that have dealt with the use of classification schemes in OPACs were reviewed in the earlier section on classification schemes.

Information Requests

The effectiveness of a delegated search, of course, very much depends on how well a request made by a user actually reflects the user's information need. Much work has been done on user-intermediary interaction in information retrieval. AUSTER and LAWTON look at various characteristics of the pre-search interview as factors affecting the success of a search. ALLEN claims that the way users understand and express their needs will be affected by the cognitive structures by which they have organised their knowledge of the topic and by the schemata introduced in the questions that intermediaries ask. Differences in personal schemata may mean that the same problem could result in completely different questions as filtered through the minds of different individuals. One major problem in user-intermediary interaction is that the personal schemata of the user and that of the information specialist may be quite far apart. Moreover, various 'external schemata' may also exert strong influence on the interactions between user and intermediary. Somewhat related to Allen's work is that of DERR, who identifies five types of expressions used by individuals in making demands on information services; he discusses the implications of the differences for practices in information retrieval. PETRUS points out that the imperfect nature of requests makes information retrieval an operation based on probability. The retrieval situation can be described by the theory of statistical solutions.

NATURAL-LANGUAGE SEARCHING

The searching of text by computer can be traced back to the late 1950s, but interest has continued to increase as more and more text becomes accessible online. Based on studies performed with the full text of popular magazines, TENOPIR presents a useful but brief discussion of the relative effectiveness of various types of strategies for full-text searching. COVE and WALSH look at the feasibility of a browsing approach to searching text online. They describe a system that will display text extracts to prompt the user to select words. These can then lead to 'associated words'—*i.e.,* words occurring as the 'nearest neighbours' of the words originally selected—which can generate further displays of text, from which additional 'browse words' can be selected, and so on.

The type of text that is generally accessible online consists of relatively brief items such as journal articles, abstracts, or patents. Because of rapidly declining costs, it is now becoming increasingly feasible to store and exploit the text of much longer items, but how useful would it be to be able to search the complete text of, say, monographs? Based on studies of how library patrons use non-fiction books, PRABHA and RICE conclude that systems that permit the searching of the full text of non-fiction books would be of value to the users of at least the academic libraries. Over the years a number of studies have compared the results of searches in humanly indexed bibliographic databases with results of searches in full-text databases.

The common finding is that full-text databases give greater recall but reduced precision. SIEVERT *et al.* confirm this by comparing results achieved in searching MEDLINE with those achieved through searching two full-text databases in medicine; RO comes to the same conclusion in a different environment.

Unfortunately, this type of result is frequently mis-interpreted. The fact that a full-text database gives better recall than a database of humanly indexed bibliographic records has nothing to do with the properties of text *per se*; it is simply due to the fact that text records tend to be longer and thus provide more access points.

A database of records indexed with an average of, say, 50 descriptors may well give better recall than a database of brief abstracts, but one could change these results dramatically by greatly increasing the length of the abstracts or drastically reducing the number of descriptors assigned. It is the length of the record that is the major determinant of what is and is not retrieved, but this fact is sometimes overlooked.

AUSTIN examines some of the implications of natural-language searching, illustrating cases in which natural-language searches have failed. These failures are analysed for possible solutions, leading the author to conclude that computers exacerbate rather than alleviate the need for vocabulary control. HOOD reaches a similar conclusion. Full-text searching tends to uncover details, whereas controlled-vocabulary searching tends to uncover broad concepts. He concludes that a comprehensive search would require more than one method. Investigators at Syracuse University have undertaken several related studies on what is assumed to be one of the problems of text searching—the implicit reference to topics through anaphora. For example, AIDS can be variously represented by 'the disease,' 'it,' and so on, in a text. In one study the anaphors occurring in abstracts were replaced by their referents. It was then determined what effect this replacement would have on term weighting, based on word frequency counts, and subsequently on retrieval.

The results were inconclusive: in some searches the replacement improved the ranking of documents in search outputs, while in others it actually caused a deterioration of the ranking. It was hypothesised that this anomaly might be caused by the fact that anaphors sometimes refer to topics that are integral to a text, while at other times they refer to topics that are peripheral. This hypothesis was tested. Using abstracts from the PsycINFO database, words or phrases serving as anaphors were judged as being integral in 52 per cent of the cases studied; the comparable value for abstracts from the INSPEC database was 68 per cent.

The authors concluded that the resolution of anaphora may indeed be important if the effectiveness of text searching is to be improved. This is an example of a conclusion that is based on the processing of abstracts but that may not apply to the full-text situation. Presumably, the redundancy of full text will create a situation wherein the frequency with which a topic occurs *explicitly* will generally reflect its importance in the text regardless of how many implicit references may be missed. DOSZKOCS gives a useful general overview of natural-language processing in information retrieval.

The relative merits of natural-language *vs.* controlled-vocabulary approaches to information retrieval are still debated. DUBOIS compares the two approaches, and SVENONIUS looks at the history of the issue and suggests areas for research that "would clarify it in such a way as to contribute to a rational basis for the design of retrieval tools such as thesauri".

BAER and JOHNSON, considering in particular the OP AC situation, conclude that vocabulary control is even more important in the online environment than it is in manual systems. As full-text databases become the norm, there looms a danger that the mere presence of the complete text may be viewed as a labour-saving substitute for subject indexing.

YANCEY points out that the growth of information through full-text services will place even more importance on relevance and warns of the loss of retrieval capability through lack of subject indexing. A combination of full-text and subject-searching techniques to link past and present knowledge is presented as the preferable alternative. TEUFEL describes an approach to text retrieval that he refers to as '*n*-gram indexing.' The texts of abstracts are reduced to significant words through use of a stop list, then reduced further to word stems.

The stems are converted into trigrams; 'high noise' trigrams are replaced by tetragrams or even pentagrams. Natural-language queries are processed in the same way. Retrieval consists of looking for the best matches between *n*-gram representations of documents and of requests. Teufel presents some results of tests using abstracts from the INSPEC database. Problems in the portability of natural-language queries from one database to another are addressed by DAMERAU.

AUTOMATIC INDEXING AND RELATED ACTIVITIES

For more than 30 years investigators have sought ways to replace human intellectual processing by computer processing of text. Methods investigated include automatic indexing by extraction or assignment, automatic extracting, the automatic organisation of terms or documents into classes, automatic approaches to thesaurus construction or the development of networks of semantic relations among terms, and methods for matching natural-language requests against the text of documents or their indexed representations. SGALL and VRBOVA have described work in automatic indexing, automatic extracting, machine translation, and related aspects of text processing under way at Charles University in Prague.

VON KEITZ presents a brief overview of the three types of automatic indexing currently available:

- Inverted-file full-text indexing;
- Dictionary-based indexing; and
- Dictionary/rule-based indexing.

The author asks what roles in automatic indexing should be played by humans and what roles should be played by machines. Although only full-text indexing is fully automatic and is the most frequently encountered, the dictionary and dictionary/rule systems provide higher precision; thus, better dictionaries and rules will yield better indexing. The author concludes that the human role should be one of continuing to develop better dictionaries and rules.

SUZUKI and TOCHINAI compare the keyword density method with a 'mean order' method for extracting sentences in automatic abstracting, and DAS-GUPTA compares the Two-Poisson model of automatic indexing with inverse document frequency and discrimination value models. While the automatic extraction of 'significant' words, phrases, or sentences from documents, based on frequency and/or positional criteria, has been successful for many years, automatic assignment indexing, involving even very small controlled vocabularies, has met with much less success.

However, natural-language processing has progressed to the point at which assignment indexing by computer should now be possible. At least, machine-aided assignment indexing should be practicable. VLEDUTS-STOKOLOV, for example, describes experiments performed at BIOSIS in which terms from a limited vocabulary of 600 biological concept headings are assigned automatically to journal articles. The assignment is achieved by matching article titles against a semantic vocabulary containing about 15,000 biological terms, which, in turn, are mapped to the concept headings.

The automatic aid to indexing developed at BIOSIS is described in detail, and the disambiguation techniques used are illustrated. While, overassignment and underassignment of terms still occur, automatic assignment indexing has certainly made some progress since, the 1960s. Machine-aided assignment indexing is also in place at the National Aeronautics and Space Administration (NASA). This work is described by BUCHAN but in insufficient detail. As might be expected, considerable interest now exists in the possibility of devising 'expert systems' to aid the indexing process. One example is the MedlndEx System being developed at NLM.

Referred to as a 'prototype interactive knowledge-based system,' it uses an experimental frame language and is designed to interact with trained MEDLINE indexers by prompting them to enter MeSH terms as 'slot fillers' in completing document-specific indexing frames derived from the knowledge-base frames. MARTINEZ *et al2.* describe another rule-based system. The American Petroleum Institute's (API) Central Abstracting and Indexing Service (CAIS) incorporates a rule-based, expert system founded on the API Thesaurus, which has been in operation since, 1985.

Terms automatically generated by the system and by API's human indexers are reviewed by a human editor, and the edited terms are added to print indexes and the online index. At present the base contains about 14,000 text rules. SALTON presents suggestions for the automatic indexing of monographs. The method proposed performs a syntactic analysis of the text, selects nominal constructs, weights the terms, and selects terms to act as index terms. Approaches to the machine-aided indexing of patents are discussed by SCHRAMM and BIELA.

ALADESULU studies methods of improving automatic indexing operations to make them more closely approach the intellectual level of human indexing. The approach used involves the recognition of phrases that are semantically equivalent but syntactically different. DYKSTRA observes that the clear rules of the PRECIS system lend themselves to the process of content analysis and automatic indexing. CONGREVE describes a project designed to evaluate the automatic production of PRECIS-based indexes. Among other methods used for automatic indexing are user manipulation of index commands imbedded in the document and system manipulation of keywords in and out of context.

LAMEIN examines the advantages and disadvantages of keyword-out-of-title indexing and describes its use in the law library of the Free University of Amsterdam. The processing of the text of a request against the text of a document collection can be considered as essentially a pattern-matching operation. The objective is to retrieve items in a ranked order, with those that best match the request at the top of the ranking. One way of achieving such a ranking is by weighting the search terms by the frequency with which they are associated with items already known to be relevant, their rate of occurrence in the database as a whole, or other statistical properties.

ROBERTSON describes one weighting formula that he considers an improvement over those previously used. SALTON and BUCKLEY summarise findings of research on automatic term weighting and present models for comparison with more complex techniques of content analysis. CHOROS and DANILOWICZ describe an approach to 'relative indexing,' in which the weights assigned to descriptors associated with documents are modified on the basis of user relevance feedback.

BUELL discusses problems associated with the fuzzy-set approach to weighted retrieval. The calculation of term discrimination values is discussed by WILLETT, EL-HAMDOUCHI and WILLETT, and CROUCH, while BARTSCHI presents a general mathematical framework for looking at retrieval approaches involving term weighting and the ranking of output, and MURTAGH describes hierarchic clustering methods applicable to information retrieval. CAN and OZKARAHAN also deal with term discrimination values. They introduce a 'cover coefficient' and describe how this can be used in computing the discrimination value for a term.

FAGAN compares two methods for automatically extracting phrases from texts to serve as content indicators. Non-syntactic methods are based on simple text characteristics, such as word frequency and word proximity, while syntactic methods selectively extract phrases from parse trees generated by an automatic syntactic analyser. Retrieval tests were inconsistent but tended to indicate that the non-syntactic methods produced better results. Nevertheless, Fagan suggests that the syntactic approach does have certain advantages and has a greater potential for improvement than does the non-syntactic method. The ranking of documents in 'automatic' information systems is usually based on probabilistic, vector, or fuzzy-logic criteria.

LOSEE building on the work of BOOKSTEIN, presents a probabilistic sequential learning model for ranking. The proposed system will retrieve documents, accept feedback on the retrieved items, and 'learn' from the feedback to enhance future performance, the relevance feedback being an intrinsic element in the sequential learning model itself. An earlier article describes how coordination-level matching can be used for ranking outputs from retrieval systems incorporating sequential learning.

CROFT describes a method for integrating Boolean approaches with probabilistic retrieval methods. He claims that term dependencies derived from queries, when incorporated into a probabilistic retrieval model, can improve performance. The term dependencies can be derived automatically from Boolean queries or from user selection of important phrases from their natural-language queries. RADECKI, MARON, LOSEE and BOOKSTEIN, FOX and KOLL, S ALTON, and COOPER all deal with the limitations of conventional Boolean searching methods and propose ways in which such approaches can be improved.

Relevance feedback is usually considered an essential element in any probabilistic retrieval method, and this implies the ability of the searcher to locate 'a few relevant items' in a database. One way of achieving this is to match the query against clusters of items rather than against individual items. PANYR considers the place of cluster analysis in information retrieval along with possible search strategies to exploit clusters. GRIFFITHS *et al.* have compared various clustering methods and found that the best retrieval results were achieved by procedures that divide a database into many small clusters. This led them to propose that the optimal cluster will consist of only two items, the ones that are most similar.

However, further tests showed that searches based on nearest-neighbour clusters did not perform any better than conventional 'best-match' searches, although they retrieved a different set of items. Consequently, these authors propose that a retrieval system incorporate both approaches. SALTON *et al.* discuss the use of automatic relevance feedback techniques with Boolean query statements. An extended or 'fuzzy' Boolean logic approach, which relaxes the normally strict interpretation of the Boolean operators, can improve search performance.

ENSER examines clustering techniques using terms from tables of contents, title, and back-of-the-book indexes, and concludes that this technique is viable in a book/text database. SHAW looks at the empirical significance of document clusters as a function of term weight and similarity thresholds. In related work SHAW also looks at the validity of partitions formed on the basis of co-citation. Approaches to the automatic indexing/classification of documents are generally based on data derived from a document/term matrix, showing which index terms or text words are associated with which documents.

Documents may be grouped according to such factors as the frequency with which a term occurs in a document and the frequency with which it occurs in the database as a whole. The relationships between documents and terms need not be considered 'absolute.' For example, words that do not occur in a document may nevertheless be judged 'close' to that document when they tend to co-occur in other contexts with the words that do occur frequently in the document. DEERWESTER *et al.* propose an approach to indexing based on the 'latent' relations among terms and documents, derivable from the document/ term matrix. They refer to this as 'latent semantic indexing.'

The model uses a reduced set of about 100 'descriptive parameters' derived by the linear decomposition of a document/term matrix. Each term, document, and query can be represented by values on this small set of orthogonal dimensions, which may be considered as 'artificial concepts.' The investigators claim that results achieved in retrieval tests for the method ranged from considerably better to roughly comparable with performance based on weighted keyword searching. A more abstract, mathematical discussion of the analysis of weighted graphs in the clustering of items is given by GOETSCHEL, while CAN and OZKARAHAN compare two clustering algorithms in terms of stability and similarity factors.

YAKUBOVITZ refers to an associative retrieval system that can overcome some problems of text retrieval without the need for daily updating of a system thesaurus. This system links keyword-bearing documents with adjacent, associated documents having only one keyword in common to form an associative path. An algorithm for the construction of a path that changes keyword three times is presented as an example. THÖNSSEN reports on an interface that connects automatic indexing programmes with automatic thesaurus maintenance programmes. The interface can be used with a personal computer.

STREETER and LOCHBAUM present details on an expert/expert locator (EEL), which matches requests for information with technical organisations. The technical organisations in EEL are represented by their documents, and these documents provide the system with input. The automatic indexing places terms and organisations in a 100-dimension semantic space and determines similarities among organisations on the basis of their use of terms. When queried, the system computes the degree of similarity between the request and all objects in this structure, retrieving those that are most similar.

The approach is similar to the latent semantic indexing described by DEERWESTER *et al.* Another approach to 'automatic' retrieval consists of the development of natural-language interfaces that allow a user to enter queries as phrases or sentences without the need to deal with controlled vocabularies or to express logical relationships among terms. Various natural-language interfaces have been developed over the years.

BISWAS *et al.* introduce an approach that uses fuzzy-set techniques, and they describe it in considerable detail. CLEMENCIN describes a natural-language interface to the 'yellow pages' of France's online telephone directory, while SPIEGLER and ELATA propose a model for analysing a query at a local workstation to determine whether it is 'answerable' before submitting it to some accessible database. Rather than mapping natural-language expressions to a limited number of controlled terms, words occurring in text can be decomposed into smaller semantic units. This is the basis of 'semantic analysis' and the 'semantic code' that was applied to information retrieval at Western Reserve University more than 25 years ago.

SMETÁÈEK describes the SEMAN system that will decompose text words into 630 distinctive 'semantic features'. He mentions several possible information retrieval applications but does not elaborate on them. BELONOGOV *et al.* compare the performance of a retrieval system based on automatic indexing with the performance of a system based on text searching. They conclude that the system with automatic indexing has significantly better recall/precision characteristics and is faster than the other approach. Also, because low-performance terms can be eliminated, the database can be smaller.

BLAIR and MARON, using IBM's STAIRS for full-text legal retrieval, reported average precision values of around 75 per cent; but recall values of only about 20 per cent. SALTON comments on these results and suggests that they are typical of conventional retrieval operations. He presents results for studies that have compared conventional with automated approaches and emphasises that the future lies with the latter. BLAIR reviews the basic model of a relational document retrieval system and demonstrates how documents can be linked during a search in a relational system. He presents an extended model that includes weighted subjects, associative features such as thesaurus links, citation indexing, and co-occurring terms.

At a more general level, CANISIUS discusses potential uses of knowledge-based systems in information service applications and argues that the information profession could become redundant if it fails to exploit the capabilities of such systems, while WORMELL and BALDACCI deal with artificial intelligence and expert systems applied to information retrieval problems. SPARCK JONES, on the other hand, questions the need for artificial intelligence applications in information retrieval systems.

CITATION RELATIONSHIPS

Related documents can be grouped on the basis of direct citation, co-citation, or bibliographic coupling as well as through the more conventional methods of subject indexing. A number of recent studies deal with various aspects of these citation relationships in information retrieval. PAO and PAO and FU have compared results of searches based on citation relationships with results from conventional subject searches in MEDLINE. Not surprisingly, they find that the two methods are essentially complementary, each retrieving some relevant items not found by the other. One conclusion was that the conventional approach by descriptors could retrieve only about half of the 'quality' papers.

In reviewing their own bibliographic references, however, it is distressing to note that none of the items cited was published before 1979, giving the impression that studies of this kind are relatively new. In fact, comparisons of citation retrieval with conventional descriptor retrieval go back more than 20 years. Moreover, the complementarity of citation and traditional approaches was demonstrated long ago and is now taken pretty much for granted. We really don't need more studies to prove it. MCCAIN reports a similar study. Results from co-citation searches in SciSearch were compared with results from conventional searches in BIOSIS Previews. The subject was the genetics of fruit flies. One of McCain's conclusions is that co-cited author searching "is capable of capturing a large percentage of relevant documents in a broad subject retrieval." TRIVISON compares items retrieved by subject indexes and citation indexes in the field of information science.

Unfortunately, neither conventional subject indexing nor citation links offer a foolproof way of linking documents or groups of documents that are 'logically' related. SWANSON points to two groups of logically related articles—one on the effects of dietary fish oils on changes in the blood and the other on the possible beneficial effects of similar blood changes for patients with Raynaud's disease—that are not closely related by co-citation, bibliographic coupling, or statistical associations among assigned descriptors. In a similar study SWANSON looks at the problems of linking the literature of magnesium to the literature of migraine.

SHAW raises doubts about the validity of some subject relationships supposedly demonstrated by co-citation. Classes formed by co-citation can be statistically invalid even at a high co-citation level. However, critical thresholds that define the limits of statistical validity can be identified. Within these limits there does exist "a narrow region of statistical validity where the associated structures are not an artifact of the clustering procedure and can be interpreted".

KWOK refers to the fact that reference/citation links can be used in information retrieval to form an 'augmented collection' of retrieved items. That is, when a search strategy is applied to a database in the normal way, using text words or controlled terms, the set of items thus retrieved can be augmented by those items linked to them through bibliographic citations. He suggests that the set of terms associated with the items originally retrieved might be augmented by the addition of terms drawn from the items that they cite.

These new terms could be index terms assigned to the cited items, or they could be text expressions drawn from abstracts or titles. He suggests that augmentation by drawing terms from the titles of cited items is most practicable. This is virtually what Mary Elizabeth Stevens was working on more than 20 years ago. SALTON and ZHANG have tested the value of augmenting the set of terms associated with retrieved items by adding title words drawn from 'bibliographically related' items.

Title words were drawn from:

- Items cited by the retrieved items;
- Items citing the retrieved items; and
- Co-cited items.

The authors conclude that while many 'useful' content words can be extracted in this way, many terms of doubtful value will also be extracted; further, the procedure is not sufficiently reliable to warrant inclusion in operating retrieval systems. KWOK, on the other hand, reinterprets their results and concludes that the enhancement may still be worth further investigation. REES-POTTER looks at the potential for using citation, co-citation analysis, and citation context analysis in the updating of thesauri or other controlled vocabularies. She concludes that the analysis of citation content may be used in the development of indexing vocabularies in specialty areas.

CONCLUSION

This review strongly suggests that subject analysis continues to be an area of great interest and activity. The increasing impact of electronic technology, combined with the ongoing expansion of that technology's capabilities, seem certain to have a profound effect on the progress of subject analysis, an effect that will no doubt be expressed in future *ARIST* chapters on this topic. The authors hope that continued technological advances will not only stimulate ever-increasing enquiry and experimentation, but that sharing these advances, enquiries, and experiments with less technologically developed countries will also bring about more efficient and more sophisticated means of subject analysis and access on a global scale.

Readers of this review who have been actively involved in information science for a considerable time will recognise that substantial progress has occurred in the past 25 years in certain areas; automatic indexing, full-text searching, and end-user searching are obvious examples. This progress has been accompanied by the increasing convergence of information science and library science. The advent of the online public access catalogue (OPAC) has promoted greatly increased interest in the library community in improving subject access. Indeed some of the most interesting work in this area is now being performed in the traditional library setting, which was not generally true 20 or more years ago. It is interesting to note how history repeats itself.

In the 1950s and 1960s much of the progress in information retrieval occurred through the efforts of scientists, engineers, lawyers, and others who were not information professionals. These individuals were not familiar with the literature of library science, and some reinvention of the wheel occurred. Today a reverse situation may be occurring, with members of the library community reinventing methods that were developed outside the community many years ago. The field of information science seems to have a short collective memory. We know of work done three or four years ago but are unaware of, or have forgotten, work done much earlier. While much of the early work is outdated, some of it is still highly relevant. *ARIST* is of immense value in providing a review and synthesis of research in broad areas performed during relatively short periods of time, but it does not obviate the need for longitudinal reviews, covering perhaps 20 or 30 years, on more specific topics.

Bibliography

Anil K. Dhiman and Yashoda Rani: *Learn Library Cataloguing*, Ess Ess Publication, Delhi, 2005.

Anthony T. Velte: *Cloud Computing: A Practical Approach*, Tata McGraw-Hill, Delhi, 2009.

C. Janakiraman: *Library Cataloguing And Multimedia Library*, Pacific Books International, Delhi, 2011.

Jogender Singh Burman: *Library Cataloguing : Principles and Practices*, Rajat Publication, Delhi, 2007.

Jogender Singh Burman: *Managing Libraries in Digital Era*, Rajat Publication, Delhi, 2007.

K.S. Dhawan: *Library Cataloguing Strategies*, Commonwealth Publication, Delhi, 1997.

K.T. Dilli: *Library and Information Science in a Digital Era*, Atlantic Publication, Delhi, 2009.

Kishor Chandra Satpathy and R. Ramachandran: *Networking of Library and Information Centres in Digital Era : Problems and Prospects*, National Library and S.K. Jain and Sons, 2011.

Kumar Saurabh: *Cloud Computing : Unleashing Next Gen Infrastructure to Application*, Wiley India, 2014.

Kumar Saurabh: *Cloud Computing*, Wiley India, 2012.

Kumar Saurabh: *Cloud Computing: Insights Into New-Era Infrastructure*, Wiley India, 2011.

M.S. Ramalingam: *Library Cataloguing and Classification Systems*, Kalpaz Publication, Delhi, 2000.

Manisha Dawra: *Modern Theories of Library Cataloguing*, Rajat Publication, Delhi, 2004.

Manohar Nanda: *Library Cataloguing*, Anmol Publication, Delhi, 2006.

Moorttimatee Samantaray: *Vibrant Children's Library in Digital Era*, Pratibha Prakashan, Delhi, 2011.

R. Rajeswara Rao and V. Subba Ramaiah: *Cloud Computing and Virtualization*, BS Publications/BSP Books, Delhi, 2014.

Rajiv Adhikari: *Library Serials Automation*, Rajat Publication, Delhi, 2000.

S.K. Chaudhary: *Library Cataloguing*, A.P.H. Publication, Delhi, 2011.

Sandhya Aggarwal and R.D. Mehla: *Library Services : Challenges and Solutions in Digital Era*, Ess Ess Publications, Delhi, 2012.

Shyama Balakrishnan & P K Paliwal: *Library Cataloguing and Multimedia Libraries*, Anmol Publication, Delhi, 2001.

Shyama Balakrishnan and P.K. Paliwal: *Automated Library Serials*, Anmol Publication, Delhi, 2001.

Shyama Balakrishnan and P.K. Paliwal: *Library Serials Management*, Anmol Publication, Delhi, 2001.

Sunil Kumar Satpathy; Chandrakant Swain and Bijayalaxmi Rautaray: *Modernisation of Libraries : A Challenge in Digital Era*, Mahamaya Publishing House, Delhi, 2008.

Superna Sharma, Arundhati Kaushik, Chanda Arya and Hema Haldua: *Redefining Libraries in Digital Era*, Daya Publication, Delhi, 2014.

T.R. Sanjiv Reddy and Shyamgopal Verma: *Library Cataloguing and Information Technology*, Pacific Books International, Delhi, 2012.

Index